RAILS
TO
INFINITY

CRISPIN WRIGHT

RAILS
TO
INFINITY

Essays on Themes
from Wittgenstein's
Philosophical Investigations

HARVARD UNIVERSITY PRESS · Cambridge, Massachusetts · London, England
2001

FOR CATHERINE

Library of Congress-in-Publication Data

Wright, Crispin, 1942–
    Rails to infinity : essays on themes from Wittgenstein's
Philosophical investigations / Crispin Wright.
        p.   cm.
    Includes bibliographical references (p.   ) and index.
    ISBN 0-674-00504-X
    1. Wittgenstein, Ludwig, 1889–1951. Philosophische
Untersuchungen. I. Title.

B3376.W563 P5328 2001
192—dc21   2001024172

CONTENTS

Contents

PREFACE

In the mid-1980s I almost published two volumes of collected papers. One, *Realism, Meaning and Truth,* was published in 1986. It gathered together a number of my essays on the debate between realism and anti-realism conceived (broadly) in the form that Michael Dummett has encouraged. In its preface, it announced a second book—*Realism, Rules and Objectivity*—which was to be a collection of papers bringing Wittgenstein's 'rule-following considerations' to bear on the debates about realism, and also encompassing the pre-Dummettian model of debate, in which realism contrasts with various forms of expressivism or instrumentalism. That book never appeared, and the second part of its project was in any case somewhat superseded by the publication of *Truth and Objectivity* (1992). However, those of the essays reprinted here which were completed during the 1980s would have been included in *Realism, Rules and Objectivity.* So if the announcement of that book was a promise, then I hereby—partially—finally keep it.

The essays in the present anthology represent a career-long fascination with the thought of the 'later' Wittgenstein. Their central preoccupation is with his ideas on rules, and their bearing on issues to do with objectivity—ideas which go to the heart of our thinking about virtually everything, and promise especially striking consequences for the philosophy of logic and mathematics on the one hand and the philosophy of ordinary intentional psychology on the other. I freely confess, though, that I have never found an account of the 'rule-following considerations' which contented me long enough to feel that I could finally take their measure. Some of the lines of development I canvass within this volume verge, like Saul Kripke's,[1] on paradox. Others seem more sober, but call for constructive philosophical developments which one can approximate but whose completion seems to remain tantalisingly out of reach. And of course one's confidence in the very attempt is continually liable to erosion by Wittgenstein's own seemingly theoretically deliberate inexplicitness and 'unconstructiveness', his seemingly stubborn refusal to respond to the sense of intellectual vacuum which the apparent negative thrust of the rule-following discussion is apt to create. There are philosophers—some of them able—whose assured style of writing suggests they believe that they have learned what Wittgenstein has to teach about these matters. I have never shared this confidence. Every time I have written or taught about the ideas at the heart of *Philosophical Investigations,* I have felt as though I was starting from scratch. The result, I'm afraid, is that a reader who works patiently through these essays will find no settled interpretation of Wittgenstein on rules, but a number of variously contrasting proposals which I find myself reluctant to try to co-ordinate further or to pass final judgement on. This is perhaps unsurprising. Wittgenstein himself had the greatest difficulty in bringing his ideas to a sufficiently finished state to consider they merited publication; indeed, he thought that he never succeeded. How might an interpreter better succeed where the author himself failed? Besides, I have persistently attempted to understand and appropriate his thinking within the resources and idiom of a philosophical tradition from which he deliberately stood aside. Perhaps nothing stateable and supportable in the style of this tradition could ever confidently be

1. See Kripke 1982.

taken to capture what Wittgenstein tried to say, or teach, or where exactly he makes mistakes. My writings here are motivated, provoked, or—at their best—perhaps inspired by reading Wittgenstein. But while they are not, I hope, unscholarly, I do not offer them as serious scholarly exegesis, still less as a key to unlock his thought. I want to make much the same disclaimer as Kripke did.[2] The value of these essays, if any, must largely depend on their own interest, not on their claim to portrayal of Wittgenstein.

I have resisted one temptation, and succumbed to another. The temptation I resisted is to change the substance of the essays, to correct what strike me now as misformulations and oversights (as is quite often done in later essays.) But I have not resisted the temptation to do some light editing for clarity, to cut some cackle, and to stave off certain (in some cases, historically occurrent) misunderstandings. The essays have been organised, perhaps a little artificially, into four groups—Wittgenstein and Rules, Wittgenstein's Argument As It Struck Kripke, Privacy and Self-Knowledge, and Rule-Following and Mathematics.[3] Rather than a single substantial Introduction, I have included four corresponding sets of introductory reflections. I have added two Postscripts, one of a piece with the discussion at the conclusion of Essay 11 on Wittgenstein's later views on philosophical method and the sources of philosophical problems, and the other reacting against, inter alia, John McDowell's interpretation of Wittgenstein's views on privacy. I also have included as part of the bibliography of references a selection of additional writings criticising or otherwise reacting to certain of the themes in the essays.

2. "I suspect . . . that to attempt to present Wittgenstein's argument precisely is to some extent to falsify it. Probably many of my formulations and recastings of the argument are done in a way Wittgenstein would not himself approve. So the present paper should be thought of as expounding neither 'Wittgenstein's' argument nor 'Kripke's': rather Wittgenstein's argument as it struck Kripke, as it presented a problem for him." Ibid., p. 5.

3. I had originally intended to include some of my essays on Wittgenstein's apparent conventionalist or 'non-cognitivist' attitude to logical and mathematical necessity in this section, but thought it better to defer them for inclusion in a later collection.

Preface

Acknowledgements associated with particular essays are noted in each essay separately. But at a more general level I'd like to express my gratitude to James Hopkins, who first kindled my interest in the later Wittgenstein when we were research students in Cambridge, and to Michael Dummett, under whose supervision I first wrote about Wittgenstein's views about mathematics, and whose incredulity has served as a spur ever since; to John McDowell and Christopher Peacocke for their long-term attention to my efforts on these matters, and for their own stimulating and important contributions on the issues; to Bob Hale, whose careful critical response to my work when he was preparing his synoptic essay[4] on the area for our *Companion to the Philosophy of Language* did much to help me understand the progression of my own thinking; and to Paul Boghossian for countless discussions of the ramifications of Kripke's ideas, and for excellent criticisms of mine. I have also had the privilege over the years of teaching or examining many outstanding graduate students who have worked on these issues—Darragh Byrne, Chris Leich, Alex Miller, the late Mark Powell, and José Zalabardo deserve special mention—and have learned much from them.

Anyone who has put together an anthology of this kind will know how protracted and time-consuming the final tasks can prove to be. I should like to thank Stephen Ferguson for assistance with the bibliographies and systematisation of references, Anne Cameron and Janet Kirk for preparing typescripts of some of the older papers, David Bemelmans, whose skillful editing resulted in innumerable improvements, Cyrus Panjvani for invaluable help with proofreading, and Donna Bouvier, my production editor. Lindsay Waters, for Harvard University Press, has been exceptionally helpful at every stage and has shown remarkable patience through a series of delays. Finally, I record my deep gratitude to the Leverhulme Trust for awarding me the Personal Research Professorship whose tenure provided the opportunity to complete this book.

4. R. Hale, 'Rule-Following, Objectivity and Meaning', in R.V. Hale and C. Wright, eds., *A Companion to the Philosophy of Language* (Oxford: Blackwell, 1997), pp. 369–96.

To what extent can the function of language be described? If someone is not master of a language, I may bring him to a mastery of it by training. Someone who is master of it, I may remind of the kind of training, or I may describe it; for a particular purpose; thus already using a technique of the language.

To what extent can the function of a rule be described? Someone who is master of none, I can only train. But how can I explain the nature of a rule to myself?

The difficult thing here is not, to dig down to the ground; no, it is to recognize the ground that lies before us as the ground.

For the ground keeps on giving us the illusory image of a greater depth, and when we seek to reach this, we keep on finding ourselves on the old level.

Our disease is one of wanting to explain.

"Once you have got hold of the rule, you have the route traced for you."

—WITTGENSTEIN,
Remarks on the Foundations of Mathematics, VI, ¶31

PART ONE

WITTGENSTEIN AND RULES

The principal philosophical issues to do with rule-following impinge on every normatively constrained area of human thought and activity: on every institution where there is right and wrong opinion, correct and incorrect practice. It is the merest platitude that where there is such a thing as following a rule or complex of rules correctly, or as going wrong, there have to be *facts* about what the requirements, in context, of the relevant rule(s) are. And whatever kind of objectivity can belong to the judgement that someone has proceeded in a manner in or out of accord with the rule(s), it cannot be greater than the objectivity pertaining to such a fact. Yet facts about what rules allow seem on reflection to raise puzzling questions of constitution and epistemology: what could be the nature of a fact which—in a context in which we've yet to be placed or to consider—somehow already makes it true that such and such a response, or course of action, is what will be required of us if we are to keep faith with a particular specified rule? How and when was it settled—again, take a case which no one has ever explicitly considered—that *this* is what complies with the rule, when everything we may so far have said or done would cohere with a quite different understanding of the rule? How is the once-and-for-all division of particular possible (so far unmade) responses into those in accord and those out of accord with the rule accomplished? And how, consistently with allowing that distinction an appropriate kind of objectivity, so that what is in accord with a rule or not really is fixed before any verdict of ours, can we account for our ability—in the normal case, effortlessly, even thoughtlessly—to be appropriately responsive to it?[1]

There is an understandable tendency of philosophers to miss the issues here. For a rule, it may plausibly be said—at least any rule of sufficient generality and definiteness—is nothing if not something that precisely does mandate (or allow) determinate courses of action in an indefinite range of cases that its practitioners will never have explicitly considered or prepared for. So there cannot be a puzzle about *how* a rule does that, or what settles what its requirements are. To ask how it is settled what complies with the rule is like asking how it is settled what shape a particular geometrical figure has. Shape is an *internal* property of the figure. What settles what shape the figure has is simply its being the figure it is.[2]

But the concerns are not, of course, to be dismissed so easily. They merely reformulate themselves. If a (suitably precise and general) rule is—by the very definition of 'rule', as it were—intrinsically such as to carry predeterminate verdicts for an indefinite range of occasions, and if grasping a rule is—by definition—an ability to keep track of those verdicts, step by step, then the prime question becomes: what makes it possible for there to *be* such things as rules, so conceived, at all? I can create a geometrical figure by drawing it. But how do I create something which carries determinate instructions for an open range of situations which I do not contemplate in making it? What gives it this

1. The overriding concerns about rule-following may thus be presented as an instance of what Christopher Peacocke has recently termed the 'integration challenge': the challenge of '[reconciling] a plausible account of what is involved in the truth of statements of a given kind with a credible account of how we can know those statements, when we do know them.' Peacocke (2000), p. 1.

2. John McDowell makes exactly this response in the context of the corresponding issue concerning intention—see McDowell (1991), pp. 163–4, discussed in Essay 10.

content, when anything I say or do in explaining it will be open to an indefinite variety of conflicting interpretations? And how is the content to be got 'into mind' and so made available to inform the successive responses of practitioners?

Someone who is responsive to these concerns is likely to be exercised—as Wittgenstein conspicuously was—by the range of implicit assumptions about the issues which we seem to make in our ordinary thinking about two quite different areas: logic and pure mathematics on the one hand, and ordinary intentional psychology on the other. Ordinary thinking about logic and pure mathematics is highly realist. It views both disciplines as tracking absolutely hard conceptual constraints. Discoveries in mathematics are merely the unpacking of (possibly) deep but predeterminate implications of the architecture of our understanding of basic mathematical concepts, as codified in intuitively apprehended axioms; and logical inference, for its part, is seen as the tracing of steps which are, in some sense, *already* drawn and which we have no rational option but to acknowledge once presented to us. This kind of thinking conceives of the requirements of rules— or at least, the requirements of logical and mathematical rules—as ultra-objective:[3] as somehow constituted quite independently of any propensities for judgement or reaction of ours. So an account seems wanted of how we might presume ourselves capable of keeping intellectual track of requirements so independently constituted. But both those issues—the ontological and the epistemological—when once exposed to the light, as it were, and so long as we are mindful that an answer to either must sit comfortably alongside an answer to the other, are apt to come across as extremely perplexing.

An essentially similar way of thinking about the requirements of rules is quietly at work in the ordinary conception that mental states and processes are items of direct acquaintance for their subjects but are strictly inaccessible to others, by whom they are knowable only by (rather problematical) inference. It is a usually unremarked part of this way of thinking to have no difficulty with the idea of simple

---

3. What Wittgenstein (*Philosophical Investigations* §192) styles 'superlative' facts.

---

recognition of the character of one's own mental states and processes: privacy is not supposed to be at odds with one's ability to know them for what they are—to the contrary, it's supposed to go hand in hand with the possibility of a special degree of certainty. Yet a judgement expressing a purported such recognition, insofar as it can be correct or incorrect, must be a rule-governed response: there has to be a fact about what one *ought* to make of a newly presented inner *gestalt*—a fact about how it *ought* to be described—with which one's judgement about it is capable, in the best (normal) case, of correspondence. So again it seems the question must be faced: what constitutes such a fact—what can make it the case that, independently of any reaction of mine, the rules of the language in which I give expression to my private mental life *require* a certain type of description of an episode therein, and *proscribe* others; and what enables me to keep track of such requirements? Or again, if it is made definitional of rules to carry such requirements and proscriptions: what can make it the case that specific such rules are associated with particular expressions in the language, and how can they be items of awareness for me in such a way that I can recognise what their specific requirements and proscriptions are?

In its most general form, and independently the subject matter concerned, we can focus the issue being raised on my assent to a particular token statement, expressed in a language I understand, on a particular occasion of use. In order for this assent to be normatively constrained, and hence a candidate to be correct or incorrect, we have to be able to conceive of whatever constitutes its correctness or incorrectness as in some way independent of my disposition to assent. What are the candidates for such a 'requirement-constitutor'? The question confronts us with a broad dilemma. One thought—the Communitarian response—is that the requirement-constitutor must somehow be located *within* the propensities for assessment of the case possessed by others in my language community—that for my assent to the sentence in question to be, in the relevant context, in or out of line with the requirements imposed by its meaning is, in one way or another, for it to be in or out of line with others' impressions of those requirements. (Of course, this response cannot engage the case of judgements about one's own mental states, understood as in the previous paragraph.) The other—Platonist—response demurs: it says that even (hypothetically) shared assessments are constitutively quite independent of the requirements they concern—that even in the far-fetched scenario where a whole speech community assents to a particular utterance, and where everybody is clear-headed, attentive, and generally competent, the communal impression of what ought to be said is one thing and what really ought to be said is something else: something settled just between the character of the context and prevailing circumstances on the one hand and the meaning (that is, the rules governing the use) of the statement in question on the other, and should therefore be conceived as a matter on which a consensual verdict, in the best case, merely alights. The dilemma is then there only seem to be thee two options; and that while the Platonist line threatens to raise baffling ontological and epistemological problems, any move to Communitarianism promises to struggle when it comes to recovering basic distinctions on which our ordinary ideas of objectivity, the growth of knowledge and the defeat of superstition would seem to depend.

The three following essays were all written under this broad impression of the 'problematic' to which the rule-following considerations are addressed[4] (though some passages in Essay 1 might encourage the suspicion that its author saw no alternative to a broadly Platonist view of the reality of rule-requirements, so that destruction of that would be destruction of the very idea of facts about rule-requirements at all).[5] I took it—and still believe—that, with a qualification I shall enter below, Wittgenstein essentially invented this philosophical problem: something which, because—unlike almost all philosophical problems of comparatively recent provenance—it

4. For the record, the rather lacklustre phrase 'the rule-following considerations' came into general currency after my use of it in *Wittgenstein on the Foundations of Mathematics*. But I believe it was Christopher Peacocke who first suggested this label for the relevant cluster of Wittgensteinian thoughts. It's now impossible to think of anything better.

5. This, of course, would be very close to the dominant strategic idea of Kripke's *Wittgenstein on Rules and Private Language*.

might in principle have been appreciated by the Greeks, before the advent of developed empirical scientific methodology or of modern mathematics and logic, was an astonishing feat of philosophical perceptiveness and creativity. Appreciating the problem, as briskly characterised above, does of course, depend upon a willingness to allow *constitutive* questions—What makes it the case that . . . ? What could constitute the fact that . . . ?—as legitimate philosophical currency, and hence implicitly credits reflective philosophy with the power to provide satisfying, non-trivial answers to such questions. Though this willingness is perhaps particularly characteristic of modern philosophical thought—it is part and parcel, for instance, of the desire for a broadly monistic ontology which inspires contemporary ontological worries about intentional psychology—it only dawned on me much later that there is as much evidence in Wittgenstein's text for *impatience* with this kind of question as argument—meted out sparingly, in suggestive and, by 'professional' standards, underdeveloped nuggets—that the Platonist direction is a cul-de-sac. This is the qualification I flagged a moment ago. In a sense, Wittgenstein invented the problem—but not as a self-standing intellectual challenge. He did not intend it as something we should try to *solve,* beyond understanding its roots. In particular, he did not intend that we should try to work our way, by constructive philosophical reflection, to a conception of requirement-constitutors which somehow provided both objectivity and unproblematical accessibility.

Still, one could realise that this was not Wittgesntein's own intention without believing that his deflationary attitude to the concerns involved was right. Whether some form of the Communitarian response lurks below the surface of his writings or not, isn't it at least worth attempting to see how the best version of it might go? Essay 2, presented at a colloquium on Wittgenstein's ideas about rules which Christopher Leich and Steven Holtzman organised in Oxford in 1979,[6] begins to go in that direction. But a central thought in it—that there is no such thing as 'unilateral' recognition of a communal mistake (one should rather conclude that one does not understand the

6. Holtzman and Leich (1981).

judgement at issue)—is a definite error. Essay 3 effects a repair, and also dissociates the anti-Platonist argument from verificationist assumptions. This essay was not published until 1986, but the essentials of its argument were conceived much earlier and first presented at Charles Travis's conference on the Psychological Content of Logic at Tilburg in 1982. It could as well have been a chapter—or worked into a revision of other chapters—of *Wittgenstein on the Foundations of Mathematics*.

It is difficult, reading work of one's own conceived twenty or more years ago, to be completely certain of the unstated assumptions and ways of thinking in play. But it's safe to say that at the time of *Wittgenstein on the Foundations of Mathematics* I took Wittgenstein's effort to be almost wholly directed at the deconstruction of Platonism, and did not sufficiently reckon with the possibility of very different conceptions of what response might be appropriate to his succeeding in that. However, I think this did no serious harm. Wittgenstein clearly *was* exercised by the Platonist tendency, recognised that it was at work all over philosophy—and in ordinary thinking too, so far as that shows itself prone to be troubled by certain philosophical problems—and wanted to bring the assumptions involved out into the open and to subject them to various kinds of dialectical discomfiture. The primary task I set myself, in these early essays, was to work out what seemed to be Wittgenstein's own and other allied points of 'dialectical discomfiture' for the Platonist conception of rule-requirements. The main section of Essay 1 focuses on problems with the first-person epistemology of rule-requirements, as conceived by Platonism. Essay 2 generalises that argument to the unintelligibility of rule-requirements, so conceived (there crystallised in the idea of the *investigation-independence* of the truth values of decidable but so far undecided statements), and suggests, as a corollary, that there is a metaphysical doubt about the very *subject matter* which a recursive theory of meaning for a natural language, in the style of Davidson, would attempt to describe.[7] Essay 3—the one in

---

7. Gareth Evans's fine paper, "Semantic Theory and Tacit Knowledge" (Evans 1981), began life as his response to Essay 2 at the 1979 conference.

this group with whose central argument I still feel most content—argues that to embrace the Platonist option is actually inconsistent with basic principles governing our conception of competence with certain secondary quality concepts, and leaves us with no entitlment to regard compliance with ordinary standards for warranted belief and assertion as tending to promote true belief save on what would appear to be an wholly unmotivated assumption of a certain form of metaphysical harmony.

If the general tendency of these three essays is accepted, the reader will be persuaded that Platonism about rules is beset by hopeless metaphysical and epistemological difficulties. But no positive alternative is developed in them, beyond the vague suggestion that we have somehow to think of rule-requirements in some sort of "constructivist" way, and that there is some sort of insight lurking in the tendency to the Communitarian response. The questions, how best to respond to the deconstruction of the Platonist response—supposing it successful—and how Wittgenstein himself should be supposed to have responded, came to occupy me more as I tried to define a re-action to Kripke's *Wittgenstein on Rules and Private Language.* They are prominent in the essays in Parts Two and Three.

1 — Following a Rule

I. INTRODUCTION

We use the idioms of a particular application of an expression 'according with its meaning', of a particular derivation being 'required' by a certain rule of inference, of a particular continuation of an infinite decimal 'complying' with its governing rule. These seemingly harmless ways of talking are subjected to recurrent scrutiny throughout Wittgenstein's later writings. Repeatedly he seems to come close to suggesting that there is in reality no substance to the idea of an expression being used in accordance with its meaning, no substantial sense in which we, as language-users, can be regarded as committed to certain patterns of linguistic usage by the meanings we attach to expressions.

Suppose, for example, that we are concerned with a formal system. When it is determined what are the axioms and rules of inference, we tend to think of that as *already* a determination of everything that is to count as a theorem. In accepting the axioms and rules, we think of ourselves as undertaking a hard and fast commitment to accepting certain things as theorems; the mathematical task is then to uncover what in particular cases our commitment is. Wittgenstein seems to suggest that this is a false picture. Notwithstanding the fact that proof in such a system is a mechanically decidable notion—that we may programme a machine effectively to check any putative proof—there is somehow in reality no rigid, advance determination of those sentences which are theorems. To put the point in its most general form: there is in our understanding of a concept no rigid, advance determination of what is to count as its correct application.

It seems that we have, according to Wittgenstein, a philosophically distorted perspective of such locutions as

'the steps are determined by the formula'
'the way the formula is meant determines which steps may be taken'
'"Fa" has to follow from "$(x)Fx$", if the latter is meant in the way in which we mean it'
'if you really follow the rule in multiplying, you must all get the same result'

We think, for example, of the meaning of '$(x)Fx$' as so determined that it simply will not cohere with an application of this sentence if 'Fa' is not allowed to follow. We think of the meaning of '$x^2 + 2$' as so determined that it is fixed in advance what the reference of this expression will be for a particular integral value of x. But for Wittgenstein it is an error to think of our understanding of such expressions as already predetermining ahead of us what sort of use of them on future occasions it will be correct to allow. It is not determined in advance what we shall accept as the value of '$x^2 + 2$' in a particular case, but only that we shall not brook more than one alternative. Similarly it is not determined in advance how we shall apply '$(x)Fx$' and 'Fa'; it is merely, so to speak, a rule of 'grammar' that if, for example, we count an individual as 'not F', we must be prepared to conclude 'not $(x)Fx$'.

Consider *Remarks on the Foundations of Mathematics* I, 113—4: Wittgenstein's objector asks, 'Am I not compelled, then, to go the way

I do in a chain of inferences?' Wittgenstein responds, 'Compelled? After all I can presumably go as I choose'. The objector continues, 'But if you want to remain in accord with the rules you *must* go this way'. 'Not at all', says Wittgenstein. 'I call *this* accord'. 'Then', according to the objector, 'you have changed the meaning of the word "accord" or the meaning of the rule'. 'No. Who says what "change" and "remaining the same" mean here? However many rules you give me, I give a rule which justifies my employment of your rules. We might also say: when we *follow* the laws of inference (inference rules), then following always involves interpretation also'.

Compare this with *RFM* VII, 39. Wittgenstein quotes the idiom, 'if you accept this rule, you must do this'. This may mean, he says, that the rule does not leave two paths open to you here, which is a mathematical proposition. It could also mean that the rule conducts you like a gangway with rigid walls, and against this picture he urges the objection that the rule could be interpreted in all sorts of ways.

II. WITTGENSTEIN AS INDUCTIVE SCEPTIC?

What is the correct interpretation of this tendency in Wittgenstein's thought? Some of his remarks might be taken to suggest that he supposed that there were always indefinitely many, equally good, alternative ways in which a given rule might in a particular case be followed. But that, we should protest, is surely quite wrong, so long as we are concerned with a rule whose sense is at all precise. Still, it might occur to someone, there is one relatively clear way in which following a rule could be regarded always as involving an *interpretation*. Any rule which we set someone to follow may be applied by him at some stage in a manner both consistent with his past application of it and other than that which we intended. That is, if somebody suddenly makes what seems to be a deviant application of a rule, there may be an interpretation of the instructions we gave him which both explains his previous use of the terms in question—which coincided up until now with the use which we intended—and also the further deviant use. We should say that such a person had *mis*interpreted our instructions, that he had hit on a different rule from the one we intended. But it is also, evidently, a possibility that nothing which we say or do will get such a person to, for example, expand an infinite decimal as we wish. However many rules we give him, he gives a 'rule which justifies his employment of our rules'—that is, he supplies an interpretation of what he has been told to do under which it can be recognised that he is indeed doing it.

It might be suggested, then, that Wittgenstein's thought here is something like the following: where we think we have grasped the rule which people intend us to follow—where we think we understand how to apply a certain predicate, how to expand an infinite decimal—and now the occasion for a new application arises, there are always open to us indefinitely many hypotheses about how the expression should be applied in the new circumstances, how the decimal should be continued, which are consistent with the applications we have made of it so far without being corrected, and which we have witnessed others make of it. Of course, there is no reason why these alternative hypotheses should occur to us, and typically they do not; typically, the use we make of an expression is quite automatic and unhesitating. Nevertheless what we regard as following the rule will in this sense involve interpretation, that we shall, perhaps *unconsciously,* have picked on one of the available hypotheses as being the one which other language-users are applying, the one our teachers intend us to apply.

So according to this suggestion, Wittgenstein's point would not be that the same rule, be it vague or not, somehow always allows of application in indefinitely many ways. Rather it would be that there are always, on the basis of any normal training in and exposure to others' applications of the concepts involved, indefinitely many equally viable interpretations of which rule it is that we are intended to follow. And Wittgenstein is drawing our attention to the possibility of someone who fixes on an unintended interpretation of the instructions we gave him, and who, having done it once, proceeds to go on doing it, despite our best efforts to clarify to him what it is that we wish him to do. This is to be expected of course if he possesses some alternative understanding of the terms in which we attempt to clarify the original instruction; and, in any case, no matter how many examples and how much patter we give him, it will all be consistent with an indefinite variety of interpretations of the intended rule.

Of course if it is the deviator himself who supplies the alternative interpretation which explains his behaviour, it seems that the difficulty is not likely to be a very deep-reaching one; for if he is in a position to explain to us what he thought we meant, we are likely to be in a position to explain to him what we really did mean. But where we are concerned with somebody who either does not understand, or who misunderstands the terms in which we might explain to him what rule it is that we intend him to follow, so that we have recourse to examples alone, there are available to him indefinitely many hypotheses to explain whatever examples we give him.

Indeed, is not the learning of a first language just this same situation writ large? But then at any stage somebody may, like the man who continues '2004 . . . 2008 . . . 2012 . . . ' in response to the rule 'Add 2', reveal that he has *all along*, as we should say, misunderstood the manner in which some expression is to be applied. And if he misinterpreted his original training, he may subsequently misinterpret any attempt to re-educate him; all this while using the expression, as it seems to him, in a perfectly consistent and regular way.

Now, how might these considerations be thought somehow to bear on the locutions which we considered: 'The way the formula is meant determines which steps are to be taken', 'If he follows the rule, he must get this', and so on? A first suggestion would be that they call in question our right to speak of *the* way the formula is meant, or of *the* rule. What reason have we to think that there *is* a shared understanding of the rule? If variations in the temperature of a room were sufficiently localised, it would make no sense to speak of the room temperature. But is not the possibility to which Wittgenstein has drawn attention just the possibility that variations in understanding are so localised? Unless we may reasonably rule out this possibility, we have no right to speak of *the* meaning of an expression; for the meaning of an expression is just the way it is generally understood.

This would be, in effect, to suggest that some sort of inductive scepticism lies at the root of Wittgenstein's comments. The suggestion might be amplified as follows. Wittgenstein apparently rejects the idea that the meaning of an expression is anything which is properly seen as constraining a certain sort of future use of it. *One* rather extreme way of supporting that view would be to propose that a correct account of the meaning of an expression is at any stage to be constituted just by an account of its past uses. In that case each fresh use of the expression would be independent of the account so far given and would, indeed, require a refinement and extension of it. Of course, a good objection to such a view of the meaning of an expression would be its conflict with standard criteria for what it is to misunderstand a meaning. It is by *misusing* an expression that someone shows that he does not understand it, however accurate his knowledge of the history of its use. Knowing a meaning is knowing how to *do* something; we are supposed to know how *in general* the expression is to be used. This position is thus not really available, nor am I suggesting that Wittgenstein held it. On the contrary. The point is rather that it is but an *inductive* step from an account of the past use of an expression to a statement of its general use. The knowledge which we derive when we learn a first language is, it might quite naturally be supposed, nothing other than inductively based conclusions about how expressions ought in general to be used, drawn from our experience of how they have been used. So to possess the same understanding of an expression as someone else will be to have formed, on the basis of suitable training, the same inductive hypothesis about its correct use. And now, what evidence is there that widespread, local semantic variation really is a practical possibility? It would seem, on the contrary, that all the evidence points to the conclusion that we have each arrived at very much the same inductive hypotheses. The suggestion that it is out of order to speak of *the* rule—that is, our common understanding of the rule—would therefore seem to require that the evidence that we do indeed possess such a common understanding, viz. our continuing agreement about how the rule is to be applied, is somehow to be discounted. Can Wittgenstein, then, be doing anything other than playing at inductive sceptic concerning general conclusions about how an expression is to be used, based on samples of its use?

If this were a correct account of it, Wittgenstein's point would seem prima facie nothing essentially to do with meaning. The point capitalises upon the supposed equiviability of an indefinite number of incompatible hypotheses, each of which accommodates one's data concerning the past use of some expression; any number of these may actually be in play in the linguistic community, awaiting only a suitable crucial case to bring the misunderstanding into the open. But, as Hume and Goodman[1] have emphasised, just this is the situation with *any* inductive inference. Thus it might appear that the proper way to combat Wittgenstein's views, on their current interpretation, would be to solve the problem of induction!—to show that it is simply untrue that there are always available indefinitely many hypotheses which, on the basis of certain evidence, may equally reasonably be adopted. If it could be shown, it might be thought, that where, when attempting a simple induction, we are confronted with indefinitely many possible hypotheses, we are nevertheless confronted with only finitely many genuinely *probable* hypotheses—hypotheses which, in some objective way, it would be rational to take seriously, given the available evidence—then inductive scepticism in general, and so in particular inductive scepticism about meaning, would be vanquished. In the case of an induction about the correct use of some expression, it could be expected, provided the language were used in a consistent way, that all reasonable beings would sooner or later arrive at the same hypothesis. There would be in practice no possibility of deep, ineradicable misunderstanding of the kind Wittgenstein imagined.

It is worth noticing, however, that it would be incorrect to assimilate the problem of countering Wittgenstein's view, on this interpretation, to that of meeting the traditional epistemological difficulties

1. Hume *locus classicus:* (1975 (1748)), section IV; Goodman (1954), chap. 3.

with induction. If Wittgenstein's position about meaning were that of inductive sceptic, it remains the case that there would be an important difference between his position and that of inductive scepticism in general. For how are we supposed to have learned which procedures are rational, which type of hypothesis, although consistent with the data we possess, we may nevertheless rationally eliminate? If it was right to admit at all that we are confronted, in the process of learning any concept, with at any stage indefinitely many possible hypotheses about its correct application, then the same admission must be made with respect to the concept of a rational inductive inference. And now our rationality could not be invoked, at any rate by an empiricist, to cut the number of possibilities open to us down to size, since it is rationality itself that is supposed to be being explained to us.

A solution, then, to the problem of induction which took the form of showing that one can always advance, given adequate data, to a situation where it is rational on the basis of that data to accept only one particular hypothesis would not effectively countermand a general inductive scepticism about the identity of people's concepts in some area, and in particular about our concepts of the correct use of certain expressions. If the problem is that of giving a reason for thinking that we all possess the same understanding of some expression, that we intend to use it in accordance with the same governing hypothesis, inductively arrived at, then it is no answer to suggest that that at any rate will be the position if, on the basis of a sufficiently wide experience, we have arrived at our respective hypotheses by purely rational methods. This reply would simply push the difficulty back into that of giving a reason for thinking that we operate in accordance with the same notion of a sound, or rational, inductive inference. If we represent inductive scepticism in general as questioning whether it is rational to believe one, rather than any other, of the indefinitely many hypotheses which can be used to explain any particular finite set of data, then it is a peculiarity of the strain which Wittgenstein, on the present interpretation, is promoting here that it is resistant to what for any other application would be an effective disinfectant. It will be no reason for supposing that we have all achieved the same understanding of a concept that we will at any rate have done so if our conclusions are all rationally based, unless a reason can be provided for thinking that we share *that* concept.

Inductive scepticism, then, is one interpretation[2] of Wittgenstein's thought on the issue. And its application in this setting would have certain points of special interest. But the fact remains that it is not a very promising interpretation. For it consists in drawing attention to a possibility which by ordinary criteria we have every reason to exclude. The amount of successful linguistic commerce which goes on, and the variety of situations in which it takes place, constitute by any ordinary standards overwhelmingly powerful inductive grounds for supposing that we share a common understanding of most of the expressions in our language. And there are independent practical reasons—apart, that is, from the success of our use of language—for thinking that this is likely to be so. For example, we should expect there to be a practical limit on the number of alternative hypotheses which people could competently handle or imagine; so in practice it would be quite likely that one's training in a concept would determine it to within uniqueness. After a certain stage we would simply be unable to see alternatives. In addition, it is likely that certain features of a situation in which a concept is applied will always strike a learner as dramatically more noticeable than others, so that certain possible hypotheses to account for the pattern of usage which he is experiencing will simply be ignored; and we learn a first language at sufficiently tender an age to make it plausible to suppose that our dispositions to be struck by certain features and to overlook others are largely innate, and so largely shared.

To a philosopher who is impressed by the inductive sceptical challenge, of course, such considerations will seem enormously feeble. But Wittgenstein was not at all so disposed. Indeed, an inductive sceptical interpretation of his ideas on rule-following runs counter to the whole

2. Cf. Blackburn (1969), pp. 141–2.

approach of his later philosophy towards traditional epistemological problems. This is the philosopher who wrote:

> The danger here, I believe, is that of giving a justification of our procedure when there is no such thing as a justification and we ought simply to have said 'that's how we do it',[3]

and:

> To use a word without justification does not mean to use it without right.[4]

Wittgenstein did not believe that we owe a sceptic-proof explanation of the justice in our ordinary procedures of belief formation;[5] on the contrary, it was for him a symptom of an erroneous philosophical outlook, a distorted perspective upon the nature of those procedures, that we find ourselves with the capacity to take scepticism seriously. So we need a better interpretation.

III. Wittgenstein as 'Anti-Realist'?

There is at several places in Wittgenstein's later philosophy evidence of sympathy with anti-realist ideas in the sense introduced by Michael Dummett: evidence, that is, of a hostility towards a notion of truth dissociated from criteria of verification or use. For example, a desire to identify mathematical truth with provability is evident in the discussion of Gödel's theorem in *RFM* appendix III. Similarly he claims (V, 11) that to say of an infinite series that it does *not* contain a particular pattern *makes sense* (my italics) only when it is determined by the rule that the pattern should not occur. And here it seems clear that he

3. *RFM* III, 74.
4. Ibid., VII, 40.
5. Cf., among many other passages, *Philosophical Grammar* I, §§55, 61; *Bemerkungen über die Grundlagen der Mathematik* VI, 31; *On Certainty* §150.

means there to be in the rule only features which we have explicitly put there, and so are in a position to recognise, for he goes on to say:

> When I calculate the expansion further, I am deriving *new* rules which the series obeys.

It is also plausible to regard the general emphasis on the necessity for proofs to be perspicuous, or *surveyable,* as an application of an anti-realist outlook. Consider, for example:

> I want to say: if you have a proof pattern that cannot be taken in and, by a change in notation, you turn it into one which can, then you are producing a proof where there was none before.[6]

If something is a proof, then, according to Wittgenstein, it must be possible for us to recognise that it is so, to 'take it in'. There is no question of something having the status of a proof which, because of its length or complexity or for whatever reason, cannot be used as a means of persuasion.

Perhaps the most conspicuous example of an appeal to anti-realist notions in Wittgenstein's later philosophy, however, is arguably to be found in the *Philosophical Investigations* in the discussion of private languages. Consider this (chopped) quotation from I, §258:

> I want to keep a diary about the occurrence of a certain sensation. To this end I associate it with the sign 'S', and write the sign in the calendar for every day that I have the sensation. . . . I remember the connection between the sign and the sensation right in the future. But in this case I have no criterion of correctness. One would like to say, whatever is going to *seem* right to me is right. And this only means that here we can't talk about 'right'.

But *why* may we not talk about 'right'? I use '*S*' correctly on any particular occasion, it may be replied, just in case the sensation which I

6. *RFM* III, 2.

---

have on that day really is the same kind as the sensation which it was my original intention to describe as 'S'. Wittgenstein's observation is that I have no criterion for saying, no method for determining, that the two sensations really are the same, that is, are relevantly similar; I have no way of making a distinction between seeming to myself to be using 'S' correctly and really doing so. Apparently he wants it to follow that there therefore *is* no distinction here between a correct description and a merely seemingly correct description. Whereas, he wants to suggest, it is a necessary condition of someone's being said to use an expression correctly that such a distinction can be significantly made. But, whatever the merits of that claim, there would seem to be a clear repudiation of a realist notion of truth in the transition from the impossibility of our effectively making a distinction of a certain sort to the conclusion that there *is* no such distinction.

It is therefore in point to consider an account of Wittgenstein's thought about the topic of following a rule of an essentially anti-realist sort. It is not difficult to see how such an account might go. Wittgenstein's examples suggest that we have no way of verifying that we share our understanding of an expression with someone else, that on some future occasion our respective uses of the expression will not diverge so radically that we shall be driven to regard the meanings which we attach to it as different. If this is allowed, then we are implicitly taking the supposition that two people *do* agree in the way in which they understand some expression as requiring the truth of some open set of statements about their behaviour in actual and hypothetical circumstances. However, since nothing can count as recognition of the truth of such a set of statements, it will follow, for an anti-realist, that nothing will count as the *fact* of its truth. From this point of view, talk of the specific way in which someone understands an expression is admissible only if we possess some means of verification of how specifically he does understand it. But we have no such means; and thus there is no fact of his understanding the expression in some particular way, a fortiori no such thing as his using the expression in a way which complies with or violates his understanding of it.

On the first, inductive sceptical interpretation of Wittgenstein's position, the trouble with talk of someone's application of an expression according or not according with the rule was the presumption of the rule as something public, the presumption of largely shared understanding of it. The problem of the sceptic was: what right have we to suppose that there is any such shared understanding? From the point of view of the current anti-realist interpretation, the very content of this question is dubious. If there is no way of knowing that people share the same understanding of an expression, then just for that reason there is for an anti-realist nothing *to be known;* there are no instantiable truth conditions for the supposition that their understanding is shared. From the point of view of the sceptic, the difficulty, of having the right to suppose that their understanding is shared transmutes, when we shift to this anti-realist standpoint, into the problem of giving sense to the supposition that it is shared. But, from either standpoint, the idea of the rule for the use of some expression as something which we do share, something which we all ingest during the period when we learn the language, is inadmissible. Either—sceptically—there is no way of justifying the presumption that anyone's understanding of an expression coincides with one's own; or—anti-realistically—there is no such thing as the fact that it does.

IV. THE SCEPTICAL AND ANTI-REALIST INTERPRETATIONS DISCOUNTED

In fact it is clear that neither the sceptical nor the anti-realist interpretations so far considered will do, and for a shared reason. On both of these interpretations, at any rate as far as they have been developed, the difficulty has to do with the understanding which *another* has of some expression, of the rule which *another* is following in writing out the expansion of some infinite decimal. For the nature of the understanding of someone else we have only the evidence of what she has so far done. Both interpretations fasten on the point that this is never a decisive verification of the nature of her understanding. But, intuitively, the situation would seem to be quite different in one's own case. Quite simply: none of us, in our own case, is dependent upon inductive means to know what our meanings are for any particular expression. Knowledge of the character of one's own understanding does not seem to be inferential at all; at any rate, it does not *have* to be based on inference. It is better assimilated to knowledge of one's own intentions.

Now, it is consistent with both interpretations of Wittgenstein's thinking so far considered that each of us may be credited with the capacity to know finally how she herself understands some expression, what rule she herself is following. We speak of ourselves, for example, as grasping 'in a flash' what rule governs a series when given the initial elements; and even if it is not the intended rule, we tend to think that we can then nevertheless be absolutely certain of the understanding *we* have of how to continue the series. Even if I cannot know for sure what rule another is following, I can be certain, we would ordinarily allow, of the rule *I* am following and of what it requires me to do. We are tempted to think that we can in some sense survey the whole future pattern of our use of an expression—assuming we go on to use it sincerely.[7] Specify circumstances to me and, in contrast with the situation with other people, I can be absolutely certain how in those circumstances I would, if I did so sincerely, apply some relevant expression.

Both the interpretations of Wittgenstein's position so far considered leave intact the possibility of such a first/third-personal asymmetry with respect to knowledge of understanding. But the idea of such strongly privileged access to the character of one's own understanding is, I believe, a main target for him. Consider the following passages:

If you use a rule to give a description,

—of what someone is to do—

7. Compare ibid., I, 123, 130. On 'grasping in a flash', see especially *Philosophical Investigations* I, §§138–9, 151–2, 179–81, 191, 197, 323. Cf. *Lectures on the Foundations of Mathematics* lecture II, p. 26 sq.

you yourself do not know more than you say; that is, you yourself do not foresee the application which you will make of the rule in a particular case. If you say, '. . . and so on', you yourself do not know more than 'and so on'.[8]

And:

Of course we say, 'all this is involved in the concept itself'—of the rule for example. But what this means is that we incline to these determinations of the concept. For what have we in our heads which of itself contains all these determinations?[9]

For Wittgenstein, we do not have, even in our own case, advance knowledge of the manner of employment of an expression which will conform to the way we understand it; the introspective knowledge which we seem to have here somehow comes to nothing. Let me try to explain why.

V. THE INSUBSTANTIALITY OF EXCLUSIVELY FIRST-PERSONAL KNOWLEDGE OF MEANING

There is a natural response to the example of the man who persistently misunderstands the rule which we are trying to get him to follow. It is to protest that while, of course, someone may always hit on an unintended meaning for some expression, or extrapolate from our examples some rule for the series other than that which we meant, it does not follow that there is no room for the idea of the objective correctness of our and his subsequent uses of the expression relative to our *respective* understandings of it, or of the correctness of our and his continuations of a decimal relative to our *respective* understandings of which series is involved. Somebody may—of course—misunderstand our explanations, and so may not use an expression in the way that we want him to. He may, for example, be struck by some,

8. *RFM* IV, 8.
9. Ibid., VII, 42.

from our point of view, incidental feature of the examples which we gave him, and so form a notion of what justifies the application of the expression quite other than what we intended. But that does not squeeze out the idea of the objective correctness of his and our uses of the expression relative to our respective notions of its meaning. In such cases we can always in principle recognise that if *that* is what he means, when the meaning is specified to us, then his use of the expression is entirely understandable and correct. And even if we cannot finally determine what he does mean, we can still recognise the correctness or incorrectness of what he does relative to some hypothesis about what he means. Perhaps it could happen, as Wittgenstein suggests, that we might never get him to see what we mean, nor be able to form any clear impression of what he might mean; but nothing has been done to rule out the supposition that, could we do both these things, we and he could recognise of each other that we were using words intelligibly and correctly. It follows that nothing has been done to *undermine* the idea of using an expression in accordance with its meaning; each of us still has the capacity to recognise the kind of use of an expression which a particular understanding of it requires and to know how we ourselves understand it.

In what sense, though, do we really know the *kind* of use of an expression which a particular understanding requires of it? Where an independent characterisation is possible, then presumably, this is just to understand the characterisation—to know the kind of use which we should be prepared to make of the expressions involved in giving it. But that is not the basic case. The sense in which I feel my own understanding of an expression to be transparent to me is rather that of possessing a *general idea* of the kind of circumstances in which I should be prepared to apply it, if using it sincerely. And the application of the expression accords with the way I understand it when it is applied in circumstances which accord, as it seems to me, with this general idea.

Wittgenstein points out that this kind of talk suggests certain phenomenological distortions. It makes the judgement that I here use an expression in a way that fits my understanding sound essentially complex, as if I somehow 'measured' the prevailing circumstances with the general idea or compared them with a set of recollected paradigms. But often, when we are disposed to apply the expression to a new case, this need be no more than a simple response, like our responses to colours.[10] And in any case the range of circumstances in which I should confidently apply an expression may very well include cases of a sort other than those I have already encountered, or which I might imagine when asked to introspect the character of my understanding of it—to conjure up my 'general idea'. So to what am I being faithful when I apply the expression to such a case?

We shall not, presumably, want to quarrel with either of these points. Recognition of something may indeed be absolutely simple and immediate; and we may find ourselves with definite linguistic responses to situations strictly unlike any previously experienced or anticipated to which we made, or would have made, a similar response. But these considerations only tell against certain notions which we might have been tempted to invoke to *support* the idea that we each are committed to certain definite patterns of use by the way we respectively understand expressions; it is harder to see that they tell against the idea itself. To be sure, we are not always committed by exact precedents; and it is not always appropriate to see us merely as tracing out the verdict of some complex test when we judge whether some expression applies. But may I still not know the kind of circumstances my use of an expression will signal just as a special case of knowledge of my own intentions—namely, of the rules I intend to follow in using it?

To see the character of the issue Wittgenstein is raising, it is in point to consider the following argument. Suppose we have a semantic rule for the application of a predicate F: F is predicable of an individual just in case that individual satisfies the condition of being ϕ. Now, recognition of understanding seems first/third-personal asymmetric just in the sense that such a rule may be recognisably correct as an account of one's own understanding, whereas as an account of the

10. *RFM*, I, 3.

understanding of another it is always hypothetical. Of course, it is not in general possible to specify such rules in what seems to be an informative way; it is not in general possible to specify an appropriate φ for an arbitrary F without *using* F. But, we may say, it is immaterial to the status of the rule as a correct description of the sense of F whether that is the situation; all that is affected is the potential utility of the rule as part of an explanation of the meaning of F to someone who does not yet understand it.

What then is the argument? Consider any such semantic rule. It is irrelevant to the argument whether φ is informatively specified, but more natural to suppose that it is. The question is, what is it for it to be true that such a rule faithfully incorporates a particular individual's understanding of F? For you and I may sincerely agree about the correctness of such a rule, and then go on, sincerely and irresolubly, to apply F in mutually inconsistent ways. No doubt I'll want to protest in that case that all that follows is that you use F in accordance with a different rule. But it is not clear that this protest is really open to me. We agreed on how the rule for F was to be characterised; but now, it seems, I want to reserve the right to offer some other characterisation of what governs your use of the expression. (Though, of course, there is no necessity that such a characterisation will occur to me.) However, from your point of view the initial characterisation may continue to seem perfectly adequate; so you can equally well say that it is of *my* use of F that a re-characterisation of the determining rule is required. But then, what content is there to the idea of one of us being right—the idea of *a correct* characterisation of your and my respective rules? And if there is none, how can I express the nature of the rule which *I* follow, if I wish to describe my use of F? And how can the rule be an object of knowledge to me?

The knowledge which we suppose ourselves to have of the nature of our own understanding of an expression is here assimilated to knowledge of the rule, or set of rules, which we follow in our use of it. And the question is: what is it to know what these rules are, if it is not to be able to recognise as such a correct characterisation of them? We should conclude, it therefore appears, that neither of us can claim to know what their rule is; for in the situation just described the same characterisation was 'recognised' to apply to what turned out to be different rules, and neither of us can enforce our respective views.

Specious as it may seem, this simple argument is decisive unless we are prepared to allow—what will doubtless seem a very natural next step—that it is only relative to her own understanding of the terms involved in it that a rule adequately characterises someone's under-standing of an expression. The picture is thus that each of us knows what rule we are following, and we both give the same characterisa-tion of the rule; each of us indeed recognises the correctness of the characterisation. It is just that the characterisation may mean differ-ent things in different mouths. But the price of allowing us this capac-ity is that our self-knowledge of our meanings floats free of any public ties: that it does not matter whether or not we can convey to *anyone else* how our understanding is properly characterised.

The dilemma is therefore this. If the disagreement in our respective uses of *F* is taken to show that one of us gave an incorrect characteri-sation of their rule, then, since there is no way of recognising who, neither of us can be said to know that their own characterisation was correct, nor therefore to know how they understand the expression—unless this knowledge is to be something which they cannot *state*. On the other hand, if it is allowed that *both of us* may have given a cor-rect account of the rules which we follow, then since, from my point of view, any old manner of application of *F* by you will now be con-sistent with what you actually said your rule was, and vice versa, nei-ther of us has actually provided *any* account of their rule for *F*; no specific expectations on my part are licensed by the supposition that you follow the rule which you stated, and you are no better placed vis-à-vis me.

The two horns of the dilemma come indeed to the same thing, more or less: my knowledge of the rule that I follow is utterly indiffer-ent to the possibility of my communicating it. But is there not inde-pendently a great temptation to think just that?—that even where the specification of ϕ contains *F*, something is intended by your assent to the rule which you may not be able to convey? If you say that you call only green things 'green', don't you at least know which circumstances you mean? You think of something green and say to yourself: 'I call *that* sort of thing green', and this information—of the *sort*, not the particular item, which you mean—is something you have whether or not you can get it across to me.

It is this conception of knowledge of one's own understanding, and hence of what conforms to it, which Wittgenstein wishes to oppose. For Wittgenstein, there is nothing in the idea of my meaning something by an assertion—'I call this sort of thing "green"'—which I cannot straightforwardly convey. But this is not our ordinary outlook on the matter. My assent to the rule, we feel, is always informative *for me*, as it were; I know what kind of pattern of use I am committing myself to. When I assent to the rule 'F is to be applied only to individuals which are ϕ', I commit myself to a quite determinate way of using F, which is quite clear to me, even if I cannot finally make plain to others what this way of using F is to be.

In Wittgenstein's view, this situation cannot be the locus of a determinate commitment. I have no privileged overview of the total range of circumstances in which, if I am faithful to my understanding, I shall be prepared to say that condition ϕ is satisfied. Partly it is, as noted, that some of these circumstances may be unlike any that I have previously visualised or encountered. Proofs are a particularly good example of this. 'But,' it will be retorted, 'they will not be unlike in any relevant respects, or you would not presumably be prepared to describe them as F.' And that is right. The key point is, rather, that my impressions of relevant likeness here are *the source* of my judgements about the instantiation of condition ϕ rather than based on some independent grip on the latter. Of course, my successive sincere applications of an expression all seem quite *familiar* to me. But the feeling of familiarity and the disposition to reapply the same expression are all the same thing, so to speak. I can do nothing to make out the thought that the former amounts to recognition of the requirements of my personal rule and hence justifies the latter.

What is the putative content that I attach to my intention to call just green things 'green', which I may not be able to convey to you? Suppose I am asked to concentrate on that content; what kind of thing will I do? I might look around the room at the various green things in it, visualise a few others, conjure up some memories of green things. '*That's* the kind of thing I mean', I might say to myself. '*That's* the kind of thing which I always call "green"'. But where in that routine is the commitment to a certain determinate pattern of future use? For the fact is that whenever in the future I find myself disposed to call something 'green', I shall count it just on that account as being *that* kind of thing. The point is essentially an extension of that in the passage quoted earlier from the *Investigations* concerning the idea of a private rule of a language of sensations. Naturally, when I use the word 'green' sincerely on future occasions, it will seem to me that my use is familiar, is of the same pattern to which I earlier committed myself; just that is incorporated in the adverb 'sincerely'. But how can I unilaterally give sense to the idea that it *really* is of such a pattern, that there is an objective similarity in the circumstances in which I apply 'green', which I may be unable to communicate to others but which I can look within and discern?

Wittgenstein wants us to realise that actually we can give no sense to this idea. I can flatter myself that I use a word in a stable, determinate way and know within myself at least what this way is, and how I intend to continue. But if there really were an objective but perhaps incommunicable pattern which I set out to follow in my use of the word 'green', then it is conceivable that while seeming to myself to be using the word in an essentially consistent way, my employment of it might actually be quite chaotic and irregular. All that I can effectively intend to do is to apply 'green' just when it *seems* to me that things are relevantly similar; but that is not a commitment to any regularity—it is merely an undertaking to apply 'green' just when I am disposed to apply 'green'.

Asked to concentrate on what we mean by an expression *F*, we tend, as remarked, to concentrate upon past occasions on which we have applied it and to visualise others in which we would apply it. We *focus*, it might be said, on our idea of what it is to be *F*; and if we do not employ the picture of carrying the idea with us as a means of assessment of future circumstances, we come very near to it. The truth is, however, that to describe our successive sincere uses of an expression as based on the intention to preserve a certain pattern, a pattern which for each of us is transparent to himself, is to misdescribe what using an expression in accordance with one's understanding of it amounts to. We simply find ourselves with a sincere disposition to apply F again in this new case, and that is the whole of the matter. If sense could be given to the idea of an objective similarity between the cases, then, to adapt a simile from the *Investigations*, God could look into our minds, see what similarity it was which we intended to describe by the use of F and so predict the future occasions on which we should use F, provided we used it in accordance with our intentions. But without such an objective notion, even God cannot know what specifically, if we carry out our intentions, we shall do; if my intention to follow a specific rule is to license any specific expectations, there has to be some other account of what the rule requires than in terms of my impressions. If there is no other account, then just to know my intention is to know nothing at all.

Are we then to deny that there is any first/third-personal asymmetry with respect to knowledge of how someone understands an expression? An asymmetry there surely is: in the normal case, I can know and tell you what I mean by an expression without inference or evidence, whereas for you to know what I mean will demand the evidence of what I say and do. The putative asymmetry we are objecting to is not that. It came out in the temptation to say that if you tell me that you intend to apply 'green' only to "green things", you may tell me nothing at all about how I may expect your use of 'green' to go; but, from your point of view, there can be a determinate pattern of use which you commit yourself to by this, and which is transparent to you. Now, however, it appears that this seeming knowledge is spurious. It is spurious because *whatever* sincere use you make of 'green' in the future will seem to you to be doing what you tried to tell me that you would. And the point, of course, applies equally to expressions whose senses are complex and for which an informative criterion of application could actually be formulated; for in employing such a criterion simple classifications must at some level be involved, and with respect to these we have no notion of objectivity, save that afforded by the backdrop of communal consensus, with which to underpin our classificatory dispositions.

There is thus no respectable sense in which, indifferently to any possibility of communication, knowledge of my own meanings enables me to be sure how I shall use some expression, if I use it sincerely, and in which I cannot be so sure about you. Of course, I *cannot* be sure about you; that is, I cannot rule out the possibility that you will later sincerely make what seem to me quite baffling uses of some expression, which force me to suppose that you understand it differently. And that much, at least, I can rule out in my own case; I shall not be baffled by whatever *sincere* uses I make of an expression in the future. What is wrong is the tendency to inflate this *being at ease* in one's own linguistic practice into knowledge of—to oneself if to no one else—manifest and intended patterns in one's use of expressions which one mostly successfully upholds. I know of no such patterns for I have no way of determining whether they are continued; I merely find myself inclined to reapply a word in this new case. If that counts as continuing a pattern, the surroundings necessary to make it so must exceed my mere good intentions.

These ideas are as fundamental to Wittgenstein's later philosophy of mathematics as to his philosophy of mind. He supposed, I believe, that the epistemology of concepts implicit in the platonist philosophy of mathematics cannot stand without the support of the notion of the personal semantic contract; that the phenomenology of "hardness" about logical and mathematical necessity has everything to do with our sense of what can be reconciled with our own, as it were, inner understanding—and that this idea of 'reconciliation' thus belongs essentially with the mythological conception of first-personal knowledge of meanings which we have been concerned with here.

✒

This essay was originally drafted for graduate classes on the *Remarks on the Foundations of Mathematics* which I gave in 1974, at a time when the rule-following ideas had attracted virtually no secondary literature at all. That was still true in 1980 when a later version featured as chapter 2 of my *Wittgenstein on the Foundations of Mathematics*. For that version I cited the following Wittgensteinian sources and further readings available at that time:

> *Remarks on the Foundations of Mathematics* (2nd ed.) I, 1–3, 113–18; III, 8–9; V, 32–5, 45–6
> *Bemerkungen über die Grundlagen der Mathematik* VI, 15–49; VII, 47–60
> *Philosophical Investigations* I, §§138–326 (but esp. §§185–242), §§692–3
> *Philosophical Grammar* I, §§6, 17–18, 52, 75
> *Zettel* §§87, 279–308
> *Blue Book* pp. 73–4
> *Brown Book* II, §5
> *Lectures on the Foundations of Mathematics* lectures II; VI; VIII, p. 124

But it was still possible, without irresponsibility, to cite no further secondary sources or recommended reading at all. The present version is closely based on that of 1980 (albeit with all references to *RFM* revised to tally with the 3rd edition), but it has jettisoned one section and has been quite extensively edited both to forestall some of the more serious misunderstandings which my enthusiastically incautious wording later proved to encourage, and to try to bring out more forcefully the significance of the central argument of its predecessor.

2

Rule-Following, Objectivity and
the Theory of Meaning

I.   Qualms about the Objectivity of Meaning

When we think of a question in some area of enquiry as an *objective* issue, what we have in mind, I take it, is—very crudely—that a two-fold distinction is required to do justice to the situation: there is our, perhaps settled, opinion on the one hand, and, on the other, the (hopefully concordant) true facts of the matter. For the believer in objectivity, human opinion in no sense constitutes truth; truth is in no sense dependent upon human opinion.

Realism about verification-transcendent statements—the view, that is, that we are capable of intellectual grasp of the character of a range of facts, or at least possible facts, to which we can have no cognitive access—obviously believes in the objectivity of such statements. With decidable statements, however—whatever may prove to be the correct general characterisation of that class—the belief in objectivity cannot have to do with possible verification-transcendence. Rather, what is in play is something like this notion: confronted with any decidable, objective issue, there is *already* an answer which—if we investigate the matter fully and correctly—we will arrive at. The objectivity of decidable statements consists, in this way, in their possession of determinate, investigation-independent truth values—in their, as I shall call it, *investigation-independence*.

I believe, rightly or wrongly, that the Wittgenstein of the *Philosophical Investigations* and *Remarks on the Foundations of Mathematics* is, rightly or wrongly, sceptical about investigation-independence, and that the grounds for that scepticism are embedded in his discussions of rule-following. In the first part of this essay, I want to try to convey, all too hastily I fear, something of the character of that scepticism. And in the second part, though again I shall have space only to pose certain questions and adumbrate certain theses, I shall attempt to sketch some of the challenges I think Wittgenstein's later thought poses to recent approaches in the philosophy of language.

II. AGAINST INVESTIGATION-INDEPENDENCE

Investigation-independence requires a certain stability in our understanding of our language. To think, for example, of the shape of some particular unobserved object as already determinately describable in a particular way, irrespective of whether or not we ever inspect it, is to accept that there are facts about how we will, or would, assess its shape if we do, or did, so *correctly*, in accordance with the meaning of the expressions in our vocabulary of shapes; the putative investigation-independent fact about the correct description of the object's shape is a fact about how we would describe it if on the relevant occasion we continued to use germane expressions in what we regard as the correct way, the way in which we have always tried to use those expressions when aiming at telling the truth. The idea of investigation-independence thus leads us to look upon grasping the meaning of an expression as grasping a general pattern of use, conformity to which requires certain determinate uses in so far unconsidered cases. The pattern is thus to be thought of as an extending *of itself* to cases which we have yet to confront.

It has to be acknowledged, however, that the 'pattern' is, strictly, inaccessible to absolutely definitive explanation. For, as Wittgenstein stresses, no explanation of the use of an expression is proof against misunderstanding; verbal explanations require correct understanding of the vocabulary in which they are couched, and examples are open to an inexhaustible variety of interpretations. So we move towards the idea that understanding an expression is a kind of 'cottoning on'—that is, a leap, an inspired guess at the pattern of application which an instructor is trying to get across. It becomes almost irresistible to think of someone who is learning a first language as if she were forming general *hypotheses*. 'Cottoning on' would be forming the right hypothesis; and failing to do so would be forming the wrong, or no hypothesis. And the leap involved would just be that with the best will in the world we—the instructors—cannot do better than leave an indefinite variety of hypotheses open for selection.

Well, what is wrong with that picture of the business? On occasion, no doubt, we do self-consciously form hypotheses in order to interpret what somebody means; people are, for example, sometimes embarrassed to confess that they do not know the meaning of a particular expression, so are reluctant to ask to have it explained. What is wrong with thinking that, when we are learning a new expression, it is always *as if* we formed a hypothesis? It rather depends how circumspect we are in our application of the resulting picture. For it makes sense to think of someone as having a hypothesis only if *she* knows what it is, that is, what its correctness will require. So the question is whether it is legitimate to think of a first-language trainee as knowing what she herself has come to mean by an expression, what hypothesis about its correct use she has formed. If the 'as if' is to be taken literally, we have to be able to credit the trainee with knowledge about what we—the instructors—will allow in a particular new case if her hypothesis is correct—if her conjectural understanding of the relevant expression coincides with ours. So the picture encourages, if it does not make absolutely inevitable, a drift into the idea that each of us has some sort of privileged access to the character of her own understanding of an expression. Each of us, that is to say, knows of a particular idiolectic pattern of use which she intends her use of an expression to subserve, and for which there is a strong presumption, when sufficient evidence has accumulated, that it is shared communally.

The hypothetico-deductive picture thus encourages us to accept as a matter of course the rider of certain knowledge of the character of one's own understanding of an expression. And this idea is fundamental to our whole conception of concepts, or meanings, as stable, on which the idea of investigation-independence feeds. But the rider is not a matter of course. It involves an overdignification. In cases where there really *is* a hypothesis, as in the case of the embarrassed person who is trying to guess the meaning of some expression, this hypothesis can be formulated and its correct application will be open to communal assessment. But when it is merely a matter of an 'as if', the trainee will not have the vocabulary to tell us—or herself—what it is she thinks we mean. To be sure, the idea of hypothesis is then psychologically artificial—but it was already conceded to be a mere picture anyway. The more fundamental objection is that nothing can be done to defend the description that the trainee *recognises* how, if her conjectural understanding is right, we will treat a particular new case, against the more austere account that she simply expects *this* application to be acceptable to us.

The trouble is to prise apart the fact of what her 'as if' hypothesis requires from her expectations about the new case—or, what comes to the same thing, her response to it. For *we* cannot tell whether she implements her hypothesis correctly, that is, whether her expectations here really are consonant with the interpretation she has put on our treatment of, say, the samples which we gave her; and *she* cannot provide any basis for a distinction between their really being so and its merely seeming to her that they are. It would make all the difference if she could tell us what her hypothesis was; then there could be a public assessment of the situation. But this is just what she cannot do in the fundamental case when the whole idea of a hypothesis about a pattern is meant merely as an 'as if' idea.

The proper conclusion is not merely that the hypothetico-deductive picture is potentially misleading, but that there cannot be such a thing as first-personal privileged recognition of the dictates of one's understanding of an expression, irrespective of whether or not that understanding can be shared. For the only circumstance in which it makes sense to think of someone as correctly applying a non-standard understanding of, 'square', for example, is where others can agree about how, given that *that* is what she means, she ought to characterise this object.

Now, how exactly do these reflections bear on the idea of investigation-independence? What they bear on is the implicit idea that if we do not allow the description of certain so far uninvestigated objects in certain particular predeterminate ways, we shall have broken faith with the patterns of use which we have given to the relevant vocabulary. The question is whether it is legitimate to think of our mastery of a language as involving anything properly seen as a capacity to recognise what preservation of such patterns requires. For suppose that you find yourself incorrigibly out of line concerning the description of some new case. We have just noted that you can't, single-handedly as it were, give sense to the idea that you are at least being faithful to your *own* pattern; that is, that you recognise how you must describe this new case if you are to remain faithful to your own understanding of the relevant expressions, no matter what anyone else may think. How, then, would your disposition to apply the expression to a new case become, properly speaking, recognition of the continuation of a pattern if it so happened that you were *not* out of line, if it so happened that there was communal agreement with you?

If there can intelligibly be such a thing as a ratification-independent fact about whether an expression is used on a particular occasion in the same way as it has been used on previous occasions, then the fact ought to be something which we can recognise—or at least be justified in claiming to obtain. Otherwise the correct employment of language would become on every occasion radically transcendent of human consciousness. But I cannot legitimately credit myself with the capacity to recognise that *I* am here applying an expression in the same way as *I* have used it before, so long as this capacity is to be indifferent to whether I can persuade others of as much or whether that is the way in which the community in general uses the expression. How, in that case, is it possible for me to recognise that I am using the expression in the same way that *we* used it before? How, where it seems that I cannot significantly claim to have grasped an idiolectic pattern, can I claim to have grasped a *communal* one? How does others' agreement with me turn my descriptive disposition into a matter of recognition of conformity with a pattern, recognition of an antecedent and independent fact about how the communal pattern extends to the new case?

To put the point another way: none of us, if he finds himself on his own about a new candidate for φ-ness, and with no apparent way of bringing the rest around, can sensibly claim to recognise that the community has here broken faith with its antecedent pattern of application for φ; the proper conclusion for him is rather that he has just discovered that he does not know what φ means. So there can be no such thing as a legitimate claim to unilateral recognition that here a community's pattern of application of a particular expression is contravened. So long as the 'recognition' is unilateral, it cannot legitimately be claimed to be recognition, nor can that state of affairs of which it is supposed to be recognition be legitimately claimed to obtain (although if the community can be brought around, it will later be legitimate to claim that the unilateral verdict *was* correct). But how, in that case, can there ever be such a thing as a legitimate claim to unilateral recognition of how, provided it is to be applied in the same manner as previously, any particular expression should be applied in particular circumstances? How can the mere *absence* of the information that the community at large does not agree legitimise the claim to recognition of the fact whose status is supposed in no sense to await our ratification?

Virtually everyone, myself included, will be tempted to reply here that a solicitable community of assent just does make the relevant difference, just does supply the objectivity requisite to transform one's unilateral response into a matter of recognition or mistake. Thus in the absence of the information that the community at large does not agree with one's verdict, standard inductive grounds will remain intact for the supposition that there will be sufficient agreement; and one's claim to have recognised how the 'pattern' extends to the particular new case will be justified accordingly. But ask, what *type* of bearing would the discovery that one was in line with the rest of the community concerning this case have on the question of the correctness of the original unilateral verdict? How does finding out that other people agree with one make it legitimate to claim apprehension of a fact whose status does not require that we acknowledge it at all? Is it that it is somehow less *likely* that lots of people are in error? To suppose that such was the correct account would be to confront the unanswerable challenge to explain how the probabilities could be established.

Assuredly, there is truth in the idea that it is a community of assent which supplies the essential background against which alone it makes sense to think of individuals' responses as correct or incorrect. The question is whether it can be explained why there should be any truth in this idea unless the correctness or incorrectness of individuals' responses is precisely *not* a matter of conformity or non-conformity with *investigation-independent* facts; for if the contrary account were correct, the role of communal assent in determining the correctness of individuals' responses would require the capacity of the *community as a whole* to recognise what conformity to antecedent patterns of use required of us. And now essentially the same problem arises again that beset the attempt to make unilateral sense of correct employment of an idiolect. What is it for a *community* to recognise that it here continues a pattern of application of an expression on which it previously embarked? What does it add to describe the situation in two-fold terms, of the fact of conformity to the pattern *and* the community's recognition of the fact, rather than simply saying that there is communal agreement about the case? It is unclear how we can answer. We are inclined to give new linguistic responses on which there is communal consensus the dignity of 'objective correctness'; but we have, so to speak, only our own word for it. If 'correctness' has to mean *ratification-independent conformity with an antecedent pattern,* the uncomfortable fact is that there is apparent absolutely nothing we can do to make the contrast active between the consensus description and the correct description. Of course it may happen that a community changes its mind; and when it does so, it does not revise the judgement that the former view at one time enjoyed consensus. But that is a fact about our cultural procedures; to call attention to it is to call attention to the circumstane that we make use of the notion that we can all be wrong, but it is not to call attention to anything which gives sense to the idea that the wrongness consists in departure from a ratification-independent pattern.

This, I believe, is the fundamental point of Wittgenstein's 'limits of empiricism' remarks.[1] None of us unilaterally can make sense of the idea of correct employment of language save by reference to the authority of securable public assent on the matter; and for the community itself there is no higher authority, so no standard to meet except in its own ongoing judgements of linguistic propriety. It is another matter why we find the idea so attractive that the communal use of language tracks a network of determinate independent patterns, and that our communal judgement is somehow in general a faithful reflection of how they extend. Probably it is because we do not pause to consider how much sense we can really give these ideas; and their opposites seem worrying.

To put the point in the starkest possible way: how can we penetrate *behind* our agreed verdict about a particular question in order to compare it with the putative investigation-independent proper description? Once we accept the double-element conception of the situation—actual verdict and investigation-independent proper description confronting one another—we feel constrained to say that all we can know for sure is how things *seem* to us to deserve description; certainly, we may come to revise our assessment—but then, again, the revised assessment would be merely what *seems* right. The

1. *Remarks on the Foundations of Mathematics* III, 71; IV, 29; VII, 17, 21; cf. *On Certainty* §§110, 204.

dilemma we then confront as a community is thus essentially that of the would-be private linguist: faced with the impossibility of establishing any technique of comparison between our preferred description and the putative objective fact about the proper description, we must construe the latter either as something we cannot know at all, or—the classic choice for the private linguist about sensations—as something which we cannot but know. But both courses are equally disreputable; and we should therefore abandon the conception of meaning which leads to the dilemma. If we do so, we shall reject the idea that, in the sense implied by investigation-independence, a community goes right or wrong in accepting a particular verdict on a particular decidable question; rather—from that point of view—it just goes.

III. A Question about the Significance of the 'Theory of Meaning'

Some philosophers, of whom Donald Davidson has been perhaps the most determined, have recommended work towards the construction of formal theories of meaning for natural languages as a fruitful way of approaching traditional problems in the philosophy of language. Others have agreed at least to the extent of accepting that extensive philosophical gains can be expected to accrue from consideration of the question: what exact form should such a theory ideally take?[2] What does Wittgenstein's later philosophy of language have to say to proponents of these views?

The question is of course very wide-ranging, and raises a host of exegetical problems about Wittgenstein's writings and an army of questions concerning the claims which might legitimately be made on behalf of the sort of recursive theory typically proposed. My aim here is not to answer questions but to ask them—questions which, I think, will quite briskly occur to anyone familiar with Wittgenstein's later

2. See, e.g., Foster (1976), p. 4; McDowell (1976), p. 97.

writings who devotes some thought to the sort of semantic pro-gramme being advocated.

The relevant sort of systematic theory of meaning for a natural lan-guage will consist in an axiomatic system whose deployment will enable us, in principle at least, to resolve any well-formed declarative sentence in the language into its essential semantically contributive constituents, and to determine its meaning on the basis of the struc-ture thereby revealed and the assigned semantic values of those con-stituents. The theory may, as Davidson proposed, incorporate a Tarskian axiomatic theory of truth; or it might utilise as its central semantic concept something other than truth. In what follows we shall be concerned with the constraints which Davidson imposes on any axiomatic theory of truth which is to be suitable for the purposes of a theory of meaning; but these constraints would be no less intu-itively attractive if the central theory was to be, say, a theory of assert-ibility. And the points to be made are applicable equally, if at all, to all theories of meaning fitting the above general characterisation.

The crucial issue is of course: to what questions is such a theory able to give answers? Clearly, there are plenty of well-established questions in the philosophy of language which a theory of this kind need not be capable of addressing at all. To begin with, a theory meet-ing the general characterisation just bruited would not be required to say anything about commanding, asking whether, or wishing; it would need supplementation with, in the Frege/Dummett terminol-ogy,[3] a theory of *force*—a theory which makes explicit what differ-ence it makes whether a sentence to which the original theory assigns a particular truth-condition, say, is understood as a command, or question, or wish, or assertion, or any other kind of linguistic act which we deem to constitute a further kind of illocutionary force with which an utterance can be made; and goes on to describe the gram-matical indicators, if any, which the studied language uses to mark these various kinds of force.

It is clear, second, that a whole range of limitations are consequent upon the fact that, in the case where the language in which the theory

3. See Dummett (1973), pp. 302–3.

is stated is the same as, or an extension of, its object-language, the theory need not, in order to comply with the characterisation given, say any more about the meaning of any particular semantically atomic expression than can be conveyed by incorporation of an appropriate 'homophonic' axiom; that is, an axiom in which that very expression is *used,* in whatever way the theory considers appropriate, to state its own semantics. For suppose that such an axiom is all the theory has to offer by way of elucidation of the semantic role of a particular predicate, ϕ. Then the construction of the theory will neither deliver nor presuppose any account of the *vagueness* of ϕ, if it is vague; the *theoreticity* or *observationality* of ϕ, if it is theoretical or observational; the *reducibility* of ϕ in terms of other predicates, if it is so reducible. In these ways, and in general, the theory will fail to speak to the question: in what does an understanding of ϕ consist— what are the criteria for mastery of the use of ϕ? And it will keep silence, third, on perhaps the most fundamental question at all: what *is* a language—what distinguishes language-use from any other rule-governed, goal-directed activity, and what makes mouthings and inscriptions into uses of language?

Where, therefore, would light be cast? One answer would be that a theory of the kind characterised can still be a theory of *speakers' understanding* of the object-language. For we ought to distinguish between giving an account of what an understanding of any particular expression *consists in*—what, that is, distinguishes anyone who possesses that understanding from someone who lacks it—and giving an account of *what is known* by anyone who understands that expression. It is in general one thing to state a particular item of knowledge, another further to explain what having that knowledge essentially is. So, prima facie, a theory of the 'modest'[4] kind may still be presented as an account of understanding; it is just that it will purport to characterise only what is understood by anyone who knows the meaning of a particular expression, and will not attempt to explain what having this understanding amounts to. It appears to be open, then, to the proponents of such a theory to present it as that less

---

4. Dummett (1975), p. 102.

ambitious kind of theory of understanding, a theory of what speakers know.

That Davidson originally so intended his particular brand is strikingly suggested by his insistence that an adequate such theory must supply the means to derive for each declarative sentence in the language a meaning-delivering theorem in (i) a *structure-reflecting way* on the basis of (ii) *a finite axiomatisation.*[5] The intention of this pair of constraints would appear to be to ensure the capacity of the theory to explain the familiarly stressed fact that mastery of a typical natural language will involve the ability, on the basis of finite training, to understand indefinitely many sentences which its speakers have never heard before. The goal is, apparently, a model of this epistemic capacity; it is desired to understand how it is *possible* for us to recognise the meaning of any given new significant sentence in our language. The answer is to be: by deploying the information encapsulated in the axioms germane to the parts of the sentence in the manner determined by the structure of the sentence, that is, the manner reflected by the mode of derivation within the theory of the relevant meaning-delivering theorem.

Naturally, it would be unwise to insist that *only* this underlying conception of the significance of such a theory could vindicate the organisation which Davidson proposed it should have. It could very well make a difference, to begin with, whether, for example, the theory was being constructed as the end of a programme of radical translation, in one language for another, or whether the goal was rather to use a particular language to state its own semantics. It might be that in the former case it would only be by observing Davidson's two constraints that we could actually construct a theory yielding a meaning-delivering theorem for each of the object-language's declarative sentences. But in the latter case, unless the conception described is presupposed, it is, to say the least, a very nice question why, assuming that we have available an effective criterion for determining whether an arbitrary sequence of symbols is a significant declara-

5. See, e.g., Davidson (1973), p. 81.

tive sentence in the language in question, we should not simply help ourselves to the general form of T-theorem, or whatever form the meaning-delivering theorems take, as an infinitary *axiom schema,* thereby saving a great deal of work. If the goal is not to provide a model of how the meaning of an arbitrary declarative sentence in the language can be recognised but merely to state what its meaning is, then—putting to one side presently irrelevant complications about the appropriate form for such a statement to take—it is hard to see what objection there could be to such a course.

How, though, ought we to receive the suggestion that a theory which both correctly characterised the meaning of all significant expressions in the object-language, and satisfied Davidson's two constraints, would *explain* the capacity of speakers of the object-language to recognise the sense of new sentences? It is part of mastery of a language neither to know a theory of this kind explicitly, nor to be able to formulate one, nor even to be able to recognise a satisfactory formulation if one is presented. (For all we know, there may *be* no such satisfactory theory for English.) But it seems that if such a theory really is to explain the performance of speakers of the object-language, then there must be a sense in which knowledge of its content can be attributed to them. Accordingly, there has been a tendency to invoke some sort of notion of *implicit* knowledge to supply the needed contact of the theory with the studied speakers' actual performance.[6]

This notion can certainly seem natural enough. Suppose, for example, we were to teach certain dumb illiterates to play chess—not merely to mimic chess play, but to play correctly and strive to win. It would seem unexceptionable to describe such people as possessing *knowledge,* albeit inarticulately, of exactly that information which someone who understands an explicit formulation of the rules of chess knows articulately. Taken in one way, there is indeed nothing objectionable about such a description. For giving such a description need commit one to no more than that the people in question habitually comport themselves in such a way when playing chess as to

6. See, e.g., Dummett (1976), pp. 69–72.

satisfy any criteria which we might reasonably wish to impose on someone's having understood an explicit statement of the rules of the game. But in that case, to attribute implicit knowledge of such a 'theory' of the game to them is to do no more than obliquely to describe their behaviour; it is to say that they behave in just the way in which someone would behave who successfully tried to suit his behaviour to such an explicit statement.[7]

It is doubtful, however, whether it can be *this* notion of implicit knowledge which is relevant to the concerns of a theorist of meaning who conceives his goal to be an explanation of how a master of the object-language is able to recognise the senses of novel sentences, and accepts Davidson's two constraints as necessary if that goal is to be achieved. For to have, in the described sense, implicit knowledge of the content of a theory of meaning amounts to no more than being disposed to employ the object-language in the manner which would be followed by anyone who, being sufficiently agile intellectually and knowing sufficiently much about the world, successfully tried to suit his practice with the object-language to an explicit statement of the theory. So construed, talk of speakers' implicit *knowledge* of the theory is, indeed, misleading; there is no real suggestion of an internalised 'programme'. All that such talk need involve is that speakers' practice fits a certain compendious description. But now the question resurges: what reason would the theorist have to accept Davidson's two constraints—that the theory be finitely axiomatisable and that the mode of derivation of each meaning-delivering theorem reflect the structure of the relevant sentence—if his objective were only the achievement of such a description? For the fact is that it is only the lowest-level output of the theory—the T-theorems, or their counterparts in a non-truth-theoretic theory—which purport to describe discernible aspects of speakers' practice. So if, as when the theory is stated in a language for that very language or a fragment of it, it is possible to peel off, as it were, the descriptive part of the theory, for example by taking the general form of T-theorems as an infinitary

7. Cf. Foster (1976), pp. 1–4.

axiom schema, there is apparent, once the objective is restricted merely to describing speakers' practice, no reason for having the full-blown theory. To suit one's beaviour to what is stated by the theory is just to suit one's behaviour to what is stated by its practice-describing part. So if the theorist's aim was merely to formulate a theory knowledge of which would suffice for competence in the object-language, there would not necessarily be any point in observing Davidson's constraints; no advance reason why it would not serve his purpose to axiomatise more simply, even if infinitistically, the descriptive part of a theory which met those constraints.

A theory of that truncated form would, of course, seem *hugely* trivial and unexplanatory. It would contribute not a jot to the purpose of devising a framework by reference to which traditional philosophical questions about language-mastery could be formulated and answered. But if the aim were no more than deliverance of an account of the meaning of each declarative sentence in the object-language, and if we were content that each instance of the relevant axiom schema was of an appropriate form for such an account to take, then what more could we want?

One reason why Davidson's idea has occasioned interest, it seems to me, is because it aspires to cast philosophical light on the concept of meaning without overt recourse to any intensional notions an attractive promise to any philosopher who sees these problems in the way that Quine encouraged us to see them. But a more fundamental reason for the 'Davidsonic boom', at Oxford at any rate, was that a framework seems to be suggested in which it would be possible to *explain* the potentially infinitary character of mastery of the sort of natural language which we all speak. What I am suggesting is that unless this prospect is to be illusion, it has to make sense to attribute to speakers of the studied language implicit knowledge of the whole of an appropriate theory of meaning for that language, and to mean by this attribution something richer than a mere imputation to speakers of a disposition to suit their practice to the theory's requirements. For implicit knowledge, in the latter, weaker sense, of the content of a Davidsonian theory would be just the same thing as implicit knowledge of its T-theorems; and it is manifestly no *explanation* of a person's ability to understand novel sentences in his language that he has *that* knowledge—to attribute that knowledge to him is no more than to attribute to him the very ability that interests us. A more substantial notion of implicit knowledge of its content is therefore going to be required if a theory of meaning is to explain how speakers of its target language are able to recognise the meanings of new sentences. the question is whether there is any respectable such 'more substantial' notion.

IV. WITTGENSTEINIAN DOUBTS

Wittgenstein's later thought contains a number of prima facie challenges to the idea that has emerged: the idea that the potentially infinitary character of mastery of a typical natural language can be explained by appeal to its speakers' implicit knowledge, appropriately richly interpreted, of the contents of a suitable theory of meaning.

First, and most obviously, the thesis seems to involve thinking of mastery of the language as consisting in (unconscious) equipment with the information which the axioms of the theory codify, information which systematically settles the content of so far unconstructed and unconsidered sentences. Such a conception is far from patently coherent with the repudiation of the objectivity of sameness of use involved in the scepticism about investigation-independence sketched earlier. The first challenge is to demonstrate *either* that it is right to repudiate that scepticism *or* that there is no real tension—that the explanatory claim made by the thesis does not require that we conceive of the meanings of novel sentences as investigation-independent, nor presuppose that people's agreement in their use of language has a foundation of the sort which the rule-following considerations would argue to be mythical. I'll return to this below.

There immediately arises, second, the challenge to show that the thesis is not, at bottom, simply an inflated version of the old muddle about 'universals' and predicate understanding. It is at best harmless to talk of understanding a predicate as 'grasp of a universal'; and it is harmless only if we do not think that we have thereby achieved some sort of *explanation* of people's capacity to agree about the application of the predicate. All that such terminology actually achieves is a measure of embroidery upon the phenomenon of agreement; for there is no criterion of what it is for us to have 'grasped' the same universal save a disposition to agree in application of the predicate. But if the fiction of universals is no explanation of people's disposition to agree in their basic predicative classifications, it is far from clear that the assumption of shared implicit knowledge of the content of a theory of meaning can provide any genuine explanation of the capacity of speakers to agree in their use of new sentences.

The third challenge is verificationist. No one is in a position to verify that a particular theory of meaning states precisely what some speaker implicitly knows. For the theorist, the theory has, like any theory, the status of a compound general hypothesis; and it ought by now to be clear just how hard it would be to defend the view that a speaker of the studied language was somehow better placed than an observer of his practice to recognise the correctness of a particular theory of meaning for his language. But it is unclear how we can achieve the kind of explanation of the open-ended character of a speaker's competence which is under consideration here unless it is legitimate to suppose that there is at large some real 'fact of the matter'—that is, that the speaker's use of his language is essentially the deployment of some *particular* body of information which some specific theory states. Each axiom of *that* theory will then actually be true of the speaker in question. And the challenge is to defend this particular invocation of a verification-transcendent notion of truth; or to show that it is not needed.

Each of these challenges deserves a separate, detailed treatment, which I cannot attempt here. Certainly, the view is not yet justified that they cannot be met, whether by an appropriate refinement of the requisite notion of implicit knowledge or by some more direct defence of it. What I do claim is that, until it is shown that the play which the thesis makes with a rich notion of implicit knowledge can be defended against these challenges at least, there is no reason to think that it is within the power of the sort of theory we are considering to serve up anything which could rightly be considered an *explanation* of the open-ended character of the competence of its object-language speakers.

Let's finish by scrutinising the first challenge a little further. As noted, it is one thing to interpret a theory of meaning as codifying information which speakers in some sense possess and deploy, another to see it merely as an attempt systematically to describe their linguistic practices. I think it is fair to say that it is the latter type of interpretation which has held sway among most of those philosophers of language who have interested themselves in formal theories of meaning, Davidsonian or otherwise. The problem, as we have seen, is then to motivate the constraints which such philosophers typically wish to impose upon interesting such theories. But supposing that this problem could be solved, there may still seem to be a very fundamental tension between thinking of linguistic practice as amenable even to bare description by the sort of theory envisaged and the rule-following considerations. For surely, it may be said, it is necessary, if such a theoretical description is to be possible, that what will constitute an admissible use of each new sentence whose construction the language in question permits is something settled in advance, predetermined by the language's 'semantic essence'. The theory is not going to confine itself to recording actual, historic uses; its role will be to formulate *generalisations,* effectively furnishing predictions about what will be counted as correct use, or appropriate responses to the use, of new sentences, and of old sentences used on new occasions. So it seems to be presupposed that the language in question *has* a certain general character, capturable by an appropriate generalisation-venturing theory. Whereas the moral of the rule-following considerations was—wasn't it?—that we have to regard correct use, or correct response to the use, of any particular sentence on a new occasion as in some fashion objectively indeterminate; it is what competent speakers do—where competence is precisely *not* a matter of a disposition to conformity with certain investigation-independent facts—which determines the correct use of expressions, rather than the other way about. How can there be such a thing as a general, correct, systematic description of a practice which at any particular stage may go in *any* direction without betrayal of its character? There is simply nothing *there* systematically to be described.

It may be replied that if this doubt were well conceived, it would not just be a certain post-Wittgensteinian concept of the proper objectives and methods of the philosophy of language which was in jeopardy. Wittgenstein's own presented methodology of assiduous attention to facts about the 'grammar' of our expressions would be equally guilty of attempting to penetrate through to general traits in our linguistic practices. In fact, though, the difficulty is surely spurious. For there is no reason to suppose that all the purposes we might have in attempting to generalise about aspects of our own or others' linguistic practices could be served only if it is legitimate to think of those practices as having investigation-independent aspects. *If* the goal of a particular theory of meaning was simply to contribute towards supplying a framework in one language for describing what counted as correct linguistic practice in the same, or another, language, no need for any assumption is apparent which the rule-following considerations would call into question—or better, if there was a need for such assumptions, then the difficulty would be one not merely for the theory of meaning but for descriptive/predictive theorising of all kinds.

In order for a particular prediction about what would be accepted as correct use of an object-language sentence in particular circumstances to have practical content from the *theorists'* point of view, it is required neither that they conceive of the relevant hypotheses in the theory as codifying certain investigation-independent general features of object-language practice, nor that they conceive of it as objectively predetermined what behaviour by object-language speakers they—the theorists—will count as meeting the relevant prediction if they judge correctly. All that *is* required is that they can agree among themselves about whether, in any particular situation, the initial conditions of the prediction are fulfilled, and about whether, if they are, the performance of object-language speakers meets the prediction's requirements. More generally, in order for any hypothesis to have a determinate meaning, it is required neither that we can render philosophically respectable the conception that it depicts some objective general trait in the studied range of phenomena, nor that it be objectively predeterminate what will have to happen if it is to be falsified in any particular situation; our securable consensus about its standing in any particular situation is enough for its utility.

The principal effect of the rule-following considerations in this vicinity is to caution a believer against allowing his interpretation of a theory of meaning to aspire to a bogus objectivity. But they do not, or so it seems to me, impugn the legitimacy of at least the most basic purpose with which such a theory might be devised: that of securing a description of the use of (part of) the object-language of such a kind that to be apprised of that description would be to know how to participate in the use of (that part of) the language.

That still leaves the problem about semantic structure, however. If the goal is to be the purely descriptive one adumbrated, there will be no point in paying attention to semantic structure unless a complete description of the use of (the relevant part of) the object-language cannot be given if we do not do so. I observed earlier that, where the metalanguage contains the object-language, there seems to be no very clear reason why it should be necessary for the theory to discern structure in order for it to fulfil that limited descriptive purpose. And, of course, almost all the philosophical interest thought to attach to formal theories of meaning depends upon preoccupation with semantic structure. So we confront a fundamental question: if, for Wittgensteinian reasons or others, an appeal to rich implicit knowledge is thought illegitimate, can any remaining adequate motive be elucidated for the belief that an interesting theory of meaning must be structure-discerning?

3   Rule-Following, Meaning
      and Constructivism

I. INTRODUCTION

John McDowell writes:[1]

> We find it natural to think of meaning and understanding in, as it were, contractual terms. Our idea is that to learn the meaning of a word is to acquire an understanding that obliges us subsequently—if we have occasion to deploy the concept in question—to judge and speak in certain determinate ways, on pain of failure to obey the dictates of the meaning we have grasped; that we are 'committed to certain patterns of linguistic usage by the meanings we attach to expressions'.[2] According to Crispin Wright, the burden of Wittgenstein's reflections on following a rule, in his later work, is that these natural ideas lack the substance we are inclined to credit them with: 'There is in our understanding of a concept no rigid, advance determination of what is to count as its correct application.'[3]

1. McDowell (1984), p. 325.
2. Wright (1980), chap. 2 (this volume Essay 1, p. 10).
3. Ibid.

If Wittgenstein's conclusion, as Wright interprets it, is allowed to stand, the most striking casualty is a familiar intuitive notion of objectivity. The idea at risk is the idea of things being thus and so anyway, whether or not we choose to investigate the matter in question, and whatever be the outcome of any such investigation. That idea requires the conception of how things could correctly be said to be anyway—whatever, if anything, we in fact go on to say about the matter; and this notion of correctness can only be the notion of how the pattern of application that we grasp, when we come to understand the concept in question, extends, independently of the actual outcome of any investigation, to the relevant case. So if the notion of investigation-independent patterns of application is to be discarded, then so is the idea that things are, at least sometimes, thus and so anyway, independently of our ratifying the judgement that this is how they are. It seems fair to describe this extremely radical consequence as a kind of idealism.

My purpose in this essay is not to try to meet McDowell's criticisms of this interpretation of Wittgenstein, but to attempt to provide a fuller perspective upon the kind of considerations[4] which suggest the 'extremely radical consequence'. Whether Wittgenstein actually ever had exactly these, or similar, considerations in mind is a question of much less interest than what force attaches to them. The exegetical issue between myself and McDowell is, I suggest, best viewed as concerning whether Wittgenstein, as McDowell interprets him, has any proper recourse to the constructivist imagery which is so prominent in the *Remarks on the Foundations of Mathematics*. I reserve pursuit of that issue to another occasion.

---

4. The account suggested here differs from Wright (1980) primarily in dissociating the argument from reliance on general 'anti-realist' premises. It is important, I think, to recognise that, as was argued in chapters 11 and 12 of that book, the sort of anti-realism about meaning developed by Dummett does command suspicion of the contractual conception of understanding illustrated by the above quotation from McDowell; but, equally important, that grounds exist for discontent with the contractual conception which depend not upon general anti-realist sympathies but only on principles which could hope to pass as platitudes.

II. Preliminaries

Three preliminary sets of remarks may assist the evaluation of what follows.

First, 'idealism' does not entirely happily characterise the adjustment required if the argument to be presented is sustained. Idealism has traditionally involved the view that human consciousness in some way creates the world; that material objects, for instance, exist only for the mind. The present target, however, is a thesis about meaning. We ordinarily think of the truth value of a statement, whether assessed or not, as depending only upon a *semantic component,* its content, and a *worldly component,* the state of those aspects of the world which it is about. This conception has, indeed, the status of a platitude and is not under challenge in what follows. What is under challenge is a certain idea of determinacy in the first component: the idea that we can, by appropriately rigorous explanations and sufficiently distinctive paradigms, lay down so specific a content for a statement that its truth value is settled, in the manner described by the platitude, quite independently of the result of any investigations we may carry out to settle it; and any correspondence between its actual truth value and our findings about it, if we bother to investigate, is utterly contingent on our capacity to keep track of our antecedent semantic obligations. The target—what I shall call *objectivity of meaning*—is the conception that the meaning of an expression stands to the unfolding tapestry of the way it is used in our linguistic practices as a person's character, according to a certain misconception of it, stands to his or her unfolding behaviour. The misconception would have it that character is, as it were, a finished design for a person's life which they usually act out, but which their behaviour may, at any particular stage, somehow betray. This has at least the virtue of explaining, but goes far beyond what is necessary to explain, the use we make of the idea that a person can act 'out of character'. But it is obvious enough that we also conceive of charcter as determined by behaviour: there are, we would like to say, *conceptual* limits to the extent and variety of ways in which a person can act out of character.

A proper account of the relations between character and behaviour would have to display both how the nature of someone's character is a conceptual construct from what is said and done, and how it is nevertheless intelligible and fruitful to allow for the sort of contrast which we describe as 'acting out of character'.

The conclusion of this essay will be that there is a structurally parallel problem posed by the concepts of meaning and use: that, whatever the proper interpretation of the *normativity* of meaning, and of what it is to use an expression in a way which fails to fit its meaning, it cannot issue from the picture of a semantic contract to which McDowell referred. Rather, the proper interpretation of these notions has to be compatible with the capacity of ongoing use to determine meaning. Our collective ability to misuse an expression—to use it in a way out of accordance with its meaning—is conceptually limited in the same sort of way as is the individual's ability to act out of character. For the believer in the objectivity of meaning, there could be no such limitation.

Idealism, it seems to me, implies that there is, in advance of appropriate human activity, an indeterminacy in the second, *worldly* component out of which the platitude manufactures truth value. The present thesis, however, entirely concerns the first component. It is that while, in accordance with the platitude, we may regard the truth values of uninvestigated statements as settled by their contents and relevant worldly aspects, we should not also think of those contents as fully settled by over-and-done-with behavioural and intellectual episodes. The positive task, if we accept this negative conclusion, will be to explain exactly how the content of a statement, and hence its truth value, must be seen as shaped by features of our ongoing linguistic behaviour. But that task will not be broached here. We shall be fully occupied with the attempt to articulate one set of grounds for the negative conclusion.

We are now in a position—the second preliminary—to see a contrast between the intended target of the argument with which we shall be concerned and that of a proponent of Kripke's Sceptical Argument, vividly expounded in his *Wittgenstein on Rules and Private*

Language.[5] Fundamental to Hume's philosophical opinions concerning ethics, and causation, is a distinction between genuinely descriptive statements—our assent to which may mark cognition of a real state of affairs—and sentences which, while possessed of the syntax of genuine statements, serve rather to *project* emotions and attitudes of ours on to the world. Now, the conclusion of the 'sceptical argument' which Kripke finds in Wittgenstein is exactly that all talk of meaning and understanding is, in essentially this sense, *projective:* there are no substantial facts concerning meaning and understanding, a fortiori none to serve as possible objects of cognition. The route to this conclusion is of no importance to us here. What is clear is that it is a yet more radical contention than any involved in a rejection of objectivity of meaning in the above sense. To be sure, Wittgenstein is not represented by Kripke as recommending, like Quine in places, that we should jettison the concepts of meaning and understanding altogether; projective discourse may, after all, have some socially valid role. (That, in effect, is the tenet of Kripke's attempted Sceptical Solution.) But there is a grave doubt whether Wittgenstein, as so represented, can be saying anything coherent. The trouble is the platitude above. If the truth value of a statement is a function of its meaning and relevant aspects of the world, then if meaning is nothing *factual,* how can truth value be? (A rough parallel: if whether it is worth going to see a certain show is a function of, inter alia, how funny the leading act is, and if we think that judgements about what is funny are projective, ergo non-factual, then that non-factuality is going to infect the judgement whether the show is worth seeing.) The result would seem to be that *every* judgement of the truth of a statement, so every statement, becomes non-factual. How then is the contrast between factual and projective statements to be drawn, in terms of which Wittgenstein's position on meaning, as interpreted by Kripke, is to be explained?

Kripke's sceptic must, of course, repudiate objectivity of meaning: if there are no genuine facts about meaning at all, there cannot be

5. Kripke (1982).

facts about what meanings require of us on new occasions. But, at the risk of leaning too heavily upon the analogy, a rejection of the objectivity of meaning should no more entail that there are literally no true statements to be made about meaning than the avoidance of the misconception about character outlined above entails that there are no true statements to be made about somebody's character. This opinion is, of course, quite consistent with holding that the argument which Kripke finds in the *Philosophical Investigations* is of great independent interest. I merely record my suspicion that nobody can coherently accept its conclusion; that, accordingly, its power can only be that of a paradox. The contrast with my present argument is that the latter, if sustained, can have the status of a result.

Let me indicate, finally, something of the structure of the ensuing argument. There is a certain basic class of judgements which, it is plausible to suppose, are crucially involved in all the judgements we make. It will be argued that the supposition that these *basic* judgements possess objectivity of meaning is at odds with one aspect of standard criteria for their appraisal as correct. Then the manner of the involvement of these judgements in *all* judgement will be argued to impose upon us a choice between abandoning the objectivity of meaning quite generally and falling prey to global scepticism.

III. BASIC JUDGEMENTS

The concluding remark of what is usually regarded as the 'chapter' on rule-following in *Philosophical Investigations* is famous: Wittgenstein wrote that not merely agreement in definitions but also agreement in judgements is a precondition of the possibility of our language serving for communication.[6] But did he mean any judgements in particular? Not, evidently, judgements concerning economic theory, or molecular biology, or the existence of a tenth planet; nor any judgements concerning matters theoretical or controversial. Nevertheless Wittgen-

6. *Philosophical Investigations* §242.

stein's remark will bear interpretation, I suggest, as concerning a specific class of judgements: roughly, those which we make responsively, without articulated reasons, under the impact of those aspects of our environment which we can most directly perceive. For it is indeed a plausible precondition of our reciprocal intelligibility that we share a network of certain basic concepts, by which we exercise perceptual recognition and in whose application to novel cases we concur (by and large) without collusion and without stateable grounds to fall back on if disagreement should arise. The most natural examples would be attributive and relational concepts of form, pattern, colour, loudness, pitch, texture, taste, smell, warmth and cold, temporal precedence, etc. Only, it seems, if we do indeed share such a system of basic concepts, furnishing corresponding agreed basic judgements, will our attempts to negotiate disagreement about judgements of a more sophisticated kind be fruitful.

The basis of this claim is the thought, on which I shall dwell below, that basic perceptual judgements are involved in all judgement: that there could not be a common conception of the conditions of justified assent to (and dissent from) judgements of any sort unless certain relevant basic concepts were also held in common. This is not to say that any *particular* basic concepts are necessary, but only that if we do succeed in understanding each other, we will share some basic concepts. Nor are we committed to supposing that any basic concepts have that status absolutely; which concepts are basic for us will be a function of our sensory capabilities, and concepts may be envisaged as shifting their status according as we imagine those capabilities enlarged or restricted in relevant ways. (A judgement of the rough similarity, for example—in the geometrical sense of 'similarity'—of a pair of drawn triangles, which the normally sighted are able to make at a glance, may be available to those with extreme 'tunnel vision' only on the basis of a series of measurements and inferences.)

A fuller account is desirable of the nature of concepts of this sort, but providing one is not entirely straightforward. We are concerned with concepts which are characteristically introduced by ostensive means, incapable of definitional paraphrase, and whose applications in at least a large class of cases are directly recognitional. Yet if the intention is to pick out the sort of concepts listed above, more needs to be said. Let us call a *recognition statement* any statement composed purely of demonstratives, predicates, and relations of arbitrary degree, of which a competent use standardly presupposes no more than normal sensory capacities and ostensive teaching. 'That is red', 'That is deeper than that' (said of sounds), 'That is salty', etc., all qualify. So, however, may recognition statements concerning cedar trees, pineapples, Geiger counters, cathode ray tubes, and telephones. We confront the familiar range of difficulties besetting the attempt to elucidate a worthwhile notion of *observation statement,* difficulties which have been the despair of so many foundationalistically inclined epistemologists and philosophers of science. So, whether or not it will involve a contribution to *that* issue, there is more to be said for our present purpose.[7] Let us stipulate that a predicate F, or a relation R, is basic just in case it satisfies all the following conditions:

1. F, or R, is capable of featuring in recognition statements.
2. Nobody counts as understanding F, or R, who lacks the capacity—even when perceiving normally in normal circumstances—competently to appraise recognition statements which contain them.

This condition excludes expressions like 'Geiger counter' and 'cathode ray tube'. For their instances, while sensorily recognisable, could in principle take any of indefinitely many various overt forms. It is thus no essential part of understanding such predicates to have the capacity to handle recognition statements involving them; you can know exactly what Geiger counters are without knowing the gross form they conventionally assume.

7. The following proposals were conceived with the benefit of discussion with Christopher Peacocke and bear analogies to material since published in Peacocke (1983), chap. 4.

The corresponding claim about 'pineapple', 'cedar tree' and indeed a whole host of natural kind terms is, however, much less plausible. Intuitively no one fully understands 'pineapple' who has no inkling of the distinctive appearance of pineapples. Here appropriate recognitional capacities do seem necessary for understanding; what distinguishes these expressions from those in the class we seek to characterise is that such capacities are not *sufficient*. We therefore stipulate:

3. It is not possible coherently to regard someone both as able to pass all reasonable tests for the ability to recognise demonstrative presentations of *F*s, or *R*-relata, *and* as simultaneously lacking a full understanding of *F*, or *R*.

Conditions 2 and 3 determine that the recognitional capacities which bestow competence with recognition statements involving *F*, or *R*, are to be constitutive of an understanding of those expressions. There is to be no possibility of understanding of what it is for such statements to be true without possessing the appropriate recognitional capacities; and no possibility of possessing the appropriate recognitional capacities without understanding what it is for such statements to be true (so no possibility of 'fools' *F*s').[8] Finally:

4. *F*, or *R*, has no analysis in terms of other predicates, or relations, meeting requirements 1, 2 and 3.

The intention of condition 4 is—perhaps unimportantly—to reflect the feeling that the sought-for characterisation should be of a class of concepts which are *primitive*.

Some commentary on this characterisation is called for. To begin with, it is worth drawing a distinction between basic *statements* and basic *judgements*. A basic judgement is any judgement which could be expressed by a recognition statement involving only basic concepts,

8. Ibid., pp. 92–3.

and which is made by exercising appropriate recognitional capacities. But the content of a statement which expresses such a judgement does not, obviously, preclude that the very same statement should be made not on the basis of exercise of the appropriate recognitional capacities but as the conclusion, for example, of a chain of inferences. There are thus no sentences which are apt *only* for the expression of basic judgements. We shall understand a *basic statement* to be a particular *historic utterance* of a recognition statement which involves only basic concepts and which, in context, expresses an exercise of the relevant recognitional capacities. In what follows, I shall work with the fiction that we have the means to coin basic statements apt for expression of any basic judgements which we are actually able to make. This is presumably a substantial idealisation: we share a huge number of basic concepts, as evinced in various discriminatory abilities which we have, for which we have no direct (non-comparative) means of expression. But the idealisation is perfectly in order in the present context: if it can cogently be argued that the vocabulary of English, enriched only by the addition of a fuller range of expressions for basic concepts, cannot serve to construct sentences with objectivity of meaning, then it is quite unclear how English as we presently have it—a fragment of that language—could somehow fare better. The point of the idealisation, as the reader will anticipate, is that we shall thereby be enabled to apply our reflections concerning the objectivity of meaning to basic judgements as a class, without the need to attempt to construct some analogous concept which might characterise, or fail to characterise, basic judgements for which we happen to have no means of expression.

Second, regarding an *observation statement,* the notion traditional in the philosophy of science—that which Carnap intended by *Proto-colsatz,* for example—is that of a statement possessed of a special epistemic security and free of theoretical presupposition. Whether basic statements, as characterised above, have either of these features is a matter for further investigation. Prima facie, at least, it is not obvious that they do: the recognitional capacity constitutive of an understanding of a particular basic concept may well, typically will, be a *fallible* capacity; and our conception of some of the conditions under which its fallibility will emerge may well be a 'theoretically conditioned' one. Enough has been said, perhaps, to make it clear that those philosophers who have thought that there is no interesting distinction between theoretical statements and records of observation may be mistaken; but whether the notion of a basic statement gives us the germ of a distinction which will subserve the traditional purposes of foundationalism in epistemology and the philosophy of science will not further be considered here.

There is a further concept of some importance, to be introduced before we tackle the main argument that basic statements lack objectivity of meaning. The most fundamental notion of objectivity is (what I propose to call) the *objectivity of judgement*. To think of a class of statements as apt to express objective judgements is to conceive of them as having a real subject matter, as dealing in genuine matters of fact, as apt to be correct or incorrect by virtue of how matters stand in certain objective states of affairs which may be the objects of human cognition. This is the notion which divides genuine statements from the sort of projective impostors postulated by Hume, and from *quasi-assertions*[9] of other sorts. Clarification of this notion of objectivity is a matter of great importance: there is a long history of philosophical disputes—about morals, aesthetics, theoretical statements in science, pure mathematical statements, etc.—all of which are precisely disputes about whether these types of statements qualify for objectivity of judgement.

What, though, is the hallmark of the genuinely factual? How should we set about deciding whether a given class of statements really do have this kind of objectivity? No doubt the disputes just alluded to would not have been so long-lived if there were an easy answer. But one important initial consideration is that cognition is *relational*: it is a matter of arriving at true opinions in a manner *sensitive* to states of affairs whose obtaining is somehow independent of one's so arriving. Moreover, such sensitivity must be conceived as

9. Dummett (1973), pp. 353–60.

———

essentially fallible; whatever the details are of the process which induces in a subject a belief that P, it must be conceivable—at least with the simple empirical judgements which basic statements serve to express—that the process should on occasion misfire, that the appropriate sensitivity should be missing. These two considerations—the independence of the objects of knowledge and the fallibility of cognitive capacities—suggest as at least a necessary condition for a class of statements to have a genuinely cognisable, ergo factual, subject matter that sense can be made of the possibility of a subject's or a group of subjects' *ignorance* or *error* concerning their truth status.[10]

I do not believe that a full account of objectivity of judgement can be anything so simple, only that it must build on the foregoing thought. If a class of statements are to be credited with objectivity of judgement, then, for arbitrarily chosen P in that class, there must be an appropriate contrast in content between:

(a) X believes that P is true; and
(b) P is true.

Only if (a) may conceivably be denied while (b) may be asserted have we made sense of the possibility of X being ignorant of the status of P; only if (a) may conceivably be asserted while (b) may be denied have we made sense of the possibility of X's being mistaken.

Now 'X' may, of course, be taken not merely as a single individual but also to range over groups of individuals including, as a limiting case, an entire community. Even so, there seems no reason to doubt that basic statements can legitimately aspire to meet the condition. Individuals can, of course, be ignorant of or mistaken about the truth status of a basic statement. And most of the explanations why—bad lighting, poor eyesight, tone deafness, not noticing, absence at the relevant time, etc.—would in principle serve equally well for whole communities. Accordingly, to have grounds for thinking that a communal

10. This thought underlies the doubt about 'private language' voiced by Wittgenstein in *Philosophical Investigations* §258 (pursued in Essay 8 below).

consensus on some basic statement is, or was, mistaken is a remote but real possibility (systematic sorts of misperception, for example, may be induced by disease). Conversely, most of the basic judgements each of us makes, with perfect justification, are made not merely in ignorance of any communal consensus that there may be about their status but with a strong presupposition that most members of our community will never consider them. So we certainly cannot affirm, even with basic statements, that 'whatever seems right to the community is right', or anything of that sort. At least, we cannot do so without betraying a class of distinctions which, as we think, we are ordinarily able to draw soundly.

At this point, it may seem that we must either sustain the objectivity of meaning of basic statements, thereby entitling ourselves to the sorts of distinction just sketched; or we must embrace some sort of crude 'consensualism' about those statements, forgoing our rights to practise the distinctions in question. Wittgenstein himself rejects the second alternative.[11] The dilemma is, however, a false one. The primary thesis of this essay is that the capacity of a class of statements to satisfy the indicated necessary condition for objectivity of judgement does not depend upon the legitimacy of crediting them with objectivity of meaning; and the reason why not is best brought out by considering why the latter is in doubt—to which task I now turn.

IV. BASIC STATEMENTS AND OBJECTIVITY OF MEANING AND JUDGEMENT

Let ϕ be some basic concept, and consider a large series of basic statements involving ϕ, about which there is, as it happens, a near universal consensus. If we are to believe in the objectivity of meaning of these statements, there has to be a possibility that this consensus is, in any particular case, misplaced: for belief in objectivity of meaning is exactly the belief that what determines the truth values of these

11. *Investigations* §241; cf. *Remarks on the Foundations of Mathematics* VII, 40.

statements is wholly independent of human assessment of them and, at best, contingently correspondent with it. Now there is, of course, a distinction between the claims:

1. For each statement in question, it is possible that our verdict and the truth status diverge.
2. It is possible that, for each statement in question, our verdict and the truth status diverge.

The question is what, if any, reason the believer in objectivity of meaning can give for accepting claim 1 but refusing to accept claim 2. Generally speaking, the transition from

$$(x) \text{ Possibly } Fx$$

to

$$\text{Possibly } (x) \, Fx$$

fails just in case F is a predicate the conditions of whose application to any particular individual in the range of quantification are a function of relevant characteristics of other members of the range Thus, familiarly, the transition fails, for example, for Fx = 'x is below average height.' More strikingly for our present purposes, it fails, letting 'x' range over episodes of Jones's behaviour, for Fx = 'x is totally out of character'. Thus the only apparent way to resist the transition from claim 1 to claim 2 is to insist that our consensus over so large a class of cases must be regarded as playing some sort of *constitutive* role in determining what counts as correct use of ϕ, just as Jones's behaviour over a sufficiently large class of cases plays a constitutive role in determining his character. But that is exactly the parallel which the believer in objectivity of meaning must resist. Letting 'x' range over the basic statements in question, and Fx = 'the community's assessment of x is out of accord with the requirements of the meaning of ϕ', the believer in ϕ's objective meaning ought to hold that the considerations which determine whether or not φ applies in any particular case will concern nothing other than the relevant facts about it (the 'worldly component' referred to above) and those episodes in the linguistic and intellectual history of the community which constituted the determination of the ('objective') meaning of φ. What is crucial is that we may think of those episodes as having entirely *antedated* the series of statements in question. And in that case, what determines whether or not φ applies in any of the relevant cases is quite independent of the communal response in other cases in that range. We should conclude that believers in objectivity of meaning have no satisfactory ground why, having accepted claim 1, they should not also accept claim 2.

What has been said is already enough to suggest how it is that one who rejects objectivity of meaning for a given class of statements might nevertheless quite consistently reserve the right to endorse objectivity of judgement for them (or at least, to endorse their capacity to pass the test on which, I suggested above, a full account of objectivity of judgement should build). Actually, it is not clear whether belief in objectivity of judgement for a given class of statements really does require that we give sense to the possibility of massive communal *error* about their status (whether it would not be enough to give sense, for example, merely to the possibility of massive communal *ignorance)*. But if it does, no more is required, at any rate, than that we substantiate claim 1 above. Belief in objectivity of meaning, in contrast, requires—if the foregoing is correct—that we additionally substantiate claim 2. And crude consensualism would reject both.

Now, what is supposed to be the difficulty with claim 2? What is wrong with the idea that as a bare and no doubt very remote possibility, all or almost all the members of a linguistic community might collectively, but non-collusively, go right off track in their applications of some basic predicate, so that the paths of truth and shared opinion over a protracted series of basic statements might radically diverge? The immediate worry has to be, of course, whether the alleged possibility is really intelligible. What would it be to have satisfactory grounds for thinking that it actually obtained? Naturally, no one can be considered competent to criticise a range of statements accepted by others unless there is a reason to think that the critic and the criticised share an understanding of those statements. But with basic concepts, the criterion for such a shared understanding is precisely the disposition to agree in basic judgements involving those concepts. How then, if somebody finds himself out of line with the verdict of his community in a protracted series of cases, can we or anyone else retain the right to think of him as a competent critic? Why is the position not rather that it has emerged that he never succeeded in understanding or no longer understands the basic concepts in question? It would seem to follow that there is no such thing as being in a position reasonably to criticise a sufficiently protracted non-collusive consensus on basic statements; so no such thing as having reason to think that a 'radical divergence' had taken place. 'Anti-realist' constraints would then enjoin that there is no such genuine possibility.

This in essentials was my argument in chapter 11 of *Wittgenstein on the Foundations of Mathematics*.[12] However, the conclusion is, at this stage, too swiftly drawn, since it overlooks the possibility that the critic *is* able to support his charge by evidence that something is interfering with the (physiological basis) of the capacities of his community. Certain sorts of environmental contaminant may, for example, be known adversely to affect people's capacity to apply certain basic concepts, but to do so in a uniform way so that the disposition to consensus is not disrupted. So could there not, in appropriately fantastic circumstances, be reason to think that *everyone* had, perhaps irreversibly, gone astray in their application of certain basic concepts? Yet a little reflection renders it doubtful whether this thought really meets the issue. There seem to be three sorts of basis on which it might be claimed that such a contaminant, or other factor, had produced an episode of radical divergence. First, and most simply, the contaminant might be associated with overt damage to its victims so gross—near-total deafness, for example—that nothing would have to be known about the detailed character of their suspect judgements in order reasonably to hold them in suspicion. Second, the judgements in ques-

12. And of Wright (1981) (this volume Essay 2).

tion might be found to betray an established correlation with some associated physical parameter: measured temperature, for instance, or the frequency of sound waves. Or, third, the contaminant might previously have been recognised to have induced disruption in the relevant recognitional capacities of a previously affected subpopulation—disruption, that is, as evinced by discord with the responses of an unaffected majority. Now, the second and third types of case both turn on the assumed reliability of certain basic judgements outside the putative episode of radical divergence—those, respectively, by reference to which the association with the relevant physical parameter and the adverse effect of the contaminant on the subpopulation were established. No doubt that might be perfectly reasonable: the judgements in question will be assumed reliable because no consideration of the three kinds adumbrated, or any other, are on hand to call them into question. But can the theorist who accepts objectivity of meaning *explain* why that is a reasonable assumption?

The real difficulty for the theorist is to keep the tiger in the cage—to disclose any reason why the range of possibilities for radical divergence is appropriately constrained by the criteria on which we should actually rely in order to affirm that such a possibility had been realised. Why shouldn't our belief in the reliability of some associated physical parameter *itself* have been the product of an extended bout of radical divergence? Why shouldn't those communal judgements with which the responses of the contaminated subpopulation were compared *themselves* have been haywire? These seem foolish questions. And the reason they seem so, I surmise, goes deep. Suppose a subject sincerely assents to a statement S in circumstances C in which we have adequate reason to believe that each of the following holds:

1. The subject has had a normal teaching in the concepts involved in S and has given every indication of a normal understanding of them.
2. The subject is functioning normally in C—is unaffected by drugs, disease, etc.

3. The perceptual conditions obtaining in *C* are normal—no funny lighting, tricky mirrors, etc.

Obviously enough, adequate reason to believe the conjunction of 1–3 cannot in general constitute adequate reason to believe *S*, since the current normality of the subject and of the perceptual conditions are no special assets if *S* does not concern what the subject is currently in position to perceive. But if *S* is a *basic* statement, the position is different: precisely because 2 and 3 constitute conditions which are optimal for the subject's exercise of the relevant recognitional capacities, and because 1 suggests that it is indeed those capacities which the subject is attempting to exercise, adequate reason to believe each of 1–3 must be, it appears, adequate reason to believe *S*.

This conclusion in fact needs a supplementary assumption:

4. *S* expresses a basic statement *for* the subject—that is, his assent to it is based entirely on an exercise of recognitional capacities.

(Otherwise it will be easy to conjure up counter-examples involving the subject's recourse, for whatever reason, to an unreliable secondary source, for example, or a problematic chain of inferences.) But granted that assumption, it is, I suggest, not merely true but *necessarily* true that sufficient reason for each of 1–4 confers a (defeasible) warrant to believe *S*. More specifically, it is impossible to understand how a recipient of adequate grounds for each of 1–4 could reasonably doubt *S* if he possessed no other relevant information.

Intuitively, the case for *S* is stronger if what is involved is a widespread non-collusive *consensus* of subjects about its truth. That, I surmise, is because the fact of such a consensus would *eo ipso* be grounds against supposing that misunderstanding, or abnormal function—usually an idiosyncratic matter—or certain sorts of tricky perceptual circumstances (misleading perspectival effects, for example) were materially involved. That is, consensus of that sort enhances the likelihood, though it does not make it certain, that 1, 2 and 3 hold for each of the participants. Whether or not that is quite the right reason, the following principle has an exceedingly powerful intuitive appeal.

P: If, without any form of collusion occurring, there is wide-spread agreement about the truth of an S which is basic for each of the judges; and if someone has adequate grounds for supposing that 1, 2 and 3 each hold of each of the judges, but no other relevant information, then he has excellent grounds for regarding S as true.

The appeal of P is, I suggest again, owing to its being analytic of the notion of a basic statement. The salient question, however, is how the principle can so much as hold, let alone how it can hold in necessitated form, if objectivity of meaning is accepted for basic statements. For in that case, what determines the truth or falsity of any S is constituted quite independently and in advance of the judges' response to it. To hold to the principle P (in necessitated form) would then be, accordingly, to hold that there is (necessarily) reason to think that those responses tend by and large to keep in step with the objective pattern of correct use of the concepts involved in S. Presumably, then, we can produce a reason for discounting as a possibility the suggestion that we may be prone, without any external interference either with us or with the conditions of observation, simply to swing collectively away, without any sense of disquiet, from the paths laid down by objective meanings and the worldly facts. If some sceptic suggests that human beings may just be rather bad, in very similar ways, at internalising the requirements of objective meanings, we presumably have ready to hand a consideration to confound him. What is it?

The proper response to this train of thought, it seems to me, is to reject objectivity of meaning for basic statements. P holds good not because objective meanings, in their and our very nature, somehow exert a tug on the responses of people who satisfy its antecedent clauses, but because the relation, for the case of basic statements, between correctness and human response—however difficult to do justice to in detail—is such as to render the principle analytic. It follows that the fantasy of a collective 'radical divergence' over a series of basic statements, where no standard grounds exist for suspicion, is incoherent.

The effect of supposing that P can be false is that satisfaction of the conditions expressed in its antecedent need provide no adequate case for regarding the relevant statement as true. Yet the fact is that—at least when the judges include ourselves—we have not the slightest idea what it would be to increase the strength of the case. The result will be that the truth, or falsity, of such statements comes to transcend our strongest standard grounds for affirming them to be one or the other. That is an extreme and unappealing form of realism: it reduces our belief in our competence to use our own language correctly to a matter of faith. There is, however, no need to assail it with the familiar anti-realist arguments of full generality. Anyone who recognises the fidelity of the principle P to their intuitive concept of reasonable belief already has decisive grounds for rejecting it.

To reject objectivity of meaning for basic statements is to come to regard their content, and so their truth status, as ever open to ongoing determination by our linguistic behaviour. The competent use of basic vocabulary, with whatever degree of confidence, should not be viewed as reflecting cognition of the requirements of objective meanings. Rather, we should view it as an expression of certain basic reactive propensities, primitive classificatory dispositions—a common human (or at least cultural) heritage without which our language would fail. We must endeavour to see the content of basic statements as plastic in response to speakers' continuing performance with the basic vocabulary which they involve. Such metaphors are, of course, unsatisfactory and are no substitute for a sharp account of the sort of supervenience relation which we now seem obliged to make out. But it is at least clear that we can no longer think of the truth conditions of basic statements as fixed quite independently of responses of ours, still to be elicited from us, involving the relevant basic concepts. It is this *openness* in the content of basic statements which is critical in what follows.

V. The Ubiquity of Basic Judgement

There is no immediate generalisation of these considerations to non-basic statements since, as noted, P holds only for basic statements. Nevertheless, the argument ought to generalise. The suggestive thought is that exercise of basic concepts seems to be involved in the formation of judgements of all kinds. Think, for example, of the judgements of shape and colour which may be involved in recognising a cedar tree outside the window; the judgements of temporal precedence involved in competently running a scientific experiment; or the judgements of congruity of pattern involved in recognising a formal proof. But the mode of involvement is not usually, or even often, inferential. Basic judgements appear to form a foundation for judgement in general, not in the sense that they supply premises from which other judgements are derived, but in the sense that getting them right is a necessary condition, in context, for arriving at any other judgement *soundly,* for having a well-founded reason for thinking that judgement true. One's warrant to make a judgement of any kind, however sophisticated the context, will, it seems, always be *defeasible* by considerations which suggest that one misapplied certain basic concepts in coming to that judgement.

Let us try to amplify this claim a little. Defeasibility comes in several kinds. One way of defeating evidence for a particular belief is to bring to bear other evidence, stronger or equally strong, that the belief is false. Another is to show that there is an alternative and equally plausible account of why the original evidence is available. A third mode of defeat is to fault the *pedigree* of the evidence in some way, to call attention to some feature of the evidence gathering (or gatherer) which disqualifies it. Examples are the disclosure of pressure leaks in the apparatus, drunkenness in the observer, or a powerful magnetic field which may have affected the gauges. Defeat of either of the first two sorts admits the data but disputes their capacity to warrant the belief in question; defeat of the third sort undermines the validity of the data. I shall say that a case for a particular belief is *impeccable* if it is immune to defeat of the third sort; and that it constitutes a *genuine warrant* for that belief if it is both impeccable and will not be defeated in either of the first two ways no matter what the additions to our knowledge. To have a genuine warrant is thus to have a case for a particular belief which both possesses a faultless pedigree and will retain its supportive character through arbitrarily extensive improvements in our state of information.

One way of expressing the involvement of basic judgements in all judgement is now to say that in order to possess a genuine warrant for a particular belief, it is necessary that a large class of relevant basic judgements, pertaining to the process whereby the belief was acquired, be true; failing their truth, the process will lack the requisite impeccability. This is not to say that the relevant basic judgements need actually have been consciously entertained by a subject in the course of his arriving at the belief; but rather that if, having arrived at that belief, the subject were to be persuaded that any of them were false, he would be rationally constrained to consider the belief unjustified. In the presence of our earlier assumption, that the language contain means for the expression of all the basic judgements which its practitioners can make, we may summarise the proposal as follows:

> T: For any context C, agent X, and statement S: if X acquires the belief that S in C, there will be certain basic statements relating to the circumstances and process whereby X's belief was acquired such that (1) if he did not actually do so, X *could* have assessed any of these statements in the course of arriving at his belief that S; and (2) X has acquired impeccable, a fortiori genuine warrant for his belief that S only if each such statement is true.

I don't know how to support this principle beyond inviting a reader who is sceptical about it to try to come up with a counter-example: a case, in effect, of reasonable belief, acquired via some process with which no basic statements are so associated that evidence of their falsity would constitute defeat of the third kind. In any event, there seems no reason to doubt that T holds in a very wide class of cases. A reader sceptical whether it holds universally may simply restrict the scope of the argument which follows to the cases where it does hold.

VI.   Non-Basic Statements and Objectivity of Meaning

We now introduce one further seemingly platitudinous principle:

> *P**:   Necessarily: if *X* has acquired, in context *C*, a genuine warrant for believing *S*, then it is reasonable for *X* to believe *S* to be true.

This principle ought to seem platitudinous since a genuine warrant is *more* than is required for reasonable belief: beliefs may reasonably be held on what are, in fact, grounds which are destined for defeat. However, if we try to retain, along with the lemma that basic statements lack objective meaning and thesis *T*, the view that the truth and falsity of non-basic statements *is* subject to determination by objective meanings, then it becomes unclear whether, so far from being platitudinous, *P** has so much as a plausible claim to truth. This is the crux of the argument.

Let *S* be a non-basic statement and consider:

1. We have, in context *C*, genuine warrant for believing *S*; and
2. *S* is true.

If objectivity of meaning continues to be assumed for non-basic statements, an asymmetry now emerges in the types of states of affairs apt to confer truth on 1 and 2 respectively. The question of whether 2 is true is a *closed* question: it is settled by the state of the world in relevant respects and the objective meaning of *S*, which in turn is settled by past episodes in the linguistic and intellectual life of the community. But the question of whether 1 is true is, in the sense canvassed on pages 71–72 above, *open*. For a necessary condition for the truth of 1 will be—given *T*—that certain basic statements are true; and the truth of those statements, in so far as it depends upon their content, has to be conceived—in the presence of the lemma—as a function of, inter alia, future and counterfactual responses, involving the relevant basic concepts, of members of the linguistic community. Rejection of objectivity of meaning for basic statements led us to the view that what it is true to say about the meaning of any basic expression, and hence the nature of that meaning, is indefinitely open to further determination by ongoing responses of members of the linguistic community; rather as what it is true to say about someone's character, and hence the nature of his character, is indefinitely open to further determination by what he says and does. In the presence of *T*, this feature of basic statements flows upwards, as it were, to affect all judgements of the sort typified by 1: their truth depends on the truth of basic statements; which depends on their content; which depends on things we have not but would have done, or will or would do.

Why does this consideration pose a threat to *P**? Because in order for *P** to hold, it is necessary that the sorts of circumstance which go to make up a genuine warrant for *S* be a *reliable indication* of the sorts of circumstance which constitute *S*'s truth; that pursuit of the policy, as it were, of aiming at genuine warrants for one's beliefs will enhance the chances of selecting true beliefs. For the believer in objectivity of meaning, however, the claim that *S* is true is a claim about the deliverance of objective meanings. The result is that, in view of the noted asymmetry, the question of the reliability of genuine warrants for statements in *S*'s class becomes imponderable. For to believe in their reliability is to believe that the obtaining of the ingredients involved in a genuine warrant, including certain non-actual but elicitable primitive linguistic responses involving basic vocabulary *which may not even feature in the non-basic statement at issue,* is a reliable indication of that statement's truth. And that demands reason to believe in what seems to be a most mysterious *felicity* in our basic conceptual responses. In order for genuine warrants and truth to tend to go in step, it has to have been contrived that our primitive dispositions with basic vocabulary somehow follow suit after the requirements of the objective meanings of non-basic vocabulary, engineering a sufficient measure of covariance, among statements in general, between truth and the availability of genuine warrants to give point to the practice of trying to secure genuine warrants as, wherever practicable, a precondition of belief. The asymmetry thus brings it about that P^*, so far from having the status of a platitude, emerges in the role of postulate of an odd sort of pre-established harmony.

Naturally it is quite unclear how it could be *necessary* that such harmony obtained. The attractiveness of P^* is merely that of a principle that is analytic of our ordinary concepts of truth and evidence. But in that case, the only way of retaining a belief in objectivity of meaning for non-basic statements while acknowledging the force of the above argument is to see it as a demonstration that the conditions for reasonable belief in the truth of non-basic statements are never satisfied. The best we can aim at is genuine warrant; and the probability that we shall thereby tend to believe more truths is inscrutable. Perhaps this outcome is only to be expected. The penalty which we risk by endorsing the kind of semantic autonomy with which objective meanings would infuse our language is that we shall find ourselves hard pressed to explain with what right we consider ourselves in any way sensitive to the course taken by the semantic tracks thereby laid down. The burden of the argument has been that, first at the level of basic statements and then with all the rest, this penalty cannot be avoided. The price of objective meaning is an *absolute* conception of truth: a conception absolved from all practical controls. This is not the notion we actually have, if P is true. It is not a notion we should want, if our cognitive endeavours are to fare better than cannon-fodder for sceptical artillery.

VII. CONSTRUCTIVISM

It was suggested earlier that 'idealism' was not a happy label for the view which repudiates objectivity of meaning. The label of 'constructivism' is another matter. There really is a point, if the argument of this essay is sustained, in seeing ourselves as the perennial creators of our concepts, not in the style of conscious architects but just by doing what comes naturally. Thereby we contribute towards the creation not of extralinguistic facts, but of true sentences. It is, however, another question whether this shift in perspective must engender revision in the classical 'non-constructive' techniques and concepts of mathematics and logic against which the twentieth-century schools of constructivism in the philosophies of logic and mathematics have rebelled. Certainly from one point of view it seems that radical methodological revisions may have to be involved. If, for example, the mathematical intuitionists' willingness to accept the law of the excluded middle for all quantifier-free statements in number theory had to be taken as evincing a belief in the validity of the principle of bivalence for those statements, then it is hard to see that that practice could now be justified. What could sustain the idea that finitely decidable, but in practice hopelessly undecidable, number-theoretic statements are in every case *determinately* true or false, except the conception that they have objective meanings capable of settling their truth values without any further contribution from us? It is, however, unobvious that the intuitionists' willingness to accept excluded middle in such cases must be interpreted in that light.[13] And the issue is, in any case, overshadowed by very delicate and unresolved questions concerning revisionism in the philosophy of logic—including, in particular, the question of what can be made of the notion of *conservativeness* of a set of principles of inference among statements for which objectivity of meaning has been rejected—which cannot be broached here.

Finally, if we take it that the target of Wittgenstein's reflections on following a rule *is* objectivity of meaning quite generally (whatever the relation of the preceding argument to the detail of his own thought), where does that leave the relation between the 'rule-following considerations' and the polemic against 'private language' which, *pace* Kripke, begins at *Investigations* §243? In §258 Wittgenstein urges,

13. Wright (1980), chap. 11, §§4–6.

famously, that the would-be private linguist ought to be disquieted by his inability to make anything of the distinction between uses of his private language which seem right to him and uses which really are. (Those of Cartesian sympathies are apt to see no force at all in the consideration, precisely because they aspire to regard one's impressions of one's own mental contents as especially sure. They entirely miss Wittgenstein's point.) Now one thing which is clear is that if expressions in a private language could have objective meaning, then there would *be* a distinction between what seemed right to a practitioner and what was right, even if he could not apply the distinction; that is, what *determined* the rightness of any particular description of his sensations, or whatever the private material was supposed to be, would be independent of the way in which the subject was inclined to describe them. Hence, a general attack on objective meaning would preempt one effective rejoinder to Wittgenstein's apparent train of thought at this point. So an extensive discussion of rule following, with objectivity of meaning as its general target, would certainly be intelligible as a *preparation* for the argument against private language. But quite other interpretations of the relations between the two *Investigations* 'chapters' are possible; someone who took the view, for example, that the material on rule-following is not directed against objectivity of meaning, could essay to see Wittgenstein's remarks about private ostensive definition as expressing the view that, in contrast to a situation in a public language, the private linguist cannot establish any objective meanings for himself. Fare that approach as it may, it is evident that a quite general assault on objectivity of meaning cannot of itself establish any *special* problem for private language.

The rule-following considerations have been fairly intensively discussed in philosophical circles for a number of years now and the impression is, I think, prevalent that while Wittgenstein may have achieved certain destructive insights into widespread lay-philosophical notions of meaning, confusion has overtaken him when he thinks that private language somehow fares especially badly.[14] (Admittedly, if

14. See especially Blackburn (1984), pp. 281–301.

confronted with the issue in these terms, a Cartesian, might well wish to invest his private language with objective meanings; so Wittgenstein could still be credited with an anti-Cartesian point.) The truth seems to me to be different. Wittgenstein does have a special query to raise about private language, even if we suppose that a successful general attack has been mounted against objectivity of meaning. The query is, precisely, whether the would-be statements of the private linguist can have *objectivity of judgement,* whether they can be so much as factual. But corroboration of that claim I must defer to another occasion.[15]

꒰

This essay expands some of the material which I presented at the conference on 'The psychological content of logic' at the University of Tilburg in October 1982, and at the Thyssen conference on 'Constructivism' at Lyme Regis in March 1983. I am grateful to the participants on those occasions for their helpful comments; to the audiences at seminars held at the Universities of Manchester, Belfast, Pennsylvania, Harvard and Stirling at which I presented ancestors of this essay; and to John Skorupski, Leslie Stevenson and Charles Travis for criticisms of an earlier draft.

15. Wright (1986a) (this volume Essay 8).

PART TWO

WITTGENSTEIN'S
ARGUMENT AS IT
STRUCK KRIPKE

Saul Kripke's *Wittgenstein on Rules and Private Language* was published in 1982, two years after my *Wittgenstein on the Foundations of Mathematics*. I'd known, however, during the final stages of preparation of my book that Kripke had been developing what was invariably reported as a remarkable account of Wittgenstein's thought about rules and privacy; and although I'd been as keen to know as little as possible about it while preparing my own ideas for publication, it was with a mixture of intense curiosity and some degree of trepidation that I came to a careful study of Kripke's text.[1]

At first I was struck by general similarities. Kripke's interpretation works within an (unexamined) contrast between statements which are possessed of genuine truth conditions, and are apt to record matters of real fact, and types of utterance which, while possessed of the surface syntax of genuine statements, do not serve to express facts and thus, although associated with conditions—assertibility conditions—under which their use is warranted, have no genuine conditions of

1. A study not indeed, in the first instance, of Kripke's book but the version of his material that appeared in I. Block, ed., *Perspectives on the Philosophy of Wittgenstein* (Oxford: Blackwell, 1981.)

truth. His discussion divided into two parts. In the first, an ingenious Sceptical Argument is developed whose conclusion is that talk of meaning, and cognate notions, lacks genuine truth conditions (and hence that there are, properly speaking, no *facts* about meanings and their kin.) In the second part, a Sceptical Solution is proposed to accommodate this conclusion: statements about meaning, etc., do nonetheless possess conditions of warranted assertibility, and—here was the surprising connection with the private language argument—when these conditions are spelled out, it turns out that utterances within a 'private language'—in particular, those of a Cartesian soliloquist—lie outside the range to which ascriptions of content, of correct and incorrect use, etc., may significantly be made. Superficial points of similarity with my treatment in *Wittgenstein on the Foundations of Mathematics* were, first, the representation of Wittgenstein as mounting a challenge against the reality of meaning as platonistically conceived—(although I felt somewhat uncertain whether that conception could be satisfactorily captured by means of the contrast between truth-conditional and assertibility-conditional discourses)—and, second, the emphasis on the role of a speech community in somehow providing the essential backdrop for any intelligible contrast between correct and incorrect uses of language. However in the course of preparing a paper on Kripke's interpretation to give at the Kirchberg Wittgenstein Symposium in 1992—the paper that eventually became Essay 4 in this volume—I began to have doubts both about Kripke's account as interpretation of Wittgenstein and about the soundness of his dialectic in its own right.

Some of these doubts concerned the stability of the Sceptical Solution; they are elaborated on in Essay 4. But the main worry lay with the Sceptical Argument itself. The overarching thought behind it is this: that claims of a certain kind cannot be supposed to deal in matters of real fact if someone could know all possible facts which might conceivably constitute the truth of such a claim yet be unable to defeat a sceptic concerning his knowledge of its truth.[2] It's obvious

2. It's striking, by the way, that this principle cannot pass muster on any broadly externalist conception of knowledge—but I do not know of any commentator on

enough that an argument driven by this principle may lead to distortions unless the correct choice is made about what comprises 'all possible facts which might conceivably constitute the truth' of a claim of the targeted kind. Kripke's Sceptical Argument starts out by targeting claims about one's own former meanings—for instance, that by 'plus' I formerly meant addition—and then is easily able to extend the non-factualist conclusion drawn for them first to their present-tense analogues, and thence, generalising over speakers and expressions, to claims about linguistic meaning in general. But of course the generalisation cannot be properly founded if the initial non-factualist conclusion, concerning claims about one's own former meanings, is based on scrutiny of too restricted a class of potential truth-makers. Kripke's sceptic allowed this class to include all facts about one's former behaviour and—in a certain sense—all facts about one's former conscious mental life. But it turns out in the course of the argument that the latter are restricted to, in effect, former occurrences in consciousness whose full recollection demands no recollection of *content*.

It might seem plausible that such a restriction is perfectly reasonably imposed. For facts about one's former mental contents are surely in exactly the same boat as facts about one's former linguistic meanings; indeed, it's hard to see that the latter are not simply a subclass of the former. (For if, in dialogue with Kripke's sceptic, I may freely help myself to the ability to recall what I formerly believed, desired, intended, and so on, then what additional difficulty could there be with a presumed ability to recall what I formerly intended to express by a certain expression?) So in circumstances where a sceptical challenge has been tabled against the factuality of former meanings, it has

---

Kripke's argument who has made anything of this. The explanation, presumably, is that knowledge of one's own (present and former) meanings is naturally viewed as a species of psychological self-knowledge; and the latter, together with general a priori reflection, goes to provide the base in terms of which the idea of self-consciously reasonable belief, on which any internalist conception of knowledge must build, is presumably to be explained. In other words: knowledge of one's own meanings ought to be internalist knowledge if anything is.

to be taken that former mental contents in general are placed *sub judice* thereby as well. Or so it might be claimed.

Kripke was, of course, alive to the concern that the Sceptical Argument might have proceeded from too narrow a fact base. It was this that precipitated his discussion of meaning as dispositional, some of the most arresting material in the book. If one's former meanings consisted in one's possession of certain dispositions, that would certainly explain why they were not to be found when the search was restricted to over-and-done-with behaviour and over-and-done-with conscious, non-contentual phenomenology. But there would be a residual problem even if, as some commentary—unconvincingly to my mind—charged, Kripke's rebuttal of the dispositional proposal had been unsuccessful. That problem is that to conceive of one's meanings as consisting in dispositions would in any case be in tension with one's ability to know of them *non-inferentially.* The warranted self-ascription of any disposition must attend, one would suppose, the possession of relevant evidence: evidence, in the best case, provided by actual manifestations of the disposition. But knowledge of what one means by 'plus' doesn't seem essentially evidence-dependent at all.

I'll come back to that point in a moment. The concern I felt about the Sceptical Argument was not that better candidates to constitute meaning-facts might be found if the search was widened beyond the individual's psychology and behaviour, but that the point just noted—that self-knowledge of meanings is typically immediate—implied that rules of debate which allowed the bracketing of all content-bearing psychological states as *sub judice* were simply prejudicial. Are not such rules guaranteed to ensure success for a Kripke-style sceptic in *any* case where a contested subject matter is thought of as known non-inferentially? If the sufficient and adequate ground of my knowledge that P is precisely my non-inferential apprehension of the very fact that P, then it is to be expected that I may fare badly if in discussion with someone who doubts that P I am allowed to proceed only by reference to considerations of a quite different kind, considerations which could in principle at best defeasibly warrant an *inference* that P.

In any case there seemed serious reason to doubt that Wittgenstein's text would sustain Kripke's interpretation. For one thing, as almost every commentator at the time remarked, the 'sceptical paradox' which is actually elicited in *Philosophical Investigations* §§198–201—even if interpreted as somehow prefiguring Kripke's more developed paradox—is not accepted by Wittgenstein. His response is not to propose an accommodation with it—a 'sceptical solution'—but to discharge what he views as a faulty premise on which it depends: the idea that determinacy of meaning somehow depends upon *interpretation* (that to mean is to have an interpretation in mind.) Second, Wittgenstein's own reaction to the thought that one's former mental life—even when allowed to include intentional episodes other than meaning—is insufficient to determine meaning is to view it not as calling into question the reality of one's meanings, but rather as teaching us 'how different the grammar of the verb "to mean" is from that of "to think"'.[3]

It came to seem to me that the real lesson of 'Wittgenstein's argument as it struck Kripke' was not to cast doubt on the factuality of meaning but to pose a sharp problem about how to conceive of one's meanings, and intentional states generally, if they are indeed to be available for non-inferential knowledge, and thus to resource a satisfying response to Kripke's sceptic. They must be *routinely possible* items of non-inferential self-knowledge. But there are puzzles about how they can be so—difficulties which variously apply not just to meaning, but to understanding, thinking, intending, hoping, expecting, and so on, and which engage Wittgenstein's attention throughout his text. The ordinary conception of self-knowledge sees it as based on what is literally a 'looking within'—something involving a capacity to notice states and changes in our consciousness other than those associated with states and changes of public exterior objects *of* consciousness. One phenomenological difficulty which Wittgenstein brings out is that it is just very implausible to think of intentional states generally as residing in such noticeable states of consciousness. (That's one point made by the meaning-without-thinking passage

---

3. *Philosophical Investigations* §693—the concluding paragraph of the book.

cited a moment ago.) A second major consideration is that the identity of a subject's intentional states is constitutively answerable to her (subsequent) capabilities and behaviour in a fashion which is broadly analogous to that of dispositional states (which is why the idea of construing meanings of dispositional does not, in advance of Kripke's critique, impress as a loser from the outset.) But how can the presence, or onset of such quasi-dispositional states be non-inferentially accessible to the subject? More: why, as attested by the authority we normally cede to a subject's claims about her own intentional states, should such accessibility be regarded as the *normal* case?

This is the problem on which Essay 4 concludes, and to which Essay 5—presented at the 1986 Kirchberg Wittgenstein symposium—begins to develop a response. The essence of that response, which undergoes further development in Essay 7 and is generalised in Essays 10 and 11, is that a subject's knowledge—indeed, authority—concerning what she means, and her intentional states generally, is non-cognitive. It is based, that is to say—at least in the most general case—not in one's occupying a cognitively superior vantage point (a position, as it were, from which an unmatchedly good view of the relevant subject matter can be enjoyed), but by the obtaining of a constitutive or determinative relation between appropriately constrained impression on the one hand and that very subject matter on the other. There are a variety of different ways of trying to give theoretical sharpness to this idea, and some of that variety is exhibited in my own approaches in this volume. But one general way of putting the point is that it is the proposal to regard a subject's meanings, and her intentional states generally, as *secondary* qualities of her, in (one common interpretation of) the sense of the Lockean contrast between primary and secondary. One who thinks of colours as secondary thinks roughly this: that the relationship between what colour something has and how it visually seems to normally sighted humans is a constitutive relationship—that the appropriate mode of impressionability of normally sighted humans under the right circumstances is not a mere *indicator* of a self-standing colour but belongs to the essence of what having that colour consists in. The corresponding thought about meaning—and one which would supply the perfect riposte to Kripke's sceptic—is that, in normal circumstances, it belongs to the essence of meaning thus and such by a particular expression, now or in the past, to seem to oneself to do so.

Crudely so characterised, this proposal would have nothing to say about the second puzzling characteristic of intentional states just noted—their disposition-like 'theoreticity'. The key thought of Essay 5, variously developed in later of the essays, is that it also belongs primitively to our conception of intentional states that (self-) ascriptions of them are defeated by appropriately discordant performance. They are indeed, in other words, answerable in disposition-like ways to a subject's sayings and doings; but the authority of a sincere self-ascription does not depend upon the presumption that it has somehow—in general, *per impossibile*—taken account of such (relevant) sayings and doings. Still less is it based on some phenomenological occurrence which somehow guarantees their accord with the state ascribed—rather, the self-ascription simply stands unless defeated by them.

Two effects of this way of looking at the matter are worthy of note. First, the constraint of having to have one's sincere self-ascriptions make sense in the light of one's outward performance in effect supplies the standard of correctness for one's impressions of self-knowledge of meaning which, as argued in the final section of Essay 1, goes missing in a setting consisting just of a speaker and his idiolect, and where there is no assumption that he can convey to anyone else what he means by, for example, 'green'. The proposal reinstates both a standard of correctness for my opinions about what I mean and the authority of those opinions—but in order for it to do so, I need to be considered as an at least potential object of *interpretation,* with my claims about my own meanings essentially defeasible in the light of the shape assumed by my actual practice. This—the second effect—is a step in the direction of a broadly Communitarian response to the original dilemma (see the Introduction to Part One, pages 4–5 above). There are indeed facts about what I mean, contra Kripke's sceptic, and they are constitutively constrained by what I take them to be; but the validity of these self-impressions is in turn constitutively constrained by their contribution to my ability to make sense of myself to others in my (speech-) community.

Thus the general direction of Essays 4 and 5. Essay 6 consists of most of a critical study of Colin McGinn's *Wittgenstein on Meaning* (1984). McGinn's book provides a very clear account and critique of Kripke's interpretation, and lays it alongside a similarly exemplary exposition of many of the crucial themes in the relevant sections of the *Investigations,* thereby bringing out a number of important contrasts. It seemed to me, however, that McGinn's reading offered us a rather *domesticated* Wittgenstein: a philosopher who, for instance, insistently warned against certain psychologistic mistakes about the concepts of meaning and understanding, and laid emphasis on the role of our basic natures and culture in determining what is intelligible to us, but had none of the exciting and threatening preoccupations which, whatever their other differences, Kripke's and my interpretations converged on. The blandness of McGinn's interpretation is, indeed, of a piece with a general tendency to under-read *Investigations* §§138–242 which, for more than twenty-five years of commentary on the *Investigations* since its first publication in 1953, had led to those sections' virtually complete neglect for a concentration on family resemblances, language games, beetles-in-boxes, forms of life and criteria. The same period had seen the *Remarks on the Foundations of Mathematics* first slated by its reviewers and then also largely ignored. I think these facts are connected. It is when the study of the *Investigations* is approached with Wittgenstein's nagging critique in *RFM* of "what a mathematician is inclined to say about the objectivity and reality of mathematical facts"[4] vividly in mind that the real animal lurking in the rule-following discussions steps out of the shadows. However that may be, it seemed to me important to show how, in effect, the very themes which McGinn expounded could be rechoreographed to provide the kind of dialectic on whose Wittgensteinian pedigree Kripke and I were broadly agreed.

4. *Investigations,* §254.

I had occasion to present that choreography again in Essay 8, written for Alex George's festschrift for Noam Chomsky. This essay returns to a question raised in Essay 2: can whatever survives of the objectivity of meaning after the rule-following considerations have done their work provide a sufficiently substantial subject matter to give point to the construction of recursive theories of syntax and meaning? The conception of meaning as a Lockean secondary quality, with secondary qualities in turn viewed as distinguished by their being response-, or more specifically judgement-dependent, is here developed in some detail along lines prefigured in Essay 5. The result—on the assumption that the principal upshot of the rule-following considerations is indeed to teach us that meaning is secondary, or 'Euthyphronic'[5]—is to sharpen the focus of the leading question: it becomes the question whether a speaker's 'tacit knowledge', or cognitive realisation, of the information formulated by a suitable generative grammar, or recursive theory of meaning, can be plausibly construed as among the conditions qualifying her opinion about the content of a novel utterance to rank as 'best'. Essay 7 does not answer the question, however. In fact, it cannot be answered—even granted a Euthyphronic account of sentence meaning—until we better understand what the relevant notion of tacit knowledge might come to. But that is not an issue further pursued here.

5. For more on the 'Euthyphro Contrast', see Wright (1992), appendix to chap. 3.

4

Kripke's Account of the Argument against Private Language

Saul Kripke's *Wittgenstein on Rules and Private Language*[1] suggests interpreting Wittgenstein's argument against private language as a direct corollary of the considerations about rule-following which immediately precede those passages in *Philosophical Investigations* (§§243 and following) on which more traditional attempts to understand Wittgenstein's thought on privacy have tended to concentrate. For a while I thought Kripke's interpretation of these matters more or less coincident with that at which I had arrived independently and which I had presented in my *Wittgenstein on the Foundations of Mathematics* and elsewhere.[2] A careful reading of Kripke's book has convinced me both that this is not the case and that the dominant impression given in my book of the relation between the private-language argument and the rule-following considerations is misleading.

The implicit suggestion about the private-language argument in my book was that it is to be viewed as *part* of the considerations about

---

1. Kripke (1982). All page references are to this text unless otherwise stated.
2. Wright (1980). See also Wright (1981) (this volume Essay 2); Wright (1982).

rule-following: an argument, essentially, that the sort of objectivity of meaning necessary if we are to think of the truth values of unconsidered, uninvestigated statements as determinate independently of any investigation we may carry out, can find no refuge in the situation of a single speaker and his possibly incommunicable idiolect. The rule-following considerations were then depicted as taking the argument outwards, as it were—arguing first that, within the sphere of communal practice, concepts and distinctions can be given currency, on the basis of which a "thinner" notion of correctness and incorrectness in linguistic usage can be rehabilitated than that sanctioned by objective meaning; but second that, as far as the propriety of objective meaning is concerned, the community at large ultimately fares no better than the would-be private linguist. With none of this, at least as a potentially fruitful framework for the investigation of Wittgenstein's later philosophies of mind and mathematics, do I now disagree. But it does seem to me now that the treatment in my book could be usefully supplemented in at least two respects.

First, I think the involvement of 'anti-realist' premises in the arguments against objective meaning was there overemphasised: it seems to me that a more sensitive, sparing, and concept-specific use of such premises may be possible without compromising the power of the argument. Second, more stress is wanted that Wittgenstein does have a *differential* claim about private language: that the would-be private linguist and the community are not, in the end, in the same predicament. I shall not, in this paper, attempt to enlarge upon either of these claims.[3] The notable point is that an analogue of each is a prominent feature of Kripke's interpretation: Kripke's Sceptical Argument needs no anti-realist (verificationist) assistance; and the bearing of his Sceptical Solution on private language admits of no community-wide generalization.

That said, I do not think that Kripke has Wittgenstein right. But my subject, except in the last section of the essay, is not the historical

3. They are enlarged on in, respectively, Wright (1986d) (this volume, Essay 3) and Wright (1986a) (this volume, Essay 8).

Wittgenstein but Kripke's Wittgenstein. I shall argue that, even if the main argument—the Sceptical Argument—which Kripke finds in Wittgenstein, is sustained, there is strong prima facie reason to doubt whether the accommodation with it—the Sceptical Solution—which Kripke represents Wittgenstein as commending, can really be lived with; whether, indeed, that accommodation is so much as coherent. And I shall canvass ways, unconsidered (or only very cursorily considered) by Kripke for resisting the sceptical argument. The upshot will be that the rule-following considerations as interpreted by Kripke are flawed by a lacuna, and that, even if the lacuna were filled, the private-language argument could nevertheless not emerge in the manner that Kripke describes.

Because the gist of my remarks about Kripke's book is going to be negative in these ways, it is perhaps worth emphasising my admiration of it. Whatever its relation to Wittgenstein's actual thought, and whether or not ultimately cogent, Kripke's exciting dialectic will surely provide a great spur to improving our understanding of Wittgenstein's philosophy.

I. THE SCEPTICAL ARGUMENT

Fundamental to Hume's moral philosophy, as to his views about causation, is a distinction between statements that are apt to express real matters of fact and certain sentences that, although possessed of standard features of the syntax of genuine statements—in particular, the capacity to serve as arguments for various types of statement-forming operator—are actually used not to state facts but rather to *project* various aspects of speakers' attitudes and affective responses. Moral discourse and talk of causation belong, for Hume, in the latter category. Moral judgements, so viewed, do not express our cognition of moral facts by which various moral sentiments in us are generated; rather they serve to project those moral sentiments upon the world. Likewise, those statements which the non-Humean takes to aver the existence of causal relations, from which certain observed regularities flow, serve for Hume to project an attitude that we take up towards those observed regularities.

It is familiar that this sort of distinction is pivotal to a whole class of important philosophical disputes. Realism not merely about ethics and causation, but also about aesthetics, theoretical science, pure mathematics, logical necessity, and Lockean secondary qualities may each be opposed by appropriate versions of Humean non-cognitive 'projectivism'.

In this light, Kripke's Wittgenstein may be seen as first, by the Sceptical Argument, confounding the ordinary idea that our talk of meaning and understanding and cognate concepts has a genuinely factual subject matter, and then, via the Sceptical Solution, recommending an alternative projective view of its content. It is worth emphasis that the Sceptical Solution is independent of the Sceptical Argument: strictly, the option is open of simply accepting the latter as demonstrating the vacuity of all our talk of meaning, etc., with no prospect of its rehabilitation. (Similarly, a sympathiser might regard Hume as having demonstrated that we should simply drop all talk of causation.) Accordingly, it might seem as though one way of resisting the private-language argument, as Kripke interprets it, would simply be to take the sceptical medicine straight, forgoing the compensating sweetmeat of the Sceptical Solution afterwards. I shall return to that thought.

There are a variety of ways in which it might be argued that a region of discourse apparently apt for the stating of facts does not really perform that role. One way, the Humean strategy, is to argue that from within the framework of a certain preferred epistemology, no reputable conception can be attained of the putative items of fact in question. Another general strategy is to let the argument flow from a topic-neutral account of the ways in which the distinction between fact-stating and non-fact-stating declarative sentences comes out in their respective modes of employment in the language. But the strategy of argument which Kripke finds in Wittgenstein is different from both of these. Roughly, the conclusion that there are no facts of a disputed species is to follow from an argument to the effect that, even if we imagine our abilities idealised to the point where, if there were such facts to be known, we should certainly be in possession of them, we *still* would not be in a position to justify any particular claim about their character. So we first, as it were, plot the area in which the facts in question would have to be found if they existed and then imagine a suitable idealisation, with respect to that area, of our knowledge-acquiring powers; if it then transpires that any particular claim about those facts still proves resistant to all justification, there is no alternative to concluding that the 'facts' never existed in the first place.

The initial target class of putative facts comprises those which you might try to express by claims of the form 'By E, I formerly meant so-and-so'. The relevant idealisation will involve your total recall of all facts about your previous behaviour and previous mental history, it being assumed that facts about your former meanings must be located in one of those two areas if they are located anywhere. The argument will then be that, even in terms of the idealisation, no such claim is justifiable. It follows that your previous life in its entirety is empty of such facts, and hence that there are none (cf. pp. 21, 39).

I have sometimes encountered in discussion the complaint that, whatever independent force Kripke's development of the argument may have, its use of scepticism betrays its claim to represent Wittgenstein's actual thought. In one way, this misunderstands the Sceptical Argument; in another way, however, it may have a point. The misunderstanding consists in a failure to see that Kripke's 'sceptic' is a mere device, annexed to the demonstration of a projectivist thesis which might well be supported in other ways. (It is notable that the historical Wittgenstein, though undoubtedly hostile to classical forms of scepticism, quite arguably does betray projectivist leanings in certain of his remarks, for example, on first-personal ascriptions of sensation and when he compares mathematical statements to rules.) Classical forms of scepticism purport to discover inadequacies in our *actual* cognitive powers: the sceptic about induction, or other minds, or memory holds that the best we can do, in attempting to arrive at justi-fied opinions concerning statements in the relevant classes, always falls short of anything that ought really to be counted as justification.

The sceptic whom Kripke finds in Wittgenstein, in contrast, is concerned to teach us something about the range of items that *exist to be known.* That said, there will still be a point to the complaint if it turns out that, despite these differences, the *techniques* utilised by Kripke's sceptic are importantly similar to those which feature in traditional sceptical arguments. Wittgenstein undoubtedly thought those arguments mistaken; it is hardly likely that he would have allowed himself to succumb to an argument which, even if tending toward a conclusion congenial to him, needed to rely upon epistemological principles that, if granted, would enormously strengthen the traditional—epistemological—sceptic's case. We shall consider the matter further in due course.

Suppose it granted that there are indeed no facts that we can express by statements of the form 'By *E*, I formerly meant so-and-so'. How exactly do destructive consequences follow about the notions of meaning and understanding in general? Kripke himself is fairly brief on the point (p. 13), but it is not difficult to see. Remember that the argument will have involved an extensive idealisation of your knowledge of your previous behaviour and mental history; you will have been granted perfect recall of all such facts. If it turned out that you still could not justify any preferred claim of the form 'By *E*, I formerly meant so-and-so', then how can you be better placed to justify a claim of the form 'By *E,* I presently mean so-and-so'? For anything true of your mental life and behaviour up to and including the present will be known to you tomorrow, in accordance with the idealisation. And the argument will have shown that tomorrow you won't be able to justify any claim of the form 'By *E,* I yesterday meant so-and-so.' Hence you cannot be in a position to justify the present-tense counterpart of that claim today. The idealisation also entails that nobody else is better placed than you to justify any such claim. It follows that nobody can justify any claim about what they, or anybody else, formerly meant or means. Hence, in the presence of the idealisation, there can be no facts about what anybody means by any expression. And it is impossible to see how, consistently with that admission, there might yet be facts about what expressions, as it were impersonally, mean.

The strategy of the Sceptical Argument thus appears sound and ingenious. Everything depends upon the details of its execution.

Simplifying the details somewhat, the execution runs essentially like this. Suppose you claim today that by 'green' you yesterday meant *green*. The sceptic challenges you to justify your claim. You are idealised to have perfect recall of all your previous linguistic and non-linguistic behaviour, together with your entire mental life—the whole pageant of your thoughts, sensations, imaginings, dreams, moods, etc. (At this point in the argument there is, of course, no doubt entertained as yet about the supposition that you *presently* know what you mean by 'green'—the sceptic gets you to stand on the rug before he pulls it away; cf. pp. 11–2.) Now no doubt you can cite a lot of behaviour that is broadly consistent with your preferred account of your former understanding of 'green'. The sceptic will point out, however, that there are no end of alternative interpretations of your former meaning, all of which rationalise that behaviour equally well. Perhaps, for example, by 'green' you formerly meant $grue_{2001}$; where for arbitrary t, an object is $grue_t$ at time k just in case k is earlier than January 1 in year t and the object is green, or k is some later time and the object is blue. Seemingly there are infinitely many such grue-interpretations that can be used to make sense of your previous applications of 'green', all of which are incompatible both with the supposition that by 'green' you formerly meant green and with each other.

It might be objected that this is to consider only one kind of use of 'green', viz., simple predications and withholdings, and that account will need to be taken of all sorts of other more sophisticated uses, including embeddings in descriptions of your own and others' propositional attitudes, which you previously will likely have made. But, of course, the point of the example is that 'green' will be assigned the same extension, up to and including the time of your dialogue with the sceptic, under infinitely many grue-interpretations; so the sceptic should have no difficulty in rationalising your previous uses both in extensional contexts and in all attributions of propositional attitudes whose possession, by yourself and others, can be explained in terms of the extension of the property of being green. And even if grue-interpretations don't work out in general, the decisive consideration is surely that your previous behaviour with 'green' is *finite;* hence it must be possible, it appears, with sufficient ingenuity, to come up with some use-saving interpretation of your previous understanding of 'green' which will be as unwelcome to you as the grue-interpretations. Finite behaviour cannot constrain its interpretation to within uniqueness.

The arena of battle now shifts to the mental. Perhaps considerations determining your previous understanding of 'green' can be recovered from your previous thoughts, imaginings, etc. It is evident, however, that, if the search is to succeed, the relevant mental items will need to have a certain *generality.* It is no good remembering imagining certain green things, or green after-images that you may have experienced, or thoughts about what you would have said if asked to describe the colour of that liqueur we had on such-and-such an occasion. For the constraints imposed by introducing such considerations cannot be stronger than if the images had been public objects or if the imaginary and hypothetical situations had actually taken place; and the effect of those transformations would merely be finitely to enlarge an inadequately finite pool of actual data. You have to come up with some mental episode that somehow has sufficient content to exclude *all* the unwanted interpretations of your former understanding of 'green', including all the grue-interpretations, at one go.

The only candidate, it appears, is some sort of general *thought:* you need to have entertained a thought that has something to say about each of the situations in which the difference between the true interpretation of your former understanding of 'green' and each of the successive grue-impostors successively comes to light. On the face of it, though, it is not farfetched to suppose that you might very well have entertained such a thought. What if you remember having thought, say, 'By "green" I certainly don't mean any concept which, at some particular time, will continue to apply to an object only if that object changes colour at that time'. Does not that at least force the sceptic to work a bit harder at the concoction of unwelcome interpretations?

It wouldn't be all that satisfactory if this were the best you could do. After all, it is pretty much fortuitous whether any such thought ever occurred to you, and your knowledge about your former understanding of 'green' will not seem to you to be contingent on such an occurrence. What you will want to be able to say is that you know what you formerly meant by 'green' *whether or not* you happen to have had a convenient thought that can be used to scotch a particular line of unwelcome interpretation. But the sceptic, in any case, has a stronger, indeed a seemingly decisive, reply. His challenge, after all, was general. No special interest attaches to the justifiability of claims about your former understanding of colour predicates: the question was, can *any* claim of the form 'By E, I formerly meant so-and-so' be justified? Clearly the challenge is not met if, in the attempt to justify one such claim, you presuppose your right to be sure of another. But just such a presupposition is made by the attempted play with the general thought above. If, for example, by 'colour' you had previously meant *schmolor* (p. 20), where the concept of schmolor stands to all grue-type concepts exactly as colour stands to blue, green, etc., then your having entertained that general thought is quite consistent with the sceptic's being correct in interpreting you as having meant $grue_{2001}$ by 'green'.

The point is perfectly general. Thoughts you may have had about how, quite generally, you would be prepared to use an expression will suffice to meet the sceptic's challenge only if you presuppose their *proper interpretation*. But that is just to presuppose that the sceptic's challenge can be met with respect to the expressions that figure in those thoughts. Yet no category of mental item can be appropriate to the challenge except a general thought; only such a thought can *have enough to say*, can cover the indefinitely many potential situations in which you would wish to regard some determinate use of 'green' as mandated by the understanding that you believe you have long possessed of that expression.

It, therefore, appears that the only ploy that has any chance of accrediting your understanding of 'green' with an appropriately general normative role (pp. 11, 23, 24) totally fails to meet the sceptic's challenge. And now "it seems the whole idea of meaning vanishes into thin air" (p. 22).

II. THE SCEPTICAL SOLUTION

Suppose that this Sceptical Argument is sound. Could we simply accept its conclusion and abandon all talk of meaning and understanding as founded upon error? Or must we seek some sort of rehabilitation of the concept of meaning, a Sceptical Solution? Kripke himself writes:

> I choose to be so bold as to say: Wittgenstein holds, with the skeptic, that there is no fact as to whether I mean [green or grue] But if this is to be conceded to the skeptic, is this not the end of the matter? What *can* be said on behalf of our ordinary attributions of meaningful language to ourselves and to others? Has not the incredible and self-defeating conclusion, that all language is meaningless, already been drawn? (pp. 70–1)

There is, however, a certain awkwardness here. Suppose someone runs a similar sceptical argument about moral obligation, concluding that statements about what people morally ought or ought not to do lack a factual subject matter. It would be, to say the least, an infelicitous expression of this result to say, 'So undertaking, and refraining from, any particular projected course of action are always both morally permissible.' For the conclusion of the argument would apply equally to judgements of moral permissibility: to claim that a course of action is morally permissible is just to say that it is not the case that it ought to be refrained from. It is natural to wonder, correspondingly, whether the conclusion of Kripke's sceptic is indeed "incredible and self-defeating" only if the notion of meaninglessness which Kripke uses in its formulation presupposes the notion of meaning as moral permissibility presupposes the notion of obligation. If that is so, the right conclusion is surely that such is not the way to formulate the conclusion of the sceptical argument. Once it is better formulated, such unhappy claims as that all language is meaningless or that nobody ever succeeds in understanding anybody else, etc., will presumably not be entailed.

If somebody wishes to reject the suitability of a certain class of concepts to figure in statements apt to be genuinely true or false, this rejection cannot coherently take the form, it appears, of *any* kind of denial of statements in which those concepts figure. What then *is* the proper way of formulating the conclusion of Kripke's sceptic? One influential view of the concepts of meaning and understanding, associated chiefly with the writings of W. V. Quine, is that their paramount function for us is as theoretical terms in a deeply entrenched but philosophically suspect scheme of explanation of human linguistic behaviour and of non-linguistic but language-related patterns of social activity. If we think of this scheme as issuing in a large class of only semi-articulated theories about particular individuals and groups of individuals, then one way of expressing the conclusion of the Sceptical Argument is that *scientific realism* about these theories is not an option: there are no facts, describable only by recourse to the concepts of meaning and understanding, which such theories might succeed in codifying. An immediate consequence of this perspective is that two quite different lines of response to the Sceptical Argument are apparently open. One is a kind of *instrumentalism:* a view which tries to retain the propriety of theorizing of the sort in question while granting its non-factual status. The Sceptical Solution attempts just this. The other response is to regard theorising of this sort as *discredited,* and to seek better approaches involving quite alternative systems of concepts. That, in general, is Quine's own response to the difficulties that he finds in meaning and other intentional notions. If it admits satisfactory development, then the Sceptical Solution—and with it Kripke's reading of the private-language argument—would seem to be *de trop.*

This picture of the role of the concepts of meaning and understanding in our ordinary thinking is, however, an oversimplification. It ignores the larger class of self-ascriptions of meaning and understanding which we make—the class that Wittgenstein himself gives special attention to—and, still more important, it makes nothing of various platitudes that articulate our conception of the connections between meaning and truth. One such platitude is that the truth value of a statement depends only upon its meaning and the state of the world in relevant respects. Equivalently:

> An utterance of S expresses a truth in a particular context if and only if what, in that context, S says is so, is so.

The obvious corollary is that, if we take the view that the Sceptical Argument discredits *all* talk of meaning, understanding, and cognate concepts—like the concept of what a sentence is used to say—it is not clear how much purchase we can retain on our ordinary notion of a statement's being true. A proponent of the Quinean view has the choice either to abandon the notion of truth altogether or to reconstruct it in a fashion that liberates it from conceptual ties with the discredited notion of meaning. The former course, however, is hardly an option unless we are prepared to abandon the idea that it is *ever* the case that language has a fact-stating function. (And if that were our view, why see the conclusion of the Sceptical Argument as calling into question the propriety of talk involving the concepts of meaning and understanding?) The reconstructive project, on the other hand, looks to be utterly daunting. (Indeed it is doubtful whether, in the present context, it is coherent to suppose that there can be such a project; for whatever reconstruction of truth, free of all play with meaning and cognate notions, were proposed, it is not clear why an analogue of the Sceptical Argument would not remain available to rob any particular assignment of truth conditions to a sentence of all possible behavioural or psychological corroboration.)

So the strategy incorporated in the Sceptical Solution may seem more attractive. It is in any case more comfortable to think of any errors involved in our talk of meaning, or our moral language, as *philosophical:* as belonging to our picture of what is going on in those areas of linguistic practice, rather than as undermining the practices themselves. Thus, Kripke suggests (pp. 73 ff.) that statements involving the notion of meaning have no *truth conditions,* properly so described, but only conditions of justified or warranted use:

> All that is needed to legitimise assertions that someone means something is that there be roughly specified circumstances under which they are legitimately assertable, and that the game of asserting them under such conditions has a role in our lives (pp. 77–8).

Kripke's interpretation of the private-language argument now follows elegantly from this reorientation. Without attempting to do justice to the detail of his exposition (pp. 81 ff., summarised at pp. 107–8), we find that the most natural account of the justification conditions of statement forms like:

(i) Jones means addition by '+'.

and

(ii) If Jones means addition by '+', then he will answer '125' when asked, "What is 47 + 78?"

involves essential reference to a community of practitioners with the symbols they mention. Very roughly, (i) will be considered justified if Jones performs satisfactorily often enough with '+' and marks his acceptance into the community of '+' users—those whose uses of '+' can generally be depended upon. And (ii) expresses a test for membership in that community, ratified by the responses of those already accredited with membership. Accordingly, such statement forms simply have no legitimate application to symbols whose use is essentially "private" and which cannot, in the nature of the case, competently be taken up by a community. So the concepts of meaning and understanding have no proper place in the description of an apparent linguistic practice of an individual, if that practice is one in which others could not competently share.

The elegance of Kripke's interpretation does not, however, long conceal its difficulties. One immediate difficulty is presented by the meaning-truth platitude. If the truth value of S is determined by its meaning and the state of the world in relevant respects, then non-factuality in one of the determinants can be expected to induce non-factuality in the outcome. (A rough parallel: if among the determinants of whether it is worthwhile going to see a certain exhibition is how well presented the leading exhibits are, then, if questions of good presentation are not considered to be entirely factual, neither is the matter of whether it is worthwhile going to see the exhibition.) A projectivist view of meaning is thus, it appears, going to enjoin a projectivist view of what is for a statement to be true. Whence, unless it is, mysteriously, possible for a projective statement to sustain an a priori true biconditional with a genuinely factual statement, the disquotational schema '"P" is true if and only if P' will churn out the result that *all* statements are projective.

Kripke's own remarks are confusing in this regard. He quotes with approval (p. 73) Michael Dummett's suggestion that the central contrast between the picture of language and meaning proposed in the *Tractatus* and that of the *Investigations* resides in a shift from a conception of statement-meaning as truth-conditional to the view that the meaning of each statement is fixed by its association with conditions of justified assertion. But Dummett, at least as I read him, never intended that reorientation to involve a total rejection of the category of fact-stating discourse. It could not be so intended with any plausibility, since, as we have noted, the historical Wittgenstein thought that we are apt to be misled by the form of our discourse in certain selected areas into thinking that its role has to be that of stating facts. He could hardly have considered that we were likely to be so *misled* unless he thought that form of discourse to be very often associated with the activity of fact-stating. In any case, whatever intention Dummett, or Wittgenstein, may have had, it is doubtful that it is coherent to suppose that projectivist views could be appropriate quite globally. For however exactly the distinction between fact-stating and non-fact-stating discourse is drawn, the projectivist will presumably want it to come by way of a *discovery* that certain statements fail to qualify for the former class; a statement of the conclusion of the sceptical argument, for instance, is not *itself* to be projective. But can Kripke's exposition make space for this admission? According to Kripke, what is distinctive of fact-stating is the possession by one's statements of 'real truth conditions' (whatever that may mean). And how can the judgement '*S* has (real) truth conditions' be genuinely factual if—in accordance with the platitude and the considerations of a moment ago—'*S* is true' is not?

Another way of seeing that the situation cannot really be satisfactory is to inquire what status, once the Sceptical Argument is accepted, is supposed to be possessed by the sort of account adumbrated by Kripke of the assertion conditions of statements about meaning and understanding. Could it yesterday have been *true* of a single individual that he associated with the sentence 'Jones means addition by "+"' the sort of assertion conditions Kripke sketches? Well, if so, that truth did not consist in any aspect of his finite use of that sentence or of its constituents; and, just as before, it would seem that his previous thoughts about that sentence and its use will suffice to constrain to within uniqueness the proper interpretation of the assertion conditions he associated with it only if he is granted correct recall of the content of those thoughts—exactly what the Sceptical Argument does not grant. But would not any truths concerning the assertion conditions previously associated by somebody with a particular sentence have to be constituted by aspects of his erstwhile behaviour and mental life? So the case appears no weaker that in the sceptical argument proper for the conclusion that there *are* no such truths; whence, following the same routine, it speedily follows that there are no truths about the assertion conditions that any of us individually associates with a particular sentence, nor, a fortiori, any truths about a communal association. It follows that the premises, requisite for Kripke's version of the private-language argument, about the community-orientated character of the assertion conditions of statements concerning meaning and understanding are not genuinely factual, and the same must presumably be said of the conclusion, that the concepts of meaning and understanding have no proper application to a private linguist.

The Sceptical Solution seems to me, therefore, to be a failure. More: to sustain the Sceptical Argument is to uncage a tiger whose depredations there is then no hope of containing.

III. RESISTING THE SCEPTICAL ARGUMENT

Kripke himself considers two possible sources of error in the argument. The first is the assumption that facts about my former understanding of E must be constituted by aspects of my former behaviour and mental life. Is not a more plausible candidate a certain former *disposition,* the disposition to use E in certain sorts of way? Against this suggestion Kripke brings (pp. 26–37) two prima facie very telling sets of considerations to bear. First, the relevant sorts of disposition are, with respect to any particular expression, presumably finite, since all my capacities are finite; whereas, intuitively, we want the meaning of E to contribute towards the determination of its correct use in literally no end of potential cases. Second, meanings are, whereas dispositions are not, *normative:* I may, in certain circumstances, be disposed to use an expression in a way which is out of accord with my understanding of it and which, therefore, constitutes wrongful use of that expression: whereas I can scarcely be said to have a disposition to use an expression; in a way out of accord with the way in which I am disposed to use it. Now there is, no doubt, scope for discussion about how decisive these two rejoinders are.[4] In particular, it need not be contradictory to suppose that someone may be disposed to act in a way in which he is not disposed to act—provided his dispositions are appropriately *stratified.* So much, at any rate, is certainly part of our

4. See, e.g., Blackburn (1984); Forbes (1984).

ordinary concept of a disposition; almost all the dispositional properties about which we ordinarily speak are such that their display is
conditional on the absence of certain interfering factors, and there is
no contradiction in the idea that such interference might be widespread and even usual. The matter is obviously one of some subtlety.
Here I can do little more than record my own view that Kripke is ultimately right, at least as far as our intuitive conceptions of meaning
and understanding are concerned. Understading an expression is,
intuitively, more like an *ability* than a disposition.[5] Roughly, it is the
(fallible) ability to suit one's employment of the expression to certain
constraints. Even at the most fundamental level, then, and when
nothing interferes with the exercise of a disposition, there ought to be
a distinction between what somebody's understanding of *E* requires
of him and the use of that expression which he actually makes: it is
just that, if nothing interferes with the exercise of the disposition, the
use he makes *will be* the use required of him. You could put the point
by saying that, intuitively, understanding generates *rule-governed*
behaviour; to suppose that it is at some fundamental level simply a
matter of a disposition is to ignore the distinction between suiting
one's behaviour to a rule and merely behaving in such a way that,
when the rule is construed as a descriptive hypothesis, it fits what
one does.

A second response to the Sceptical Argument which Kripke discusses (pp. 41–50) is the idea that meaning green by 'green' 'denotes
an irreducible experience, with its own special *quale,* known directly
to each of us by introspection'. If there were such an experience 'as
unique and irreducible as that of seeing yellow or feeling a headache',
then—in the presence of the relevant idealisations—it could simply be
recalled in response to the sceptic's challenge and that would be that.
Kripke's response to this proposal, drawing extensively on themes
explicit in the *Investigations,* is surely decisive. Quite apart from the
introspective implausibility of the suggestion, it is impossible to see
how such an experience could have the *content* that understanding is

5. Cf. Baker and Hacker (1983), chap. 16.

conceived as having—could have, as it were, something to say about the correct use of *E* in indefinitely many situations. There might, indeed, be a distinctive experience *associated* with meaning so-and-so by *E;* but then, in order for recall of the experience to meet the sceptic's challenge, it would be necessary additionally to recall the association—and that would presuppose recall of one's former understanding of *E,* the possibility of which is exactly what is at issue.

There are, however, a number of other ways in which the sceptic's routine, seductive though Kripke's presentation makes it seem, is open to serious question. One concerns the play the sceptic makes with the *finitude* of previous linguistic behaviour. There is no question, of course, but that the relevant behaviour is finite and that it is thereby debarred from supplying a *conclusive* ground for affirming that your former understanding of *E* was, indeed, so-and-so. But to suppose that it follows that there is no rational basis for preference among indefinitely many competing hypotheses, all of which are consistent with your previous linguistic behaviour, is tantamount to the supposition that Goodman's 'new riddle of induction' admits of no solution. This point does not, of course, depend on the fact that we actually used a Goodman-type example in the development of the sceptical argument. Rather, Goodman's riddle is exactly the challenge to explain in what, if any, sense it is rational to prefer, on the basis of finite evidence, the sorts of general hypotheses which we invariably do prefer to any of the other indefinitely many alternatives whose formulation he illustrates. Of course, this assimilation is not in itself a satisfactory rejoinder to Kripke's sceptic. But it does at least show him up for a fairly familiar animal. And it teaches us that we ought not to regard the Sceptical Argument as, so to speak, establishing a theorem unless we think it right to despair of a solution to Goodman's riddle.[6]

6. Afficionados of Kripke's text might feel that he, in effect, answers this point (p. 38):

> Let no one—under the influence of too much philosophy of science—suggest that the hypothesis that I meant plus is to be preferred as the *simplest* hypothesis. I will not here argue that simplicity is relative or that it is hard to define, or

What *is* unsatisfactory about the suggestion is that it gets the intuitive epistemology of understanding wrong. Recognition that a certain use of an expression fits one's former (and current) understanding of it would not, it seems, except in the most extraordinary circumstances, have to proceed by inference to the best semantic explanation of one's previous uses of that expression. The kind of fact—if, against the Sceptical Argument, there can indeed be such a fact—which having formerly had a particular understanding of an expression is, is misrepresented by any broadly inductive conception of how one may know it.

There is, however, a further response, focusing on the second stage of the Sceptical Argument, at the point where it is argued that, no

---

that a Martian might find the quus function simpler than the plus function. Such replies may have considerable merit, but the real trouble with the appeal to simplicity is more basic. Such an appeal must be based on a misunderstanding of the skeptical problem, or of the role of simplicity considerations, or both. Recall that the skeptical problem was not merely epistemic. The skeptic argues that there is no *fact* [my italics] as to what I meant, whether plus or quus. Now simplicity considerations can help us decide between competing hypotheses, but they obviously can never tell us what the competing hypotheses are. If we do not understand what two hypotheses *state,* what does it mean to say that one is 'more probable' because it is 'simpler'? If the two competing hypotheses are not genuine hypotheses, not assertions of genuine matters of fact, no 'simplicity' considerations will make them so.

I do not wish to suggest that canons of simplicity provide an appropriate response to Goodman's riddle. However, Kripke's point is general. Whatever criterion of preferability among competing hypotheses we come up with, its application can be appropriate only if we do genuinely have competing *hypotheses,* only if there is some 'fact of the matter' about which we are trying to arrive at a rational view. Therefore—or so Kripke's thought presumably runs—we beg the question against the sceptic in appealing to any such criteria at this stage. But this surely gets everything back to front. It is only *after* the Sceptical Argument has come to its conclusion that the sceptic is entitled to the supposition that there is indeed no such fact of the matter. In the course of the argument, *he* cannot assume as much without begging the question. At the stage at which we might appeal to the sort of refined methodology which could be used to answer Goodman's riddle, there simply is not yet any basis for thinking that talk of meaning and understanding is not factual. For what is, I think, a better response to the point, see the sequel in the text.

matter how rich a battery of explicit thoughts you may formerly have entertained concerning your understanding of *E*, these thoughts will not turn the trick. Kripke's sceptic discounted the attempt to bring your previous general thoughts against unwelcome interpretations of your previous use of *E*, on the grounds that you thereby presuppose knowledge of the proper interpretation of those thoughts—which is, in detail, knowledge of the very putative species currently under suspicion. This can seem reasonable. On inspection, however, it cannot *always* be possible to justify a presumed genre of knowledge 'from without' in the way the sceptic is here demanding. At any rate, it is obvious enough that, if we were to allow the propriety quite generally of this sceptical move, the results would be calamitous. Imagine, for example, a sceptic who questions a claim about my former perceptions, say, 'Yesterday, I saw it raining'. And suppose the ground rules are as for the dialogue with Kripke's sceptic; that is, I am to be permitted to adduce any relevant fact so long as I do not thereby presuppose that there is such a thing as knowledge of what I formerly perceived—since it is of belief in the very existence of that genre of knowledge that the sceptic is demanding justification. So I cannot simply claim to remember what I perceived: my ammunition will be restricted to my present *seeming-memories,* the presently available testimony of others, presently accessible putative traces, like damp ground and meteorological office and newspaper records. It ought to be a straightforward, if tedious, exercise for the sceptic to accommodate all that without granting me the truth of my claim about my perception of yesterday's weather. So I can know 'all relevant facts' without knowing anything about what I formerly perceived. So there is no fact of the matter about what I formerly perceived. So, since the arguments will work just as well in the future when now is 'then', there is no fact of the matter about what I *presently* perceive. So, since the argument applies to all of us, there is no such thing as perceptual knowledge. 'There's glory for you!'

The trouble, evidently, is the assumption that knowledge of a former perception has to be *inferential,* that the ultimate grounds for such knowledge must reside in knowledge of a different sort. That is true only if knowledge of what I am *presently* perceiving is inferential; otherwise, the sceptic may satisfactorily be answered simply be recalling what one formerly perceived. So, too, Kripke's sceptic persuades his victim to search for recalled facts from which the character of his former understanding of E may be *derived*. And that is fair play only if knowledge of a *present* meaning has to be inferential; otherwise the sceptic is satisfactorily answered simply by recalling what one formerly meant.

The claim, then, is that the methodology of the Sceptical Argument is appropriate, if ever, only in cases where it is right to view the putative species of knowledge in question as essentially inferential. And no ground for that supposition in the present case has so far been produced. But if it is to be possible simply to recall the character of former meanings, can the requisite presupposition—that knowledge of present meanings may be non-inferential—really be made good? Kripke, in effect, confronts this suggestion when he considers the possibility (pp. 50–1) that meaning so-and-so by E might simply be an irreducible, *sui generis* state, a state 'not to be assimilated to sensations or headaches or any "qualitative" states, nor to be assimilated to dispositions, but a state of a unique kind of its own.' His reply, only very briefly developed (pp. 52–3), is that it is utterly mysterious how such a state could have the requisite properties, in particular how, although a finite state realised in a finite mind, it could nevertheless have the potential infinity of content that the normativity of meaning requires. How can there be a state which each of us knows about, in his own case at least, non-inferentially and yet which is potentially infinitely fecund, possessing directive content for no end of distinct situations?

This may be a good question. But Kripke's discussion contrives to leave the impression that it is rhetorical, that we have not the slightest idea what such a state might be. Whereas a little reflection shows that both these features—non-inferentiality and indefinite 'fecundity'—are simply characteristic of the normal intuitive notion of *intention*. Normally, we are credited with a special authority for the character of our own intentions; asked about them, it is considered that we ought to know the answer, and, saving lying and slips of the tongue, etc., that our answers should be given a special weight. Admittedly, this authority does not have to be taken to suggest non-inferential knowledge; it might be, for example, that it derived from authority for the premises of an inference—say, certain occurrent thoughts. But to think of self-knowledge of intention, in any case where the subject would be credited with authority, as invariably based on inference from associated occurrent thoughts is to caricature the ordinary notion. For one thing, each of us regularly carries out intentional acts without necessarily thinking about what we are doing at all. Usually these are routine activities in which we are expert. It is perfectly proper to say of such activities that they are knowingly and intentionally performed and, indeed, that they are preceded by the appropriate intention. (If you were asked, in advance, whether you had the appropriate intention, you would unhesitatingly confirm that you did.) Notice also that we can in general make no ready sense of the question 'How do you know?' directed at an avowal of intention; if there were an inference in the offing, the question ought to admit of a straightforward answer. But the decisive consideration is this: even when an intention is accompanied by certain occurrent thoughts relating to its content or the circumstances of the (envisaged) course of action, one's knowledge of the character of the intention is not to be thought of as achieved via reflection on the content of those thoughts. If it were, by what principle could I assure myself that *those* were the thoughts on which I should be concentrating, rather than some other recent (or, if I am clever—or distracted—enough, simultaneous) train? To come to know that you have a certain intention is not to have it dawn on you that you have an intention of *some* sort and then to recover an account of what the intention is by reflecting upon recent or accompanying thoughts. It is the other way round: you recognise occurrent thoughts as germane to content of an intention that you have *because* you know what the intention is an intention to do.

What of the 'mysterious fecundity'? Well, suppose I intend, for example, to prosecute at the earliest possible date anyone who trespasses on my land. Then there can indeed be no end of distinct responses, in distinct situations, which I must make if I remember this intention, continue to wish to fulfil it, and correctly apprehend the prevailing circumstances. But *if* we are at ease with the idea that my intention has a general content, non-inferentially known to me, then there is no more a puzzle about the 'infinity' of this content than there is a puzzle about the capacity of any universally quantified conditional, $(x)(Fx \rightarrow Gx)$, to yield indefinitely many consequences of the form $Ga, Gb, \ldots$, when conjoined with corresponding premises of the form $Fa, Fb, \ldots$

I want to stress that this is merely to describe what seem to be features of our intuitive notion of intention. The notion is not unproblematic. It could be that it is radically incoherent. The fact remains that it is available to confront Kripke's sceptic, and that, so far as I can see, the Sceptical Argument is powerless against it. The ordinary notion of intention has it that it is a characteristic of mind—alongside thought, mood, desire, and sensation—that a subject has, in general, authoritative and non-inferential access to the content of his own intentions, and that this content may be open-ended and general, may relate to all situations of a certain kind. In order, then, to rebut the Sceptical Argument, it would have sufficed, at the point where the sceptic challenged you to adduce some recalled mental fact in order to discount the grue-interpretations, to recall precisely your former intention with respect to the use of 'green'. To be sure, any *specification* that you might give of the content of that intention would be open to unwelcome interpretation. But, if you are granted the intuitive notion of intention, you can reply that you do not in any case know of the content of an intention via (interpretation of) a specification of it; to repeat, you recognise the adequacy of the specification because you know of the content of the intention.

The point, in summary, is not that it is particularly *comfortable* to think of your former meaning of 'green' as consisting in your having had a certain general intention, construed along the lines of the intuitive conception, but rather that the Sceptical Argument has absolutely no destructive force against that proposal.

IV. KRIPKE'S WITTGENSTEIN

I conclude with but the briefest indication of the most important difference, as I see it, between Kripke's Wittgenstein and Wittgenstein.

There is an evident concern in the *Investigations* with a large class
of psychological predicates which, like intention intuitively conceived, *seem* to have a content that can somehow transcend that of
any accompanying thoughts in the subject's mind. Examples are
recalling how a piece of music goes (without hearing it right through
'in one's head'); deciding to have a game of bridge (without thinking
through all the rules); realising how to continue a series (without *per
impossible,* thinking through the entire infinite expansion); grasping
the meaning of an expression "in a flash" (without having all its possible uses run before one's mind); and so on. Each of these predicates,
it seems, can come to be true of a subject quite abruptly, yet involves
some sort of reference to things he need not, on that occasion, think
about explicitly. Wittgenstein thought that we were greatly prone to
misunderstand the 'grammar' of these notions and to form quite false
pictures of the nature of the connection that obtains between the psychological state of someone of whom such a predicate comes to be
true and the 'absent aspects' noted in the parentheses above. In particular, there need be *no* connection between the subjective content,
properly so regarded, of such states and the detail of the 'absent
aspects'.[7] Accordingly, the *normative* power of intention—the determinacy, when it is determinate, in the matter of whether a particular
course of conduct fulfils a prior intention—cannot always be accounted for by reference only to the previous subjective content of the
subject's psychological states. Wittgenstein's conclusion, however, is
emphatically *not* that there is no such thing as the fulfilment of a prior
intention—the conclusion, in effect, of Kripke's sceptic.

> Is it correct for someone to say: 'When I gave you this rule, I meant you
> to . . . in this case'? Even if he did not think of this case at all as he gave

7. For an excellent discussion of these examples, see Budd (1984).

the rule? *Of course it is correct.* For 'to mean it' did not mean: to think of it.[8]

Rather, a satisfactory philosophy of intention has to validate our claim to non-inferential authority for our present (and previous) intentions without succumbing to the mythology of infinite, explicit introspectible content. The intuitive conception of intention utilised against Kripke's sceptic above perennially tempts us towards this mythology. But there has to be something right about it if—*pace* those who would wish to reanimate a dispositional account of meaning and intention—Kripke's sceptic is not to win the day.

It is this dilemma which is prominent in the last sections of part I of the *Investigations* (§§591 to the conclusion), sections about whose evaluation there is so far little consensus. The insight that there *is* a problem here, of the most profound importance for the philosophies both of language and of mind—whether or not Wittgenstein solved it—is one of the principal lessons of the *Investigations,* and one which Kripke's book ought to make it easier to learn.

✠

This paper amplifies part of the discussion of my "Kripke's Wittgenstein," presented (in my absence, at the birth of my son) at the 7th International Wittgenstein Symposium in Kirchberg-am-Wechsel, Austria, in 1982, but omitted from the associated published volume.

8. Philosophical Investigations §692 (my italics).

5

On Making up One's Mind:
Wittgenstein on Intention

This essay is a sequel to an earlier discussion[1] of Kripke's *Wittgenstein on Rules and Private Language*.[2] That earlier work concluded with some somewhat compressed remarks about the differences between Kripke's Wittgenstein and Wittgenstein. My principal purpose here is to relieve some of that compression: to explain in more detail how, as it seems to me, the two are related and what is the real moral of Kripke's argument.

I. KRIPKE'S ARGUMENT

We shall need, as briefly as may be, to outline the Sceptical Argument which *Philosophical Investigations* §§184–202 suggested to Kripke. The conclusion of the argument is that there are no states of affairs for whose description it is necessary to have recourse to the concepts of meaning, understanding or any other concepts cognate to them. So

1. Wright (1984) (this volume Essay 4).
2. Kripke (1982).

there are, accordingly, no facts about what any particular expressions meant or mean, and, consequently, no facts about what constitutes correct use of an expression on any particular occasion. The argument proceeds, as is familiar, in the setting of a debate with a sceptic who doubts your knowledge of what you formerly meant by some randomly chosen expression, *E*. The facts which constitute your erstwhile understanding of *E*, it is assumed, will have to be found in aspects of your former behaviour and/or mental life. Accordingly, if you are idealised to have perfect recall of the events in both provinces, then you ought to be in a position to know the relevant facts and hence to see off the sceptic. Conversely, if the sceptic wins his debate with you, then the requisite facts cannot be there to be found in those two provinces—so, on the assumption that there, if anywhere, is where they must be, they do not exist at all. Since the same debate can be constructed for any particular agent and any particular expression, it follows that there are no facts about what anyone formerly meant by any expression. Since the debate will have the same result tomorrow with respect to your claim then to know what you meant by *E* today, it follows that there are no facts about what anyone *presently* means either. But the, as it were, impersonal meaning of an expression must supervene upon what individuals mean by it: so it follows, finally, that there are no facts about what any expression means or meant.

So much, then, for the setting of the Sceptical Argument—a setting for which there is, Kripke would have to admit, little if any indication in Wittgenstein's text.[3] A prima facie successful argument within this

---

3. A remark on the relation between the 'paradox' of which Wittgenstein speaks in *Philosophical Investigations* §201 and Kripke's. The former is indeed to the effect that there is no such thing as accord or conflict with a rule. But it is explicitly conditional on the assumption that what complies with a rule is determined via *interpretation* of the rule, and seems to consist essentially just in the reflection that, with ingenuity, any particular rule can always be so interpreted as to sanction any particular piece of behaviour. By contrast, the second phase of Kripke's paradox explicitly concerns the fugitive character of *non-interpretative* knowledge of one's own (former) rules and meanings. It will be clear as this essay proceeds that I believe Kripke's second phase

setting would, however, be of the greatest philosophical interest in any case—and Wittgenstein's preoccupation with, if not exactly Kripke's problem, then anyway a cluster of related questions concerning the nature of determinacy of meaning—a preoccupation which is pivotal to so much of the thought both of the *Investigations* and of the *Remarks on the Foundations of Mathematics*—lends urgency to the question: does his mature philosophy contain the resources for a satisfactory response to Kripke's sceptic, even if that character is never sharply delineated in Wittgenstein's own work?

The actual contest with the sceptic, you will remember, is a somewhat one-sided affair. He points out, reasonably as it seems, that the totality of your previous behaviour, a fortiori your actual historical uses and responses to uses of *E*, must be reconcilable with indefinitely many alternative interpretations of your former understanding of *E*, since it is a merely finite pool of data. (The underlying assumption is that finite data may always be subsumed under indefinitely many distinct generalisations.) So the sought-after facts must be found, it seems—if they can be found at all—in the pageant of episodes of your former mental life: your imaginings, sensations, dreams, thoughts and so on. But understanding an expression in a particular way is a state of a certain *generality*: a state whose content bears on the use of that expression in an open-ended set of circumstances. So the aspects of your former mental life, which you are to recall in response to the sceptic's challenge, have to subserve that generality: what you recall has to be capable of constituting a state which can have something to say about the proper use of *E* in no end of situations. This would seem to exclude images, visualisations, sense experience—for no such process in consciousness has the requisite general content. Minutely faithful documentation of all such processes could, it appears, be

---

does indeed pose a problem which Wittgenstein attempted to solve and which is prominent elsewhere in the *Investigations*. But the 'paradox' of §201 is only part of the paradoxical train of thought which Kripke expounds, and exegetes will search §§184–202 in vain for an unmistakable anticipation of the latter.

added to the description of your total previous behaviour without significantly restricting the range of available unwelcome interpretations of your former understanding of E. All, it appears, that can stand a chance of effecting such a restriction would be a certain kind of general *thought*: a thought somehow encompassing all of the unwelcome interpretations and branding them as foreign to your intentions with E. From here the sceptic wins in three moves. First, it is not at all clear how such a general thought might be formulated. Second, the strategy of seeking such a thought gets the intuitive epistemology of understanding wrong: your confidence that you know what you formerly or presently mean by an expression is not at all contingent upon your ability to recall or conjure a thought which somehow uniquely nails down that meaning. Third, and most important, the strategy is question-begging. Thoughts are thought in symbols. To assume the ability to recall a thought is therefore to assume the ability to recall the signifance you attached to certain symbols. That is just to take it that you have the capacity which the sceptic is disputing—the capacity to know your former meanings.

II.   THREE POSSIBLE RESPONSES

The Sceptical Argument is more suggestive than coercive, involving various challengeable assumptions. One such explicit assumption was that facts about your former understanding of E must somehow be constituted by aspects of your former behaviour and episodes in your consciousness. Is not understanding better construed as a *disposition*? That you mean, for instance, green rather than $grue_{2001}$ by 'green' may be manifest only in your responses to certain future and/or counterfactual situations—there may be no recovering the fact from anything you have so far actually said or thought.[4] Kripke discusses this

---

4. In case someone doesn't know: an object is $grue_{2001}$ just in case it is green at all times in its history up to midnight on December 31st, 2000, and blue at all times in its history thereafter.

response in some detail, bringing to bear upon it two powerful-looking objections. First, there is the question whether our dispositions are not altogether too impoverished to provide the basis for an account of meaning. The meaning of the plus sign in arithmetic, for instance, has—in conjunction with other relevant semantic facts—something to say about the truth values of literally infinitely many simple arithmetical equalities about which we have no dispositions of judgement at all. In fact, our dispositions for arithmetical judgement are presumably finite. So the original problem, of extrapolating a unique account of your understanding of E by consideration of a finite pool of data, remains—it is merely that the originally finite pool is finitely enlarged by the addition of certain indicative and counter-factual conditionals. Second, meaning is normative: the meaning of an expression determines how it ought to be used, not necessarily how it actually is. But I am, in a large class of cases, disposed to use expressions in ways that actually fail to fit my understanding of them—because I tend to make mistakes, or misperceive or whatever. Yet if the meaning I attach to an expression were constituted by how I am disposed to use it, it would make no sense to suppose that I could be disposed to behave in ways that ran counter to it. If I were so disposed, I would not have the original disposition.

There has been some discussion whether a dispositionalist account may not have the resources to meet Kripke's objections.[5] I shall not try to decide that issue now, but will interpolate two considerations which will suggest that the dispositionalist can at best aspire to a revisionary conception of meaning and understanding, even if Kripke's objections can somehow be surmounted.

Note that understanding cannot straightforwardly be a disposition any more than belief and desire can, and for the same reason: understanding interacts holistically with other psychological states, including beliefs and desires, in the explanation of (linguistic) behaviour. How I am actually disposed to use an expression on a particular occasion will depend not just on how I understand it, but on the way I

5. See, e.g., Blackburn (1984); Forbes (1984).

apprehend the circumstances, my other background beliefs, my intentions in so using it and my other background desires. It is no exaggeration to say that *any* sort of performance with the expression can be reconciled with a subject's possessing some specified understanding of it, if one is willing to make sufficiently elaborate adjustments in these other parameters. It will be felt, no doubt, that while this point occasions some complications for the dispositionalist response to Kripke's sceptic, it involves no serious compromise: we are still at liberty to see somebody's understanding as determined by their dispositions of use, *modulo* some fixed set of assumptions about them in the other relevant parameters. But there is a further point which now becomes salient, and which may well have been what Kripke, in invoking the idea of normativity of meaning, fundamentally had in mind. Assume some such background. Then the dispositionalist is taking it, in effect, that *whatever* the subject does, he cannot but behave in a way that is appropriate to expressing his understanding, relative to that background. That is, while sense may be attached to the idea of a speaker's using an expression in a way which does not strictly accord with the way he understands it, this failure of accord must—in the dispositionalist view—be explained by appeal to what is true of him in respect of the *other* background parameters. He misuses the expression, for instance, because he intends to deceive his audience, or is attempting irony or is mistaken about the prevailing circumstnces. Thus if, in particular, the subject correctly cognises the relevant facts, and intends a literally informative use of the expression in question, the dispositionalist view would have it that he *must* then be disposed to use the expression appropriately (as far as his own understanding of it is concerned). Now, whatever the merits of this view, it is unquestionably a fundamental adjustment in traditional thinking about meaning. The *objectivity* traditionally associated with meaning would have it that what sort of use of an expression is appropriate, modulo a suitable set of background assumptions, is settled *independently* of the subject's response. What one ought to say, modulo the background assumptions—the requirement imposed by one's understanding—is something to be *cognised*. There is a question of fitting one's behaviour to antecedent semantic tracks. It makes no difference whether we think of these tracks, after the style of medieval realism, as constituted in the nature of platonic universals, or whether we think of them as a man-made contract. Either way it cannot, on this way of thinking of the matter, be taken for granted that, *ceteris paribus*, one will be disposed to do what, semantically, one ought.

This idea of the objectivity of meaning cuts immensely deep in our ordinary thinking. It is unclear, for instance, that, unless we appeal to it, any good sense can be made of the idea that currently undecided issues, in whatever sphere of inquiry, may *already* possess determinate answers settled by the content of relevant statements and the state of the world in relevant respects. A fortiori, it is unclear whether it can be permissible to think—in the style of realism as conceived by Michael Dummett—that statements may be determinate in truth value which, in the nature of the case, we cannot appraise. The dispositionalist account thus brings into question our picture of an external world which is determinate in no end of respects for which we have adequate descriptive resources, irrespective of our cognitive achievements to date and of the limits of principle on such achievements in the future.

I have suggested elsewhere, and will suggest again later in this essay, that this is something which is at issue anyway. My immediate purpose is merely to urge on those who would favour a dispositionalist response to Kripke's sceptic the recognition that *they* are bringing it into question.

That was the first point. The second point is an application of something which we have, in effect, already noticed and which will be important to us in the sequel. Self-ascriptions of a specific mode of understanding of some expression, like self-ascriptions of a large class of beliefs, intentions and sensations, are a kind of *avowal.* There is more to be said about the characterisation of this notion,[6] but here it will suffice to recall that subjects are credited with a special authority for their avowals, that we think of the knowledge which they thereby

6. A useful discussion is Hacker (1972), chap. 9. See also Hamilton (1987).

express as groundless and immediate. It is hard to see what justification there could be for this practice if what one ascribed, in self-ascribing a particular understanding of some expression, was a *disposition*. How can I know without evidence that I have a particular disposition or complex of dispositions, and why should I be credited with any kind of authority on the matter? What substitute could there be for *empirical* appraisal, of a kind which anyone else could as well engage in as myself? The dispositionalist account, as much as the move which tried to hold off the sceptic by appeal to the occurence of some appropriately general thought, misrepresents the intuitive epistemology of self-ascriptions of understanding.

The same complaint is to be levelled against another, otherwise intuitively fair response to Kripke's sceptic: namely, that at the very first stage of the debate there is a presupposition of the cogency of what is, in effect, Goodman's version of inductive scepticism. The fact that no end of alternative generalisations are consistent with any finite accumulation of behavioural data is a ground for holding that there can be no rational preferences among them only if the 'grueish' projections which Goodman describes are supposed to be as rational as the kind of inductions that we actually favour. Yet even if Goodman's sceptic can be defeated and a more refined methodology exposed which rationally bars the Goodmanian inductions—however exactly they are to be characterised—it remains that knowledge of one's own meanings seems to owe nothing to the application of such a methodology but may be consistent with, for example, large-scale amnesia concerning one's previous linguistic behaviour.

There is a connection here with what is, I believe, the proper reading of *Investigations* §201. Wittgenstein writes:

This was our paradox: no course of action could be determined by a rule, because every course of action can be made out to accord with the rule. The answer was: if everything can be made out to accord with the rule, then it can also be made out to conflict with it. And so there would be neither accord nor conflict here. It can be seen that there is a misunderstanding here from the mere fact that in the course of our argument we give one interpretation after another; as if each one contented us at least for a moment until we thought of yet another standing behind it. What this shows is that there is a way of grasping a rule which is *not* an *interpretation*, but which is exhibited in what we call 'obeying the rule' and 'going against it' in actual cases.

In allowing, apparently, that there is indeed an ineliminable multiplicity of conflicting possible interpretations, I read Wittgenstein as granting that, if I may so put it, a *merely rational* methodology can indeed yield no determinate conclusions when it comes to disclosing what meaning is incorporated in someone's practice with an expression hitherto. His conclusion, however, is explicitly not the sceptic's, that there is no fact of the matter concerning the character of the subject's understanding, but rather 'that there is a way of grasping a rule which is *not* an *interpretation*'—that is, I take it, that something other than the exercise of interpretative (rational) faculties enters into the capacity to 'read' another's linguistic behaviour. And the additional something is, crudely, human nature: certain subrational propensities towards conformity of response, towards 'going on in the same way', which alone make possible the formation of the common conceptual scheme within which our rational capacities can be exercised. A quite common thought in recent moral philosophy in Britain has been that a sharing of certain basic human concerns is prerequisite for the formation of certain of our moral concepts.[7] The thought which Wittgenstein is putting in opposition to the, by comparison with Kripke's, rather straightforward form of scepticism set up in *Investigations* §§185 and following[8] is a generalisation of that: it is not merely concerns which must be shared but a whole plethora of natural classificatory dispositions if we are to find each other's linguistic behaviour intelligible.[9]

7. See, e.g., McDowell (1981), pp. 144–5.
8. Cf. note 3 above.
9. Cf. Wright (1985), section III (this volume Essay 12), and the Introduction to Wright (1986c), pp. 27–9.

This simple point is of great importance, and armed with it, we can perhaps explain how my former understanding of E could be salient in a sufficient sample of my behaviour, even if no fully rational ground could be given for discounting various unwelcome alternative accounts of it. But, again, that is a point to use against Kripke's sceptic only from an assumed *third-personal* point of view, as it were, with respect to one's own linguistic past. It would do nothing to legitimate the idea of one's present and former meanings as apt for *avowal* in the germane sense. And it is in the legitimation of that idea that a satisfying response to the sceptic must ultimately be found.

III. THE (W)RIGHT RESPONSE

Kripke does consider the response that meaning so-and-so by E might be a *sui generis* state,[10] like the experience of yellow or a toothache, and rightly emphasises the point I built into the summary of the argument above, that no such state can have the general, directive content essential to meaning. Later[11] he briefly considers the idea that meaning so-and-so by E might, as it were, be more *sui generis* yet, beyond illustration by comparison with states of any other familiar kind. But this he presents as merely obscurantist. How could there be such a state, available immediately to the subject, apt for authoritative avowal and non-inferential recall, yet possessing determinate, potentially infinite content?

In my previous discussion I set in opposition to this the reflection that, so far from finding any mystery in the matter, we habitually assign just these characteristics to the ordinary notion of *intention*. To summarise: the intuitive notion of intention has it that it is a state of mind, alongside mood, thought, desire, sensation, etc., for which, in at least a very large class of cases, subjects have a special authority, and whose epistemology is first/third-personal asymmetric. I can be

10. Kripke (1982), pp. 41–50.
11. Kripke (1982), pp. 50–3.

presumed to know, at least in a very large class of cases, what my intentions are, and this knowledge does not proceed, or does not have to proceed, by reflection on what I say and do—the only basis that you can have for an opinion about what my intentions may be. As far as the relation between intention and thought is concerned, it can come to be true of me that I have a certain intention without my engaging in any process of conscious deliberation or thinking any thought which specifies that intention's content. Rather I may simply find myself with my mind made up, as it were—able to give an account of my intentions if asked, but with no story to tell about the when or why of their onset. More important in the context of the Sceptical Argument, it is a feature of the intuitive concept of intention that, even when there is an association with a content-specifying train of thought, the subject does not know of his intention *via* that train of thought. It is not, for instance, because I visualise a golf ball disappearing down a hole that I know that I am currently attempting to putt out; rather it is because I know my current intention that I recognise the visualised sequence of events as germane to specifying its content. Knowledge of one's own intentions, in the cases which interest us, is based on inference neither from one's behaviour nor from other occurrent aspects of one's mental life. Finally, intentions may be general, and so may possess, in the intuitively relevant sese, potentially infinite content. I may have the intention to sue if anybody slanders me, to follow Kipling's advice and always respond alike to Triumph and Disaster, and to use 'green' to express green. How can an intention bear on a potential infinity of cases? Well, just because it may be the intention to respond in a certain way to any case of a certain sort, and because there may be a potential infinity of cases of that sort.[12]

Had the Sceptical Argument been directed against intention in general, rather than at what it is tempting to regard as the special case of meaning, there is no doubt that the intuitive concept seems to contain the resources for a direct rebuttal. Since I can know of my present intentions non-inferentially, it is not question-begging to respond to the sceptic's challenge to my knowledge of my past intentions to reply

12. Cf. Wright (1984), pp. 775–7 (this volume Essay 4).

that I may simply remember them. And this is just the reply that Wittgenstein does, in effect, give. At the conclusion to part I of the *Investigations* he writes:

(692)   Is it correct for someone to say: 'When I gave you this rule, I meant you to . . . in this case'? Even if he did not *think* of this case at all as he gave the rule? [My italics.] Of course it is correct. For 'to mean it' did not mean: to think of it. . . .

(693)   'When I teach someone the formation of the series . . . I surely mean him to write . . . at the hundredth place'—Quite right; you mean it. And evidently without necessarily even thinking about it. This shows you how different the grammar of the verb 'to mean' is from that of 'to think'. And nothing is more wrong-headed than calling meaning a mental activity!

If we may think of meaning so-and-so by *E* as either consisting in, or relevantly similar to, possession of an intention or complex of intentions,[13] then the Wittgensteinian response to Kripke's sceptic would evidently be to confront him with the 'grammar' of the ordinary notion, and in particular its distinction from any kind of episodic state of consciousness. The diagnosis would be that the sceptic has fallen prey to the kind of misunderstanding from which, in Wittgenstein's view, so many philosophical perplexities arise—a misunderstanding based on superficial similarities in functionally quite different forms of discourse. Seeing a verb—'I *intended* him to write thus—and-such at the so-and-so manyeth place'—we are inclined to cast about for a state, or process or activity of consciousness for that verb to report, which contains, as it were, an instruction for the so-and-so manyeth place. But there need not and, in the case of an open-ended general intention, cannot always be any such appropriately explicit happening in consciousness. The proper conclusion is that the connection between an intention and the act which implements or frustrates it need not and in general cannot be anticipated by states or

13. Cf. *Investigations* II, §xi, p. 214: 'In a law-court, for instance, the question might be raised how someone meant a word. And this can be inferred from certain facts.—It is a question of *intention*'.

processes of consciousness distinct from intending. To suppose otherwise is to cause the downfall of the notion—as the Sceptical Argument shows.

IV. THE REAL PROBLEM

We cannot leave matters like that, however, for now it is apt to seem utterly mysterious how the connection—between the prior intention and the performance which implements or goes against it—is forged at all. Wittgenstein writes:

> (197) There is no doubt that I now want to play chess, but chess is the game it is in virtue of all its rules (and so on). Don't I know, then, which game I want to play until I have played it? Or, are all the rules contained in my act of intending? Is it experience that tells me that this sort of game is the usual consequence of such an act of intending? So is it impossible for me to be certain what I am intending to do? And if that is nonsense—what kind of super-strong connection exists between the act of intending and the thing intended?—Where is the connection effected between the sense of the expression 'Let's play a game of chess' and all the rules of the game?

This brings us to a central, perhaps the central, preoccupation of the philosophy of mind of the *Investigations*. How can there *be* a state, or act or however one wants to regard it, with the features I characterised of the intuitive notion of intention? And what is the basis for the authority allowed to the intending subject? What is striking is that Cartesianism, whatever other difficulties it may encounter, is not even of prima facie service to us here. Cartesianism would view the authority as having the same kind of basis which it finds for a subject's authority concerning his or her occurrent sensations. The subject has privileged access to the state, is immediately aware of it in consciousness. Others, in contrast, can approach it only by an indirect, inferential route. But how, for instance, can my authority for the claim that at the so-and-so manyeth place I intended you to write down thus-and-such be based on introspection, if, as has been stressed, nothing which went on within me and which has any plausible claim to be regarded as a state of consciousness explicitly anticipated the case of the so-and-so manyeth place at all? An unthinking reply would be: but may not proper performance at the so-and-so manyeth place have been anticipated *implicitly*? But that gets us absolutely no further. For *what* was introspectibly true of you, at the earlier time, which made it the case that it was *that* kind of performance at the so-and-so manyeth place, rather than something else, which was implicit in the way you meant the rule to be taken?

The problem is not peculiar to meaning and intention and is illustrated in the *Investigations* by a variety of examples.[14] Here are some relevant passages.

(139)   When someone says the word 'cube' to me, for example, I know what it means. But can the whole *use* of the word come before my mind when I *understand* it in this way? Well, but on the other hand isn't the meaning of the word also determined by this use? And can these ways of determining meaning conflict? Can what we grasp in a *flash* accord with a use, fit or fail to fit it? And how can what is present to us in an instant, what comes before our mind in an instant, fit a *use*?

(151–3)   Let us imagine the following example: A writes a series of numbers down; B watches him and tries to find a law for the sequence of numbers. If he succeeds he exclaims: 'Now I can go on!'—So this capacity, this understanding, is something that makes its appearance in a moment. So let us try and see what it is that makes its appearance here.—A has written down the numbers 1, 5, 11, 19, 29; at this point B says he knows how to go on. What happened here? Various things

14. I draw here on Malcolm Budd's and Peter Carruthers' excellent respective discussions in Budd (1984) and Carruthers (1985).

may have happened; for example, while A was slowly putting one number after another, B was occupied with trying various algebraic formulae on the numbers which had been written down. After A had written the number 19 B tried the formula $a_n = n^2 + n\ 1 - 1$; and the next number confirmed his hypothesis. Or again, B does not think of formulae. He watches A writing his numbers down with a certain feeling of tension, and all sorts of vague thoughts go through his head. Finally he asks himself: 'What is the series of differences?' He finds the series 4,6,8,10 and says: Now I can go on. Or he watches and says 'Yes I know *that* series'—and continues it, just as he would have done if A had written down the series 1, 3, 5, 7, 9.—Or he says nothing at all and simply continues the series. Perhaps he had what may be called the sensation 'that's easy!' (Such a sensation is, for example, that of a light quick intake of breath, as when one is slightly startled.)

(152)   But are the processes which I have described here *understanding?* 'B understands the principle of the series' surely doesn't mean simply: the formula '$a_n = \ldots$' occurs to B. For it is perfectly imaginable that the formula should occur to him and that he should nevertheless not understand. 'He understands' must have more in it than: the formula occurs to him. And equally, more than any of those more or less characteristic *accompaniments* or manifestations of understanding.

(153)   We are trying to get hold of the mental process of understanding which seems to be hidden behind those coarser and therefore more readily visible accompaniments. But we do not succeed; or, rather, it does not get as far as a real attempt. For even supposing I had found something that happened in all those cases of understanding—why should it be the understanding? And how can the process of understanding have been hidden, when I said 'Now I understand' because I understood?! And if I say it is hidden—then how do I know what I have to look for? I am in a muddle.

(184)   I want to remember a tune and it escapes me; suddenly I say 'Now I know it' and I sing it. What was it like to suddenly know it? Surely it can't have occurred to me *in its entirety* in that moment!—Perhaps you will say: 'It's a particular feeling, as if it were *there*'—but *is* it there? Suppose I now begin to sing it and get stuck?—But may I not have been *certain* at that moment I knew it? So in some sense or other it was *there* after all. But in what sense?

(187)   'But I already knew, at the time when I gave the order, that he ought to write 1002 after 1000'—Certainly; and you can also say you *meant* it then; only you should not let yourself be misled by the grammar of the words 'know' and 'mean'. For you don't want to say that you thought of the step from 1000 to 1002 at that time—and even if you did think of this step, still you did not think of other ones. When you said 'I already knew at the time . . . ' that meant something like: 'If I had then been asked what number should be written after 1000, I should have replied "1002".' And that I don't doubt. This assumption is rather of the same kind as: 'If he had fallen into the water then, I should have jumped in after him'.—Now, what was wrong with your idea?

(197)   'It's as if we could grasp the whole use of a word in a flash.'—And that is just what we say we do. That is to say: we sometimes describe what we do in these words. But there is nothing astonishing, nothing queer, about what happens. It becomes queer when we are led to think that the future development must in some way already be present in the act of grasping the use and yet isn't present—For we say that there isn't any doubt that we understand the word, and on the other hand its meaning lies in its use.

These are highly suggestive passages. The most noticeable similarity running through them is that each is concerned with what appears to be a routinely psychological concept—grasping a meaning, understanding how to continue a series, remembering how a tune goes, etc.—which, like a headache or sensation, for instance, may have an abrupt onset, as it were, and may be recognised to do so by the subject. The problem Wittgenstein is concerned with is that, in contrast to a headache or sensation, these concepts contain a load which may—and in certain cases must—go quite unreflected in the subject's consciousness as onset takes place. Thus each of the following is a perfectly coherent claim:

X suddenly grasped the meaning of E—without having its whole use come before his mind.

X suddenly understood how to continue the series—without having the whole series come before his mind.

X remembered how the tune went—without playing it through 'in his head'.

X meant Y to continue '1002' after '1000'—without consciously thinking of that particular case.

X decided to play chess—without thinking of all the rules.

Now, the application of each of these predicates to X will be defeasible if his subsequent performance is inadequate when measured by a standard implicit in the things he didn't explicitly think about—if he goes on to misuse E, miscontinue the series, cannot whistle the tune, rejects Y's continuing '1002' after '1000' or shows he doesn't understand the rules of chess. But it is not that developments of this kind are taken to be a symptom that certain constitutive events or processes, of a kind of which X *would* have been fully conscious, did not take place. The point is rather that the events of X's consciousness, whatever in fact they were, do not suffice for the applicability of such predicates in the first place. Whatever took place in X's consciousness at the time he decided to play chess, for instance, that very same phenomenology could have accompanied a decision of a quite different sort. And as the quoted passages bring out, there is a case to be made that any actual phenomenology is also not necessary. A formula, for instance, may occur to X when he understands how to continue the series, but need not.

These concepts, then, seem to incorporate a tension. You could say: some aspects of their employment seem proper only if they characterise states of consciousness while others suggest something quite different. How, if nothing happening in the subject's consciousness is uniquely distinctive of the concept that comes to apply to him, can he be in *position* to apply it, usually with complete confidence? The matter is apt to seem all the more puzzling when the subject's awareness is retrospective—as Wittgenstein brings out beautifully for the case of intention:

(633) 'You were interrupted a while ago; do you still know what you were going to say?—If I do know now, and say it—does that mean that I had already thought it before, only not said it? No. Unless you take the certainty with which I continue the interrupted sentence as a criterion of the thought's already having been completed at that time.—But, of course, the situation and the thoughts which I had contained all sorts of things to help the continuation of the sentence.

(634) When I continue the interrupted sentence and say that *this* was how I had been going to continue it, this is like following out a line of thought from brief notes. Then don't I *interpret* the notes? Was only one continuation possible in these circumstances? Of course not. But I did not *choose* between interpretations. I *remembered* that I was going to say this.

(635) 'I was going to say . . . '—You remember various details. But not even all of them together show your intention. It is as if a snapshot of a scene had been taken, but only a few scattered details of it were to be seen: here a hand, there a bit of a face, or a hat—the rest is dark. And now it is as if we knew quite certainly what the whole picture represented. As if I could read the darkness.

(636) These 'details' are not irrelevant in the sense in which other circumstances which I can remember equally well are irrelevant. But if I tell someone 'For a moment I was going to say . . . ' he does not learn those details from this, nor need he guess them. He need not know, for instance, that I had already opened my mouth to speak. But he *can* 'fill out the picture' in this way. (And this capacity is part of understanding what I tell him.)

(637) 'I know exactly what I was going to say!' And yet I did not say it.—And yet I don't read it off from some other process which took place then and which I remember. Nor am I interpreting that situation and its antecedents. For I don't consider them and don't judge them.

This is a graphic expression of the non-inferential character of knowledge of one's own intentions. But Wittgenstein's point is not just that the recollection of events in consciousness of other *sorts* may provide an insufficient basis for a judgement about the former intention. It is that recollection of *anything* properly viewed as an event, state or process of consciousness is so insufficient—that the intention, construed as such an event in its own right, is evanescent.[15]

---

15. Compare *Investigations* II, §xi, pp. 216–7:

Someone tells me: 'Wait for me by the bank'. Question: Did you, *as you were saying the word,* mean this bank?—This question is of the same kind as 'Did you intend to say such-and-such to him on your way to meet him?' It refers to a definite time (the time of walking, as the former question refers to the time of speaking)—but not to an experience during that time. Meaning is as little an experience as intending.

But what distinguishes them from experience?—They have no experience-content. For the contents (images for instance) which accompany and illustrate them are not the meaning or intending.

The intention *with which* one acts does not 'accompany' the action any more than the thought 'accompanies' speech. Thought and intention are neither 'articulated' nor 'non-articulated'; to be compared neither with a single note which sounds during the acting or speaking, nor with a tune.

V. Towards a Solution

The general problem being posed, it will be evident, has two distinct aspects. First, there is the question of with what to replace the Cartesian conception of these concepts. When such a concept comes to apply to a subject—perhaps quite abruptly—what *kind* of change in him does it mark, if not one in his conscious mental state? The kind of answer which Wittgenstein seems to want to accept is, very crudely, that the change marked is the onset of some kind of capacity or complex of capacities, or of a range of dispositions. Thus in §187, quoted above, he offers:

> When you said 'I already knew at the time . . . ' that meant something like: 'if I had then been asked what number should be written after 1000, I should have replied "1002"' and that I don't doubt. This assumption is rather of the same kind as 'If he had fallen into the water then, I should have jumped in after him'. (Compare §§682–4, quoted below.)

If *X* comes to grasp the meaning of a particular expression, or to understand how to continue a particular series, or remembers how a tune goes, he does so only if in each case he acquires certain constitutive *abilities* which he did not possess just beforehand. On the other hand what has to be true of him, if it is to be said that he, at some specific earlier time, meant *Y* to continue subsequently in a particular way, is that he had certain *dispositions* at the earlier time—roughly, to allow or reject certain responses by *Y*; while the decision to play chess is answerable to the disposition to go on to do so, provided no interfering factor intrudes. This all seems unexceptionable as far as it goes, and there is a temptation to see the purpose of Wittgenstein's discussion as being no more than to effect a certain kind of overall adjustment in the way we think of the kind of concept in question—an adjustment, summarised in the slogan that 'Understanding is not a mental state', which takes us away from the Cartesian picture of intention and its kin as movements within an inner theatre and in the direction of something more functional.

That is, no doubt, an adjustment which needs to be learned, even if to take the point is hardly to swim against the tide. But matters will not rest there. We want more detail, of course.[16] It is not, however, lack of detail but the second aspect of the overall problem which now presses us. In recognising that the facts marked by the application of these concepts are persistently fugitive if sought within the sphere of consciousness, we seem to have made a mystery out of the phenomenon of first-person *avowal* of the application of such concepts. This was the point with which we earlier faced the dispositional and other responses to Kripke's sceptic. How is the *subject* to know of the application of such a concept to himself if nothing of which he is conscious intimates the fact to him? And how, moreover, can it be reasonable to credit a subject—in the cases where we do—with a *special* authority concerning such states of himself if the Cartesian picture quite misrepresents their epistemology? The authority is easily understood if the subject is conceived as the sole witness, as it were. But when that is no longer the picture, what sense can be made of this aspect of our linguistic practice? There are plenty of dispositions and capacities for which there is no institution of authoritative self-ascription—the confident self-ascription, without behavioural grounds, of intelligence, courage, patience, or endurance, for instance, is, so far from being authoritative, a mere conceit. Why is it not a conceit throughout the range of concepts with which we are concerned?

The question is difficult and probably admits of no uniform answer. If a subject's knowlege or—in cases where he has it—his special authority is not owed to the introspectibility of the relevant kind of state of affairs, only two possibilities remain. The first is that it is based on introspection of something else; and the second is that it is not

---

16. Though more refined accounts of the conditions of application of concepts of the kind in question are unlikely to throw up anything of comparable philosophical importance to that of grasping in general, in advance of the detail, these concepts' role in marking the presence of capacities and dispositions.

based on introspection at all. The former is at least the natural place to start in the case of the first three concepts illustrated—grasping the meaning of an expression 'in a flash', suddenly understanding how to continue a series, and remembering how a tune goes. In these cases there is no institution of avowal in the strict sense—the subject's word carries no *special* authority. What needs explanation is rather how a subject can be so much as in position to be *reliable*. If the proof of the pudding is in subsequent performance, what basis can there be for an opinion at a stage at which a third party can (justifiably) have none? The beginnings of an answer would be that there *are* certain kinds of phenomenological episodes—flashes of imagery, surges of confidence, and so on—which, experience teaches, correlate often enough with the capacity to go on to deliver the right kind of performance, whatever it may be, and which accordingly provide an experimental basis for claiming that capacity. But this cannot be the right place to look with the other two examples—meaning Y to continue 1002 after 1000, and deciding to play chess—or with self-ascriptions of intention generally. What I actually feel when I exclaim, for example, 'Now I can go on' may be the same in different cases involving different series. Not only may this be so—it must be so if I am to have an *inductive* basis for expecting my confidence to be fulfilled. For the series in question may be one which I have never encountered before. But the striking feature about the self-ascription of an intention is that one *identifies* it at the time: there is no such thing as knowing that one has an intention of some sort but not knowing *what* is intended. Since we are able confidently and authoritatively to self-ascribe intentions which we have never had before, it simply cannot be that we identify our intentions in general by inductive association with other, genuine states of consciousness. (Because this point is decisive, we may prescind from consideration of the additional difficulties, associated with the question, how such an inductive association might anyway be established.)

For these cases, then, we require a different explanation, dissociated from introspection. So far as I can see, there is only one possible broad direction for such an explanation to take. The authority which our self-ascriptions of meaning, intention, and decision assume is not based on any kind of cognitive advantage, expertise or achievement. Rather it is, as it were, a *concession,* unofficially granted to anyone whom one takes seriously as a rational subject. It is, so to speak, such a subject's right to declare what he intends, what he intended and what satisfies his intentions; and his possession of this right consists in the conferral upon such declarations, other things being equal, of a *constitutive* rather than descriptive role.

Authoritative utterance of this constitutive sort is not without analogues. Someone umpiring a tennis match, for instance, may declare 'The ball was good', intending only to report the physical fact of where the ball bounced. But if he speaks as *umpire,* then what he says will determine another, institutional fact, which is constituted by his decision, and which—to the possible chagrin of the players—contributes towards a resolution of the outcome of the game (in a way in which the actual physical fact may not.) If the analogy is to go further, of course, we shall require that the umpire's decision be not final but, at least exceptionally, defeasible (in the light, perhaps, of the judgement of the tournament referee)—just as avowals of intention may on occasion reasonably be discounted by a third party. Even so, the analogy limps in this respect: the umpire's pronouncements are made in the light of physical facts which are available to anyone, and the sole ground for criticism of them is the appraisal of these facts. By contrast, an avowal of intention need have no basis, and insofar as it may be criticisable, the basis for the criticism may only be constituted by states of affairs that were not salient, or even did not exist, at the time of the avowal—par excellence, the subject's subsequent behaviour.

Wittgenstein writes:

(682) 'You said, 'It'll stop soon'.—Were you thinking of the noise or of the pain?' If he answers 'I was thinking of the piano-tuning'—is he observing that the connexion existed, or is he making it by means of these words?—Can't I say *both?* If what he said was true, didn't the connexion exist—and is he not for all that making one which did not exist?

(683) I draw a head. You ask 'Whom is that supposed to represent?'—I: 'It's supposed to be N.'—You: 'But it doesn't look

like him; if anything, it's rather like M.' —When I said it represented N.—was I establishing a connexion or reporting one?
And what connexion did exist?

(684)   What is there in favour of saying that my words describe an
existing connexion? Well, they relate to various things which
didn't simply make their appearance with the words. They say,
for example, that I *should have* given a particular answer then,
if I had been asked. And even if this is only conditional, still it
does say something about the past.

This is encouragement that the present suggestion is, for the relevant
class of concepts, on the right exegetical tracks. But what more definite cast can we give it? One strategy is to proceed by asking under
what circumstances we would discount a subject's avowal of an intention. Well, supposing that we are concerned with someone who is in
general deemed *able* to be reliable on such matters—so not some form
of delusional psychotic, for instance—we would do so only in fairly
special circumstances: when there was independent evidence of insincerity, or of some sort of muddle about the content of the intention
claimed, or of some relevant self-deception, or—in the case of a retrospective avowal—of some major disorientation of memory. Suppose
that the range of grounds on which such an avowal may be legitimately discounted is both finite and circumscribable.[17] Then we may
expect that some such biconditional as this will hold a priori:

X intends that P if and only if X is disposed to avow the intention that
P, and would be sincere in so doing, and fully grasps the content of that
intention, and is prey to no material self-deception, and . . . and so on.

Now, such a biconditional may be read in two contrasting ways.[18]
One reading—the *detective*—would hold that the left-hand side serves
to describe a determinate state of affairs which, if all the provisos on

17. Actually, it is not important to the suggestions which follow that this should
be so.
18. Compare the concluding pages of Wright [1987b]. I owe this form of contrast
to Mark Johnston.

the right-hand side are met, the subject is able to *apprehend*. On this view, the provisos collectively determine the conditions for a cognitive success, which an avowal may then serve to report. The alternative, however, is to accord priority to the right-hand side. The resulting view would see the disposition to make the avowal as *constituting* the state of affairs reported by the left-hand side when the provisos are met. So the subject's cognition of an independent state of affairs does not come into the picture. Rather, he is *moved* to make the avowal and, subject to the provisos, it stands. Accordingly, any ground for discounting the avowal has to be cast in the form of reason to say that some one or more of the provisos was not really satisfied.

It can be similar with the authority for retrospective avowals of intention, etc. Rather than as based on recollection of an antecedent fact, the non-detectivist will regard it as owing to the operation of a similar right-to-left priority, only with the right-hand side of the biconditional modified so as to include at least the proviso that there is no major disorientation of memory at work. Cartesianism would, of course, enjoin a detective reading of such biconditionals. But its failure to deliver any credible conception of the constitution or episte-mology of the states of affairs in question may be taken to suggest not that we should dismiss them as fiction, but that the relevant biconditionals should be read the other way round.

I do not expect this proposal to be satisfying at this stage of development, but I cannot take it further on this occasion. The view at which we have arrived—I would like to think that it might be close to something Wittgenstein might endorse—can be summarised as follows. It is part of regarding human beings as persons, rational reflective agents, that we are prepared to ascribe intentional states to them, to try to explain and anticipate their behaviour in terms of the concepts of desire, belief, decision and intention. And it is a fundamental anthropological fact about us that our initiation into the language in which these concepts feature results in the capacity to be moved, who knows exactly how, to self-ascribe states of the relevant sorts—and to do so in ways which not merely tend to accord with the appraisals which others, similarly trained, can make of what we do but which provide in general a far richer and more satisfying framework for the interpretation and anticipation of our behaviour than any at which they could arrive if all such self-ascriptions were discounted. The roots of first-personal authority for the self-ascription of these states reside not in cognitive achievement, based on cognitive privilege, but in the success of the practices informed by this cooperative interpretational scheme.

How do matters now stand with the recommended response to Kripke's sceptic? The response was, in effect, that your former understanding of E either resided in, or may appropriately be compared to, your possession of certain former intentions, which you may now non-inferentially recall. This response is intact but is cast in a totally different perspective. The conception of meaning as a 'sui generis' mental state involved regarding your authority for your intentions, present and former, as based on privileged access to a condition of consciousness, of such content as to determine of a potential infinity of doings and sayings whether they fit or fail to fit it. Such fit, or failure of fit, is conceived as settled just by the character of the intention, independently of any judgement of yours, though—except where you misapprehend *what* is said or done—it is supposed that it is only in exceptional circumstances that your judgement about such fit or failure to fit would go astray.[19] In short: the sui generis mental state conception goes for a detective reading of the biconditionals whose left-hand sides describe your former meanings or intentions. The new perspective reverses the reading. Avowals of present or past intention are disbelievable only in special circumstances—those embraced by the provisos in the (complete) biconditional—and elsewhere are authoritative not because the subject is uniquely well placed to know but just because he or she is the subject.

A corollary: since to identify a *former* intention is to identify what would fit or fail to fit it, taking a non-detective view of a subject's avowal of a former intention involves taking the same view of his

19. Quite what is the *ground* for this belief, according to the detective view, is of course dark.

judgement about what, if anything, now implements or frustrates that intention. Accordingly, what, if any pattern of performance is imposed on a subject by the constraint of compliance with a former intention *is not settled independently of his judgement of the matter.* His judgements may be discounted—in the special circumstances when some one or more of the provisos is not met—but otherwise they serve to determine, rather than objectively accord with or violate the content of his anterior intention. Elsewhere[20] I have urged that one central moral which Wittgenstein wished to draw from his discussion of rule-following was that the notion we tend to have of the objectivity of meaning is untenable: the idea that meanings can somehow be constituted, once and for all, either within a community or by a single subject, by finitely many events—explanations, uses, episodes in consciousness—so that thereafter there is only the objective question of *fit* between new uses of the relevant expression and the meanings thereby laid down. There are a variety of grounds for disquiet with this notion, and I am now suggesting that the real message of Kripke's dialectic is to teach us one more. For intention, when non-detectively construed, *offers no resources for the construction of such objective meanings.* And the Sceptical Argument succeeds only if it is allowed to restrict the search for the fact constitutive of what I meant by E at t in such a way to exclude my *subsequent* determination of it. It is a reductio ad absurdum of meaning, understanding and intention when, but only when, they are detectively construed.

20. See in particular Wright (1980), passim; Wright (1986d) (this volume Essay 3).

6

Excerpts from a Critical Study of Colin McGinn's *Wittgenstein on Meaning*

Colin McGinn's book belongs to the reaction to, and against, Saul Kripke's *Wittgenstein on Rules and Private Language*.[1] The book is in four chapters. The first and third are respectively devoted to exegesis of Wittgenstein's ideas on rule-following and understanding, and to criticism of them. The second attacks Kripke's famous tandem of Sceptical Argument and Sceptical Solution as an interpretation of Wittgenstein; and the fourth criticises Kripke's dialectic on its own terms.

Because the view is widely received that Kripke's book fails as strict exegesis of Wittgenstein, and because there has been so much independent discussion of its Sceptical Argument and Solution, I shall here mainly concentrate on McGinn's own interpretation of Wittgenstein and his criticisms of the views which he finds. But I shall begin, in Part I, by noting certain respects in which McGinn seems to misrepresent the structure of the train of argument which Kripke's Wittgenstein is riding, or to underrate its power and resources. In particular, I shall suggest that McGinn's principal point of response to

1. Kripke (1982).

Kripke is, in a sense, facile, and that he is encouraged in this response by a reading of *Philosophical Investigations* which is, in certain crucial respects, superficial.

Parts II and III will be concerned with the account of Wittgenstein which McGinn wishes to oppose to Kripke's. I shall give grounds for rejecting certain of McGinn's criticisms of Wittgenstein. But my principal point will be that, despite his careful rehearsal of central Wittgensteinian themes, McGinn never brings Wittgenstein's most basic concerns in the discussions of rule-following into a proper perspective.

I. McGinn's Response to Kripke

Kripke's sceptic insists that whatever is to constitute the meaning of an expression must discharge the *normative* role of meaning. It is for its alleged failure to meet this constraint that the dispositional response to the Sceptical Argument is dismissed. McGinn seems to accept this criticism of the dispositional response.[2] But later he canvasses a 'straight solution' to the paradox, which he evidently believes is not vulnerable to the same difficulty, in terms of the idea of a *capacity*—to mean, for instance, green by 'green' is to have, not a disposition, but a capacity of a certain kind. He writes:[3]

> Does the capacity suggestion account for normativeness? . . . We have an account of this normativeness when we have two things: (a) an account of what it is to mean something at a given time and (b) an account of what it is to mean the *same* thing at two different times. . . . Put in these terms, it is easy to supply what we require: to mean addition by '+' at t is to associate with '+' the capacity to add at t, and to mean the same by '+' at t^* is to associate with '+' the *same capacity* at t^* as at t.

2. McGinn (1984), pp. 172 ff.
3. Ibid., p. 174.

But if that is all it takes to 'account for normativeness', then a transposition of the same solution could have saved the dispositional account. Simply replace the occurrences of 'capacity' in the last part of the quoted passage by occurrences of 'disposition'.[4]

What exactly is the normativity constraint which McGinn, apparently, misunderstands? The basic problem posed by the normativity of meaning for the dispositional response is that, whereas how I understand an expression contributes towards determining how I *ought* to use it, all that apparently can be recovered from a description of the way in which I am disposed to use it are claims about how I habitually do, will or would use it. A solution to the problem would accordingly be to show how suitably circumscribed facts about how one does, will or would use a particular expression actually constitute facts about how one ought to use it. This would call, clearly, for an account which non-arbitrarily idealised certain elements in a subject's actual dispositions of use. One will accordingly be inclined to accept, or dismiss, Kripke's criticism of the dispositional response depending on whether one believes that such an idealising account can satisfactorily be accomplished.[5]

Whether one believes that or not, it is hard to see any prospect of an advantage to be gained, in respect of the normativity constraint, by dropping dispositions in favour of capacities. If we ask, *what* capacity is constitutively associated with an understanding of 'green'?, the natural answer is: the capacity to use the word *correctly*. And here 'correctly' means, roughly: in ways which are appropriately sensitive to its meaning. This answer is, precisely, an intuitive expression of the normativity of meaning. But a proponent of McGinn's 'straight solution' would have to dismiss it as misleading or, at any rate, nonfundamental. For it apparently sets up the meaning of 'green' as an *independent* constraint to which a capacity for using the word must conform if it is to constitute a correct understanding of it. And that

---

4. This is pointed out by Paul Boghossian (1989b) in his review of McGinn (1984).

5. For sympathy with a defence of the dispositional response along these lines, see Blackburn (1984); Forbes (1984).

cannot be the right criterion for the capacity in question if it is to be in terms of possessing it that a proper understanding of 'green', and thence the meaning of 'green', are to be philosophically constituted, as it were. Rather, the line must be, understanding 'green' just is possessing a particular capacity of use of it, not to be identified—or only in a non-fundamental sense to be identified—as the capacity to suit one's use of the word to its meaning.

Well, what then is the capacity, allegedly constitutive of an understanding of 'green', most fundamentally a capacity to *do*? McGinn's discussion contains, so far as I have been able to see, no clear suggestion about how a proponent of his "straight solution" should respond to this question, nor any clear perception of its importance. Capacities may *seem* better adapted than dispositions to cope with problems of normativity because we typically invoke the notion of capacity where there is some connotation of discharging a role, accomplishing an objective or meeting a constraint. But just for that reason the use of the notion creates an obligation to characterise the relevant role, objective or constraint. To be sure, we cannot assume, without question-begging against McGinn, that meeting this obligation in the present case would involve thinking of the proper use of 'green' as determined quite independently of anyone's capacities of use, or of those capacities as qualifying as understanding only in so far as they are capacities to track that pattern of proper use. But it remains that the relevant capacities have to be singled out somehow, and the problem is structurally reminiscent of—indeed, in no way interestingly different from or more promising in outcome than—the problem, confronted by the dispositional response, of saying what puts a particular disposition in the idealised, meaning-constituting class which it is obliged to define.

McGinn's apparently imperfect understanding of the role of the normativity of meaning in Kripke's dialectic does not, however, prevent him from isolating its most vulnerable point. This is that there is an unsupported reductionism involved at the stage at which the sceptic challenges his opponent to cite some feature of his previous mental life which could constitute his having formerly meant green by 'green', for instance. It will not do, it seems, if the opponent attempts to cite that very fact. Rather the challenge is implicitly taken to be to recall some state of affairs characterised in such a way as not simply to assume that there are states of affairs of the disputed species. And it then has to be *argued* of the state of affairs so characterised that it has the properties requisite to constitute meaning. So the ground rules of Kripke's debate have the effect of restricting the search to phenomena of consciousness which are not simply characterised as having a recollectable content. States having content are somehow to be constituted out of materials whose description, at the point where they are introduced into the debate with the sceptic, does not presuppose their contentfulness.

The implicit assumption here will not strike any philosopher as uncongenial who accepts the traditional Quinean idea that the good-standing of semantic or, more generally, intentional states depends on their reducibility to something extensional, or physical or wherever the thick ice is thought to be. But the route from such a presupposition to scepticism about meaning can in that case be rather more direct than the one provided by the Sceptical Argument, which now emerges as merely an implicit prejudice against the idea that we may and usually do non-inferentially know of our current meanings and intentions, and may and often do non-inferentially recall them later.[6]

Even here, however, where he seems to me entirely right, McGinn's discussion is somewhat unsatisfying. He notes[7] Kripke's stigmatisation of such a response as "desperate" and "completely mysterious", but is content with rejoinders which, by their preoccupation with finessing the letter of Kripke's text, mask rather than clarify the genuine problems in the vicinity. For genuine problems there surely are. McGinn attributes to Kripke the thought that

> once we abandon the idea that meaning is an irreducible experiential state, we have no account of the nature of our first-person knowledge of meaning—we have no conception of how the primitive, non-experiential

6. Cf. Wright (1984) (this volume Essay 4); Wright (1987a) (this volume Essay 5).
7. McGinn (1984), p. 160.

state of meaning something is an object of distinctively first-person knowledge.[8]

And against this he is content to set the ordinary idea of first-person authority for psychological states—like believing, thinking, intending, etc.—which, unlike sensations, may be associated with no individuative affective phenomenology. He acknowledges that '[h]ow to give a philosophical *theory* of this kind of knowledge is of course a difficult and substantive question', but rejoins that '[l]ack of a theory of a phenomenon is not in itself a good reason to doubt the *existence* of the phenomenon'.[9] This is true, of course. But surely the relevant feature of the concepts in question—the combination of first-personal avowability with disposition-like connections to behaviour in circumstances which the avower need not have envisaged—is no sooner marked than anyone of genuine philosophical curiosity will feel his intellectual conscience pricked. How is it possible to be, for the most part, effortlessly and reliably authoritative about, say, one's intentions if the identity of an intention is fugitive when sought in occurrent consciousness, as McGinn grants that Kripke's sceptic has shown, and the having of an intention is thought of as a disposition-like state? There are plenty of dispositions—wisdom, tolerance, laziness—the self-ascription of which is warranted only on grounds which any third party could employ. If, notwithstanding points of disanalogy generated, for example, by the holism of the mental, content-bearing psychological states like belief, intention and hope *resemble* dispositions in the manner in which they have to answer to an indefinitely circumscribed range of behavioural manifestations, how is the institution of non-inferential first-personal authority with respect to such states not simply a *solecism*—evidence of the permeation through into ordinary discourse of a discredited Cartesian typology of the mental which takes sensation as its paradigm?

8. Ibid., pp. 160–1.
9. Ibid., p. 161.

The matter is a central preoccupation of the *Investigations* and Wittgenstein's other late writings on the philosophy of psychology. The examples vary—Wittgenstein moves between meaning, understanding, expecting, wishing, fearing, hoping and others. But the central problem is the same in each case. It is posed by the way these concepts seem to hover, puzzlingly and unstably, between two paradigms. One is constituted by states like pain, tickles, the experience of a red after-image and ringing in the ears, all of which may have a definitely dated onset and departure, which may be interrupted by breaks in consciousness, and whose occurrence seemingly makes no demands upon the conceptual equipment of the subject. Such states are authoritatively avowable, and it comes easily to us to think we understand why. The subject is authoritative about such states because, since they are events in his consciousness, he is in the nature of the case conscious of them. Further, because such states are essentially *of* a consciousness, they constitute distinct existences from their outward and behavioural expressions. For the latter are states (or events, or processes) which are not essentially of a consciousness and are therefore ontologically independent of things which are. So the relation, we conceive, of for example pain to its expression, can only be that of antecedent state to symptom or trace. By contrast, in the case of the other paradigm—that of the dispositional psychological state—the connection with behavioural display is not symptomatic but constitutive. And—or so one would think—subjects can generally know that they themselves possess such a state only in so far as and in the same way that others can know that they do. If Cartesian psychology was dominated by the first paradigm, the Rylean reaction was dominated by the second. But neither is adequate for the class of psychological concepts with which Wittgenstein was most concerned.

While it is fair to say, then, that the Sceptical Argument, as far as Kripke explicitly takes it, is open to the charge of relying upon an unargued reductionism, and may be rebutted by the adduction of ordinary features of the epistemology of intention, meaning, etc., it would be a very short step to continue the argument by pressing questions which the actual Wittgenstein was intensely concerned with, and to which I do not think that philosophy of mind has yet disclosed satisfactory answers. To repeat: how is it possible to be effortlessly, non-inferentially and generally reliably authoritative about psychological states which have no distinctive occurrent phenomenology and which have to answer, after the fashion of dispositions, to what one says and does in situations so far unconsidered? Perhaps Kripke's use of 'desperate' in response to the idea of meaning, etc., as sui generis states was uncalled-for. But the characterisation 'mysterious', it seems to me, was not. And the problem is, to stress, one of Wittgenstein's own central preoccupations in the *Investigations*.

That McGinn's principal point of response to Kripke should bring us, in this way, to one of Wittgenstein's own principal quarries is striking in two respects. First, it is striking that the matter goes unremarked in McGinn's book, in which the comparison of Wittgenstein with Kripke is an overriding concern. Second, the thought now suggests itself that, despite the shortcomings tabled by McGinn of Kripke's book as textual exegesis, the Sceptical Argument of Kripke's Wittgenstein may still correspond to something real and central in the *Investigations*—a powerful and expanded development of a train of thought tersely prefigured there, which brings home the hopelessness of a Cartesian conception of intentional states and, at the same time, teaches how vital—and problematical—the ordinary epistemological 'grammar' of these states is. One way or another we have to answer, or undermine, the question: how is first-personal authority for intentional states possible? Until we do, we have not really answered the Sceptical Argument. Wittgenstein thought the question could be answered by attention to detail—to the surroundings and everyday phenomenology of ascriptions of intention, expectation and hope. However that may be, Kripke should at least be granted that the Sceptical Argument—while Wittgenstein did not clearly develop it and would not have accepted it—still takes us, in the way I have described, to the heart of the *Investigations*.

II. McGinn's Exegesis of Wittgenstein

McGinn finds four principal themes, three negative and one positive, in Wittgenstein's treatment of meaning and understanding. Summarised early in his book,[10] they are:

   (i)   To mean something by a sign is not to be the subject of an inner state or process.

   (ii)   To understand a sign is not to interpret it in a particular way.

  (iii) Using a sign in accordance with a rule is not founded upon reasons.

  (iv) To understand a sign is to have mastery of a technique or custom of using it.

The ascription of these lines of thought to Wittgenstein is hardly controversial. But it is nevertheless very useful to have the patient and effective assembly of source material, interspersed with some of the clearest commentary on Wittgenstein to be found anywhere, which McGinn provides.

McGinn, for his part, is largely content to record his agreement with the four theses, as he amplifies them, although with two important exceptions. One is that, in his view, Wittgenstein habitually overstates thesis (i), and that there is no real objection to thinking of understanding or meaning something by a sign as an inner state or process provided we are clear that it is not an occurrent or episodic state of consciousness. Wittgenstein's stronger formulations should be viewed, he believes, as 'misplaced linguistic legislation in the interests of philosophical prophylaxis'.[11] I think the issue here is partly verbal, but partly substantial and difficult. First, is Wittgenstein's objection to 'state' or to 'inner'? McGinn, somewhat tentatively, suggests the latter,[12] but the footnote to page 59 of the *Investigations*—which

10. Ibid., p. 3.
11. Ibid., p. 117.
12. Ibid., p. 166.

McGinn cites—seems to be quite definite in his favour. Baker and Hacker[13] regard the footnote as aberrant, and claim that the notion that meaning something is *any* sort of state is clearly repudiated in *Brown Book* §66. In fact, though, Wittgenstein is there speaking of *abilities* in general—he nowhere says that understanding, meaning, etc., simply *are* abilities—and there is no clear repudiation. Rather he writes that

> we are strongly inclined to use the *metaphor*—[my italics]—of something being in a peculiar state for saying that something can behave in a certain way. And this . . . metaphor is embodied in the expressions 'He is capable of . . .', 'He is able to multiply large numbers in his head', 'He can play chess': in these sentences the verb is used in the *present tense,* suggesting that the phrases are descriptions of states which exist at the moment when we speak. The same tendency shows itself in our calling the ability to solve a mathematical problem, the ability to enjoy a piece of music, etc., certain states of mind; we don't mean by this expression 'conscious mental phenomena'. Rather a state of the mind in this sense is the state of a hypothetical mechanism, a mind model meant to explain the conscious mental phenomena. . . . Note also how sure people are that to the ability to add or to multiply or to say a poem by heart, etc., there *must* correspond a peculiar state of the person's brain, although . . . they know next to nothing about such psychophysiological correspondences.

This suggests that Wittgenstein has points to make about both 'inner' or 'mental' *and* state'. The point about 'inner' is the one with which McGinn agrees and which he thinks Wittgenstein overstates. And there we can surely say what we like provided we acknowledge Wittgenstein's point. The point about 'state' is that its application to abilities and ability-like items, including perhaps understanding and meaning so-and-so by such-and-such an expression, is merely a metaphor—an optional 'form of representation'—rather than anything imposed by the nature of these items. On this account, it would

13. Baker and Hacker (1983), p. 284.

not be *wrong,* in Wittgenstein's view, to describe understanding as a mental state; but it might encourage either of two errors.

But is the second an error? Perhaps we would not now be tempted by the idea that a state of a *mental* mechanism must underlie the ability to add, but *doesn't* there have to be a brain state? Notoriously, Wittgenstein explicitly and forcefully denies that there does in *Zettel* §§608–10. The passage amounts specifically—of course, Wittgenstein does not express himself in such terms—to a denial of the *supervenience* of the psychological on the physiological: there may be psychological differences to which no physiological differences correspond. McGinn discusses the matter in some detail[14] but I do not think he takes the measure of Wittgenstein's view. His counter-argument[15] is that if understanding, for instance, does not supervene upon a person's internal physical constitution—and if differences in understanding must issue, as presumably on Wittgenstein's view is so, in differences in use, ergo in *behaviour*—then

> there are events which differ physically but which have no differentiating physical explanation. . . . This is tantamount to the admission or claim that some physical events have no physical explanation.

One could reproach McGinn's resort to the indicative here: denying the supervenience claim would not commit Wittgenstein to the *actuality* of what McGinn describes. It would involve at most that nothing precludes its possibility. But in fact even that does not follow. What follows is only that, *for all the concept of understanding has to say about the matter,* there could be behavioural, ergo physical events whose explanation was not to be found in the *internal* physical state of the behaving subject. That may seem bizarre. But it falls well short of the claim that such events would be physically inexplicable. Nothing in physics rules out the idea that the movements of a body be explained not in terms of any internal change in it but as a direct

14. McGinn (1984), pp. 112–6.
15. Ibid., p. 113.

result of external influences, for instance. And, to stress: Wittgenstein's claim is one about what is compatible with our concepts of the psychological, not about what is possible *tout court*. Maybe it is profoundly in error. But if so, it remains to be shown.

McGinn's other major point of disagreement with his Wittgenstein concerns thesis (iv). He has no quarrel with what he regards as its principal burden: the conception of understanding as a practical capacity, with which he attempted a 'straight' rejoinder to Kripke's sceptic. But he does take issue with the associated 'multiple application thesis' which Wittgenstein expresses like this:

> It is not possible that there should have been only one occasion on which someone obeyed a rule. It is not possible that there should have been only one occasion on which a report was made, an order given or understood; and so on.—To obey a rule, to make a report, to give an order, to play a game of chess, are *customs* (uses, institutions).[16]

Some of McGinn's criticism of what he takes such passages to be advancing is based on saddling Wittgenstein with an idea for which there is simply no warrant in the texts—that all is well provided there has been *more* than one occasion! Thus the 'subtraction argument', which McGinn finds telling, runs:

> [C]onsider a possible situation in which . . . actually followed rules are not obeyed. Imagine we carry out this thought-experiment one rule at a time gradually whittling the applications away. Wittgenstein in effect allows that we can carry out this procedure very extensively: in fact, the thought-experiment is deemed coherent until we get to the final rule grasped by the subject . . . at which point, he thinks, we must call a halt to our supposings. We can also, he allows, remove large segments of the actual application made of [the final rule], but we must leave intact at least *two* applications of this rule. . . . The problem is to see why what seems such a small change in the actual situation [viz. deleting the

16. *Philosophical Investigations* §199.

penultimate surviving application of the final rule] could have such momentous consequences.[17]

But Wittgenstein said nothing to lay himself open to this. His claim was that the very existence of any rules depends on some rules actually being applied; and that one rule being applied only once would not be enough. No claim was made about what would be enough—still less was anything said about a definite numerical threshold.

McGinn's antipathy to the multiple application thesis is led by the physicalism for which, he believes, Wittgenstein's thesis (i)—the repudiation of understanding as an inner state or process—must be made to make room. For if understanding an expression is a capacity—a state of readiness for appropriate use, as it were—and if any such state must ultimately be constituted in the condition of the body and central nervous system, then there seems to be no conceptual barrier to piling up such states within a 'totally indolent' subject, as McGinn puts it, nor to imagining that all actual subjects are indeed totally indolent. Isn't it just like imagining leopards which never hunt, or swim, or mate or climb trees, but which *can* do all these things?

The real issue here, however, is not physicalism but normativity. Let us grant, for the sake of argument, that, for any capacity I have, there must be some state of my physiological constitution in which my possession of that capacity consists *as matters stand*. The qualification is, of course, essential. I can swim; but the physiological condition which makes that true does so courtesy of a co-operative physical environment. Constituted as I am, I would not, for instance, be able to swim if suddenly subjected to massively increased gravitational forces. Likewise, I can add; but the physiological condition which—by the terms of our assumption—makes that true does so courtesy of a co-operative *institutional* environment. There has to *be* such a thing as adding correctly before any physiological condition can constitute the ability to add. And Wittgenstein's contention is precisely that,

17. McGinn (1984), p. 131.

with the demise of Platonism, there can be such a thing as adding correctly—such a thing as a determinate requirement imposed by the rules of addition—only within a framework of extensive institutional activity and agreement in the judgements which participation in those institutions involves us in making. The very existence of our concepts depends on such *activity*.

The proper interpretation and appraisal of the multiple application thesis raises issues of the greatest difficulty. The passages in which Wittgenstein gives it expression go right to the heart of his ideas on rules and rule-following. The thesis is not an aberrant dangler alongside the basically sound capacitive conception of understanding, as McGinn would have us believe—another example where, according to McGinn's interpretation and for reasons which remain obscure, Wittgenstein has overcooked a simple insight. Rather it belongs with his attempt to point to an alternative account of normativity to the "rules-as-rails" imagery of Platonism, to explain how there can be occupiable middle ground between the Platonic hypostatisation of rules and the denial of their existence. The multiple application thesis is believed by Wittgenstein, it is fair to assume, to be a *consequence* of the proper account of the middle ground and is therefore a vital clue to the character of Wittgenstein's view. In any case, its assessment has to be set in the context of the issues to do with objectivity to which the Platonistic conception of rules and rule-following is a response in the first place, and which is Wittgenstein's principal concern in the passages of which McGinn is so keen to controvert Kripke's account. McGinn fails so to set it, and his disagreement with this aspect of Wittgenstein's thought is misconceived in consequence.

There are a number of other points of detail in McGinn's discussion of Wittgenstein—on the interpretation of *Investigations* §202, for instance, and its relation to the private-language argument—which deserve extended discussion but which I have here no space to engage. The question which has to be paramount is: how does Wittgenstein come out of McGinn's book? What estimate could somebody properly form of Wittgenstein as a philosopher who knew of him only through McGinn's presentation? The answer would have to be that he was a thinker who mixed a number of insights that were important in their historical context with as many obscure or obscurely motivated themes. Wittgenstein would emerge as a philosopher who contributed greatly to the slow post-Cartesian revolution in our thinking about the psychological. But the judgement would be hard to resist that, by the mid-1970s say, his most distinctive ideas had been thoroughly absorbed into the general philosophical consciousness, his writings assuming the status merely of pedagogically important tracts—a mine whose viable ores had largely been extracted.

The contrast with Kripke's book is thus very marked. The Wittgenstein who emerges there is a contemporary philosophical antagonist, the inventor of a startling and unignorable paradox, and an ingenious if flawed resolution of it, bearing in a profound way on our thinking about almost everything but about logic, mathematics and the mental in particular.

Which Wittgenstein should we believe in? Has the study of the *Investigations* nothing substantive to teach us now? Or are there still rich seams of philosophy, which we have failed to mine only by digging insufficiently deep?

I have already indicated one respect in which, as it seems to me, McGinn missed a chance to explore a genuine Wittgensteinian concern: the first-person epistemology of intentional states, and the task of achieving an understanding of how it is reconciled with their disposition-like qualities. That is an example of a theme which McGinn overlooks, or underplays, because his primary purpose is to controvert Kripke, and Kripke himself makes nothing of it. But the real failing of the parts of McGinn's book that are concerned with Wittgenstein is less a matter of overlooking, or playing down, Wittgensteinian themes of importance than of failing to grasp the choreography of ideas he is aware of or even actually highlights. It is for this reason that there is no focused attention in McGinn's book on perhaps the most profound of all the concerns in Wittgenstein's later philosophy: the exposure of certain bogus ideas to which we are inclined concerning what the objectivity of a linguistic practice can consist in, and the relations of those ideas to misconceptions concerning the nature of language-mastery and the conditions for its existence. In this respect, because it places such matters in the forefront and makes Wittgenstein speak to them in clear, if highly controversial ways, Kripke's book, whatever its shortcomings as philosophical scholarship, seems to me to be superior as a guide to the spirit of the *Investigations*.

III. CONCLUSION: SUGGESTED CHOREOGRAPHY

Let me conclude, then, with an indication of what I take to be some of the choreography: a way of arranging some of the themes which McGinn highlights, together with others to which he gives less prominence, in such a way that we are led directly to the cluster of concerns I have claimed to be fundamental to Wittgenstein's later work. I shall stay, for the most part, within the bounds of §§185–219 of the *Investigations* and 23–47 of part VI of the *Remarks on the Foundations of Mathematics*.

It must be stressed that the characteristic concerns of these passages have, *pace* Kripke, nothing to do with the *reality* of rules, but are epistemological. Wittgenstein is concerned to examine the idea that a rule can be genuinely an object of intellection, something whose requirements we keep track of by grace of some intuitive or interpretative ability. Undoubtedly the tone of the passages is negative. The working assumption is that we tend badly to misunderstand the nature of the accomplishment involved in competent rule-following, and that our misunderstandings lead us to a mythology of the character of the constraint imposed by a rule, and of what successfully following it actually consists in. But there is nowhere to be found any explicit denial of the existence of such constraints, or any consequential rejection of the very notion of accomplishment in this context.

Following McGinn's example, we can usefully highlight four themes. The third and fourth collectively encompass McGinn's main theses (ii)–(iv); the second is briefly glossed by McGinn[18] as part of his thesis (iii); and that, I believe, is how he would view the first, which he does not explicitly advert to, if asked to locate it in his scheme of interpretation. The first is:

> One's own understanding of a rule does not exceed what one can explain.[19]

The temptation to think otherwise arises from the reflection that the explanation of a rule must eventually culminate in, or anyway ultimately be founded upon, the giving of illustrations of its application; and that any such illustrations are finite, and hence open in principle to an indefinite variety of interpretations. Yet explanations do usually, or so we suppose, secure mutual understanding. So somehow more is got across—the thought continues—than the pursuit of explanations can ever make completely explicit. Correct uptake of an explanation is having the *right* 'something' come into one's mind as a result of the explanation; and the resulting informational state, though it is expressed in one's subsequent practice with the concept concerned, essentially transcends it.

Now, it is essential to recognise that this notion of what is involved in successfully giving and receiving explanations is a consequence of another notion, elaborated in the 'rules-as-rails' imagery of *Investigations* §§218–9. This is the idea that, as Wittgenstein characterises it at *RFM* VI, 31:

> Once you have got hold of the rule, you have the route traced for you.

Suppose the rule governing a particular arithmetical series, for example, really was somehow able to determine its every *n*th place quite independently of any judgement or reaction of ours. Then since any feasible illustration of the rule will sustain alternative interpretations

---

18. Ibid., pp. 21–2.
19. *Investigations* §209–10; *Remarks on the Foundations of Mathematics* VI, 23.

generating conflicting verdicts about what happens at nth places which were not explicitly illustrated, the every-nth-place-determining "something" which someone who correctly receives the illustrations somehow comes to have in mind—the 'essential thing' which we 'have to get him to *guess*'[20]—is clearly at best imperfectly conveyable by illustration. Of course, we can maybe say in other words what the rule is. But that will help only if the recipient is already a master of the vocabulary used in the alternative formulation. And such mastery cannot always be the product of explicit definition; sooner or later, we have to hit concepts acquired by witness of illustrative practice.

The upshot is, then, that the picture of rules as rails forces us to think of our ability to follow them, to know in a potential infinity of cases what moves are in accord with them, as owing to a kind of hyper-cognitive felicity. Explanations come to be viewed not so much as communicating understanding as *triggering* the jump to an informational state by which the accord or clash with the rule of any proposed move is settled. Every competent rule-follower is the beneficiary of such informational states—and each of them packs in more than explanations ever made explicit to him or her can ever make explicit to others. When Wittgenstein sets himself against this idea, as when he writes:

> If you use a rule to give a description, you yourself do not know more than you say. . . . If you say 'and so on', you yourself do not know more than 'and so on'.[21]

his concern is, of course, to challenge a mistaken epistemological picture; but he *thereby* challenges the parent rules-as-rails imagery which is simply a figurative expression of Platonism.

The second theme I want to highlight might be expressed like this:

> It might be preferable, in describing our most basic rule- governed responses, to think of them not as informed by an *intuition* (of the requirements of the rule) but as a kind of *decision.* [22]

20. *Investigations* §210.
21. *RFM* IV, 8.
22. *Investigations* §§186, 213; *RFM* VI, 24; *Brown Book* §5.

The point of the contrast between "intuition" and "decision"[23] is that the former implies and the latter repudiates the suggestion that— even in the most basic cases, where one can say nothing by way of justification for one's particular way of proceeding—rule-following is a cognitive accomplishment, success in tracking an independently constituted requirement. "Intuition" suggests an unarticulated *ur-cognition,* a form of knowledge too basic to admit of any further account. But this very primitiveness has the effect that there can be no further story to be told about how the relevant sort of intuitive faculty might accomplish the harmony, which it would supposedly generate, between the real requirements of a rule and a subject's impression of them. For that reason, it is wide open to sceptical challenge:

> If intuition is an inner voice—how do I know *how* I am to obey it? And how do I know that it doesn't mislead me? For if it can guide me right, it can also guide me wrong. (Intuition an unnecessary shuffle.)[24]

There is no response to this challenge because nothing can be done by way of *filling out* the thought that, in the most primitive cases of rule-following, when everything seems immediate and beyond further account, we nevertheless track a set of independent requirements. The fact is, though, that neither the sceptical thought, nor the intuitional epistemology which it challenges, are really intelligible. We have no accountable idea of what would constitute the direction taken by the rule off its own bat, as it were, if the deliverances of our intuitive faculties were to take us collectively off track—'no model of this superlative fact' (*Investigations* §192). And that is just to say that we have no model of what constitutes the direction taken by a rule, period—once the direction is conceived, after the fashion of Platonism, as determined autonomously, and our performance, whether communal or solitary, as merely an exercise in tracking. That is why it 'would almost be more correct to say' that decision rather than intuition is involved (*Investigations* §186). Such a way of putting the matter

23. *Intuition* and *Entscheidung.*
24. *Investigations* §213.

would have disadvantages of its own, not least in its connotation of a felt absence of constraint. But at least it would be free of the cognitive pretentiousness of Platonism.

The third theme is complementary to the second, and elaborates Wittgenstein's critique of a 'tracking' epistemology of rule-following:

> Supposing that grasping a rule were a matter of coming to have something 'in mind', how would one thereby be enabled to recognise, step by step, what its requirements were?[25]

It is in the context of this theme that the 'paradox' is presented which inspired Kripke:

> "But how can a rule show me what I have to do at *this* point? Whatever I do is, on some interpretation, in accord with the rule."—That is not what we ought to say, but rather: any interpretation still hangs in the air along with what it interprets, and cannot give it any support. Interpretations by themselves do not determine meaning.[26]

Suppose I undergo some process of explanation—for instance, a substantial initial segment of some arithmetical series is written out for me—and as a result I come to have the right rule 'in mind'. How, when it comes to the crunch—at an nth place which lies beyond the demonstrated initial segment, and which I have previously never thought about—does having the rule 'in mind' help? Well, with such an example one tends to think of having the rule 'in mind' on the model of imagining a formula, or something of that sort. And so it is natural to respond by conceding that, strictly, merely having the rule in mind *is* no help. For I can have a formula in mind without knowing what it means. So—the response continues—it is necessary in addition to *interpret* the rule. But then we immediately get the 'paradox' which Wittgenstein's interlocutor blunders into in *Investigations* §198. *Any* selection for the nth place can be reconciled, on *some*

25. Ibid., §§198, 209–13; *RFM* VI, 38, 47.
26. *Investigations* §198.

interpretation, with the rule. An interpretation is of help to me, therefore, in my predicament at the nth place only if it is *correct*. But to invoke the idea of correctness at this point makes the play with interpretation nugatory. To describe someone as 'knowing the correct interpretation of the rule for the nth place' becomes just a piece of patter equivalent to saying that he knows how to *apply* the rule at the nth place. And then we might just as well have put the initial question in the form: how am I to know what interpretation of the rule for the nth place *is* correct?

It should be reasonably evident how these three themes interrelate. Suppose that what I take up from an episode of explanation, if it is successful, does indeed transcend that explanation and any other that I might give in turn. I come to have the right rule in mind but might, save for a kind of felicity, equally well have arrived at a wrong one, despite having missed no overt feature of the explanation. This idea, explicitly challenged by the first theme, connects with the second and third in that they jointly confront it with a dilemma. How does the explanation-transcendent rule which I supposedly have 'in mind' tell me what to do in novel cases? How does the rule, once grasped, help—what is the epistemology of acting on it? If it requires interpretation, that could be done in lots of ways. So how do I tell which interpretation is correct? Does that, for instance, call for a *further* rule—a rule for determining correct interpretation of the original— and if so, why does it not raise the same difficulty again, thereby generating a regress? If, on the other hand, it is not necessary to interpret the original rule, then the only possible answer appears to be that I have some unmediated, intuitional contact with its requirements, and this is the thought challenged by the second theme.

So the overall structure is this. It comes naturally to us to think, with the Platonist, of the objectivity of many of our practices,— including par excellence logic and mathematics—as residing in our following rules-as-rails, rules which somehow reach ahead of us and determine of themselves their every actual and counterfactual proper application. But if we have the capacity to keep track of rules when so conceived, we must be capable of somehow getting them 'in mind', notwithstanding the necessarily imperfect character of explanations—ultimately illustrations—of their application. The grasp of such a rule is thus the internalisation of an open-ended set of preordained requirements, an informational state accessible, as Wittgenstein had his interlocutor put it, only by a kind of guesswork. Well, let it be so. Wittgenstein's question is then: what does the deployment of this 'informational state' consist in: *how* does it inform the actual practice of following the rule? Thinking of the rule as literally an object of consciousness—as a formula, or whatever—either raises the regress-of-interpretations paradox, or requires construal of the rule as 'self-interpreting', as it were; which is to say that the epistemology of it is conceived as intuitional, too primitive to allow of an account, and hence as vulnerable to the simple sceptical thought— not, of course, that of Kripke's sceptic—of *Investigations* §213. If, however—as is perhaps more likely if autobiography is any guide— one is thinking of the way in which the rule allegedly informs one's ongoing practice not in terms of something which is literally an object of consciousness—like a formula, or picture, or whispered instructions in the ear[27]—but just in terms of a kind of inner confidence or sense of directedness, the epistemology of the step-by-step judgements involved in applying the rule remains irremediably intuitional, and thus vulnerable to the same sceptical attack. In short: think of the objectivity of rule-following on the model of the rules-as-rails picture, and you will be completely beggared for any satisfactory account of our ability to stay on track.

I do not present this, as it seems to me, simple yet powerful train of thought as the spine, so to speak, of the 'rule-following considerations'. I claim for it only that it is one very important development contained in the relevant passages in Wittgenstein's writings, and that it brings out the fundamental preoccupation that I advertised at the conclusion of the preceding section. Its connection with Platonism in the philosophy of mathematics is perhaps obvious

27. Ibid., §223.

enough,[28] but I would suggest that a bearing on the private language argument is also evident. For what does the would-be private linguist do except *platonise* his baptismal intention? If you think that, just by concentrating inwardly upon a sensation and labelling it 'E', you can thereby create—in advance of your own response to the cases as and when they occur—indefinitely many truths about the proper use of 'E' on subsequent occasions, then you are thinking of your original intention in a way which is going to give rise to exactly similar—and similarly hopeless—epistemological problems.

How do the ideas which I have adumbrated relate to those developed by Kripke? One point of difference between Kripke's Wittgenstein and Wittgenstein which has not been generally noted is that the regress-of-interpretations paradox of *Investigations* §§198–201 actually diverges in focus from Kripke's Sceptical Paradox. Kripke's sceptic challenges his adversary to substantiate a claim to know what rule he formerly followed—the problem is to describe aspects of his former behaviour and/or mental life which take us *to* an identification of the former rule. The regress-of-interpretations paradox, by contrast, focuses on a particular conception of the path *from* a rule to a judgement about its proper application in a new case. The rule is assumed from the outset to be in place—'in mind'—and the issue is, how does it help to have it there? Further, the problem is conceived as arising as a result of a certain specific (mis)conception of what rules are, one which pictures the relation between receiving an illustration of a practice and going on to participate in it successfully as essentially mediated by cognition of the requirements of something which has been interiorised.

---

28. Though one should not lose sight of the consideration that the aspect of mathematical Platonism targeted is not the ontology of abstract objects but something which Platonism shares with the sort of structuralist conception of the subject matter of number theory, famously advocated for example in Benacerraf (1965). This is the notion that we can somehow pack more into our mathematical concepts and rules than need ever be elicitable by proof—and that proof is accordingly a mere cognitive auxiliary whereby finite minds may unlock implications of the understanding of mathematical notions to which they subscribe.

So not merely do the two paradoxes focus on different—though of course connected—kinds of question concerning rules, namely:

How is it possible to know which rule I (used to) follow?

versus

How is it possible to know what the rule which I grasp requires of me here?

In addition, while Kripke's sceptic directs his paradox at the very existence of rules and rule-following, Wittgenstein's 'paradox' is directed, in intention at least, at what he regards as a misunderstanding of the nature and epistemology of rule-following—something which it should be possible to correct without calling into question the reality of rules.

Well, that may have been Wittgenstein's general intention. The question is: did he succeed in carrying it through? For, to stress: if the interiorised, explanation-transcendent rule, with all its hopeless epistemological difficulties, is merely the upshot of a Platonist conception of the autonomy of rules, then that has to be a casualty too. So the distinguishability of his view from that of Kripke's sceptic is totally dependent on Wittgenstein's ability to dislodge the opposed thought that rules can be *nothing* if not autonomous in that way. Unless that thought is dislodged, then while Kripke's account of the route in, as it were, may have involved somewhat free play with Wittgenstein's text, the terminus of the train of thought which I have described and that of Kripke's sceptic will be the same.

Dislodging that thought requires indicating an alternative: a conception of rules and rule-governed practices which allows a sufficient gap between the requirements of a rule and a subject's reaction in any particular case to make space for something worth regarding as normativity, yet abrogates the spurious—Platonist—autonomy which gave rise to the difficulties. It is clear enough what Wittgenstein regards as the *sort* of considerations which should point us towards the right perspective on the matter. They are the considerations which constitute the fourth theme which I wish to highlight:

> Language, and all rule-governed institutions, are founded not in
> our internalisation of the same strongly autonomous, explanation-
> transcendent rules, whose requirements we then succeed, more or less,
> in collectively tracking, but in *primitive* dispositions of agreement in
> judgement and action.[29]

There is no essential inner epistemology of rule-following. To express
the matter dangerously, we have *nothing* 'in mind'. The connection
between the training and explanations which we receive and our subsequent practices is no doubt effected in ways which could only be
sustained by conscious, thinking beings; but it is not mediated by the
internalisation of explanation-transcendent rules that, in our training,
we (something like) guessed at. It is, for epistemological purposes, a
basic fact about us that ordinary forms of explanation and training
do succeed in perpetuating practices of various kinds—that there is a
shared uptake, a disposition to concur in novel judgements involving
the concepts in question. The rules-as-rails mythology attempts an
explanation of this fact. But the truth is the other way round: it is the
basic agreement which sustains all rules and rule-governed institutions. The requirements which our rules impose upon us would not be
violated if there were not this basic agreement; they would not so
much as exist.

This aspect of Wittgenstein's thought is very familiar and, as the
familiar often does, it can seem quite clear. But it is not clear at all. The
great difficulty is to stabilise it against a drift to a fatal simplification:
the idea that the requirements of a rule, in any particular case, are simply *whatever we take them to be*. For if the requirements of the rule are
not constituted, as the Platonist thought, independently of our reaction to the case, what is there available to constitute them *but* our reaction? But that idea effectively surrenders the notion of a requirement
altogether. And Wittgenstein in any case explicitly cautions against it
as a misreading of his text.[30] In which case how do matters stand?

29. *Investigations* §§211, 217, 242; *RFM* VI, 39.
30. *Investigations* §241; cf. *RFM* VII, 40.

Wittgenstein tells us that the requirements of rules exist only within the framework of institutional activities which depend upon basic human propensities to agree in judgement; but he reminds us that such requirements are also, in any particular case, independent of our judgements, supplying standards in terms of which it may be right to regard those judgements, even if they enjoy consensus, as incorrect. So we have been told what does *not* constitute the requirement of a rule in any particular case: it is *not* constituted by our agreement about the particular case, and it is *not* constituted autonomously, by a rule-as-rail, our ability to follow which would be epistemologically unaccountable. But we have not been told what *does* constitute it; all we have been told is that there would simply be no such requirement—the rule could not so much as exist—but for the phenomenon of actual, widespread human agreement in judgement.

It is probably vain to search Wittgenstein's own texts for a more concrete positive suggestion about the constitutive question. His later conception of philosophical method seems to be conditioned by a mistrust of such questions. Consensus cannot constitute the requirements of a rule because we do, on occasion, actually *make use* of the notion of a consensus based on ignorance or a mistake. That is a distinction to which our ordinary practices give content. The thing to guard against is the tendency to erect a mythological picture of this content, the myth about rule-following challenged by the first three themes. The myth is active in the Platonist philosophy of mathematics, and in the Cartesian philosophy of inner experience. So it is important to expose it. But, once exposed, it does not need to be supplanted:

> Our mistake is to look for an explanation where we ought to look at what happens as a 'proto-phenomenon'. That is, where we ought to have said: *this language-game is played.*[31]

No further *account* of the distinction is necessary. Enough has been done when we have preempted philosophical misunderstandings of

---

31. *Investigations* §654.

our linguistic practices in a way that avoids misdescription of their details.

I mean that to be recognisable as an "official" Wittgensteinian line. I do not know whether it is really Wittgenstein's own; and insofar as it may be, I suspect that he did not succeed in clearly representing to himself a sound theoretical basis for declining rather than—perhaps quixotically—rising to the challenge posed by his own thought which I have tried to describe. In any case, *we* now confront a challenge: make out the constitutive answer which Wittgenstein's fourth theme does not deliver, though it imposes constraints upon it;[32] or make out the necessary theoretical basis for the analytical quietism which, 'officially', he himself adopted.

Three things are worth stressing. First, these are not issues from a mined-out corpus, but remain of great interest and importance. Second, Kripke's sceptic continues to loom over them: it is still to be shown that the ideas of Wittgenstein which I have described can be prevented—quite contrary to his intentions, no doubt—from spiralling into some kind of incoherent irrealism about meaning. Third, this agenda which Wittgenstein's writing sets us—this whole clutch of issues concerning meaning, intention, content, truth and objectivity—comprises some of the most exciting and profound questions in contemporary philosophy. The agenda is, of course, broader than the Wittgensteinian legacy: there has been important input from Quine, Putnam and, indeed, Kripke, in Wittgenstein's name. It is regrettable that, though often tantalisingly within range, *these* issues are never in focus in McGinn's book.

32. For one effort in this possibly quixotic direction, see Wright (1989c) (this volume Essay 7).

7

Wittgenstein's Rule-Following Considerations and the Central Project of Theoretical Linguistics

✍

I

The Central Project of theoretical linguistics, for present purposes, is to achieve an understanding of one component in what Chomsky has termed the 'creative aspect'[1] of our language use—our ability, after exposure to the use of no more than a small part of our language, to recognise of indefinitely many unencountered strings both whether they constitute well-formed sentences and what, if anything, they could be used in a particular context to say. No doubt this ability admits of *some* kind of scientific theoretical explanation. What is characteristic of the Project is the thought that, in the first place anyway, it is appropriate to seek an explanation in, broadly, *cognitive-psychological* terms: that it is an ability which we have because we are appropriately related to a finite body of *information* which may be

---

1. The other component, as is familiar, is that uses of language are characteristically *stimulus-free;* language is 'undetermined by any fixed association of utterances to external stimuli or physiological states (identifiable in any non-circular fashion)' (Chomsky (1966), pp. 4–5). Chomsky speaks (1964), p. 7, of the first component as 'the central fact to which any significant linguistic theory must address itself'.

inferentially manipulated in such a way as to entail, for each novel string on which we can successfully exercise our 'linguistic-creative' power, appropriate theorems concerning its grammaticalness and content.[2]

It is a basic and familiarly thorny question how the 'appropriate relation' which is to mediate between the contents of a suitable grammar, or theory of meaning, and the abilities of actual speakers may be best conceived—whether, for instance, it is happy to involve a notion of *knowledge,* however attenuated. But that is not now my immediate concern.[3] My question, perhaps even more basic, is whether, even in this inchoate and highly general formulation, the Central Project is not somehow already at odds with lessons to be learned from Wittgenstein's discussions of rule-following in *Philosophical Investigations* and elsewhere.[4]

2. In Chomsky (1967), pp. 4–5, for instance, he writes: "A person's competence can be represented by a *grammar,* which is a system of rules for pairing semantic and phonetic interpretations. Evidently, these rules operate over an infinite range. Once a person has mastered the rules (unconsciously, of course), he is capable, in principle, of using them to assign semantic interpretations to signals quite independently of whether he has been exposed to them or their parts, as long as they consist of elementary units that he knows and are composed by the rules he has internalized." Compare Dummett (1976), p. 70: "A theory of meaning will, then, represent the practical ability possessed by a speaker as consisting in his grasp of a set of propositions; since the speaker derives his understanding of a sentence from the meaning of its component words, these propositions will most naturally form a deductively connected system." A useful assembly of source material for this basic thought is provided, their deflationary purposes notwithstanding, by Baker and Hacker (1984a), chaps. 8–9.

3. I have considered some of the issues involved in Wright (1986c), chap. 6, 'Theories of Meaning and Speakers' Knowledge'.

4. Both the present chapter and my 'Theories of Meaning and Speakers' Knowledge' are attempts to pursue issues raised in the symposium I had with Gareth Evans (Evans (1981); Wright (1981) (this volume Essay 2)). The principal purpose of my contribution (cf. Wright (1980), chap. 15), was to raise the question to which the present paper is addressed. But Evans's reply focused on the more specific questions to do with the notion of implicit knowledge which 'Theories of Meaning and Speakers' Knowledge' tried to pursue further. Somehow or other, with the obvious exceptions of Kripke's brief remarks and Chomsky's response (1986), there has been virtually no discussion of the present question since.

The tension is very immediate on Kripke's widely discussed inter-pretation (1982) of Wittgenstein. According to Kripke's Wittgenstein, all our discourse concerning meaning, understanding, content and cognate notions fails of strict factuality—says nothing literally true or false—and is saved from vacuity only by a 'Sceptical Solution', a set of proposals for rehabilitating meaning-talk in ways that prescind from the assignment to it of any fact-stating role. If that claim were correct, there would be nothing strictly and literally true to say about the con-tent of a novel utterance nor, therefore, anything to be strictly known or recognised concerning its content. So linguistic creativity, conceived as the ability to *know* the syntactic and semantic status of encountered strings, would be a myth: there would be, simply, no such knowledge-forming power. The apparently remarkable, unbounded character of our linguistic competence would no more demand a deep, *cognitive* explanation than would a disposition to consensus about the *comic* qualities of an indefinite variety of situations (if indeed we were so dis-posed, and assuming, for the sake of argument, the non-factuality of claims concerning comedy). It would still, no doubt, be possible to raise the question what *does* explain our ability to communicate using novel linguistic constructions, if it is not that we deploy essentially the same store of syntactic and semantic information to arrive at the same answers to the same problems. Maybe the question could be so cast as to admit of some sort of natural scientific treatment. But we would have surrendered the vision which inspired the Project: the vision of basic English, say, as an articulate system of syntactic and semantic *fact,* whose mastery consists in the internalisation of a store of principles out of which all aspects of the system are generated. That vision calls for the existence of *truths* concerning the content of novel utterances, truths which Kripke's Wittgenstein repudiates. There would still be something, our 'agreement in semantic reactions', which might seem remarkable. But since it would be, precisely, no longer an agreement in *judgements,* properly so described, there would seem to be no legitimate project of enquiry into its cognitive provenance.

There is an additional, more specific point of tension between Kripke's Wittgenstein and the Central Project. The latter is a project in *psychology*, a project of explaining manifest abilities of the individual in terms of his cognitive-psychological (and ultimately, neurophysiological) equipment. Explanans and explanandum are thus both exhausted by characteristics of individuals 'considered in isolation'. By contrast, so Kripke's Wittgenstein argues, we can refashion the notion of meaning in the wake of the Sceptical Argument only by recognising that a proper account of the (non-fact-stating) use of statements essentially involving it and other cognate notions must make essential reference, one way or another, to the purposes and practices of linguistic *communities*. Meaning—what the Sceptical Solution saves of it—cannot lie within the province of individual psychology, so the methodological individualism which characterises Chomsky's work[5] would apparently be guilty of a compound error. There are no facts of the kind which it seeks to explain by reference to (non-existent) states of individuals; and the concept of meaning, as entrenched in our (non-fact-stating) talk of meaning, has an essentially *social* character which the methodologically individualistic perspective imposed by the spurious explanatory project makes it additionally difficult to recognise.

Kripke's own remarks on the relations between the ideas of his Wittgenstein and the Central Project are somewhat low key. He writes, for instance, that

> *if* statements attributing rule-following are neither to be regarded as stating facts, nor to be thought of as *explaining* our behaviour . . . it would seem that the *use* of the ideas of rules of competence [in Chomsky's technical sense] in linguistics needs serious reconsideration, even if these notions are not rendered 'meaningless'.[6]

Maybe such a 'serious reconsideration' might in the end succeed in conserving a use for the ideas of 'rules' and 'competence' in some kind of theoretical description of our linguistic practices. But Chomsky has

---

5. Cf. d'Agostino (1986), chap. 1.
6. Kripke (1982), pp. 30–1, n. 22.

conspicuously declined to take up the invitation, preferring a frontal attack on the Sceptical Argument and its alleged Sceptical Solution.[7] Concerning the first, the essence of his response, if I may simplify somewhat and presuppose some familiarity with Kripke's dialectic, is that the search for facts constitutive of what you formerly meant by a particular expression, or of its being a particular rule that it was your former practice to follow, is only improperly restricted by Kripke's sceptic to the domains of your former linguistic behaviour and former conscious mental life. Rather, the claim, for example, that you formerly followed a certain specified rule is a *theoretical* claim, and answerable, therefore, in the context of an appropriate embedding theory, to an indefinite pool of past, present *and* future evidence.[8] Any fact may seem fugitive if we do not look in the right place.

If that reflection rebuts the Sceptical Argument, there is of course no need for a Sceptical Solution. But Chomsky finds the Sceptical Solution 'far from descriptively adequate'[9] in any case, demurring at what he takes to be the suggestion of Kripke's Wittgenstein that the assertibility, by the members of a given speech community, that some third party is following rules, requires that 'his responses coincide with theirs'.[10] For this would frustrate the often unproblematic identification of practices governed by rules different to any pursued by the community in question. It is open to question whether this complaint does justice to the resources of the Sceptical Solution.[11] But whether it does or not, it would anyway now be widely accepted that no refinement of the Sceptical Solution can *be* a solution.[12] The crucial ques-

---

7. Chomsky (1986), pp. 223–43.

8. Which need not be restricted to aspects of behaviour and conscious mental life. See ibid., pp. 236 ff.

9. Ibid., pp. 227 ff.

10. Ibid., p. 266.

11. See George (1987), pp. 158–60. Chomsky replies to George's criticism in the same number of the journal (1987, pp. 189–91).

12. For a variety of points of dissatisfaction, besides Chomsky's, see, e.g., Baker and Hacker (1984b), pp. 429–32; Goldfarb (1985), pp. 481–4; McDowell (1984), pp. 329–30; McGinn (1984), pp. 180–91; Wright (1984), pp. 768–70 (this volume Essay 4).

tion concerns what is wrong with the Sceptical Argument—for it can only have the status of a paradox—and what relation it bears to (the real) Wittgenstein's discussion.

Chomsky's response to the Sceptical Argument is unsatisfying, it seems to me, for reasons which also apply to the dispositional response[13] effectively criticised by Kripke himself.[14] Kripke himself objects to the dispositional response that it cannot account for the normativity of understanding an expression in a particular way, intending to follow a particular rule, and so on. The reason for dissatisfaction which I have in mind, however, is not this. It is rather that Chomsky's suggestion, that the identity of followed rules is a strictly theoretical question, threatens, like the dispositional account, to make a total mystery of the phenomenon of non-inferential, first-personal knowledge of past and present meanings, rules and intentions. The whole temptation to think of understanding, intention, etc., as mental

---

13. Kripke (1982), pp. 22–3, characterises it like this:

According to this response, the fallacy in the argument that no fact about me constitutes my meaning plus lies in the assumption that such a fact must consist in an *occurrent* mental state. Indeed the sceptical argument shows that my entire occurrent past mental history might have been the same whether I meant plus or quus, but all this shows is that the fact that I meant plus (rather than quus) is to be analyzed *dispositionally*, rather than in terms of occurrent mental states. Since Ryle's *The Concept of Mind,* dispositional analyses have been influential; Wittgenstein's own later work is of course one of the inspirations for such analyses, and some may think that he himself wishes to suggest a dispositional solution to his paradox.

The dispositional analysis I have heard proposed is simple. To mean addition by '+' is to be disposed, when asked for any sum 'x + y' to give the sum of x and y as the answer (in particular, to say '125' when queried about '68 + 57'); to mean quus is to be disposed when queried about any arguments, to respond with their quum (in particular to answer '5' when queried about '68 + 57'). True, my actual thoughts and responses in the past do not differentiate between the plus and the quus hypotheses; but, even in the past, there were dispositional facts about me that did make such a differentiation. To say that in fact I meant plus in the past is to say—as surely was the case!—that had I been queried about '68 + 57', I *would* have answered '125'. By hypothesis I was not in fact asked, but the disposition was present none the less.

14. Ibid., pp. 24–32.

---

states, against which Wittgenstein repeatedly inveighs in the *Investigations*, flows from this point of analogy with things which *are* genuine mental states and processes—sensations, after-images, having a tune go through one's head. Each of us is, for the most part, effortlessly authoritative, without inference, about our past and present intentions, about the rules we 'have in mind', about how we understand or have understood particular expressions. An account of the truth conditions of such claims which, like Chomsky's or the dispositional account, makes a puzzle of this aspect of their first-personal epistemology should be rejected.[15]

The Sceptical Argument is flawed in any case and needs no response of the sort which Chomsky proposes. For there is an explicit and unacceptable reductionism involved at the stage at which the sceptic challenges his interlocutor to recall some aspect of his former mental life which might constitute his, for example, having meant addition by 'plus'. It is not acceptable, apparently, if the interlocutor claims to recall precisely that. Rather the challenge is to recall some *independently characterised* fact, in a way which does not simply beg the question of the existence of facts of the disputed species, of which it is then to *emerge*—rather than simply be claimed—that it has the requisite properties (principally, normative content across a potential infinity of situations). The search is thus restricted to phenomena of consciousness which are not—for the purposes of the dialectic—permissibly assumed 'up front' to have a recollectable *content*. (For to suppose that one could recall the content of a mental state would just be, the sceptic will claim, to assume a positive answer to the question at issue—namely, whether there is such a thing as knowing one's former meanings.) If the sceptic is allowed to put the challenge in this way, then it is no doubt unanswerable. But so put, it is merely an

15. Cf. Wright (1987a), pp. 393–5 (this volume Essay 5).

Of course, one will be inclined to play down, or query, the claimed feature of the first-personal epistemology of intentional states if one is independently convinced of the 'theoretical' view. And this, unsurprisingly, is what Chomsky does. See, for instance, the rebuttal of Dummett's claim that knowledge of meaning is conscious knowledge in Chomsky (1986), p. 271.

implicit prejudice against the ordinary notions of meaning and intention, according to which we may and usually do non-inferentially know of our present meanings and intentions, and may later non-inferentially recall them.[16]

This somewhat flat-footed response to Kripke's sceptic may seem to some to provide a good example of 'loss of problems'. (The phrase is Wittgenstein's own, of course, from *Zettel* §456.) In fact, though, and on the contrary, I think the real problem posed by the Sceptical Argument is acute, and *is* one of Wittgenstein's fundamental concerns. But the problem is not that of *answering* the Argument. The problem is that of seeing how and why the correct answer just given can *be* correct.

A central preoccupation of the *Investigations,* and Wittgenstein's other late writings on the philosophy of psychology, is with concepts which—like meaning, understanding, intending, expecting, wishing, fearing, hoping—seem to hover, puzzlingly and unstably, between two paradigms. To the left, as it were, stand genuine episodes and processes in consciousness: items which, like headaches, ringing in the ears, and the experience of a patch of blue, may have a determinate onset and departure, and whose occurrence makes no demands upon the conceptual resources of the sufferer.[17] To the right, by contrast, stand qualities of character—like patience, courage, and conceit—which are naturally viewed as constituted in the (broadly) behavioural dispositions of a subject, are fully manifest in things he is inclined to say and do, and advert to no inner phenomenological causes of these inclinations. Descartes's conception of the mental tended to draw everything towards the left-hand pole. The Rylean reaction, by contrast, attempted to colonise as widely as possible on behalf of the right. And the difficulty raised by the concepts with which Wittgenstein was preoccupied is that we are pulled in both

16. Cf. Wright (1984), pp. 771–8 (this volume Essay 4); Wright (1987a), pp. 395–403 (this volume Essay 5).

17. There are also genuinely episodic states whose occurrence is conditional on the conceptual resources of the sufferer. Having a tune run through one's head is arguably of this character.

directions simultaneously. Their first-personal epistemology pulls us to the left—since explaining it seems to call for construal of such states as objects of consciousness. But, as Wittgenstein and his Kripkean ersatz both effectively argue, nothing strictly introspectible has, in the case of these concepts, the right kind of characteristics. We cannot, honestly, find anything to *be* the intention, etc., when we turn our gaze inward; and anything we might find would have no connection or, at best, the wrong kind of connection with those subsequent events—what we go on to count as fulfilment of an intention or expectation, etc.—on which the correctness of an earlier ascription to us of the intention, etc., depends. But if we accordingly allow ourselves to be pulled towards the right-hand pole—interestingly, Chomsky's response—we encounter the difficulties with normativity (at least in some cases), and with saving ordinary first-personal epistemology, which have already been noted. We need, accordingly, some account or perspective on these concepts which is conservative with respect to the features which give rise to the difficulty—their combination of first-personal avowability and 'theoreticity'—yet dissolves the temptation to assimilate them to cases which they do not fundamentally resemble.

Supposing that it is via provision of such an account that the Sceptical Argument can and must ultimately be defused, does any point of contact, or abrasion, remain between Wittgenstein's thought about rule-following and the Central Project? If there is no compelling argument to the conclusion that meaning, etc., are non-factual, is not the Project simply in the clear? Well, whether Wittgenstein's later discussions should be seen as issuing a challenge to the factuality of meaning and rule-following, they undeniably feature a recurrent, explicit discomfort with a certain conception of the *autonomy* of rules, the image of a rule as a rail laid to infinity, tracing out a proper course for a practice quite independently of any judgement of the practitioners (*Investigations* §218). And it is hard to avoid finding this conception of autonomy in the picture of language and linguistic competence which drives the Central Project: the picture of language as a kind of syntactico-semantic mechanism, our largely unconscious knowledge of which enables us to compute the content which, independently and in advance of any response of ours, it bestows on each ingredient sentence. Chomsky wrote, over forty years ago:

> It is not easy to accept the view that a child is capable of constructing an extremely complex mechanism for generating a set of sentences, some of which he has heard, or that an adult can instantaneously determine whether (and if so, how) a particular item is generated by this mechanism, which has many of the properties of an abstract deductive theory. Yet this appears to be a fair description of the performance of the speaker, listener, and learner.[18]

Note that the *mechanism* does the generating, and the competent adult merely *keeps track* of what (and how) it generates. The conception of language manifested in those remarks—a continuing fundamental theme of Chomsky's thought—is all one, it seems, in its implicit conception of the character of rule-following, with what Wittgenstein has in view in his remarks about mathematical rules:

> But might it not be said that the *rules* lead this way, even if no one went it? For that is what one would like to say—and here we see the mathematical machine, which, driven by the rules themselves, obeys only mathematical laws and not physical ones.[19]

What motive could there be for such a view of, for example, the rules of multiplication which would not also motivate:

> But might it not be said that this sentence is grammatical, and has the meaning it does, even if no one ever considers it? For that is what one would like to say—and here we see the language-machine which, driven by the rules of the language themselves, obeys only linguistic laws and not physical ones.

18. Chomsky (1959), p. 57.
19. *Remarks on the Foundations of Mathematics* IV, 48.

Unquestionably, Wittgenstein came to regard this conception as deeply misconceived.[20] But why? And is there any good reason for that verdict which does not in the end lead to the same place as the argumentation of Kripke's sceptic—the conclusion that there are, in truth, no such things as the requirements of rules? Anything which is genuinely an instance of rule-following, it is natural to think—rather than mere charade—has to consist in keeping abreast of certain objective requirements. If it is not that, if the requirements are not settled independently of the way I find myself inclined to go, then I do not *follow* anything—any more than, when walking in bright sunlight, I follow my shadow.[21] Is not the image of the syntactic-semantic engine simply a graphic expression of the rule-governed nature of linguistic practice? And if we reject it, are we not, in effect, rejecting the idea that proper linguistic practice *is* rule-governed—and thereby rejecting the notion of strictly *correct* linguistic practice, and with it the notion of meaning?

II

A reminder is desirable of the general gist of Wittgenstein's discussions of rule-following. I shall try, briefly, to provide one by concentrating (largely) on §§185–219 of the *Investigations*, and 23–47 of part VI of *Remarks on the Foundations of Mathematics*.

20. Or better, the conception which someone who expressed themselves in this way would be likely to intend to convey. Wittgenstein's conservatism almost always leads him to fight shy of direct criticism of a problematical form of expression. Cf. *Philosophical Investigations* §195:

'But I don't mean what I do now (in grasping a sense) determines the future use *causally* and as a matter of experience, but that in a *queer* way, the use itself is in some sense present'—But of course it is, 'in *some* sense'! Really the only thing wrong with what you say is the expression 'in a queer way'. The rest is all right . . .

The problems reside in our *interpretations* of what we say.

21. The comparison is James Hopkins'.

It's notable that the characteristic concerns of these passages seem to have nothing at all to do with the *reality* of rules. Rather, they are epistemological: Wittgenstein is preoccupied with the sense, if any, in which a rule can be genuinely an object of intellection, something whose requirements we *track*—to use a more recent piece of jargon—by grace of some intuitive or interpretative power. Undoubtedly the intention—or one might better say, the suspicion—of these passages is negative. Wittgenstein thinks we tend to badly misunderstand what the accomplishment is of someone who is a competent rule-follower, and that our misunderstandings lead us to overdignify the nature of the constraint imposed by a rule, and the character of our accomplishment in following it. But there is, emphatically, no explicit denial of the *existence* of the constraint, and no consequential rejection of the very notion of accomplishment. It is not *impossible* that their absence is to be accounted for by Wittgenstein's failure to follow through all the way on his own thought, but I shall try to suggest a better explanation.

Four interlocking themes are prominent. First:

One's own understanding of a rule does not exceed what one can explain. (Investigations §§209–10; RFM VI, 23)

The temptation to suppose otherwise arises from the reflection that any explanatory process is finite and, hence open in principle to an indefinite variety of interpretations. Yet explanation does usually—or so we suppose—secure mutual understanding. So, somehow, more is got across—the thought continues—than an explanation makes explicit. Correct uptake of an explanation is having the *right* 'something' come into one's mind as the result of the explanation; and the resulting informational state is then expressed in, but essentially transcends, one's subsequent practice with the concept concerned.

It is important to see that this picture of what is involved in successfully giving and receiving explanations is a cornerstone for the thought:

'Once you have got hold of the rule, you have the route traced for you'. (*RFM* VI, 31; Wittgenstein's own scare quotes) which is elaborated in the 'rules-as-rails' imagery of *Investigations* §§218–9. For if the rule governing a particular arithmetical series, say, really does determine its every *n*th place quite independently of any judgement of ours, then—since any feasible explanatory performance will allow of alternative interpretations generating disputes about the identity of *n*th places which were not explicitly covered— the every-*n*th-place-determining 'something' which someone who follows the explanation correctly comes to have in mind—the 'essential thing' which we have to 'get him to *guess*' (*Investigations* §210)— must somehow have been at best clumsily and imperfectly conveyed. The idea which Wittgenstein is opposing when he writes:

> If you use a rule to give a description, you yourself do not know more than you say. . . . If you say 'and so on', you yourself do not know more than 'and so on'. (*RFM* IV, 8)

is hence a direct consequence of the rules-as-rails picture, joined with the supposition that, by dint of ordinary training and explanations, we do indeed succeed in perpetuating a community of mutual understanding of arithmetical and other rules.

The second theme is:

> *It might be preferable, in describing one's most basic rule-governed responses, to think of them as informed not by an* intuition *(of the requirements of the rule) but a kind of* decision. (*Investigations* §§186, 231; *RFM* VI, 24; *Brown Book* §5)

The point of contrast between the terms 'intuition' and 'decision'[22] is that the former implies, and the latter repudiates, the suggestion that following a rule is, even in the most basic cases when one can say nothing by way of justification for one's particular way of proceeding, a matter of *cognition* of an independent requirement. 'Intuition'

---

22. *Intuition* and *Entscheidung*.

suggests a primitive, unarticulated apprehension, a form of receptive knowledge too basic and immediate to admit of any further account. Such an intuitive faculty would ensure that, once we have mastered, for example, an arithmetical rule, our successive applications of it are disposed to be appropriately sensitive to its requirements—either already in line or able to be brought into line. But it seems there could be no further story to be told about how the intuitive faculty accomplishes this harmony. For precisely that reason, however, we have no means to resist a sceptical suggestion:

> If intuition is an inner voice—how do I know *how* I am to obey it? And how do I know that it doesn't mislead me? For if it can guide me right, it can also guide me wrong. (Intuition an unnecessary shuffle.) (*Investigations* §213)

The reason why there is no response to this is because we have done, and can do, nothing to *fill out* the thought that, in the most primitive case of rule-following, we track a set of independent requirements. But the sceptical thought is barely intelligible. For we have no accountable idea of what would constitute the direction taken by the rule by itself if the deliverances of our intuitive faculties were to take us collectively off track—'no model of this superlative fact' (*Investigations* §192). That the sceptical thought makes no even apparent sense[23] but arises inevitably out of the intuitional epistemology of rule-following, brings out the cognitive pretentiousness of the latter, and the purpose of:

> It would almost be more correct to say, not that an intuition was needed at every stage, but that a new decision was needed at every stage. (*Investigations* §186)

23. Contrast, say, Cartesian scepticism about other minds, where we precisely do have an apparent conception of the truth-conferrers for descriptions of others' mental states, based on a seemingly plausible projection from one's own case, which sets up an epistemological problem.

The third theme is complementary to the second and elaborates Wittgenstein's doubts about the possibility of a 'tracking' epistemology of rule-following:

> *Supposing that grasping a rule is a matter of coming to have something 'in mind', how am I supposed to recognise what its requirements are?* (*Investigations* §§198, 209–13; *RFM* VI, 38, 47)

It is in the context of this theme that the 'paradox' is presented on which Kripke's exegesis concentrates:

> 'But how can a rule show me what I have to do at *this* point? Whatever I do is, on some interpretation, in accord with the rule'.—That is not what we ought to say, but rather: any interpretation still hangs in the air along with what it interprets, and cannot give it any support. Interpretations by themselves do not determine meaning. (*Investigations* §198)

I undergo some process of explanation—somebody writes down for me a substantial initial segment of some arithmetical series, say—and as a result, let us suppose, I come to have the right rule 'in mind'. But now consider any nth place in the series which lies beyond the demonstrated initial segment and which, in coming to a correct understanding of the intended rule, I nevertheless did not think about at all. How, when it comes to the crunch—at the nth place—does having the rule 'in mind' help? A natural response—because one tends to think of 'having the rule in mind' on the model of imagining a formula or something of the sort—is to concede that, strictly, merely having the rule in mind is no help. For it is possible to have a formula in mind without knowing what it means. So—the response continues—it is necessary in addition to *interpret* the rule. But then we immediately get the 'paradox' which Wittgenstein's interlocutor[24] blunders into in *Investigations* §198. *Any* selection for the nth place can be reconciled, on *some* interpretation, with the rule. An interpretation is of help to me, therefore, only if it is *correct*. But the fact that the idea of correctness has to be invoked at this point makes the play with interpretation idle. 'Knowing the correct

24. For note the quotation marks.

interpretation of the rule' becomes just a piece of patter equivalent to 'knowing the rule'. Or if it is not—if we try to think of it as the having of something further in mind, some expanded account, for instance, of the content of the rule—then the problem will simply recur.

That is, if having the expanded account in mind is having an uninterpreted object in mind, then I get no guidance; but if its guidance is conditional on an interpretation, then I need to arrive at *its* correct interpretation, and an account is still owed of how I am to recognise *that*.

The relations between the three themes should, I suggest, be viewed like this. Suppose that what I take up from an episode of explanation, where it is successful, does indeed essentially transcend that explanation and any other that I might give in turn. I come to have the right rule in mind, but might, save for a kind of felicity, equally well have arrived at a wrong one despite having missed no overt feature of the explanation. This idea, challenged in the passages cited in connection with the first theme, connects with the second and third themes in that they jointly confront it with a dilemma. How does the explanation-transcendent rule which I supposedly have 'in mind' tell me what to do in novel cases? If I have to interpret it, that could be done in lots of ways. So how do I tell which interpretation is correct? Does that call for a further rule—a rule for determining correct interpretation of the original—and, if so, why does it not raise the same problem again, and so generate a regress? If, on the other hand, I don't have to interpret the original rule, then the only possible answer appears to be that I have some unmediated, intuitional contact with its requirements—the thought challenged by the second theme.[25] The upshot is, accordingly,

25. There is some question, I think, whether the third theme really strikes home at what someone is likely to be thinking who is working with the conception of the rule as explanation-transcendent but manifest to the subject. One is—I suppose this is a point of autobiography—much more likely to be thinking in terms of a kind of *inner illumination* than in terms of having the rule as, literally, an object of consciousness. But the connection between the inner illumination and the step-by-step judgements involved in applying the rule remains irremediably intuitional, in the sense that opens it to the sceptical attack of the second theme. For an elaboration of the attack, see Wright (1980), pp. 36–8 (this volume Essay 1, pp. 28–31).

that if we attempt to construe grasp of a rule as the presence in mind of an explanation-transcendent item, as the conception of the autonomy of rules expressed in the rules-as-rails imagery dictates, we are beggared for any satisfactory epistemology of step-by-step rule-following.

How do these ideas relate to those developed by Kripke? Several commentators[26] have challenged Kripke's interpretation on the ground that the second paragraph of *Investigations* §201 makes it plain that Wittgenstein did not accept the 'paradox' which Kripke makes pivotal. These commentators might also have emphasised the point, noted above, that the paradox is first presented, in §198, in 'interlocutor-quotation', as a suggestion for correction. And a third point of disanalogy, not generally noted, is that the focus of the regress-of-interpretations paradox of §§198–201 does not coincide with that of Kripke's sceptic. Kripke's sceptic challenges his interlocutor to substantiate a claim to know what rule the interlocutor formerly followed—he is to call attention to facts concerning his former behaviour and/or mental life which nail the rule down. So the problem is to describe a cognitive pathway *to* the (former) rule. By contrast, the regress-of-interpretations paradox focuses on a particular conception of the path *from* the rule to a judgement about its proper application in a new case. The rule is assumed to be in place—'in mind'; the question is, how does it help me to have it there?[27] And the problem arises only on a certain conception of what rules are, one which conceives of the relation between receipt of an explanation and successful ongoing practice as essentially mediated by cognition of the requirements of something interiorised. So not merely do the

26. For instance McDowell (1984); McGinn (1984); Baker and Hacker (1984b). See also Malcolm (1986), p. 154.

27. I am not, in presenting this contrast, forgetting that Kripke's sceptic is a device for focusing on an *ontological* issue. It remains that the device works by raising, at the relevant stage of the dialectic, an epistemological worry. The transition to an ontological conclusion is mediated by the further assumption, disputed for example by the dispositionalist, that facts about (former) rules—if they existed—would have to be accessible, at least in principle, via reflection on (former) behaviour and conscious mental episodes.

two paradoxes focus on ostensibly different—though of course connected—kinds of question concerning rules, namely:

How can I tell which rule I (used to) follow?

and,

How can I tell what the rule I grasp requires of me here?

In addition, while Kripke's paradox is directed at the very existence
of rules and rule-following, Wittgenstein's paradox is directed, in
intention anyway, at a misunderstanding of the epistemology of rule-
following competences, which—he apparently believes—can be corrected without calling into question their reality.

If that was Wittgenstein's intent, however, the question remains
whether he succeeded in carrying it through. If the interiorised,
explanation-transcendent rule, with its attendant hopeless epistemological difficulties is, as I suggested, the inevitable upshot of a certain
conception of the autonomy of rules, then that has to be a casualty
too. So unless the thought that rules are nothing if *not* autonomous in
that way is somehow disturbed, the upshot of the three themes which
I have been describing is going to be the same as that of Kripke's Sceptical Argument. Does Wittgenstein manage to disturb that thought?

Disturbing it would seem to require indicating an alternative: a
conception of rules, and rule-governed practices, which allows sufficient distance between the requirements of a rule and the subject's
reaction in a particular case to make space for something worth
regarding as normativity, yet abrogates the spurious autonomy which
generates the difficulties. It is clear enough what Wittgenstein regards
as the *kind* of considerations that point us towards the right perspective on the matter. They are the considerations which constitute his
fourth principal theme:

*The foundations of language, and of all rule-governed institutions, re-
side not in the circumstance that we have internalised the same strongly
autonomous, explanation-transcendent rules, whose requirements we*

*then concur—or concur enough—about, but in primitive disposi-
tions of agreement in judgement and action. (Investigations §§211,
217, 242; RFM VI, 39)*

There is no essential *inner* epistemology of rule-following. The connection between the training and explanations which we receive and
our subsequent practices, although effected in ways which, no doubt,
could be sustained only by conscious, thinking beings, is not mediated
by the internalisation of explanation-transcendent rules that have to
be guessed at. It is a basic fact about us that ordinary forms of explanation and training do succeed in perpetuating practices of various
kinds—that there is shared uptake, a disposition to concur in novel
judgements involving the concepts in question. The rules-as-rails
mythology attempts an explanation of this fact. But the reality is the
other way about: it is the agreement which sustains all rules and rule-
governed institutions. The requirements which our rules impose upon
us owe their existence to it.

This aspect of Wittgenstein's thought is familiar enough to need no
further elaboration here—familiar, and ill understood. The great difficulty is to stabilise it against its natural drift to a fatal simplification:
the idea that the requirements of a rule, in a particular case, are simply *whatever we take them to be*. That idea would, in effect, surrender the notion of a requirement. And Wittgenstein, it seems, explicitly
cautions against it. (See *Investigations* §241; *RFM,* VII, 40.)[28] But
then what is the upshot? We are told that the requirements of rules
exist only within the framework of institutional activities which
depend on basic human propensities to agree in judgement, but reminded that such requirements are also, in any particular case, independent of our judgements, supplying genuine norms in terms of
which those judgements, even consensual judgements, may be evaluated. We have accordingly been told what does *not* constitute the
requirement of a rule in a particular case: it is *not* constituted by
our agreement about the particular case, and it is *not* constituted

28. But a distinction is necessary here. See p. 210 below.

autonomously, by a 'rule-as-rail', our cognitive connection with which there would be no accounting for. But we have not been told what *does* constitute it; all we have been told is that there would be no such requirements in the first place but for the phenomenon of human agreement in judgement.

I believe it is vain to search Wittgenstein's texts for any more concrete positive suggestion about the constitutive question. His later conception of philosophy is, indeed, conditioned by a mistrust of such constitutive questions. Thus, consensus cannot constitute the requirements of a rule because we do, on occasion, make use of the notion of a consensus based on ignorance or mistake. But we must guard against the tendency to erect out of a practice in which that notion is given content the mythological picture of rule-following challenged by the first three themes. The mythological picture is at work in the Platonist philosophy of mathematics, and in the ease with which it comes to us to think that a private linguist could establish objective standards of correctness and incorrectness for himself. So it is important to expose it. But, once exposed, it does not need to be supplanted. Any further urge for clarity can be gratified only by a kind of natural-historical *übersicht* of rule-governed institutions and practices.

I mean the foregoing to be recognisable as an 'official' Wittgensteinian line.[29] The most striking thing about it for present purposes is that it is hardly more hospitable to the Central Project than Kripke's Sceptical Argument. The Central Project is fuelled by the demand for a *deep* explanation of our ability to recognise the meanings of novel utterances. The Sceptical Argument entails that there is no such ability, since there is nothing to recognise. So the demand for deep explanation is misplaced; and insofar as candidate deep explanations advert to covert structures of tacitly known rules, they advert to nothing real. The 'official' response, by contrast, allows us to think, as we ordinarily do, that there is some fact about what a particular novel

---

29. I am thinking especially of Baker and Hacker's exegesis (1983a, 1983b) of the *Investigations*. But it is a nice question whether, if at all, John McDowell (1984), in his conception of semantic facts as kind of bedrock, departs from the official line.

utterance, used in a particular context, means: a fact which it is possible to mistake, and which is normative with respect to appraisals of and responses to that particular utterance in that context. So facts about meaning are safe. But it does not follow that we may immediately raise the question which drives the Central Project. It may be granted that, in any ordinary sense, our agreement about the meaning of a novel utterance, like our agreement about a hitherto unconsidered nth place in some arithmetical series, is a rule-guided agreement. But it is quite another thing to accept that it calls for an account in terms of covert cognitive operations. The whole lesson of the negative parts of Wittgenstein's discussion was—wasn't it?—that not *all* human agreement in judgements can coherently be thought of as a product of covert cognitive operations. Phenomenologically, at any rate, construal of a novel utterance is often immediate and spontaneous; what obstacle is there to the suggestion that agreement about content is, in such cases, in no way different to agreement about hitherto unconsidered places in simple mathematical series? If some of our judgemental agreement neither calls for nor admits of any further cognitive account, why should not our agreement about the content of novel utterances come into that case?

To stress: the transition from linguistic training to linguistic competence may be mediated in ways which are possible only for certain sorts of conscious, thinking beings. But that is not to say that it is informed by rules—whether put there by the training or, in part at least, in place already—of which linguistic competence works by repeated but unconscious consultations. If we reject the constitutive question—what makes it the case that this is a correct application of the rule at this point? what makes it the case that this novel utterance means just that?—the phenonenon to be explained, it seems, can only be our agreement in judgements on the relevant point, and on similar matters. And if one message of Wittgenstein's discussion is that it is philosophically misguided to ask for an account of that in general, what is special about the particular case of agreement about the content of novel utterances? Can the sort of story which the generative grammarian tells be given without commitment to the mythology at which the negative part of Wittgenstein's discussion is directed? The 'official' Wittgensteinian view is apt to encourage a dismissal of the Central Project altogether.[30]

III

I want to canvass a third possibility: a response to the central insight of Wittgenstein's discussion of rule-following which is neither Kripkean nor 'official'. It may be that the 'official' view is exegetically correct, and that I here part company with the intentions of the actual, historical Wittgenstein. But it seems to me that it is an important methodological precept that we do not despair of giving answers to constitutive questions too soon; if the accomplishments of analysis in philosophy often seem meagre, that may be because it is difficult, not impossible.

The rule-following considerations attack the idea that judgements about the requirements of a rule on a particular occasion have a 'tracking' epistemology, answer to states of affairs constituted altogether independently of our inclination to make those judgments. How can judgements lack a substantial epistemology in this way, and yet still be *objective*—still have to answer to something distinct from our actual dispositions of judgement?

A good example of a broadly parallel problem is provided by secondary qualities of material objects—qualities of colour, taste, smell, palpable texture, audible sound and so on. It is an old idea that, in our judgements concerning such qualities, we respond more to aspects of our own affective phenomenology than to anything real in nature, and there is a corresponding perennial temptation towards an irrealist construal of such judgements.[31] But the irrealist response is, in this case, an overreaction. What may be true, I believe, is that (a

30. For elaboration, see Baker and Hacker (1984a), pp. 345–56.

31. Famously succumbed to by Locke, of course, and more recently by J. L. Mackie (1976), pp. 17–20.

large class of) judgements of colour, for instance, fail what I have elsewhere called the *order-of-determination* test.[32] Judgements of shape, by contrast, to take the most often discussed example of a Lockean primary quality, arguably pass the test. The order-of-determination test concerns the relation between *best* judgements—judgements made in what are, with respect to their particular subject manner, *cognitively ideal* conditions of both judge and circumstance—and truth. Passing the test requires that there be some content to the idea of best judgements *tracking* the truth—the determinants of a judgement's being true and of its being best have to be somehow independent. Truth, for judgements which pass the test, is a standard constituted independently of any considerations concerning cognitive pedigree. For judgements which fail the test, by contrast, there is no distance between being true and being best; truth, for such judgements, is constitutively what we judge to be true when we operate under cognitively ideal conditions.

The contrast, then, is between judgements among which our best opinions *determine* the extension of the truth predicate, and those among which they at most reflect an extension determined independently—henceforward *extension-determining* and *extension-reflecting* judgements respectively. So expressed, it is an intuitive and inchoate contrast, which can doubtless be elaborated and refined in a variety of ways. To fix ideas, let us look a bit more closely at the way matters might proceed first in the cases of (primary) colour and (visually appraisable, three-dimensional) shape, and then in the case of psychological characteristics.

Consider a plane surface one foot square. What conditions on the circumstances of judgement should we impose in order to ensure that a thinker's (visual) judgement will be that the surface is, say, uniformly royal blue only if it is? Well, the surface must be in full view and in good light, relatively stationary, and not too far away; and the thinker must know which object is in question, must observe it attentively, must be possessed of normal visual equipment and be other-

32. In Wright (1993).

wise cognitively lucid, and must be competent with the concept *blue*. In addition, the thinker must be free of doubt about the satisfaction of any of these conditions—for a doubt might lead to an unwillingness to make any judgement, or even to the making of some bizarre, compensatory judgement, in circumstances which were otherwise ideal for the appraisal of colour.

Now, it is presumably necessary, in order for our judgements, when appropriately constrained, (partially)[33] to *determine* the extension of some concept, that it be a priori true that the concept applies when, so constrained, we judge that it does. And it is, I suggest, a priori true that when all the foregoing conditions are met, the fact of the object's colour—at least at the level of refinement captured by a predicate like 'blue'—and the thinker's judgment of the fact will, as it were, covary.[34]

---

33. 'Partially' because we are, in effect, considering something of the form:

If S judges under conditions C, then (P if and only if S believes P),

which says nothing at all about the truth conditions of P-type propositions under non-C-conditions. But we cannot plausibly consider, for present purposes, the stronger *basic equation* (to use Mark Johnston's term), namely:

P if and only if (if S judges under conditions C, S believes P),

unless we can foreclose on the possibility that bringing about conditions C might materially affect the truth-status of P. And that cannot be done with colour, or any characteristics sustained by a causally active and acted-upon base. Cf. note 26 in Wright (1988). For fuller discussion, see the Appendix to chap. 3 in Wright (1992).

34. Two possible doubts about the sufficiency of the listed conditions would need to be addressed before this claim could be finally sustained.

(I) Might a subject not be possessed of eccentric background beliefs—for instance, that there are no blue things at all—which would prevent his formation of the appropriate belief about the object's colour, even though he met the conditions as stated? (I am here indebted to Paul Boghossian.) It is not clear. If the object is blue, it will look blue to him under the stated conditions; and then, if he believes that

Blue things look blue to *normally visually equipped* subjects in *good light,*

he is going to be constrained by the eccentric belief—if cognitively lucid—to doubt whether both those conditions are met. So he will violate the extremal condition, of being free of doubt, etc. But if he doesn't believe the principle connecting blueness and

It is another question whether such a priori covariance is sufficient for the judgements to enjoy extension-determining status. But there are, in this case, three supplementary considerations which, if correct, arguably confer such sufficiency.

First, apriority in such a claim—a claim that, under certain conditions, C, a thinker will hold a certain belief if and only if it is true (henceforward, a *provisional equation*)—may be the product of a certain triviality, consequent on C's receiving no substantial specification but being described purely in terms of 'suitability', 'conduciveness', or, generally, as whatever it takes to appraise judgements of the relevant sort correctly. Clearly, we would have made no case for regarding best opinion as *determining* the extension of the truth predicate among a given class of judgements if, although we had constructed an appropriate kind of provisional equation whose instances held a priori true, their apriority was owing to this kind of trivial specification of the C-conditions. For it is an a priori truth of *any* kind of judgement whatever that, if I operate under conditions which have everything it takes to ensure the correctness of my opinion, then it will be the case that P if and only if I take it to be so. But the conditions listed above for the appraisal of colour allow, it is plausible, substantial, non-trivial elaboration in a manner conservative of the a priori connection between their satisfaction and the correctness of the thinker's

---

blue appearance, does he count as appropriately competent with the concept *blue*? Still, that is just one kind of eccentric belief.

(II) Background colour affects colour appearance; a cream circle, for instance, may look pink, or eau-de-Nil, even in normal light, depending on the colour of the surface behind it. May we not need to strengthen the C-conditions to contain some stipulation of an appropriately coloured background? There would be great difficulties with the important independence condition (see p. 195) if we do. But does the phenomenon affect *royal blue, scarlet, emerald green, lemon yellow* to any extent which might result in a subject's erroneously judging (or withholding the judgement) that an object meets one of those descriptions? And would it anyway be absurd to think of colour as involving an element of situation-relativity—so that the judgements about, for example, the cream circle are all correct?

opinion. We can, for instance, specify normal visual equipment on the part of the thinker as: equipment which is actually statistically usual among human beings. Likewise, good lighting conditions can be specified as: conditions like those which actually typically obtain out-of-doors and out-of-shadow at noon on a cloudy summer's day.[35]

The second supplementary consideration is that the question whether the C-conditions, so substantially specified, are satisfied in a particular case is logically independent of any truths concerning the details of the extension of colour concepts. If this were not so, it would be open to question whether thinkers' opinions, formed under these C-conditions, could be extension-determining; for satisfaction of the C-conditions would always presuppose some anterior constitution of colour facts. It is here that one disanalogy opens up with the case of shape, as we shall see in a moment.

The final supplementary consideration is that there is to hand no *other* account of what does determine the extension of the truth predicate among simple judgements of colour, of which the apriority of provisional equations of the kind in question, whose C-conditions are substantially specified and, in the requisite way, free of logical presupposition about the extension of colour concepts, would be a derivable consequence. So there is, to put the matter another way, no *explaining away* the case which the other considerations supply for saying the judgements formed under the conditions in question are extension-determining rather than extension-reflecting.

The suggestion, in summary, is that there is at least a strong prima facie case for regarding a base class[36] of our best judgements about

---

35. The occurrences of 'actually' in these two specifications are to be understood as securing rigidity of reference to the status quo. So counterfactual situations in which other states of affairs are statistically usual are not C-conditions as specified.

36. A base class, rather than merely a proper subclass, because our beliefs about objects' colours under non-C-conditions are variously constrained by the characteristics of colours as determined by C-conditioned judgements. It is, for instance, conclusive justification for the belief that something is blue in the dark to justify the claims (i) that we would judge it to be blue if we saw it in good light and under the other C-conditions; and (ii) that bringing these conditions about would effect no changes in

colour as extension-determining. The case consists in the circumstances (i) that we can construct a priori true provisional equations
for such judgements; (ii) that the C-conditions in these equations can
be substantially specified, in a manner free of the triviality associated
with whatever-it-takes formulations; (iii) that the satisfaction of the
C-conditions is, in any particular case, conceptually independent of
the details of the extensions of colour concepts; (iv) that no other
account is available of what else might determine the extension of the
truth-predicate among judgements of colour, of which the satisfaction
by the relevant provisional equations of conditions (i)–(iii) would be a
consequence.[37]

---

any determinable (contrast: determinate) aspect of the object which would need to be
mentioned in an explanation of the form which our C-conditioned response would
assume.

A connected point, which may help to forestall possible confusion, is that the relationship between the characteristic being-judged-to-be-blue-under-C-conditions and
being blue is not to be compared to that between the characteristic marks of the
instance of a natural kind and being an instance of that kind. It is true that the marks
of gold, for example—its colour, lustre, heaviness, resistance to corrosion, etc.—are in
some sense a priori; we do not learn what gold is and then discover that it has these
characteristics. But in the case of genuine natural kinds we are (a) open to the discovery that some things which have the marks whereby we succeeded in identifying the
kind are not actually instances of the kind; and (b) open to the discovery that actually
no genuine kind of thing *is* individuated by those marks. By contrast, if what I have
been suggesting about colour is correct, we are not open to the discovery that some
objects judged to be blue under C-conditions are not blue; nor open to the discovery—
should the microphysics of blue things prove bizarrely heterogeneous—that there is no
such thing as an object's being blue.

37. It is not inconsistent with thinking of best judgements about colour as being
extension-determining simultaneously to hold that the extensions of colour concepts
are determined by microphysical characteristics of objects—supposing that the
physics *doesn't* prove bizarrely heterogeneous. For it will be best judgements about
colour which determine *which* microphysical characteristics are fit to play a (supplementary) extension-determining role. And no obstacle to colour's satisfying condition
(iv) is posed by this view of the relationship between colour and the microphysical,
since the microphysical account of the determinants of the extension of 'blue', for
example, will not, presumably, entail that appropriate provisional equations can be
formulated satisfying conditions (i)–(iii).

Contrast now the situation of shape. Suppose *x* is some nearby middle-sized object, and consider the judgement, '*x* is pear-shaped'. We will want to characterise the conditions which are cognitively ideal for the visual appraisal of *x*'s shape in terms very similar to those suggested for the case of colour. But there are differences. One, relatively unimportant, is that the lighting conditions do not have to be as good; sodium street-lighting, for instance, is suitable enough for recognising shapes. But a second, much more important, consideration is that a single thinker's *best* opinion about three-dimensional shape, if visually grounded, must needs be the product of *several* observations, from a suitable variety of spatial positions. And in order for it to be a priori true that, subject to whatever other conditions we wish to impose, such a subject's opinion about the shape of *x* will be correct, we must ensure that no *change* in *x*'s shape takes place through the period of these several observations. But that calls for some ingredient in the C-conditions of which it is an *a priori* consequence that whatever it is true to say of *x*'s shape at any time during the subject's observations is also true at any other time within the relevant period. Some independent determinant is therefore called for of what it *is* true to say about *x*'s shape during that period—independent, that is, of the opinion formed by the thinker. There is accordingly, it seems, no immediate prospect of a provisional equation for '*x* is pear-shaped' meeting both conditions (i) and (iii) above.

A natural response is that there is no reason why a particular kind of subject-matter might not dictate that the formation of a best opinion required *teamwork*. What if we discharge the single observer and consider instead the opinion concerning *x*'s shape which would be arrived at cooperatively by a number of strategically positioned subjects who observed *x* at the same time? That should filter out the problem of instability. But there is a deeper problem which brings out, I think, the real point of disanalogy between shape and colour. The application of shape predicates, even ones as rough and ready as 'pear-shaped', is answerable to a variety of considerations besides visual appearance. For instance, a solid is pear-shaped only if any maximal two-dimensional section of it describes two contiguous circles of substantially different sizes. But it cannot be an a priori truth that conditions of the kind which we regard as optimal for the visual detection of shape are adequate for the reliable visual detection of characteristics which are in this way answerable to such operational considerations. The operational criteria dominate the visual—that is why the Müller-Lyer illusion is a *visual* illusion. And we can well enough imagine starting out again, as if at the dawn of our intellectual history, armed with the concepts which we have now but with no experience of the world, and finding that the cost of maintaining the thesis that reliable visual appraisals of shapes are generally possible would be a disorderly plague of hypotheses about changes in shape, forced on us by the need to reconcile our visual appraisals with operational ones. It is an a posteriori courtesy of experience that the world in which we actually live is not of this awkward kind. And if that is right, then no kind of true provisional equation for visual judgements of shape, even if it invokes teamwork and thereby meets the independence condition (iii), can be both a priori and substantial.[38]

I am not, of course, presenting these remarks as establishing conclusively that (a base class of) judgements of colour fail the order-of-determination test, while judgements of shape pass it.[39] Nor is it clear that the considerations advanced, even as far as they go, will generalise to other instances of the primary/secondary distinction. My pur-

---

38. This train of thought is elaborated somewhat in Wright (1988), pp. 19–20.

39. Various interesting further questions have to be negotiated which I cannot go into here. For instance, might best *operationally determined* (contrast: visually determined) beliefs about shape arguably play an extension-determining role, or are even such beliefs at most extension-reflecting? One germane consideration would be that very many shape concepts—'pear-shaped' is an example—are, while operationally constrained, subject to no obvious operational, as opposed to tactuo-visual criteria of application. Another would be that we would expect to need stability provisos in the appropriate lists of C-conditions for operationally determined beliefs, since proper execution of the appropriate kinds of operation is essentially subject to invalidation by instability. It would be pleasant if that consideration were decisive, but I do not think that it is. For it may perhaps be mitigated by some play with the *positive-presumptiveness* of assumptions of stability, along the lines illustrated in the next section of the essay for the role of lack of self-deception in the C-conditions for appraisal of one's own intentions.

pose is, rather, to indicate one framework for the discussion and development of the test: to give credence to the thought that there is a distinction here—perhaps a number of distinctions—and an explanatory programme of potential importance.

Nevertheless, if the gist of the foregoing is correct, visual judgements of colour will emerge as an interesting mix of subjectivity and objectivity. They should not, at least in a basic class of cases, when appropriate C-conditions are met, be regarded as responsive to states of affairs which are constituted independently—our best opinions about colour do not, in that sense, *track* colour. But neither is it the case that there is no standard to meet, that whatever we say about colour goes or—what comes to the same thing—that there is no such thing as an object's real colour. Rather, it is a perfectly objective question what, in a particular case, the deliverance of best opinion would be; and that deliverance is something with which a majority, or even a whole community, may for some reason be out of accord.

IV

I pass now to the second set of potential examples which I want to air, namely, self-ascriptions of psychological states like sensation, emotion, mood, belief, desire, and intention—the traditional category of *avowals*. The proposal that such judgements are extension-determining is an extremely attractive one. The traditional Cartesian epistemology attempts to construe avowals in general on the model of a certain conception of what is involved in competent self-ascription of *sensation*—a model which draws heavily on a comparison with perception of material objects, but with the crucial differences that the sensation, *qua* 'inner' object, is accessible only to the subject, whose gaze is conceived as all-seeing and error-proof. As a picture of knowledge of one's own sensations, this generates problems enough, principally by its presupposition of the operability of private schemes of classification—'private languages'. But, even if we let the Cartesian account of sensation pass, it provides only the most feeble basis for an account of the self-ascription of other kinds of psychological states. For there are no plausible introspectible processes or states which are candidates to be, for instance, beliefs and intentions. And besides— and more important—to think of, for example, intention as an introspectible episode in consciousness generates no end of difficulties and contortions when we try to make sense of the necessarily holistic character of the scheme of beliefs, desires and intentions by reference to which we explain subjects' behaviour, and of the notion of *fit* between an intention and the behaviour which implements it. One of the most central themes in Wittgenstein's later philosophy of mind is the idea that Cartesianism is based on a *grammatical* misunderstanding, a misinterpretation of the language-game of self- and otherascription of mental states. The Cartesian takes the authority of avowals as a symptom f, as it were, a superlatively sure genre of detection. We should accomplish a very sharp perspective on the sense in which this is a 'grammatical' misunderstanding if it could be shown that avowals fail the order-of-determination test—in other words, that subjects' best opinions determine, rather than reflect what it is true to say about their intentional states, with the consequence that the notion of detection or 'inner tracking', as it were, is inappropriate. (Naturally, it would have to be part of a satisfying development in this direction that best opinions about one's own intentional states turned out to be very easily accomplished and normal; otherwise, the authority of avowals would be unaccounted for.)

Can we, then, provide a set of conditions whose satisfaction will ensure, a priori, that subjects will believe themselves to have, for example, certain particular intentions if and only if they do? Well, how might a subject who had the conceptual resources to form a belief appropriate to the presence, or absence, of a certain intention, nevertheless fail to do so? Self-deception is one possibility, whatever the correct account of that puzzling idea. A subject may, as many people think, be simply unable to bring to consciousness the real intentions which inform certain of his courses of action. Conversely, we are familiar with the kind of weak-mindedness which can lead subjects into deceiving themselves that they have formed certain intentions—usually ones which are desirable but difficult of implementation—when in truth they have not done so.

In both these kinds of case, we typically regard the self-deceptive (lack of) belief as *motivated*. But in certain other circumstances it would be better to think of it as having a primarily physiological—perhaps a pharmacological—explanation. The cause of a subject's mistaken belief about her intentions need not reside in other aspects of her intentional psychology. Anyway, one way or another, an appropriate set of C-conditions will have to ensure that nothing of this kind is operative. And in addition, we need only include, it seems, a condition to the effect that the subject be appropriately attentive to the question what her intentions are. However, nothing in what follows will depend on whether these three conditions—grasp of the appropriate concepts, lack of any material self-deception or anything relevantly similar, and appropriate attentiveness—do indeed suffice.

The most salient difficulty, for our purposes, with the provisional biconditional which will emerge from these suggestions is that of making a case that it meets condition (ii)—the condition that the C-conditions be substantially specified. The motive for condition (ii) was not a distaste for triviality as such, it will be remembered, but rather for the particular kind of triviality involved in 'whatever-it-takes' formulations. Such formulations are always possible and, by prejudicially representing matters in terms of the jargon of tracking, leave us with no way of getting at the distinction which it is the point of the order-of-determination test to capture. And on the face of it, unfortunately, we are some considerable distance from a formulation of the no-self-deception condition which can count as non-trivial in the relevant sense. The problem is, first, that 'self-deception' covers, for the purposes of the biconditional, *any* motivated condition which might lead to a subject's ignorance or error concerning his or her intentions; and, second, we need, as noted, to allow for the possibility of *un*motivated conditions—chemically induced ones, or whatever—with the same effect. So we seem to be perilously close to writing in a condition to the effect that the subject be 'free of any condition which might somehow impede her ability reliably to certify her own intentions'. And that, of course, is just the sort of insubstantial, whatever-it-takes formulation which condition (ii) was meant to exclude.

Perhaps it is possible to do better, to produce some descriptions which exclude the relevant class of states but does so non-trivially. But none comes to mind, and it would of course be pointless to wait on the deliverances of empirical science if one is hoping for vindication of an extension-determining view of the beliefs expressed by avowals, and so requires something which will subserve the *a priority* of the resulting biconditional. So how to proceed?

We have, I think, to depart somewhat from the approach which emerged in the case of colour. But a possible variant of it is suggested by the reflection that the troublesome no-self-deception condition is *positive-presumptive*. By that I mean that, such is the 'grammar' of ascriptions of intention, one is entitled to assume that a subject is *not* materially self-deceived, or unmotivatedly similarly afflicted, unless one possesses determinate evidence to the contrary. Positive-presumptiveness ensures that, in all circumstances in which one has no countervailing evidence, one is a priori justified in holding that the no-self-deception condition is satisfied, its trivial specification notwithstanding. Suppose, then, that we succeed in constructing an a priori true provisional biconditional:

$$C(\text{Jones}) \rightarrow$$
$$(\text{Jones believes he intends to } \phi \leftrightarrow \text{Jones intends to } \phi),$$

where C includes the (trivial) no-self-deception condition but no other trivially formulated conditions. Then if—lacking evidence to the contrary—we are a priori justified in holding the no-self-deception condition to be met, we are also a priori justified in believing the result of deleting that condition from the provisional biconditional in question. Likewise for any other positive-presumptive conditions listed under C. In this way we can eventually arrive at a restricted provisional biconditional in which all the C-conditions are substantially specified and which, in the absence of any information bearing on whether the conditions are satisfied which we have deleted from it, it is a priori *reasonable* to believe.

It is true that we are now dealing with something a priori credible rather than a priori true. But the question still arises: what is the *explanation* of the a priori credibility, in the relevant kind of circumstances of ignorance, of the restricted version if what determines the fact of Jones's intention, under the residual C-conditions, is something quite detached from his belief? The explanation cannot be that the C-conditions are trivially formulated, for they are all, by hypothesis, substantial.

Suppose that the three conditions suggested above—possession of the appropriate concepts, attentiveness, and lack of self-deception—do indeed suffice a priori for Jones's opinion about his intention to covary with the facts. But suppose also that possession of the relevant concepts and attentiveness raise, unlike lack of self-deception, no problems of triviality. Then the matter for explanation is: why is it a priori reasonable to believe that, provided Jones has the relevant concepts and is attentive to the matter, he will believe that he intends to ♀ if and only if he does? The key thought of the variant approach will be that the matter will be nicely explained if the concept of intention works in such a way that Jones's opinions, formed under the restricted set of C-conditions, play a *defeasible* extension-determining role, with defeat conditional on the emergence of evidence that one or more of the background, positive-presumptive, conditions are not in fact met.

To elaborate a little. There are, in contrast to the case argued for colour, no conditions which can be characterised non-trivially but independently—in the sense of condition (iii) above—whose satisfaction a priori ensures covariance of a subject's beliefs about his intentions and the facts. But there are such non-trivially, independently specifiable conditions whose satisfaction ensures, courtesy of no a posteriori background beliefs, that, failing any other relevant information, a subject's opinions about his or her intentions should be accepted. And the proposed strategy of explanation is, roughly, as follows. What determines the distribution of truth values among ascriptions of intention to a subject who has the conceptual resources to understand those ascriptions and is attentive to them are, in the first instance, nothing but the details of the subject's self-conception in relevant respects. If the assignment of truth values, so effected, generates behavioural singularities—the subject's behaviour clashes with ingredients in her self-conception, or seems to call for the inclusion of ingredients which she is unwilling to include—then the self-deception proviso, broadly interpreted as above, may be invoked, and the subject's opinion, or lack of it, overridden. But that is not because something is shown, by the discordant behaviour, about the character of some *independently constituted* system of intentions which the subject's opinions at best reflect. When possession of a certain intention is an aspect of a self-conception that coheres well enough both internally and with the subject's behaviour, there is nothing *else* that makes it true that the intention is indeed possessed.

The view proposed is minimalist. Nothing leaner has any prospect, so far as I can see, of accommodating both the avowability and the theoreticity of intention. To be sure, explaining the a priori reliability of a subject's C-conditioned beliefs about her intentions will do nothing to explain the reliability of her avowals—even assuming our right to regard her as honest—unless the C-conditions in question are likely to be met. But there seems no cause to anticipate problems on that score. Attentiveness—however precisely it should be elaborated—is presumably, like lack of self-deception, a positive-presumptive condition; and a subject's possession of the appropriate concepts is prerequisite for her being able to effect the avowal in the first place. So there is every promise of a straightforward kind of explanation of the authority which avowals of intention, *qua* avowals, typically carry.

Suppose, by contrast, that subjects' best opinions about their intentions are at most extension-reflecting. Then the a priori reasonableness, when nothing else relevant is known, of the restricted provisional biconditional needs another explanation. And providing one will require explaining how it coheres with the view that subjects' best opinions track independently constituted states of affairs to suppose it a priori reasonable to think, failing evidence to the contrary, that some of the conditions on an opinion's being best are satisfied. Why, in the absence of germane evidence, is *agnosticism* about the satisfaction of, for example, the self-deception condition not a preferable stance? The three conditions collectively formulate, on this view, what it takes to ensure a certain kind of cognitive accomplishment, a feat of detection. Why is it a priori warranted to assume, failing information to the contrary, that a subject satisfies any such conditions?

To avoid misunderstanding, I do not mean to present the question as rhetorical. There are various ways in which it might be approached by an opponent of the extension-determining view. Perhaps it could be made out that the warrant somehow flows from the subject's nature, *qua* subject, or from the nature of the states of affairs—the intentions in question are *hers*, after all—of which the conditions ensure her detection. Alternatively, perhaps other examples can be produced where best opinions are extension-reflecting and yet certain of the conditions on their being best are likewise positive-presumptive, for general reasons which might be argued to apply to the present case. But it is fair to say, I think, that the onus is now on someone who prefers to think that one's best opinions about one's own intentions, etc., are extension-reflecting. Why are we, apparently, so cavalierly optimistic about our general fitness for such detection? And what, fundamentally, when we succeed in holding best opinions, *does* determine the extension of the truth predicate among the class of judgements in question, if not those opinions themselves?

My purpose in introducing the psychological was only the limited one of canvassing a second shape which the attempt to refine and apply the order-of-determination test might assume. Perhaps enough has been said to accomplish that. But note a prospective corollary, if the extension-determining character of subjects' best opinions about their intentions and similar states, and the authority typically carried by avowals of such states, can indeed be accounted for along the lines proposed. Earlier, I criticised responses to Kripke's Sceptical Argument which—like the dispositional conception, or Chomsky's own proposal—locate the called-for meaning-constitutive facts only at the cost of obscuring subjects' non-inferential knowledge of their own meanings. It would be appropriate to level a similar complaint against dispositional or theoretical construals of the notion of intention. But no such complaint is appropriate against an account of self-knowledge of intention further developed along the lines canvassed: one according to which subjects' best opinions about their intentions, *both past and present,* are properly conceived as provisionally extension-determining, and which explains how and why the opinions which they typically hold are indeed best. It will be, similarly, a perfect answer to Kripke's sceptic to explain how judgements concerning one's own meanings, both past and present, are likewise provisionally extension-determining in the most ordinary circumstances. Challenged to justify the claim that I formerly meant addition by 'plus', it will not be necessary to locate some meaning-constitutive fact in my former behaviour or mental life. A sufficient answer need only advert to my present opinion, that addition is what I formerly meant, and still mean, and to the a priori reasonableness of the supposition, failing evidence to the contrary, that this opinion is best.

Responding to Kripke's sceptic in this way does not require construal of meaning precisely as a species of intention; it is enough that the concepts are relevantly similar—that both sustain authoritative first-personal avowals,[40] and that this circumstance is to be explained in terms of failure of the order-of-determination test. However, I can go no further into the matter here except to record the view that it is indeed with the conception of meanings as items which our best opinions may *reflect,* rather than with their reality *tout court,* that the Sceptical Argument engages.[41]

40. Note that the most likely reservation about the claim that they do—the thought that certain elements of *convention,* which have no counterpart in the case of intending in general, sustain my ability to mean anything in particular by a word—will undercut the sceptic's strategy in any case, since restricting the search for facts about my former meanings to aspects of my former behaviour and conscious mental states will precisely exclude the relevant conventional (presumably social) elements. I am here indebted to Bob Hale.

41. For further discussion, see Wright (1987a) (this volume Essay 5).

V

Correctly applying a rule to a new case will, it is natural to think, typically involve a double success: sensitivity is necessary both to the relevant features of the presented situation and to what, in respect of those features, will fit or fail to fit the rule. Correctly castling in the course of a game of chess, for instance, will depend both on apprehension of the configuration of chessmen at the time of the move, and on a knowledge of whether that configuration (and the previous course of the game) permits castling at that point. In this respect the simple mathematical examples on which Wittgenstein's discussion concentrates are apparently untypical. Knowing how to continue a series does of course require knowledge of what point in the series one has reached, and also in certain cases some knowledge about the preceding constitution of the series beyond the identity of the immediately preceding element. But there need be no *perceptual* input, corresponding to perception of the board configuration in chess. Wittgenstein's examples thus approximate as closely as possible to cases of *pure* rule-following, where only one kind of sensitivity—that concerning the requirements of the rule—is necessary for success, and failure has to be attributed to an imperfect understanding of the rule or to some technical slip in applying it. That is, presumably, why he selects just those examples. In order to focus on questions concerning the objectivity and epistemology of rule-following, it is obviously best to consider cases where our judgements about what accords with the rule are most nearly pure and unconditioned by the cognitive effects upon us of the prevailing circumstances.

Absolute purity is, however, impossible. The judgement that *this* move accords with a particular rule can never be informed only and purely by one's understanding of the rule. So much is clear when one reflects that aberrant performance, even in simple arithmetical cases and when there is no question of insincerity, can always in principle be explained in ways which conserve the hypotheses that the subject correctly understands the rule and, relative to what she took to be the situation, applied it correctly. The subject may, for instance, have lost her place, misremembered what she had done before, or misunderstood some relevant symbol not involved in the expression of the rule.

The ability successfully to follow a rule is thus to be viewed as, at each successive instance, the product of a number of cognitive responses which interact holistically in the production of the proper step. And some of these responses—correctly perceiving the set-up on the chess board, for instance, or recollecting the expansion of the series to this point—do not strictly pertain to the rule but are possible for subjects who have no inkling of it. Where R is the rule or set of rules in question, let us call the others 'R-informed'. Now, an R-informed response need not be encapsulable in any judgement which the subject can articulate distinct from the output judgement, as it were—the judgement into which her R-informed and non-R-informed responses conjointly feed. In that respect, the chess example, in which the R- and non-R-informed components could be respectively explicitly entertained as the major and minor premises for a modus ponens step, is untypical. I cannot always have concepts *other* than those whose governing rules I am trying to observe in a particular situation in terms of which I can formulate a separate judgement of the input to which these rules are to be applied. So I cannot always extricate and articulate a judgement which, conditionally on such a separate judgement of the input, formulates my impression of the requirements of the rules in a fashion which is neutral with respect to the correctness of my R-*un*informed responses to the situation.

It is a platitude that the existence of a rule requires that some sort of content be given to the distinction, among responses which are informed by it, between those which are acceptable and those which are not. The fundamental question raised by the topic of rule-following concerns the ground and nature of this distinction. However, the points about holism and inextricability counsel caution in the formulation of this question. There is, for instance, because of the point about holism, no simple relation between questions concerning what makes for acceptable R-informed responses and questions to do with *truth*, as applied to the output judgements to which those responses holistically contribute. Indeed, we cannot always—because of the point about inextricability—equate the acceptability of a rule-informed response with the truth of any judgement made by the subject—at least, not if such a judgement has to consist in an articulate belief.

Clearly, then, there is some awkwardness in attempting to apply the distinction drawn by the order-of-determination test to the question of the ground and nature of the requirements of a rule. The test, as so far considered, calls for a class of judgements about which we can raise the question of the relation between best opinion and truth. And the existence of such judgements is just what the inextricability point counsels us not to expect in general. Still, there are extricable cases. The example of castling in chess provided one. And, most significant in the present contest, the comprehending response to a novel utterance provides another. Such a response will involve a set of beliefs about the utterance which someone could have who had no understanding of the language in question; but it will also involve a belief about what, modulo the former set, has been said—a paradigm, it would seem, of a rule-informed judgement. Rather than confront the awkwardnesses presented by inextricability, therefore, let me concentrate for our present purposes on such favourable cases: cases where the acceptability of a rule-informed response can be seen as a matter of the truth of a judgement which the responder may be thought of as making. Our question, then, is: what makes for the truth of such rule-informed judgements?

Irrealism is an option. One could hold that such judgements answer to nothing real, not even the deliverances of best opinion. Rather, making acceptable such judgements really is just a matter of keeping in step with the community of followers of the relevant rules. This would be, in effect, the opinion of Kripke's Wittgenstein.

A variation—no longer strictly irrealist—would hold that such judgements are true just in case there is agreement *in* them, and that this is the 'agreement in judgements' which is a precondition for the possibility of language serving as a means of communication (*Investigations* §242). It might be thought that, as an interpretation of

Wittgenstein anyway, this variant of the irrealist thought is ruled out by his explicit repudiation[42] of any identification of truth with consensus. But that would be a bad reason. Consensualism about the truth-conditions of R-informed judgements would be quite consistent with repudiating consensualism concerning the output judgements to which, in association with relevant non-R-informed judgements, they contribute on particular occasions.

Platonism is also a possibility. Platonism is, precisely, the view that the correctness of a rule-informed judgement is a matter quite independent of any opinion of ours, whether the states of affairs which confer correctness are thought of as man-made—constituted by over-and-done-with episodes of explanation and linguistic behaviour—or truly Platonic and constituted in Heaven. For the Platonist, correctly following a rule in a particular situation involves a double-feat of tracking: one has to detect both all relevant aspects of the situation and the relevant requirements of the rule. But the principal negative point of Wittgenstein's discussion of rule-following was precisely that the ability to make acceptable rule-informed judgements allows of no coherent construal as a tracking ability, in the fashion which Platonism requires.

That leaves the possibility for which I have been labouring to prepare. Abandoning Platonism need not involve abandoning the objectivity of rule-informed judgements. There remains the option of regarding such judgements as extension-determining, of seeing *best* opinion as constituting their truth. I would like to be in a position to offer a supported opinion about whether this idea can be approached along the lines sketched for the cases of colour and intention. But I have, at the time of writing, no settled opinion to offer about that, let alone about whether the idea can ultimately be made good.

In summary: once it is agreed that the essential Platonist thought is that best opinion about the correctness of rule-informed judgements is extension-reflecting, and that part of Wittgenstein's purpose was, in effect, to demonstrate the untenability of that view, the would-be

42. See references on p. 188 above.

interpreter of Wittgenstein on rules faces four broad choices. First, there is 'official' Wittgensteinianism, of which the hallmark is scorn of constitutive questions. Asked what constitutes the truth of rule-informed judgement of the kind we isolated, the official Wittgensteinian will reply: 'Bad question, leading to bad philosophy—Platonism, for instance, or Kripkean scepticism'. If official Wittgensteinianism is rejected, on the other hand, and the constitutive question is allowed, there seem to be three options, each consistent with the repudiation of Platonism. First, there is the thesis that *nothing* constitutes the truth of such judgements, and that this is an important and disturbing contrast which marks them off from judgements of other kinds. This inherently unstable view is in essence that of Kripke's Wittgenstein. Second, there is consensualism, as canvassed above. And finally there is the proposal that the truth-makers for such judgements—the facts in which their correctness consists—are constituted by the deliverances of best opinion.

VI

The concern of the Central Project was to explain our recognition of the syntax and sense of novel sentences. The judgements accomplished by such recognition are, as noted, naturally taken to be rule-informed judgements par excellence, which in turn contribute holistically, in association with other judgements of features of the presenting circumstances and with certain background beliefs, to opinions concerning the proper use, or specifically the truth or falsity, of the sentence in the circumstances. So, if the options are as just described, what now are the prospects for the thought that our recognition of (agreement in judgement about) the meanings of novel sentences calls for a deep cognitive-psychological explanation, the *ur*-thought of the Central Project? Platonism might sustain it; but if that is the only way it can be sustained, then there is after all, a real collision between Wittgenstein's thought and the Central Project, and one might well want to side with Wittgenstein. 'Official'

Wittgensteinianism, as we have seen, and Kripkean Wittgensteinianism, by contrast, both undermine the thought. And the same is presumably true of the consensualist option. If the correctness of a rule-informed judgement is simply constituted by our agreement in it, there seems to be no call for a cognitive-psychological account of that agreement. On the contrary, the provision of such an account would immediately restore the idea that, since consensus in a rule-informed judgement would be the product of certain purely cognitive accomplishments, there ought to be some fact about what in any particular case, independently of our actual dispositions of response to it, the *proper* exercise of the relevant cognitive skills and informational states would culminate in; space, in other words, for the idea that an actual consensus might, in a particular case, be misplaced.[43]

With Platonism out of the way, the Central Project, as a project in cognitive psychology, would thus appear to demand the view that the correctness of the relevant rule-informed judgements—semantic responses to novel utterances—is objective but best-opinion-determined—the view that semantic content is, if you like, *secondary* in Lockean terms. If that view can be sustained, then the cognitive-psychological project is properly seen as directed not at the description of the conditions for a certain kind of tracking accomplishment—that conception has to fall with Platonism—but at the detailed elaboration of the C-conditions whose realisation ensures that a subject's judgement of the content of a particular novel utterance will be *best*. The Central Project is thus prima facie compatible with Wittgenstein's thought-about rules, if the upshot of the latter is indeed (at least compatible with the claim) that judgements of content, and of the requirements of rules in general, are extension-determining.

Whatever the proper interpretation of Wittgenstein, the outstanding substantive questions are accordingly whether the order-of-determination test can be refined and developed sufficiently to allow a clear-cut application to judgements of content, with their failure of

---

43. Exactly the idea enshrined in the distinction between *competence* and *performance*, of course.

the test—their classification as extension-determining—as the outcome; and whether the then emergent notion of *best* opinion will contain components whose proper description will require—or, less, allow—invoking the apparatus of theoretical linguistics. We are a long way from knowing what is correct to think about either question. But it may be some advance to be a little clearer about some of the respects in which matters are unclear.

🖋

I am very grateful to Paul Boghossian and Bob Hale for helpful discussion of an earlier draft of this essay.

PART THREE

PRIVACY AND

SELF-KNOWLEDGE

The four essays I have grouped together here are devoted to the dominant themes in the latter half of *Philosophical Investigations*, from §242 onwards. They are focused on Wittgenstein's rejection of the Cartesian conception of psychological privacy, and on the light which his discussions cast on the asymmetries between our knowledge of others and our knowledge of ourselves.

Essay 8 is an extended discussion of the central point of *Investigations* §258—the famous passage about the private diarist which, prior to Kripke's interpretation, had usually been regarded as the heart of the 'private language argument'. The main ideas of this paper formed part of the presentation on Kripke's book which I prepared for the 1982 Wittgenstein Symposium at Kirchberg, but it soon grew into a self-contained talk, and then beyond one, under the stimulus of various colloquia and presentations. According to Kripke's exegesis, the argument against private language is essentially merely a corollary of the rule-following considerations (the latter viewed as the harnessed pair of Sceptical Argument and Sceptical Solution); so to challenge Kripke's interpretation is, naturally, to invite the question how better the relationship between the critique of private language and the discussion of following a rule should be conceived. My view was (and is) nearer to the older interpretation than to Kripke's: there is an all but self-contained argument against private language pointed to in §258. Moreover, not merely is this argument not a direct corollary of anything that has happened before §202: it is actually one strand in the weave that goes to make up the rule-following considerations—an argument that a Platonist conception of rules, and of the epistemology of following them, can find no refuge in the situation of a thinker whose conceptual resources are presumed independent of the possibility of their communication to another. The argument is not quite self-contained, however, for it emerges that driving it home does presuppose something close to the constructivist or 'secondary' conception of intention and cognate concepts which came to the forefront in the essays in Part Two.

For his private diarist, Wittgenstein charges, there would be no— or anyway insufficient—distance between circumstances when it *seemed* to her that a new sensation merited an entry as 'S again' and circumstances when a sensation *really did* merit that entry. And that, he suggests, subverts the whole idea of correctness as applied to such entries. As explained in Essay 8, such a distinction is required in order for there to be any content to the idea that the diarist's impressions are *of* anything, that they are responsive to self-standing events and states of affairs, just as ordinary observation reports are responsive to events and states of affairs in public space. But granted that the distinction is required, why is Wittgenstein so confident that it cannot be drawn? It may seem obvious enough that the diarist won't be able to *practise* the distinction: on any particular occasion, she will be unable to contrast what seems right to her on the occasion and what really is so. But why, in order for that contrast to have content, does she have to be able to practise it at all? Isn't that a tacit assumption of some form of verificationism? And even if that assumption is granted, why is it of *contemporaneous* impressions and facts that she is required to make some sort of contrast—why would it not suffice to make the contrast *retrospectively*?

A suggestion about how the diarist might indeed make principled retrospective contrasts between private facts about her experience and her impressions of those facts was in the wind when I was a graduate student in Cambridge, and later surfaced in the writings of some of my contemporaries.[1] The thought was, in brief, that there are two principled ways of correcting one's impressions of things: one—which Wittgenstein seems to presuppose to be the only way—is on the basis of conflict with the impressions of other competent judges; but the other—to which he pays no heed in this context—is on the basis of conflict with well-established generalisations and theory. Let the diarist be not merely a chronicler but a *theorist* of her sensations—in other words, let her have access to a well-tested theory which predicts patterns of recurrence and co-occurrence in her sensations, for instance—and she can get into position, in the light of the established success of her theory, to discount an impression that a certain sensation has occurred in just the way that well-established scientific theory can stand in the face of a recalcitrant but amateur experiment. As Simon Blackburn put it, 'System soon enforces recognition of fallibility'.[2]

The principal task of Essay 8 is to show that this prospect is bogus. More specifically: although one can readily foresee simple little theories which—to the extent that theory may ever be held reasonably to overrule apparent observation—would prima facie require the diarist to correct certain of her impressions, the capacity of a theory genuinely to carry an overall content capable of delivering this result will depend, so it is argued, on its ability to deliver corrections in principle for *every* type of 'observation' which can bear on the acceptability of its lower-level hypotheses. In other words, the theory must be such that for each observation which one can formulate in its language, it would be reasonable, in certain circumstances, to reject that observation on the basis just of other observations and (justified) acceptance

1. Ross Harrison (1974) and Simon Blackburn (1984)—details in Essay 8.
2. Blackburn (1984), p. 300.

of the theory. One finding of the essay is that no matter how (finitely) many types of sensation the diarist chooses to record,[3] there *will* indeed be possible theories which have this property. But a second finding—which I confess to pursuing somewhat as a *jeu d'esprit*—is that such theories become vanishingly scarce the larger the variety of presumed phenomenal kinds that the diarist wishes to document. For example, if she chooses to record occurrences of just five sensation types, the chances of their falling into a phenomenological pattern which is prima facie corroborative of a theory with the required potentiality for corrections are a paltry 1 in 8,192!

A proper generalisation of this 'scarcity' result is actually quite difficult to obtain. After I'd finished the philosophical part of the paper and had the technical problem sufficiently sharply formulated, I wrote round to a number of logicians to see if I could interest them in it. The only one to manage a positive response was Warren Goldfarb, who showed essentially that as the number of sensation types recordable within the private language increases, so the ratio of instances of the needed kind of theory to all possible theories tends to zero. A version of the essentials of his reasoning appears in the Appendix to Essay 8. I'm glad to have the opportunity to acknowledge his friendly contribution to my project once again here, which I've always regarded as an act of unusual scholarly generosity.

Formal pyrotechnics apart, the philosophically serious point is that the 'let-the-diarist-be-a-theorist' response to Wittgenstein's point has very limited mileage in it: in particular, it is incapable of saving the very Cartesian intuitions which motivate its proposal in the first place. For they certainly provide no room for the thought that whether the diarist is dealing in contents apt for the expression of genuine self-knowledge or not has anything to do with the slim chance that she has been moved to construct a theoretical structure of the necessary kind.

None of this, however, engages the other reservation about Wittgenstein's train of thought in §258: why should it be necessary, in

3. Provided there are more than two!

order for the distinction between the diarist's impressions and the real facts to have any content, that it be a distinction which she, or anybody else, can *practise?* Anyone who really was infallible and all-seeing about a certain subject matter—as Cartesianism envisages each of us to be with respect to our own sensations—would indeed never have any *use* for a contrast between what seemed correct to them and what really was so. But if their infallibility was properly so termed—if it were a matter of their impressions genuinely *mirroring* the facts, rather than merely being operationally incorrigible—then there *would* be a distinction in the fashion demanded by objectivity: the facts and the impressions would be constitutionally separate, but march in step. Why couldn't it be like that for the diarist's impressions of her sensations?

Essay 8 takes some steps towards the treatment of this proposal, but a full discussion of it is reserved to Essay 9. This essay was first presented at the Eastern Division meeting of the American Philosophical Association (APA) at Atlanta in 1989, in a symposium with Warren Goldfarb and John McDowell on the thought of Wittgenstein. It's argument, in brief, is that the infallibilist pretensions of Cartesianism are unsustainable in any case—that fallibility must go with the very idea of representation, even when the possibilities for mishap are as restricted as in the case of judgement of one's own sensations. A fallibilist version of Cartesianism, on the other hand, has to explain what provides for the fact that a certain private concept applies, or fails to apply, in a case where the impression of the diarist is to the contrary. This is the point of engagement, signalled above, for the 'secondary quality' conception of intention. For the possibility the fallibilist must contemplate is precisely that what constitutes compliance with the diarist's erstwhile intentions is determined wholly independently of her impression of the matter.

Essays 10 and 11 constitute the two Whitehead Lectures I gave at Harvard in the spring of 1996. They represent a natural generalisation of the foregoing discussion. The primary philosophical problem of self-knowledge is not the current obsession—the prospects for its reconciliation with semantic externalism—but that of accounting for the apparent asymmetries, manifest in features of the use of 'avowals', between our knowledge of our own psychological states and our knowledge of those of others. Essay 10 offers analysis of these asymmetries in some detail and argues that the importation of the notion of privileged observation, which is the cornerstone of Cartesianism, should be viewed as an attempt to provide an *explanation* of them. Wittgenstein's various criticisms of the Cartesian notion, both for the case of phenomena of consciousness like sensations and for attitudinal and other intentional states, are reviewed; and the essay takes the opportunity to rebut certain criticisms of Essay 9 which were lodged by John McDowell in his commentary at the 1989 Eastern Division APA symposium at which that essay was originally presented. Essay 11 considers various non-Cartesian responses to the problem, including recent proposals of Tyler Burge, Donald Davidson and Christopher Peacocke, as well as the more traditional 'expressivist' conception of avowals, suggested to certain commentators by *Investigations* §244, which, it is argued, has greater resources than is usually supposed. All, however, are found wanting. And we therefore confront the question: how, if not in any of these ways, are the puzzling features of self-knowledge to be explained, and how did Wittgenstein himself propose to explain them?

In fact, these questions go to the heart of the agenda of Wittgenstein's later philosophy. All along he spares himself the labour of providing more satisfactory alternatives to the accounts he aims to demolish or make us uncomfortable with. The Platonist conception of rules and of their requirements is thoroughly debunked, but no alternative account of what constitutes the requirements of a rule, or of how we are supposed to recognise what its requirements are, is offered. (In effect, we are told only that there could be no such requirements but for our propensity to agree in judgements.) The Cartesian conception of the source of the asymmetries between self-knowledge and knowledge of others is debunked, but no better account is so much as gestured at. It's true that Wittgenstein wrote in the preface to the *Investigations* that he had no wish to spare his reader the labour of thinking the issues through for herself, but his reticence surely goes beyond anything that might be licensed by the restraint which that wish might justify! The explanation has to be, rather, that—exactly as his remarks about philosophical explanations and the roots of philosophical problems suggest—he did not believe that there was anything substantial to be said. The philosophical questions to which Platonism and Cartesianism are respectively bad answers do not need better answers: they need no answers.

This overarching 'quietist' tendency in Wittgenstein's thought is elaborated in the final section of Essay 11 and touched on again in the first of the two Postscripts. It contains certain internal tensions. But there is no doubt to my mind that contemporary analytical philosophy is far too unclear about its methods and objectives—of what it would be, for example, to 'give an account' of psychological self-knowledge in a fully satisfying, conservative, and yet non-Cartesian way—to allow us to be sure that Wittgenstein's quietism is not excellent advice.[4]

4. I have pursued some aspects of this issue in Wright (1992) chap. 6.

8   Does *Philosophical Investigations* §§258–60 Suggest a Cogent Argument against Private Language?

I.   What Is a 'Private' Language?

As the notion is usually understood in the literature, a private language is one which, necessarily, only one person can understand. Wittgenstein's own remarks (§§243, 256)[1] may encourage such an interpretation. But it is not quite right. Intuitively, two people share an understanding of a predicate if what qualifies an item to fall within its extension is the same for both of them. Accordingly, if I somehow invented a language apt for the description of material—sensations, or whatever—in principle accessible only to myself, someone else might nevertheless understand the language: he would do so if he associated with its various descriptions material of the same respective kinds as I associated with them. This is just the natural and familiar thought that, while the phenomenological qualia associated by each of us with the word 'pain' are unknowable by anyone else, and

---

1. All references in the text are to *Philosophical Investigations* unless otherwise stated.

are regarded as playing a constitutive role in our respective under-standings of 'pain', there may nevertheless *be* mutual understanding if, as it happens, our qualia are appropriately similar. Only, if at all, in the case of proper names for which knowledge of reference is held necessary for understanding would the inaccessibility of my material to others be an essential bar to shared grasp.

A successful polemic against private language is meant, inter alia, to refute this picture of the meaning of sensation vocabulary. Since the picture does not entail that each of our idiolects of sensation is private in the standard sense,[2] we need to qualify somewhat the usual terms of the discussion. Private language had better be, not a language which necessarily only one person can understand, but a language which necessarily no two people can have adequate reason to believe they share. If your pain-quale is inaccessible to me and constitutive of your understanding of 'pain', what (uncontroversially) follows is not that your understanding cannot coincide with mine but only that I cannot have adequate reason to think that it does.

It merits remark that the inaccessibility, to others, of a speaker's material would not be the only possible source of private language (in the qualified sense). For the condition presented above as sufficient for shared understanding is also necessary: even if we are speaking of material accessible to everybody, shared understanding of an expres-sion requires, in addition, that our uses of it be informed by the same conception of what qualifies an item to fall within its extension. So evidence of shared understanding has to involve evidence of a certain community of intention: evidence that we intend to let our respective uses of the expression be answerable to the same constraints. Now, a familiar sceptical line of reasoning aims to generate doubt whether a third party can ever have satisfactory evidence for the content of another's intention. If that were so, it would follow that intentions are, by their very nature, things which no two people can reasonably

2. As Edward Craig notes (1986), this point blocks any interpretation of Wittgen-stein's argument which would build directly upon the impossibility of *consensus* in the description of private material.

believe they share; so *all* language would be private, whether concerned with a publicly accessible subject matter or not.

The scepticism in question trades on the apparent first/third-personal asymmetry in our knowledge of intention. *My* intentions (to prescind from consideration of the unconscious) are immediately, that is non-inferentially, available to me, and my beliefs about them are authoritative. For *your* intentions, on the other hand, I have only the evidence of what you say and do. What you *say*, however, is of no evidential use to me until it is interpreted; that is, until I have arrived at grounded hypotheses concerning the intentions which inform (your use of the ingredients in) your utterances. So your linguistic behaviour, it appears, can justify me in attributing a certain intention to you—because, for example, you say you have it—only if I assume knowledge of others of your intentions—those which underpin what you mean by the various words you use. Presumably, therefore, the *ultimate* basis for my beliefs about your intentions must lie in your non-linguistic and uninterpreted linguistic behaviour. And now it appears that this 'basis' must inevitably be hopelessly crude: that no end of alternative construals of your intentions, beliefs and desires will be reconcilable with it. So, in outline, runs the sceptical argument: a prototype of the refinements respectively developed by W. V. Quine, in his writings on meaning and translation, and by Saul Kripke, in his exegesis of Wittgenstein.

II.   THE SIGNIFICANCE OF THE ISSUE

The reinterpretation of 'private' changes little: the philosophical consequences of the impossibility of private language remain extensive. First, solipsism will be an untenable position. Solipsism holds that no subject can have adequate reason to believe in the existence of any consciousness besides his own. It follows that no subject can have adequate reason to believe that he shares a language with another—since that would require belief in the *existence* of the other. From the standpoint of solipsism, language is essentially private; if there can be no such language, the solipsist is deprived of the medium in which to conduct his solipsist dialectic. A demonstration of the impossibility of private language will therefore be a demonstration that there is error in any philosophy of mind, or epistemology, which has the consequence that the existence of another consciousness is at best a groundless assumption.

Second, a remodelling will be required of the natural pre-philosophical conception, touched on above, of the kind of meaning possessed by our talk of sensations and other mental states. We tend to view the understanding each of us has of a word like 'pain' as possessing both a public and a subjective component. The public component is conceived as graspable by one incapable of feeling pain: it is constituted by our shared concept of what pain-behaviour is and of the consequences, personal and social, of someone's being in pain. The subjective component, in contrast, is fixed by the character of painful experience; only one who can suffer pain can imbue his understanding of the word with such a component, and the component is, in the nature of the case, idiosyncratic. Now, the niche here granted to a public component may be held to obviate any implication that the language of sensation, and of the passions generally, is already for each of us a private language. But if the felt quality of my experience has *some* part to play in determining the content of the relevant parts of my vocabulary, and if it is accepted that this quality can be known only by myself, it must follow, it seems, that we cannot have reason to think that we *fully* understand each other's talk of sensations, and so on. Besides, if it is coherent to grant that material in principle accessible only to me contributes at all towards determining what I mean, what obstacle can there be to the fiction of a language in which it makes the *sole* contribution—a full-fledged private language in just the sense we are concerned with? The natural pre-philosophical conception, even if it escapes the outcome that the language of sensations is already, for each of us, private, must at least, it appears, be committed to the *possibility* of a private language. Accordingly, a demonstration of private language's impossibility will be a demonstration that that conception cannot be the basis for a satisfactory philosophical understanding of the language of mind.

The issue is potentially of significance in at least one other important respect, connected with the crude Sceptical Argument adumbrated a moment ago. The first/third-personal asymmetry which we are tempted to find in the epistemology of intention is no less tempting, of course, in the case of a speaker's meaning; what *I* mean by an expression is available to me directly and with special surety, whereas the meaning *you* assign to that expression is, for me, a theoretical construct, earned by inference, and as precarious as any (strictly) unverifiable hypothesis. Once a speaker's meaning is so conceived, we can hardly avoid thinking of a communal language as itself a theoretical postulate; something which, if it exists at all, is constituted by the overlapping of first-personal transparent idiolects, but whose existence can be at best a good conjecture. Now, if the sceptical argument succeeds, 'good conjecture' has to be replaced by 'assumption'; and communal languages, if any exist, will have to be constituted by the overlappings of private languages. So if the sort of sceptical argument adumbrated is sound or, more generally, if the first/third-personal asymmetrical view destablises, under one form of pressure or another, to a point where only unjustifiable conjecture about my meanings is available to a third party, then a demonstration of the impossibility of private language will accomplish a proof that the intuitive asymmetry is already a misconception; that no priority can coherently be accorded to the notion of an idiolect, conceived as first-personally transparent, in an account of what a *communal* language is.[3]

The issue, then, is a pivotal one in general epistemology, in the philosophy of mind and in the philosophy of language. Not that I think that many doubt it. But a reminder may be salutary, when so much

---

3. Such a result would not have to be the death warrant of programmes—the most famous is H. P. Grice's—in which the notion of individual speaker's meaning is assigned priority. But it would require such programmes so to construe individual speakers' meanings as to build in third-personal availability from the outset.

of the literature has been preoccupied with its success or failure, of how deep the significance of a successful argument against private-language would penetrate. And we need to be clear, as I hope the above makes it clear, that this depth is in no way compromised by the modest reinterpretation of 'private language' with which I am going to work.

III. CONSTRAINTS ON A COGENT ARGUMENT AGAINST PRIVATE LANGUAGE

A genuinely cogent argument against private language will have to observe a number of special constraints.

First, whatever the detail of the argument, it had better not have the additional strength sufficient to make trouble for Robinson Crusoe. A private language is to be a language which no two people can *in principle* have adequate reason to believe they share: if the argument seems to show that merely *practical* obstacles—like desert island isolation—defeat the possibility of language, then, even if we can find no fault in it, it will fail of cogency because seeming to prove too much. To suppose that a solitary individual, even if isolated from birth, could not invent and utilise consistently (or as nearly consistently as need be) a system of notation could only be defensible, it seems, if it could be shown that *any* sort of rule-following was impossible for such an individual. And that seems preposterous: there is no limit to the kinds of behaviour in which such an individual might engage which would be utterly inexplicable unless construed as involving purpose, insight and the mastery of rules. (A nice example of Michael Dummett's: suppose Robinson finds a Rubik's Cube washed up on the beach, and learns to solve it.)

A second constraint is similar but more immediate: 'going public', as it were, must make all the difference. There are two ways in which this constraint might be violated. First, a seemingly genuine problem might be disclosed in private language which, however, would remain even after sufficient alteration in the content of its vocabulary to enable a number of speakers reasonably to believe that they had the language in common. Obviously, whatever independent interest the problem might then possess, it could not provide the basis of a specific argument against private language. And the same holds, second, if, although going public would solve a specific difficulty disclosed with private language, some relevantly *analogous* difficulty could plausibly be argued to beset language in general. A cogent argument against private language must leave communal language alone. Abstractly so presented, the point might seem hardly worth stating. But it has been violated by a number of interpretations of Wittgenstein, favoured both by sympathisers and critics; and it should anyway alert us to the risk attending the reading of Wittgenstein in this context as any sort of epistemological *sceptic,* despite the temptations posed by passages like §265.

A third desideratum, if not quite a constraint, is that the argument should be effective against two quite different opponents. The usual antagonist, for most commentators, has been *Cartesianism* about sensations: a standpoint according to which not merely are sensations private to a subject, but they constitute necessarily self-intimating material—no aspect of whose character can pass unnoticed—about which the subject's opinions have an error-proof authority. Now, no doubt the privacy of sensation has some connection, in Cartesian thinking, with its putatively self-intimating and indefeasibly certain character. But that there is at any rate no entailment is evident in the possibility of a weaker standpoint—that of the *fallibilist*—according to which the subject may be sincerely mistaken, or fall prey to oversight, in the description of his sensations or other psychological material, its privacy notwithstanding. The Cartesian conception encourages us to think of our sensations as events played out on a stage to which necessarily we alone are witness, but there is no reason why such a picture has to involve the idea that our witness has to be all-seeing and error-proof. Yet the fallibilist standpoint—well represented in recent literature[4]—is as much committed to the possibility of private language: if you are privy, albeit fallibly, to events and

4. See, e.g., Harrison (1974), chaps. 3, 6; Blackburn (1984).

processes of a kind of which you and I can never be *jointly* aware, even in principle, there is no means whereby I can make the sort of comparison between our respective linguistic behaviour necessary if I am to arrive at reasons to think that we share an understanding of the language we use to describe that material. Something worthy of the title of a demonstration of the impossibility of private language ought, therefore, to be effective against this weaker position. An argument of less general bearing, trading upon the additional features present in Cartesianism proper, might still be of some intrest. But it would necessitate no more than repair to the Cartesian philosophy of mind; it would not extract the root. And it could not have the wider sort of philosophical significance outlined in Section II.

IV. THREE INTERPRETATIONS OF §§258–60

It is worth quoting in full G. E. M. Anscombe's translation of the passage in *Philosophical Investigations* with which we are especially concerned:

(258) Let us imagine the following case. I want to keep a diary about the recurrence of a certain sensation. To this end I associate it with the sign 'S' and write this sign in the calendar for every day on which I have the sensation.—I will remark first of all that a definition of the sign cannot be formulated.—But still I can give myself a kind of ostensive definition—how? Can I point to the sensation? Not in the ordinary sense. But I speak, or write the sign down, and at the same time I concentrate my attention on the sensation—and so, as it were, point to it inwardly.—But what is this ceremony for? For that is all it seems to be! A definition surely serves to establish the meaning of a sign.—Well, that is done precisely by the concentrating of my attention; for in this way I impress on myself the connection between the sign and the sensation.—But 'I impress it on myself' can only mean: this process brings it about that I remember the connection *right* in the future. But in the present

case I have no criterion of correctness. One would like to say: whatever is going to seem right to me is right. And that only means that here we can't talk about 'right'.

(259) Are the rules of the private language *impressions* of rules?— The balance on which impressions are weighed is not the *impression* of a balance.

(260) 'Well, I *believe* that this is the sensation *S* again'. Perhaps you *believe* that you believe it! . . .

The principal question is: what is the thought at the end of §258? Why should it follow, if 'whatever is going to seem right to me is right', that the very notion of the *correctness* of the private linguist's would-be descriptions is emptied of content? Wittgenstein's transition has, indeed, the appearance of simple question-begging against the Cartesian; for if infallible authority, about any subject matter, were ever a possibility, then—trivially—whatever seemed right to the authority would be right. The Cartesian conception is exactly that each of us is an infallible authority for the character of their own sensations. A reader could be forgiven the impression that Wittgenstein has done nothing to disclose a specific fault in that conception of *sensation;* his reservation, whatever it is, would apply, it seems, to any such putative cognitive authority. And, whether one intuitively suspects the coherence of the idea of such authority or not, it does seem unclear what exactly the reservation is.

It will be useful to consider a number of interpretations which contrast with the one I want eventually to recommend. There is, to begin with, the possibility of reading the passage along the following, broadly verificationist lines. Meaning is an essentially normative notion: if an action—like making a noise, or marking down a symbol—is to be credited with meaning, there must accordingly be sense in the distinction between situations in which tokens of that action accord with this meaning and situations in which they do not. This is as much as to say that, from the point of view of a subject, trying to keep his actions in accordance with the meaning, there must be sense in the distinction between what seems right to him and what is right. For someone of verificationist sympathies, however, there has to be doubt about the *content* of a distinction which no one can possibly be in a position to exploit: a distinction, that is, between states of affairs which, in the nature of the case, cannot be verified to obtain independently of each other. For the verificationist, then, there is, in the case of putatively private language, doubt about the sense of a distinction which *has* to make sense if the notion of meaning, and with it that of language, is to have any proper application.

The spirit of this train of thought could, of course, be formulated and refined in various ways. It is notable, in particular, that its purpose would be as well served by the slogan 'Meaning is Use' as by explicit versions of the verification principle. For it is exactly the lack of any contrastive *uses* for 'seems right to me' and 'is right' which Wittgenstein seems to be presenting as undermining any contrast in their content. I myself would not regard the presence of verificationist premises in this context as necessarily importing any error of substance. Indeed, I had better declare now that the interpretation I shall eventually concentrate on is not guaranteed to disturb the privacy of a theorist who is *sufficiently* resolute and comprehensive in his fidelity to the verification-transcendent. Nevertheless, the rather *direct* play which the kind of argument sketched makes with a quite general verificationism about meaning has to be associated with costs in point of cogency.[5]

The answer provided by this first interpretation to our title question is, in effect: yes, provided there is a cogent argument for the veri-

---

5. The point is simply the unlikelihood that purely theoretical argument can provide absolutely compelling support for such a general principle: however well grounded it may seem, in the abstract, to be, consequences of a sufficiently *outré* character will generate suspicion. Anyone who wishes to base far-reaching metaphysical conclusions on (an analogue of) the verification principle had better recognise the substantial body of philosophical opinion which is prepared to find others of the known consequences of the principle to be sufficiently implausible to discredit its use as a tool of persuasion.

fication principle, or for the principle that differences in meaning must correspond to differences in use. What, I am suggesting, is doubtful is whether we have any conception of what it would be for argument in support of a principle of such generality to be *cogent* if 'intuitions' about the plausibility or implausibility of consequences are not allowed to come into play; and doubtful, in consequence, whether something as controversial as the present question can be resolved by an argument which relies directly on a general principle of this sort.

A second, quite natural interpretation finds Wittgenstein's thought to be that the private linguist has no basis for trust in his own judgement, no effective controls on his own competence to practise the system of concepts he believes his private language to encode. Now this is, I believe, a point that Wittgenstein is keen to have recognised; it may plausibly be read into §265 and seems to be exactly the thrust of:

> Always get rid of the idea of the private object in this way: assume that it constantly changes, but that you do not notice the change because your memory constantly deceives you.[6]

It is, from the inner perspective of the private linguist, all the same whether his ongoing practice keeps accord with the original, putatively definitive use of 'S', or whether his memory of the kind of sensation he wished to mark lets him down repeatedly and in diverse ways, so that his use of 'S' is actually quite chaotic. And there is, of course, no *other* perspective to be had. But what exactly does the point show? Well, that the Cartesian conception of the inner, characterised above, is itself unstable under sceptical attack. Wittgenstein is urging on the Cartesian the realisation that there is a difference between a guaranteed *fit* between impressions and fact and a mere inability to distinguish them. Once it is insisted that there really is to be such a thing as a *correct* description, in the private language, of the

6. *Investigations* II, §xi, p. 207.

subject's occurrent sensation, whose correctness is settled by the character of that sensation and the original private ostensive definition, there is absolutely no basis for an opinion about the reliability or otherwise of the subject's impression—so scepticism seems to be the only rational standpoint.

The point is well taken. But, whatever Wittgenstein's intention, it is plain that it is effective only against the Cartesian and does not tell against the possibility of private language as such. The fallibilist counter will be to acknowledge that, ultimately, there is no decisive riposte to sceptical doubt about his private linguistic competence, but then to enquire how exactly 'going public' would get around the difficulty. For one thing, the subject will still need to rely upon his own memory, and other faculties, if he is to make effective use of others' judgements as a check on his own, since ultimately he must judge for himself what their judgements are and whether they accord or conflict with his.[7] For another, no sooner do we admit—as we are inclined to do—that correctness is never *constituted* by a community-wide consensus than we leave scope for a similar kind of sceptical doubt about the shared judgements of the speakers of a public language: if coincidence between correctness and communal consensus is a matter of the proper functioning of individuals' faculties, it is difficult to see what could obstruct the possibility of sceptical query, of one or another familiar sort, about whether, in any particular case or range of cases, such proper functioning had taken place. If, on the other hand, there proved to be some sort of *conceptual* connection between correctness and the considered verdict of a whole linguistic community, that might well exempt the community from forms of sceptical doubt to which the private linguist is vulnerable; but it would be a conclusion for which we still await the supporting argument—which would have to embrace considerations quite beyond the scope of the interpretation we are presently considering. If this interpretation were correct, indeed, the verdict would have to be that, as a purported demonstra-

7. A point first made, I believe, by A. J. Ayer (1954) in the symposium with Rush Rhees.

tion of the impossibility of private language, §§258–60 falls foul of *each* of the three constraints outlined above.

There is evidence, however, that Wittgenstein may have wished a would-be believer in the possibility of private language to ponder what is apparently a deeper-reaching sceptical doubt.[8] A little earlier (§237) he writes:

> Imagine someone using a line as a rule in the following way: He holds a pair of compasses, and carries one of its points along the line that is the 'rule', while the other one draws the line that follows the rule. And while he moves along the ruling line he alters the opening of the compasses, apparently with great precision, looking at the rule the whole time as if it determined what he did. And watching him we see no kind of regularity in this opening and shutting of the compasses. We cannot learn his way of following the line from it. Here perhaps one really would say: 'The original seems to *intimate* to him which way he is to go. But it is not a rule'.

The quotation reminds us that there is a difference between following a rule and acting under a sense of constraint; it is even possible, as a result of hypnosis or in the throes of some sort of manic episode, to have the impression that you are rule-following, that your performance is guided by a concept, when that is not the case. The practice of private language is to be, at least, a rule-governed practice. What reason, then, can the private linguist offer *himself* for thinking that he genuinely has such a practice, that his performance is not to be compared to that of the lunatic with a pair of compasses?

This train of thought is in one way more, and in another less, sceptical than that which we have just discarded. It is more sceptical because what is in doubt is not the *reliability* of the judgements of the private linguist but whether he is so much as making judgements at all; at issue is not what grounds there are to think that the private linguist is competent to follow certain rules but what grounds there are

8. This line is briefly canvassed, if I read him correctly, in Stevenson (1982), pp. 45–6.

to think that there are any appropriate rules in the offing. But the train of thought is, at least arguably, also less sceptical inasmuch as it does not seem to need recourse to doubt about the subject's memory. Under the second interpretation, we were to imagine that changes in the type of sensation which the subject was willing to describe as 'S' are compensated for by changes in his memory of the kind of sensation which he originally so baptised; but the delusion, whatever exactly its nature, suffered by the lunatic with the compasses need not involve, it seems, his misremembering anything. This asymmetry suggests that the second interpretation may serve better than its predecessor. Challenged to produce a reason for thinking that he is using 'S' correctly, the private linguist will naturally refer to his memories of his previous practice; the challenge, if it is to continue, must then assume the form of a demand for reason to rely on those memories. But, challenged to give himself reason to think that he is so much as following rules at all, it is not clear that the private linguist has even the beginnings of a reply. If the lunatic need be under no *further* illusion about his previous conduct and experience, a debate (with his doctor, say) about whether he really is rule-following will have to involve considerations of a quite different kind. And now what could such debate pivot around except the capacity of the lunatic to explain, or of others to interpret, the specific rule which he believes himself to be following—or, at least, the kind of rule it might be, even if one too complex for others to follow, say– and what is at stake for him in his pursuit of it? The emergent suggestion is, accordingly, that nothing counts as giving yourself, or anyone else, reason to take certain episodes of your behaviour as genuine cases of rule-following which does not consist in supplying reason for thinking that it could reasonably be so interpreted by *others*.

This seems a promising outline, whose detail it may well be possible to fill in convincingly. If so, the private linguist does confront a distinctive difficulty: he cannot give himself even the weakest reason for thinking that he has a rule-governed practice. Robinson Crusoe, in contrast, need confront no such difficulty; at least, it is not an *immediate* consequence of his social isolation that nothing in the course of his experience, as he interacts with his desert island environment, can give him reason to think that others would reasonably regard him as rule-following if appropriately placed to attempt to interpret his behaviour. Naturally, he may have no defence against a *sceptical* doubt on the point; but the challenge to the private linguist, under this third interpretation of the argument, is not to produce sceptic-proof reason to think that he is rule-following, but merely to show that he is in no way disadvantaged by comparison with Robinson or the individual in the community. Since it seems clear, in addition, that it is merely privacy, rather than the assumption of any sort of Cartesian certitude, which gives rise to the difficulty, we appear to have the germ of an argument which, if successfully developed, might succeed in observing all the outlined constraints.

However, second thoughts are less encouraging. First, accepting that no one can have even the weakest reason for supposing that the private linguist has a rule-governed practice, the transition to the conclusion that it cannot be *true* that he does would still seem to require mediation by some general form of verificationism, so that the cogency of the argument confronts the same impediment as afflicted the first interpretation. Second, whatever the extent of one's sympathies with verificationism, the fact is that there is a large class of propositions whose acceptance is normal among us, and whose non-acceptance, in very many cases, would be unthinkable, for which we nevertheless can supply no solid reason. Examples like 'There exist other consciousnesses besides my own', 'The world did not come into being five minutes ago', 'There are material bodies' all have the feature that they are *beyond* evidential support: that unless they are presupposed, nothing counts as support for the sort of more specific claims from which they may be inferred. Simon Blackburn[9] makes a case for supposing that a similar groundlessness ultimately belongs to the belief that we share communal language; if that is so, the third interpretation does not, after all, fully satisfy the second of our earlier constraints. But whether Blackburn is right in detail matters less than

9. Blackburn (1984), pp. 291 ff.

the reflection that we do not in general wish to equate groundlessness with unacceptability (or, if we do, it is only human irrationality which explains why scepticism is not a dominant ideology). Accordingly, the groundlessness of the private linguist's belief that he has a rule-governed practice would not be *eo ipso* a criticism of that belief; it would remain to be shown that it is not a belief to which he is perfectly entitled, a framework belief, as it were, comparable in its own sphere to our belief in the existence of other minds or of material bodies.

Each of the three interpretations, even if not providing something fully cogent, nevertheless affords a useful and instructive version of the argument. Collectively, they suggest that a defender of private language had better be anti-verificationist, anti-Cartesian and a proponent of the propriety of groundless belief. It immediately occurs to one to wonder whether this is a consistent set of characteristics; whether, in particular, an anti-verificationist can make a decent fist of explaining our entitlement to beliefs which, on his construal, are associated with transcendent truth conditions for whose obtaining we can, in the nature of the case, have absolutely no evidence. One possible way of completing the demolition of private language would be to show that there is indeed an irresoluble tension here. Another would be to show that the province of legitimate but groundless belief cannot extend to the case in point. And a third would be, of course, further research into the semantic presuppositions of verificationism. In each of these various ways, then, the issue is very open. I do not think that we have yet considered the most persuasive version of Wittgenstein's train of thought, however, a version which, although textual evidence can be found in support of each of the interpretations so far considered, arguably best fits the actual letter of §§258–60. Before we do so, let me briefly explain why I believe the interpretation which takes centre stage in Saul Kripke's *Wittgenstein on Rules and Private Language*[10] ultimately affords no cogent argument against the possibility of private language.

10. Kripke (1982).

V. KRIPKE'S INTERPRETATION

A wide class of long-standing philosophical disputes pivots on the question whether the statements of some problematic region of discourse—ethics, aesthetics, theoretical science, and pure mathematics are the most immediate examples—should be regarded as having a *genuinely factual* subject matter, or whether—as argued for example by certain forms of ethical prescriptivism and by scientific instrumentalism—their grammatical form contrives to mask the fact that their role is not that of fact-stating at all.

There are a variety of ways in which an anti-factualist standpoint might be supported. One way—essentially Hume's strategy with statements about causation—would be to argue that a preferable epistemology countenances no means for our attaining any adequate conception of the putative species of fact. Thus there is, for Hume, within the means provided by his preferred empiricist epistemology, no way of attaining any satisfactory idea of the *necessitation* which the causal relation is supposed to involve; the way is then open—or so Hume believes—to regard that component as marking, rather, the projection of an attitude which human beings naturally take up towards tried and tested regularities. A second approach would be to attempt to establish a topic-neutral account of ways in which the distinction between fact-stating and non-fact-stating declarative sentences emerges in their uses, and then apply that account to the problematic class in question. The difficulty with this way of proceeding, of course, is that the general topic-neutral account has not merely to isolate marks of a distinction which we already perfectly understand but must, in addition, go some way towards legitimating it.

There is, however, a rather ingenious third strategy. The leading idea is that any genuine species of fact ought to be knowable by an appropriately endowed subject. Accordingly, if we can specify what powers a subject would have to have in order to be in a position to know a fact of some putative species, and if it then emerges that even such a subject could make no such defensible knowledge claim (could provide no compelling reason for preferring one such claim to another incompatible with it), it must follow that there cannot be any such facts in the first place. It is this third strategy which informs the Sceptical Argument which Kripke finds at the heart of Wittgenstein's discussion of following a rule in §§185–242. The conclusion of the argument, as Kripke interprets it, is that all talk of meaning and understanding ceases to qualify as factual, so that there are no objective truths about, for example, what particular expressions mean, or how subjects understand them or what specific uses accord with their meanings.

An argument against private language now emerges under the aegis of a non-factualist reconstrual of this region of discourse. It is this reconstrual which Kripke, following the Humean model, calls a Sceptical Solution. Sentences like 'Jones means addition by "plus" ' and 'If Jones means addition by "plus", he will answer "259" when asked "What is 132 + 127?" ' may still, according to the Sceptical Solution, possess a determinate use even if divested of objective truth conditions. And the respective uses which they have are, roughly, to ratify Jones's membership of the class of speakers whose uses of 'plus' are generally reliable, and to express a test for membership in that class which the speaker believes would be ratified by the responses of those already accredited with membership. The suggestion, in general, is that once we prescind from the idea that talk of meaning and understanding is apt to convey substantial matters of fact and look instead to an account of the role and purposes which such talk plays in our lives, we find that there is invariably a reference, explicit or implicit, to the linguistic practices of a speech *community*. Kripke's interpretation of the private-language argument would then draw the conclusion that such a reference is essential to the legitimate use of those concepts, and that they can accordingly have no proper application to the activities of a would-be private linguist.

The foregoing is just the barest outline of Kripke's interpretation: it can convey little of the fascination of Kripke's account. But it will serve to indicate various points at which, in my judgement, Kripke's version of the private-language argument fails of cogency. To begin with, the whole package can succeed—obviously—only if the Sceptical Argument succeeds, and it is open to serious question whether it does so; I have already had occasion to try to indicate places where the Sceptical Argument seems to me to go astray, and I will not elaborate on that discussion here.[11] There are, however, two slightly less obvious points. First, even if the success of the Sceptical Argument were assumed, much more would need to be done to explain why the Sceptical Solution is not just an optional extra. Hume *could* quite consistently have drawn the conclusion that we should simply drop the notion of causation as a piece of discredited mythology. Kripke writes as though a parallel option was not available in the case of meaning, since it would involve us in the 'incredible and self-defeating conclusion that all language is meaningless'.[12] But that cannot be the right way of formulating the conclusion of the Sceptical Argument, since it involves, in effect, descriptive use of the very notion whose grip on reality the Sceptical Argument aims to dislodge. It is rather as if we construed the conclusion of Hume's argument as being that all regular associations between events are *coincidental,* when the point is rather that nothing in the world—if the argument is sound—corresponds to our distinction between causal and coincidental regularity. The conclusion of the Sceptical Argument must—at least if it is to be a factual claim—be something expressible without recourse to any notion cognate to that of meaning; so it cannot be the 'incredible and self-defeating' conclusion described by Kripke.

Quite how it should be formulated is a question which we can leave to be pondered by a proponent of the argument. For present purposes it suffices merely to note that it is at least not obvious that the conclusion has to take a self-defeating form; and that what would be called for would presumably be something akin to the Quinean programme for an account of language, and language-related institutions, in which the traditional notion of meaning plays no part. It is

---

11. See Wright (1984) (this volume Essay 4). For additional criticism of the way Kripke involves the community in the Sceptical Solution, see Goldfarb (1985).
12. Kripke (1982), p. 71.

accordingly an *assumption* that the Sceptical Solution is so much as called for, and any conclusion about private language, drawn in the manner indicated, can so far at best be provisional. The argument needs a back-up demonstration either that no Quinean account of language can be satisfactory or that such an account would independently be inhospitable to private language.

It is in any case open to question whether the Sceptical Solution is so much as coherent. The problem is that the notion of meaning is platitudinously connected with that of truth; whether an utterance expresses a truth is a function only of its content and the state of the world in relevant respects; and the content of the utterance is, in turn, a function of the meanings of its constituents, the way in which they are therein put together, and the context. So if there were no facts about meaning, it would appear to follow—by the compelling principle that non-factuality among the parameters in a question must divest the question of factuality too—that there can be no facts about an utterance's truth value either. Such an outcome would call into question the very possibility of explaining what exactly it is that the non-factualist about a given region of discourse intends to hold.

There is no doubt a great deal of scope for further exploration of the implications of and possibilities for Kripke's interpretation. But perhaps enough has been said to justify the claim that, whatever else such exploration might teach us, it is unlikely to disclose the cogent argument we seek.

VI. THE RECOMMENDED INTERPRETATION

Why is a 'seems right'/'is right' distinction needed? The verificationist interpretation appealed, in effect, to the idea that the independence of the requirements of a rule from what anyone takes them to be is a precondition of genuine rule-following; so that the need for a distinction between what seems right to the private linguist and what really is right is a simple consequence of the consideration that private language, like all language, is to be a rule-governed practice. But the trouble is that exactly this platitudinous-seeming conception of the autonomy of rules is one of the things under scrutiny in the discussion of rule-following in the *Investigations* and *Remarks on the Foundations of Mathematics*. A typical passage:

> Then might it not be said that the *rules* lead this way, even if no-one went it? For that is what one would like to say—and here we see the mathematical machine, which, driven by the rules themselves, obeys only mathematical laws and not physical ones. I want to say: that the working of the mathematical machine is only the *picture* of the working of a machine. The rule does not do work, for whatever happens according to the rule is an interpretation of the rule.[13]

I do not believe that Wittgenstein intended to question the *correctness* of the platitudinous conception; his intention was rather to expose certain misunderstandings of it to which he believed we are prone. But we would need to be sure, it seems, exactly how matters stand with the autonomy of rules before the earlier verificationist interpretation of the private-language argument could be considered cogent, even if the correctness of some appropriate form of verificationism were assumed. Fortunately, we can bypass the issue. There is a different, somewhat more subtle route to the perception that a 'seems right'/'is right' distinction is prerequisite for the private linguist's enterprise, which there is some textual evidence that Wittgenstein may have had in mind.

The suggestive passage is the exchange in §260 quoted above:

> 'Well, I *believe* that this is the sensation *S* again.'—Perhaps you *believe* that you believe it! . . .

Wittgenstein's response to his interlocutor has no point unless he thinks that he—the interlocutor—may believe that he has such a belief yet be wrong. But in what circumstances can a second-order belief—a belief about one's beliefs—be incorrect? The sort of cases

---

13. *Remarks on the Foundations of Mathematics* IV, 48.

that most immediately spring to mind would involve the idea that the true character of one's (first-order) beliefs can be veiled in the sort of way that notions like self-deception, or the psychoanalytic idea of the unconscious, standardly presuppose. But that sort of example is not to our purpose. A quite different possibility—the one which, I suggest, Wittgenstein is getting at—is that *X*'s belief that he believes that *P* is false because there is *no such thing as* the belief that *P*. That will be the situation whenever the clause apparently specifying the propositional content of the supposed first-order belief, although prima facie apt for that role, actually fails to have the appropriate kind of content. A genuine belief is an attitude to the type of state of affairs described by the clause which specifies the content of the belief, namely, the conviction that it is realised. So if there simply is no such thing as that type of state of affairs (which is not, of course, the same issue as whether there exists a particular state of affairs of that type), no more can there be any such belief. Accordingly, if the clause purportedly supplying the content of the belief belongs to a family of declarative sentences which correspond to no genuine matters of fact, it cannot be used to specify the content of a possible belief. You can no more believe something which is not apt to be genuinely true or false than you can wonder what is the answer to something which is not really a question.

On this interpretation, then, Wittgenstein's suggestion is that the existence of a genuine distinction between what 'seems right' to the private linguist and what 'is right' is necessary if the private language is to be apt for the making of *genuine statements*. And so there would be a point of affinity with Kripke's discussion. Only Wittgenstein's point would not be that talk of meaning and understanding *in general* lacks a factual subject matter, but that the 'sentences' of a private language cannot qualify as having a factual subject matter unless the 'seems right'/'is right' distinction can be made good for them—which, he has suggested in §258, it cannot.[14]

---

14. What will follow, if Wittgenstein is correct, is not, strictly, that private language is impossible, but that it cannot provide a medium for the formulation of genuine

Argument is now needed for two claims: first, that there is indeed the connection between the 'seems right'/'is right' distinction and factuality which the interpretation demands; and second, that the distinction eludes the resources of the private linguist.

The grounds for the first claim are relatively straightforward. What, more exactly, is at issue is whether the sentences of a given family are apt for the expression of fact only if:

(a)   X believes what '*P*' expresses,

and

(b)   What '*P*' expresses is true,

have an appropriately contrasting content where '*P*' is any of (appropriately many of)[15] the sentences in question. Now, it is in the nature of facts to stand to us in various cognitive relations—like being known, overlooked, reasonably supposed and so on. A realist (contrast: verificationist) may press us to countenance in addition a class of facts which are cognitively inaccessible, about which neither knowledge nor reasonable opinion can be achieved. Whatever the merit of

---

statements, commands, questions, wishes, the framing of hypotheses or any kind of speech act which presupposes the availability in the language of the means for depicting genuine state of affairs. It is a further question whether anything so impoverished as to lack all these expressive resources could qualify as a language (perhaps a private language apt only for the expression of expletives would still be a possibility). However, since all the lines of thought which attract, or pressure, towards the possibility of private language involve regarding it as a medium for expression of knowledge, there is no comfort for anyone in such a possibility—if possibility it be.

15. There are very delicate questions here concerning what, if any, notion of a *family* of sentences would sustain the validity of the principle that if some members of a family are factual, all are: and whether every member of such a family should be required to admit the (a)/(b) contrast: and who X may be. Presentation of the argument which follows does not require us to engage them—though a supporter of the Blackburn/Harrison strategy (see below) would have a definite interest in doing so.

that thought, it at least suggests an argument by dilemma. If '*P*' is apt for the expression of fact, then there must at least be sense in the idea of a subject's standing in one of the various possible cognitive relations to facts which are relevant to the appraisal of '*P*'. So if—going along with the realist—all such facts are inaccessible, *X* can only be ignorant of them, and any belief he has about the status of '*P*' can have no bearing on the likelihood of its truth. If, on the other hand, certain relevant such facts are accessible, the cognitive processes involved in their investigation must nevertheless be *fallible,* and hence any opinions formed by *X* as a result of such investigation can be at best a fallible guide to the likelihood of the truth of '*P*'. Either way, there will be no entailment from (a) to (b); either way, then, there has to be an appropriate contrast in their content.

An immediate afterthought is that this reasoning begs the question against the Cartesian, whose conception is exactly that a subject's sensations, for instance, constitute a domain which is transparent to him, about which his judgements cannot be mistaken; so if '*P*' and the other sentences in the family are apt for the description of such a domain, the entailment from (a) to (b) must go through. Admittedly, we have already recorded a doubt, in discussion of the second interpretation above of Wittgenstein's argument, whether the Cartesian account can defend itself against scepticism. But that would not exonerate the present interpretation from the charge of question-begging. It would be better to show that the Cartesian is committed to upholding a contrast in content between (a) and (b) for a different reason.

Well, that can be shown quite easily. For the Cartesian claim is precisely that *X* possesses certain *guarantees* when it comes to judgement concerning the character of, for example, his own sensations which he does not possess elsewhere. This claim has to be understood as comparable to the claim, for example, that the arithmetical functions, x^2 and $8(x - 1) - 4$, although divergent in value generally, necessarily coincide in value when $x = 6$. There is no way of understanding what the Cartesian believes is guaranteed to *X* unless we take it that the sentence-forming operators, '*X* believes what—expresses' and 'What—expresses is true', have their standard senses. Any substitution, within their gaps, of a sentence with a factual subject matter about which X has no Cartesian authority will reveal, by the argument just run through, that those senses are different. Hence the Cartesian has to grant that there will be some sort of difference of sense in the sentences which result respectively from substitution of a sentence about whose subject matter X *does* have Cartesian authority, notwithstanding the mutual entailment which he then wishes to claim.

So much, then, for the first claim. The second claim is that such an 'appropriately contrasting content' cannot be given to (a) and (b) if '*P*' is a sentence of a putative private language. But what exactly should count as the existence of the appropriate kind of contrast? The Cartesian at least is in no position to advert to a difference in the *truth conditions* of sentences corresponding as (a) and (b).[16] And a moment's reflection discloses that the obvious thought—namely, that (a) and (b) differ in content merely because the sentence-forming operators which they respectively involve are different—is merely question-begging. For that consideration suffices for them to differ in content only if '*P*' expresses an argument appropriate for those operators to be applied to, that is, expresses a thought apt to be believed or true—the very point at issue.[17] So how should matters proceed?

The least that is required, it seems, is that the *information* conveyed by (a) should differ from that conveyed by (b). And it is plausible that, for a large class of examples, two items of information differ just in case there can be such a thing as reasonably regarding oneself as possessing one without the other. It is in exactly this sense that the informational content of two logically equivalent sentences may

16. How far the fallibilist, on the other hand, might get with a purely truth-conditional construal of the (a)/(b) contrast is a question for section IX of this essay.

17. I do not mean to deny that '*X* believes what "*P*" expresses' and 'What "*P*" expresses is true' have different meanings even if '*P*' is not so apt, or is not a declarative sentence at all. But the Cartesian requires, in addition, that they be capable of simultaneous *truth*. It is that which the 'argument' from difference of composition cannot, unsupplemented, give him.

diverge, since unawareness of a logical equivalence need not be unreasonable. So let us propose as a general, though perhaps not exceptionless, principle that items of information coincide for a subject just in case to have reason to accept either, in a sense which need not involve closure under logical implication, involves his having reason to accept both. Now there ought, presumably, to be no objection to supposing, of any particular belief held for good reason, that the subject is aware he has reason for that particular belief. (That is, if there is no conceptual difficulty in the idea of a particular subject having reason for a particular belief, it cannot *introduce* a difficulty to suppose that he is aware of the fact.) It follows that—unless they are to be exceptions for the principle—we are entitled to regard (a) and (b) as conveying different items of information only if someone could have reason to believe one but not the other and could be aware of the fact. The argument will now be that when 'P' is, putatively, a sentence of a language which no two people can reasonably believe they share, that is not a possibility.

It will suffice to consider four cases. Letting A range over believing subjects, we have

(i)   A is aware of possessing both reason to believe (a) and reason to doubt (b);

(ii) A is aware of possessing both reason to doubt (a) and reason to believe (b);

(iii) A is aware of possessing both reason to believe (a) and no reason to believe (b);

(iv) A is aware of possessing both reason to believe (b) and no reason to believe (a).

Our question is whether any of (i)–(iv) represents a possible conscious state of information either for an A who is some Y other than X, or for X himself. But no Y distinct from X can, it appears, enjoy any of the four states. Consider states (ii) and (iv). Both involve Y's possession of reason to believe that 'P' expresses a truth. But he cannot have reason to think that he knows *what* truth it expresses since, by hypothesis, '*P*' is a sentence of a language private to *X*, a language which no one could have reason to think he shares with *X*. So the only ground *Y* could have for supposing '*P*' true would be *X*'s authority on the matter—which contradicts the supposition that *Y* has reason to doubt (a), or at least to believe it, which (ii) and (iv) respectively involve.

State (i) involves *Y*'s possession of reason to doubt that '*P*' expresses a truth despite accepting that *X* believes that it does: that would require either that *Y* has some independent purchase on what '*P*' says—contrary to hypothesis—or, at least, that he has reason to think that some third party does who does not share *X*'s view and in whom *Y* places greater trust. But what reason could *Y* have for thinking that *X* and the third party share an understanding of '*P*' when the hypothesis of privacy dictates that the third party could have no such reason?

Y's enjoyment of state (iii) might seem less problematic. If, after all, *Y* has no conception of the meaning of '*P*', he can have no reason to think either that *X* is, or that he is not, more likely than not to be reliable about the sort of subject matters with which it deals. Hence he has no reason to regard grounds for thinking that X believes '*P*' to express a truth as tending to support (b). But one trouble with this thought is that it illicitly equates the supposition that the sense of '*P*' is private to *X*—that is, that it is impossible for *Y* to have reason to think that he shares an understanding of '*P*' with *X*—with its being impossible for *Y* to have *any* conception of the kind of subject matter that '*P*' deals with. That is not an equation which can be endorsed by the defender of the possibility of private language about the psychological. It is, for example, supposed to be consistent with my recognition that I can know neither the specific character of your sensations nor (in full) the meaning of the language in which you describe them that I can nevertheless apply the concept of sensation to you and hence have a general idea of the kind of thing which, when you give voice to the character of your sensations, you seek to describe. Generally, if one may at least suppose that '*P*', as used by *X*, concerns some aspect or other of *X*'s psychological state, then one is bound to take reason for (a) as supporting (b); and note that the point is not dependent on crediting X with Cartesian authority for his psychological states—it is enough that he be any sort of (fallible) authority about them, that his opinions about them count for something.

In Section II I noted a different kind of pressure for admitting private language, exerted by sceptical predations on the communicability of intention in general and hence of idiolectic semantic rules in particular. If the possibility, indeed the universality, of private language were granted for that sort of reason, there would not, presumably, be the sort of difficulty with (iii) just described. But there is a different, prospectively insuperable difficulty, connected with an aspect of the holistically interlocking character of psychological concepts. Without attempting detailed argument, it is at least highly plausible that it is only on the hypothesis of a subject's possession of certain intentions that his linguistic or non-linguistic behaviour can be regarded as expressive of a certain belief. The relevant sort of example is familiar: dashing out into a street full of traffic may evince the belief that there is space to cross safely to the other side, if we assume, say, that the subject intends to make an appointment in fifteen minutes' time; but the same action may also evince the belief that there is no such space, if we assume the subject's intention to be suicide. The point, then, is that if we really took seriously the idea that all intention is inscrutable from a third person's point of view, we should surely be committed to saying the same about belief; and case (iii) would be precluded not because reason to believe (a) would give Y reason to believe (b) but because he could not have reason to believe (a) in any case.

Let us try matters from X's own point of view. We can immediately discount (i) and (ii). If X were to enjoy the state of information described by (ii) he would be in a position to claim '"P" is true but I do not believe it'—precisely Moore's Paradox—and state of information (i) would put him in a position to claim the equally paradoxical obverse: 'It is not the case that "P" is true but I do believe it'. Whatever the correct analysis of utterances of this bizarre sort, it is clear that they are not apt for the expression of self-consciously held reasonable belief and so do not correspond to possible states of information in the sense which concerns us. Further, it is not clear that the distinction between (iv) and (ii) can now be upheld: at any rate, if it can, it is because it is possible for X to be aware that he has no adequate reason for supposing that he has a particular belief without thereby acquiring reason to think that he lacks it. No doubt there is scope for further discussion of the matter, and it would be unwise to be dogmatic that the separation cannot be affected in certain sorts of (psychoanalytical) case. But it seems a dangerously nice distinction on which to rest a defence of private language.

A further point about (iv) emerges when we consider (iii). What the latter seems to describe is a state of information which X would occupy if he found himself smitten, as it were, with a belief for whose truth he recognised he had no adequate ground. Isn't that a possibility? Well—again—not if the subject matter of the belief is such as to render X's very possession of it a ground for supposing it to be true; so not if the private language is to have a psychological subject matter about which a Cartesian, or weaker, authority is claimed. But a more general consideration is that, independently of the subject matter of 'P', (ii) does not describe a state of information which a *rational X* can achieve for arbitrary 'P'. No doubt restriction would be necessary on the thesis that a rational subject believes only what he has reason to believe. But this had better be true in general. The result is that a proponent of private language ought to regard X's idiolect as containing the resources for expression of a wide class of statements for which (iii) can represent, for X, a possible state of information only if X is imperfectly rational. The same point applies to (iv). But the possibility of (iii) or (iv) for an imperfectly rational X had better not be the *only* thing that a proponent of private language can oppose to the claim that the needed contrast cannot be made between the content of (a) and (b); otherwise the conclusion will stand that a private language could not be employed by a perfectly rational subject—an interesting enough conclusion, and quite sufficient seriously to damage any philosophical thesis about language, or mind, which demanded the possibility of private language.

VII. DOES THIS INTERPRETATION MEET
THE CONSTRAINTS ON COGENCY?

So much by way of outline is the interpretation of §§258–60 which I wish to recommend. I am not, of course, claiming that Wittgenstein had exactly these thoughts but then mysteriously chose to put no more than a do-it-yourself kit on paper. What I claim for this interpretation is that it elaborates the *kind* of doubt which Wittgenstein's text seems to be urging us to have about private language, and that it promises a cogency missing from the other lines of interpretations considered. One thing necessary, in order to make good the latter claim, is to consider how the interpretation fares in relation to the constraints listed earlier, which is the task of this section. Then, in the next two sections, I shall review two lines of objection which force interesting further extensions of the argument.

First, the Crusoe constraint. Let '*P*' be any statement, of whatever subject matter, in Crusoe's invented language. It would appear, taking Crusoe as *X*, that he is as badly placed to draw a distinction between (a) and (b) as the private linguist, and for exactly the same reasons: none of (i)–(iv) represents a state of information which he can achieve if he is entirely rational. It is also plausible that, so long as Crusoe remains isolated on his desert island and no one else has the slightest idea of what, if anything, any of his utterances means, no third party *Y* can achieve any of the states of information (i)–(iv) for the reasons described above. (I say 'plausible' because at least one of the considerations relevant to the discussion of private language—namely, sceptical pressure towards third-personal inscrutability of intention—would not be relevant.) Accordingly, let us suppose that Crusoe's isolation de facto prevents anyone else from arriving at any of the states of information whose possibility is demanded by a distinction in content between (a) and (b). We can even suppose Crusoe's isolation to be permanent and unalterable. Still, the difficulty about concluding that the argument, if sustained, defeats Crusoe's language too is that we do not ordinarily suppose that it suffices for a distinction to be unreal that nobody is *in fact* going to be able to make any use of it. The crucial matter is, putting it crudely, whether we know *what it would be, as rational subjects, to have occasion to make use of the distinction.* No doubt clarification is desirable of what exactly such knowledge should be held to consist in. But, whatever the truth about that, it is surely highly questionable a priori whether there can be such a thing as knowing what, counterfactually, it *would be* to be in a certain state of information if that state of information *necessarily* cannot be achieved. The thought governing the whole argument was that (a) and (b) possess an appropriately contrasting content only if the information which they convey is different; which it is only if there *could be* such a thing as having one item of information without the other. Any reader who found the principle plausible will not have supposed that the 'could' was meant to be constrained by contingent obstacles to investigation; but if it is not constrained by *conceptual* obstacles, it is doubtful whether it can mean anything at all.

There were two aspects to the second constraint, that 'going public' must remove the difficulty. First, the precise difficulty besetting the private linguist must disappear; and second, there must be no analogous difficulty for public language. Now, the precise difficulty is that, when X is taken to be the private linguist, neither he nor anyone else can attach appropriately contrasting informational content to (a) and (b). But 'going public' means: bringing it about that 'P' has sufficient public content to enable others, at least in favourable circumstances, to form a well-founded opinion about its truth value independent of X's opinion. That ought to make space for (iv). Of course X may still be invested with authority about the truth value of 'P'. But the possibility of independent assessment is likely to involve that that authority is, if only in special circumstances, defeasible—which is to say that there ought to be space for some or all of (i)–(iii). In any case, whether or not the feasibility of (i)–(iv) follows from the very publicity of the meaning of 'P', the important point is that there is never any significant obstacle to establishing the (a)/(b) distinction for the statements of a public language. What counts as enjoying one of the states of information, (i)–(iv), varies depending on the subject matter of 'P'; but there is in general no difficulty in explaining what it would be to enjoy one of those states of information vis à vis some third party X.

Whether the second aspect of the 'going public' constraint—the demand that there be no analogous difficulty for a public language—is satisfied may seem less straightforward. Suppose we take X as the entire linguistic community. Then may not the argument for the case A = X proceed more or less as before? Analogues of Moore's Paradox and its obverse may as well be formulated using 'we' rather than 'I'; and it is presumably legitimate (if fanciful) to hypothesise that the community is collectively rational, so that at least the final consideration urged against the possibility of (iii) and (iv) in the relevant part of the earlier discussion can survive. As for the situation from the point of view of Y distinct from X, the fact is that there is, by hypothesis, no such Y who understands the language. So the argument can proceed much as before with, perhaps, only the additional consideration, for the case of (iii), that confrontation with a solid communal consensus about the truth of a sentence would have to provide an observer with *some* reason to suppose that sentence to be true even if he had not the slightest idea what it meant.

The thought is, in effect, that the argument outlined has no special bearing on private language but may be run for any entire linguistic community, whether of one or many members. It is a nice question what the proper response to the argument would be if that were so. But if we were right to conclude that the Crusoe constraint is satisfied, it cannot be so. And, in fact, the relevant consideration here is the same: the existence of contingent barriers to anyone's achieving one of (i)–(iv) provides no decisive basis for the conclusion that no one understands *what it would be* to achieve one of those states of information. The community will no doubt have a conception of the circumstances in which it would subsequently be forced to judge that such a consensus about the truth of 'P' *had been* mistaken. So we know *now* what it would be for there to be a Y who was in a position to make that judgement about us; such a Y would be an additional member of the linguistic community who had adequate reason for supposing that the circumstances had indeed induced mass error. There is, by hypothesis, no such *Y*, but there could be—just as there could be a translator of Crusoe's language. Accordingly, there can be no special difficulty with this aspect of the second constraint if it was right to conclude that the argument satisfies the Crusoe constraint.

The third constraint, conceived for the special case of the psychological private language on which Wittgenstein himself concentrates, was that the argument should be effective against both Cartesian and fallibilist opposition. It will suffice to remind the reader that, by and large, the argument proceeds without special assumption concerning the subject matter of the private language or the authority, if any, about the truth value of his utterances supposedly possessed by the private linguist; and that at both points where such authority is presented as contributing towards the difficulties, it is of no consequence whether it is thought of as Cartesian or fallible.

Arguably, then, all three constraints are satisfied. Since he can make out no (a)/(b) contrast—either truth-conditionally, or by appeal to difference of composition, or by appeal to difference of informational content, in accordance with the principle of section VI—and since the reasons for demanding the contrast seem absolutely compelling, we discharge the Cartesian from further punishment at this point. But the fallibilist is not yet done for.

VIII.   The Return of the Community

One important line of objection to the argument is suggested by the thought, three paragraphs above, that even a community-wide consensus may legitimately be regarded as mistaken *at another time*. Moore's Paradox and its variant depend upon present-tense formulation: there is nothing bizarre about for example '"*P*" was true but I did not believe it'. But nothing in the original argument, that (a) and (b) must possess contrasting content if '*P*' is to count as apt for expression of fact, seems to require the present-tense formulations which (a) and (b) actually assumed—the fallibility of our cognitive powers would be as well reflected by a contrast in the content of cor-responding past-tense formulations. Such reformulation would not, to be sure, affect the course taken by the argument for the case $A = Y$, distinct from X. The objection, rather, will be that the discussion of the case $A = X$ was at best incomplete: we have simply not considered, in particular, whether a private linguist could get in position to pass principled *retrospective* verdicts of ignorance or error on himself. Should it emerge that he can, the argument would be met head-on; it would be possible to grant its claims about what is necessary for factuality, while contending that the thought which Wittgenstein expressed by 'whatever is going to seem right to me is right' in §258 is just mistaken.

The question, then, is whether X, the private linguist, can himself assign an appropriately contrasting content to:

(a)* X believed what 'P' expressed,

and

(b)* What 'P' expressed was true.

Let the private language be one for the recording of sensation types; and let 'P' be 'This sensation is S'. No doubt it may happen that X is afflicted with a sensation which, at first, he wishes to record as an occurrence of sensation S but which, as it continues, comes to seem to him significantly different. He may then want to say with respect to some recent past time that (a)* is true but (b)* is not. But that, so far, is not good enough. With what right does X propose to regard his for-mer impression of the sensation as having been mistaken, rather than view the sensation itself as having subtly changed from an instance of type S to something different? If the latter were the correct account, both (a)* and (b)* should be allowed to stand. Hence there can be, for X, such a thing as a state of information warranting assertion of (a)* but denial of (b)*—a state of information of type (i) with respect to (a)* and (b)*—only when he has equipped himself with a criterion for marking off the irrelevant kind of case when it is the sensation itself which has undergone subtle change. But it is utterly unclear what form such a criterion might take: all *X* has to go on, it appears, is his own conscious phenomenology; and phenomenologically there simply *is not* any difference—things will seem the same 'on the inside' whichever of the two descriptions is supposed to be accurate.

The point is vivid in the case of sensation, but in fact it is of general bearing. More needs to be done by a proponent of private language, whatever the envisaged subject matter, than simply to invoke the possibility that the private linguist might find himself inclined to correct a former judgement. We considered two ostensibly contrasting accounts of the situation in respect of sensation *S*. We could in fact have considered three, the third being that it is *X*'s inclination at the later time not to regard his then-occurring sensation as being of type *S* which is astray. So: on the basis of what principle should *X* give his present descriptive inclination priority over the previous one? This question must arise even if, for whatever reason, the subject matter of the private language is not conceived of as giving rise to the possibility of the kind of gradual transformation which would allow both of *X*'s descriptions to stand. What needs to be shown by someone who would have us believe that a retrospective analogue of (i) is accessible to the private linguist is that a situation may arise in which it is *rational* to accept both (a)* and the negation of (b)*; that has not been accomplished if the contrasting uses envisaged for (a)* and (b)* are based on nothing more substantial than the subject's arbitrarily giving priority to his present over his previous descriptive inclinations.

There is, as far as I am aware, only one line of thought extant in the literature which promises a reply. This is Simon Blackburn's expression of it:

> [I]n the usual scenario, the correctness or incorrectness of the private linguist's classification is given no consequence at all. It has no use. He writes in his diary, and so far as we are told, forgets it. So when

Wittgenstein imagines a use made of the report (e.g. to indicate the rise of the manometer) he immediately hypothesises a public use. He thereby skips the intermediate case where the classification is given a putative private use. It fits into a project—a practice or technique—of ordering the expectation of the occurrence of sensation, with an aim at prediction, explanation, systematisation, or simple maximising of desirable sensations. To someone engaged on this project, the attitude that 'whatever seems right is right' is ludicrous. System soon enforces recognition of fallibility.[18]

Blackburn does not elaborate, but it is not difficult to imagine the kind of thing he could have in mind. The essential idea is to let the private linguist become a *theorist,* concerned not just with the recording of sensations, say, but with anticipation of their future character and the disclosure of patterns of occurrence among them. And the thought is that, once he embarks on this theoretical project, the routine constraints on all scientific theorising (of comprehensiveness, predictiveness, simplicity and so on) will supply a framework in terms of which it may be rational, on occasion, to discount former, or even present, descriptive inclinations.

Let us construct a simple example. Suppose the private linguist is afflicted, as it seems to him, with three distinct sensation types which within any instance of some specified period—one hour, say—invariably comply with the following two hypotheses:

H_1: if no instance of S_1 occurs, then an instance of S_2 occurs.
H_2: if an instance of S_3 occurs, then no instance of S_2 occurs.

Imagine now an occasion on which the private linguist sets himself to record the occurrence of his sensations over an instance of the specified period. We can list the various possibilities in the form of a truth table:

18. Blackburn (1984), pp. 299–300. Cf. Harrison (1974), p. 161. And see Walker (1978), p. 115, for a terse gesture at the same idea.

	S_1	S_2	S_3
1*	T	T	T
2	T	T	F
3	T	F	T
4	T	F	F
5*	F	T	T
6	F	T	F
7*	F	F	T
8*	F	F	F

Line 1, for instance, is to be taken, in the obvious way, as expressing the possibility than an instance of each of the three types of sensation occurs during the specified period. The reader will note that the possibilities expressed at the asterisked lines 1, 5, 7 and 8 are at variance with the two hypotheses, while the remaining four possibilities are consistent with them. Now, the general point is that although, ultimately, theory must be the slave of observation, a theory can fare sufficiently well over a sufficient period of time to make it rational to discount a prima facie discordant set of data. H_1 and H_2 may together constitute a repeatedly corroborated, long-standing little theory; or they may represent the output, for the three sensation types, of a well-entrenched theory of wider content. Either way, it could be rational for the private linguist, if at the end of the specified period he finds that his record is of one of the four types at variance with the theory, to look askance at his 'observations' rather than at the theory.

Let his policy in such circumstances be the commendable one of making the simplest adjustment to his findings consistent with retention of his faith in the theory and in his own powers to, by and large, record his sensations properly. And now ask, what, if that is his policy, ought he to say in each of the four possible cases of discordance? The answers are interesting. Clearly he will not make two adjustments if one will do. But if he has recorded occurrences of all three sensation types, that is, we are concerned with line 1, there are two possibilities open, namely, rejecting the verdict that an instance of S_2

occurred, so transforming the data into line 3, and rejecting the verdict that an instance of S_3 occurred, so transforming the data into line 2. And *two* choices is one too many. The objection to which the introduction of theory was a response was precisely that the private linguist had no principled basis for according priority to a present preferred description over a former one. But, in the situation envisaged, a preference for his verdict about S_2 over that about S_3 or vice versa is open to just the same reproach. The lesson is that the objection is met only when there is some *uniquely* best way to resolve the inconsistency between theory and data; so long as there are choices, the decision among which is arbitrary, the invocation of theory in the present context has no point.

Matters are no better with line 8, when it seems to the private linguist as though no sensation of any of the three relevant kinds has occurred; either of the suppositions that S_2, or S_3, did in fact occur (unnoticed?) transforms the data into an acceptable set, and no non-arbitrary basis for a choice between them presents itself. But it is different with line 5: here re-assessment of the verdict about S_3 represents the best, indeed the only suitable transformation. So it would appear that this theory does indeed provide for the possibility of a state of information in which the private linguist may reasonably deem the impression that an instance of S_3 occurred to be mistaken: the state of information is that constituted by the grounds for the theory itself and his other recorded data. A similarly favourable case is presented by line 7 for the statement that no instance of S_1 occurred. The Blackburn/Harrison idea is accordingly a prima facie feasible one: equip the private linguist with well-entrenched theoretical beliefs and he may very well get into situations in which he may rationally discount verdicts which he would otherwise have endorsed and may indeed have endorsed for a time. Have we got private language off the ground?

It certainly is not as easy as that. Remember, to begin with, that the establishment of an appropriate distinction between (a) and (b) (or (a)* and (b)*) is only a *necessary* condition for qualification of a class of statements as factual. Suppose you found it possible, for example, to draw up an integrated system of moral principles in such a way as to coincide with the pattern of your untutored moral responses and to predict new ones. You might then have a theoretical basis, in just the sort of way envisaged, for describing certain of your moral judgements about particular situations as involving error or ignorance. But no non-factualist about morals need be dismayed by the prospect of such system; he will hold that it is one thing to talk as if moral judgements have a factual subject matter and another thing for them really to do so (though it would remain a decisive point in his favour if we could not so much as establish the practice of talking as if they did). We do not at present have an account of conditions both necessary *and* sufficient for a class of statements to qualify as genuinely factual; a proof of the possibility of private language would have to appeal to such an account.

Still, in fairness, Wittgenstein's apparent claim in §258 is that a necessary condition cannot be met. And now we have a competitive-looking suggestion to the contrary. However the appearance is not very long-lived: cause for dissatisfaction with the sort of theoretical scenario depicted emerges, in any case, once we reflect on what further conditions are necessary for factuality. One compelling principle— (T)—is that a class of statements can qualify as factual only if every truth-functional compound of them does so; hence in particular the negation of any factual statement must itself be factual. But the theory described does nothing to establish the possibility of contrasting uses for (a)/(a)* and (b)/(b)* when 'P' is taken as 'No sensation of type S_3 occurred'. So arguably what the theory does achieve for 'A sensation of type S_3 occurred' is not enough.

In addition, the theory goes no way at all towards establishing the (a)/(a)*–(b)/(b)* contrast for either 'A sensation of type S_2 occurred' or its negation. A proponent of the Blackburn/Harrison strategy is, I suggest, going to be hard-pressed to explain why that sort of omission does not set up a kind of 'rotten apple' effect. There are two reasons for anticipating such an effect. The first, somewhat intricate, involves appeal to the principle—(U)—noted above in discussion of Kripke, that if the acceptability—to use a neutral term—of a statement is a function of that of others, some of which are deemed not to be genuinely factual, then the original statement may not be regarded as genuinely factual either. The theory described, when well established, puts X in position to deny the appearance of acceptability of 'An instance of S_3 occurred' when and only when 'No instance of S_1 occurred' and 'An instance of S_2 occurred' are both acceptable with respect to the relevant period. Accordingly, if the latter does not qualify as factual, then—by (U)—neither, when asserted on that basis, does the conjunction of (a)* and the negation of (b)* with 'A sensation of type S_3, occurred' substituted for 'P'. Hence—by the principle (T)—not both its conjuncts qualify as factual. Since it is completely unclear what ground sympathetic to a proponent of Blackburn could be given for regarding the first conjunct as failing in factuality, the trouble, it seems, would have to lie with the second: the statement, 'It is not the case that what "A sensation of type S_3 occurred" expressed was true'. And if that is not a factual statement, it ought to be permissible to say the same about 'What "It is not the case that a sensation of type S_3 occurred"expressed was true' and hence about the statement mentioned therein.[19] A further application of the principle (T) then gives the result that 'A sensation of type S_3 occurred' does not qualify as factual after all.

The second reason for anticipating a 'rotten apple' effect concerns whether the presence of statements in the situation of 'A sensation of type S_2 occurred' in the example described leaves open any possibility of a coherent account of the private linguist's methodology. No problem, of course, if all the ingredients in the private linguist's record of his observations may be regarded as factual: in that case the three observations represented by line 5, for instance, are straightforwardly *inconsistent* with the theory, retention of which will therefore demand some reappraisal of them. But it is not clear whether it is legitimate to invoke the notion of consistency in this kind of way if certain of the

19. The two principles implicit in this transition are: (a) 'Not: what "P" expresses/ed is/was true' is factual iff 'What "Not: 'P' expresses/ed is/was true" is factual; and (b) 'What "P" expresses/ed is/was true' is factual iff 'P' is factual.

ingredients in a putatively inconsistent set are not genuine statements. I do not mean to dispute, of course, that perfectly respectable notions of consistency and inconsistency are applicable beyond the domain of genuine statements—to commands, for instance, and rules, as well as to moral judgements (if they are indeed thought to be a doubtful case). The fact remains that the notion of consistency has its *primary* place when we are concerned with genuine statements. It is applied elsewhere, I suggest, only in a derivative sense. (Commands, for example, are inconsistent when and only when those corresponding statements are, which articulate the conditions under which the commands are complied with.) In any event, anyone who wants to apply the notions of consistency and inconsistency outside the domain of genuine statements, and to sustain their ordinary connections with the notion of rationality, owes an account of what exactly inconsistency among the relevant sentences amounts to and why it is to be avoided. It is quite unobvious how such an account should proceed in the present case; certainly, nothing like the story appropriate for the case of commands can be appropriate here.

The foregoing remarks are premised on the assumption that unless the theory provides for the possibility, with respect to each particular 'observation' statement, of a state of information in which some sort of $(a)/(a)^*-(b)/(b)^*$ contrast may be drawn, no sense has yet been attached to the contrast in that particular case. But someone may be inclined to question this assumption. In discussion of the Crusoe and publicity constraints above, it was contended that it suffices, in order for (a) and (b) to contrast in content, that we possess a clear account of what it *would be* to enjoy any of the states of information (i)–(iv); and that it is not required that any of those states of information *actually* be attainable. Now, cannot the private linguist claim to have such an account for each of the statements which he wishes to regard as a possible report of his sensations? For he would be in a position to make the appropriate contrast, in each such case, just when he happened to be impelled towards a theory which furnished a line in the truth table standing to that statement as line 5 stands to 'A sensation of type S_3 occurred' in our example. There is thus, it may be contended, no need to aspire to some *single* theory which can provide the needed contrast in every case; it is enough, for each putative report of sensation, to be hospitable towards the possibility of *some* theory's providing a basis for its correction.

This point, if sustained, would certainly be convenient for the private linguist. It would mean that he did not *actually* have to engage in any theorizing at all! It would be enough to indicate that he was 'hospitable' to the possibility of sometime attempting to integrate his 'reports' within the framework of a theory; and that if the theory then proved to supply a criterion for his self-attribution of ignorance, or error, concerning the status of some particular such report then—no matter which it might be—he would be willing to reappraise it. But this implication should make us wary. If we deem that the occurrence of no *actual* attempt at theorising, or only of an unsuccessful attempt, is quite compatible with the existence of all the requisite distinctions, so long as the private linguist acknowledges that the drawing of each of them could be appropriate under theoretical pressure, we would seem committed to the view that his 'observation' statements may already be credited with a meaning which will be more or less invariant across the various theory-inclusive systems of beliefs in which they may come to be embedded. If that commitment seems untroublesome, we shall do well to remember how difficult it has proved to sustain the corresponding claim about the content of reports of observation in the context of our ordinary scientific theories (and, indeed, to sustain so much as the claim that there is a well-defined class of 'observation statements' at all).

There is a second, more fundamental point. A theory ought not to require the truth of any particular observation statement *unconditionally*. Naturally, depending on whether a particular observation statement is supposed to be true or false, a theory may enjoin a differential assessment of other such statements; but *both* the union of the theory with any single observation statement *and* its union with the negation ought to express coherent possibilities. We have not pressed the fallibilist for an account of the *sources* of possible error in the private linguist's reports of his sensations; but such an account is owing, and it is hard to see how a satisfactory story could avoid sanctioning the possibility that error might take place, in any particular case, *whatever* theory, if any, the subject held about the dependable patterns of occurrence among his sensations. So much is demanded by the analogy with observation and ordinary empirical theorising which the Blackburn/Harrison proposal invokes. If, accordingly, it is on the intelligibility of error that the supporter of private language wishes to base the needed (a)/(a)*–(b)/(b)* contrast, it is perfectly fair to insist that he explain how the private linguist might achieve a state of information of type (i) compatibly with a reasonable confidence in whatever theory he had arrived at.

To relate the point to the example above. A satisfactory explanation of what it is for the private linguist to have been in error about 'A sensation of type S_2 occurred' ought to represent it as a possibility consistent with the truth of his belief in H_1 and H_2. The conjunction of 'X erroneously believed "A sensation of type S_2 is occurring" ' with H_1 and H_2 ought therefore to represent a conceivable, self-consistent item of information—differing, for instance, from the information represented by the result of replacing 'erroneously' by 'erroneously but excusably'. But, so long as we stay with the principle about information content which has governed the discussion to this point—that two items of information differ only if there could be such a thing as having one without the other[20]—no way presents itself for giving sense to that sort of contrast. There is, simply, no prospect of an account of what it would be for X to have just the theoretical information

20. Of course, this principle may be called into question; and it will be the task of the next section to review how. But what seemed interesting about the Blackburn/Harrison proposal was exactly that it promised the private linguist the prospect of drawing the requisite sorts of distinction in *operational* terms, compatibly with the requirements of our governing principle. (The invocation of theory would be pointless if that principle were no longer accepted, since the enjoyment of an appropriately contrasting content by instances of (a)* and (b)* would no longer have to answer to the possibility of states of information of type (i)–(iv).)

incorporated in H_1 and H_2 plus reason to think that his prior acceptance of 'A sensation of type S_2 is occurring' was mistaken.

Let us see where we have got to. I have argued for two theses. *Thesis A* affirms that the private linguist can satisfactorily draw the (a)/(a)*–(b)/(b)* contrast for a particular S_k only if he can draw that contrast both for *every* such statement which, he conceives, may contribute with S_k to a body of evidence for or against his theory, and for *the negations* of all such statements. The grounds for this thesis are the principle (T), the argument for the 'rotten apple' effect and the doubt about the capacity of the private linguist to justify the play he will need to make with the notion of consistency unless the thesis is respected. *Thesis B* affirms that if—which is the private linguist's situation—*only* theory can assist in the drawing of these contrasts, then they are drawn satisfactorily only if drawn within the framework of a *single* theory. In particular, it is not good enough merely to advert to the possibility of different theories which might repair the omissions of whatever theory the private linguist happens to respect. The grounds for this thesis are two. First, the private linguist needs to suppose that the 'omitted' cases *already* enjoy the content which they would possess when harnessed to a theory which actually drew the (a)/(a)*–(b)/(b)* contrast for them—otherwise he will run afoul of the 'rotten apple' and consistency points; and he holds out a substantial hostage to fortune if he undertakes to defend that supposition against the familiar difficulties which beset the notion of the continuity of 'observational' contents through theoretical change. Second, it is part of our ordinary concept of observational error that it may occur whatever theory we hold. Accordingly the private linguist has not attained a satisfactory conception of what it is to be in error about, for example, the occurrence of an instance of S, if he does not understand what it would be both for that to be so and for his current theory to be correct. The operationalism implicit in the Blackburn/Harrison response—that the 'seems right' / 'is right' distinction should be one the private linguist can actually draw—entails, accordingly, that reason to suspect observational error—error in the appraisal of some S_k or its negation—should always be attainable compatibly, at least when taken in isolation, with *whatever* theory the subject is inclined to endorse. (Or, if it does not, it has suddenly turned suspiciously eclectic.) Of course there is no difficulty in meeting this condition when, as is usual, the criteria for observational error are, at least in part, of a largely non-theoretical sort—discord with others' reports, poor lighting, mislaid spectacles, and so on. But in the present case such criteria *have* to be theoretically generated.

Putting *Theses A* and *B* together, we arrive at the intriguing result that Blackburn's and Harrison's strategy can be both pointful and successful for the private linguist only if his theory can indeed do for *each* member of the relevant class of 'observation statements' and their negations what the theory in the example does for 'A sensation of type S_3 occurred'. Could there be such a theory, and what would it look like?

Consider the total set of rows of Ts and Fs which specify all possible truth-value assignments to the ingredient variables in a formula in n variables of classical sentential logic—let us call this structure of Ts and Fs the *assignment block*. Let us say that one row is an n-transform of another just in case the first results from the second by changing the assignment to exactly n of the variables. Then the theory in the example does what it does for 'A sensation of type S_3 occurred' because the relevant assignment block contains a row—line 5—which falsifies the theory as a whole, assigns T to S_3, has a 1-transform which verifies the theory as a whole and is achieved by changing just the assignment of T to S_3, and has no other 1-transform which verifies the theory as a whole. All that is the formal reflection of the point that the findings which line 5 represents are inconsistent with the theory but can be restored to consistency with it by a reappraisal which is *uniquely* least disturbing of them. The upshot is that if the private linguist wishes to bring what strike him as different sensation types under theoretical rein, and satisfactorily to meet Wittgenstein's argument in the Blackburn/Harrison way, his 'theory' had better take a form whereby its output for the n relevant types of 'observational 'statement' corresponds to a classical truth function, ϕ in n variables with the following features:

For each variable V_i there are rows in the assignment block, $V_j(v_1 \ldots v_n)$ and $V_k(v_i \ldots v_n)$, such that:

$V_j(v_i) = T$; $V_k(v_i) = F$

V_j falsifies $\phi(v_1 \ldots v_n)$; V_k falsifies $\phi(v_1 \ldots v_n)$

$V_j^*(v_1 \ldots v_n)$, differing $V_k^*(v_1 \ldots v_n)$, differing
from $V_j(v_1 \ldots v_n)$ only in   from $V_k(v_1 \ldots v_n)$ only in
the assignment to v_i,   the assignment to v_i,
verifies $\phi(v_i \ldots v_n)$;   verifies $\phi(v_1 \ldots v_n)$

There is no other   There is no other
1-transform of   1-transform of
$V_j(v_1 \ldots v_n)$ $V_k(v_1 \ldots v_n)$
which verifies $\phi(v_1 \ldots v_n)$;   which verifies $\phi(v_1 \ldots v_n)$

We now need to do some formal work whose details I relegate to an Appendix. But here are some pertinent results. If $n = 2$, there are no theories of the requisite sort. If $n = 3$ or 4, all the theories of the requisite sort correspond to truth functions which are verified only by a pair of complementary rows in the assignment block; for example, by [TTF] and [FFT]—lines 2 and 7 in the assignment block for H_1 and H_2 above—which would correspond to the theory:

H_3: a sensation of type S_1 occurs if and only if a sensation of type S_2 occurs; and

H_4: a sensation of type S_2 occurs if and only if a sensation of type S_3 does not occur.

Indeed one way to arrive at a suitable theory, irrespective of the size of n, is simply to write up the chain of biconditionals which correspond to any single row in the assignment block in the manner in which $\{H_3, H_4\}$ corresponds to line 2 in the three-variable assignment block tabulated earlier. But this is not the only way of finding a suitable theory if n is greater than or equal to 5. For example, the function in 5 variables which is verified at each of [TTFFT], [FFFTT] and [FTTTF] but nowhere else corresponds to a suitable theory for a language of five sensation types; as does that which is verified at each of [TTTTT], [TTFFF], [FFFTT] and [FFTFF], but nowhere else. (The alert reader will spot that the crucial consideration is that each designated row be at least a 3-transform of all the others, and that the designated rows collectively comprise assignments of both T and F to each variable.)

The resulting situation is somewhat peculiar. The feeling that a private language, in particular a private language of sensation, is possible is intuitively quite indifferent to the degree of complexity and variety of the material to be described. But if the private linguist happens to have only two sensation types, or if only two out of a larger number of types by which he is afflicted prove to be theoretically tractable, the Blackburn/Harrison strategy is no good to him. And if his inner world is richer, and a threefold or larger variety within it does seem to prove amenable to theoretical regimentation, the chances that his experience will suggest a theory falling within the range of those which deliver all that has been argued to be necessary are signally slim. There are, for example, half as many distinct biconditionally constituted theories, of the sort illustrated, in n types of 'observation statement' as there are rows in the assignment block; so the ratio of the number of such theories to all possible theories, where each possible theory corresponds to a distinct truth function in n variables, is

$$\frac{2^{n-1}}{2^{2^n}} \, .$$

Since the biconditionally constituted theories are the only suitable theories when $n = 3$ or 4, this gives the would-be private linguist a 1 in 64 chance of meeting Wittgenstein's objection if his theory deals in three sensation types, and a 1 in 8,192 chance if it deals in four! Even the most determined soliloquist ought to be dismayed by such odds. The reader will anticipate that matters get worse as n increases, and so indeed they do. In particular, the limiting frequency of suitable theories among all possible theories tends to zero as n tends to infinity. (For proof, see the Appendix.)

I conclude that the Blackburn/Harrison objection can at most oblige some refinement of Wittgenstein's claim; it does not, in the end, qualify its force. The argument proposed a necessary condition for a class of statements to qualify as genuinely factual and suggested that private language could not meet it. Not so, said Blackburn, provided the language embeds an appropriate theory. And thus far, except for the case $n = 2$, he is entirely right. But we have seen that Wittgenstein's objection can be amplified in such a way that only possession by the private linguist of a very special sort of theory can put him in position satisfactorily to respond to it in the Blackburn/Harrison way. The result is that although we find in favour of the *bare possibility* of private language—or, more accurately, of surmounting the barrier to it adverted to in §258—enough has been done to undermine the *motivation* of each of the foreseeable species of believer in private language distinguished in section I. One who believes in the essential privacy of large parts of his mental life will surely want to suppose that his capacity to record its character in terms no one else can have reason to think he understands would be *in no way contingent* on the particular form of the patterns, if any, of concomitance which the various event types display, but would depend only on the adequate functioning of his faculties. One who succumbs to sceptical pressure towards the third-personal inscrutability of intention, or to solipsism, will want to say the same. The extra element of contingency might be tolerated if it was associated with high probability; but quite the reverse is true. Blackburn's objection forces a concession which offers absolutely no comfort to Wittgenstein's traditional antagonists.

It remains to draw a further moral. It is a fact that we actually possess an 'operational' grasp of the notions of error and ignorance for statements of every sort, including everything we might incline to regard as a report of observation. One implication of the preceding is that it is wildly unlikely that this could be so unless this grasp owed more to our membership in a language community in which we have faith in others' corrections than to our engagement in theory-building. This is one crucial difference which a community, actual or potential, makes: only by reference to a (potential) community of speakers of his language can a subject guarantee himself any reasonable likelihood of globally applicable, operational notions of ignorance and error.

IX. Drawing the 'Seems Right' / Is Right' Distinction Non-Operationally

I warned in section IV that the interpretation to be recommended would not entirely distance itself from verificationism. Such verificationism as it involves is implicit in the erstwhile governing principle that—at least for a very large class of cases, including relevant instances of (a)/(a)* and (b)/(b)*—statements may be regarded as differing in their informational content only if there could be such a thing as having reason to believe one without the other. For the principle leaves no space for the possibility (as some will see it) of grasping that the informational content of a pair of statements differs although there can be no such thing as having even the weakest reason to accept *either.*

Anyone who was not already dissatisfied with the governing principle when it was introduced but now dislikes its Wittgensteinian consequences should probably have a bad conscience about dramatising this verificationist aspect. But, in any case, the belief in the possibility that verification-transcendent statements may differ in informational content is not to the purpose for a supporter of private language, since he will not wish to maintain that there is no such thing as having either piece of information conveyed by statements of types (a)/(a)* and (b)/(b)*. Prima facie, then, the verificationist aspect of the governing principle plays no part in the argument.

The reply should be that the principle actually imports verificationist cargo in two places. It entails, as noted, that the informational content of a pair of statements can be contrasted only if there can be reason to believe one of them: but it also entails that if possession of reason to believe either involves reason to believe both, we cannot attain *distinct* conceptions of their informational content, that is, understand them as depicting different states of affairs. And that is tantamount to the assumption that the meaning of a statement cannot be determined by truth conditions over and above the possible grounds for believing it. Since (prescinding from presently irrelevant considerations about conversational practice) grounds for belief and grounds for assertion coincide, the assumption is, in effect, that the contrast between (a)/(a)* and (b)/(b)* has to be drawn by reference to conditions of warranted assertion; that it cannot coherently be allowed that their assertion conditions might coincide while the *truth conditions* diverged, with the latter divergence supplying the requisite contrast in content.

It would be natural to suppose that this reflection takes the private language issue up into the general dispute between realists and anti-realists in the theory of meaning, which has recently increasingly resembled a dialogue of the deaf. It is true of course that if we were to decide—for example for the sort of reason developed by Michael Dummett—against the realist conception of truth, then that would be that. But I do not think that this is the best way to look at the matter. Rather, suppose we find *against* verificationism in general; that is, we satisfy ourselves that there are at least some areas of discourse for which the sort of idea of truth which the verificationist complains about can be made intelligible and is suitable to serve as the basis of a truth-conditional conception of meaning. Still, the victory over verificationism has to be gained piecemeal; persuading ourselves that the verificationist has no cogent *general* point would still leave open the task, for any particular class of statements where realism is our antecedent conviction, of showing that we have indeed attained the kind of conception of truth which the verificationist believes we cannot attain. Even someone who is persuaded that there are no compelling general arguments for verificationism ought not to find it simply *obvious* that the private linguist can intelligibly draw the needed contrasts in the sort of truth-conditional way proposed. It demands a special idea of truth, which has to be earned.

I continue to concentrate on the example of sensation (though the considerations which follow will generalise). The notion which has to be earned is that the private linguist may simply mistake how he ought to describe an occurrent sensation without its being in any way possible for him, then or later, to acquire evidence of the mistake. One consequence of admitting this idea is that he divests himself of any worthwhile reason for supposing that this situation is not *frequently* realised. When the idea of mistake is bound to (at least a high probability of) detectability, it is possible to get some purchase on the question of how error-prone a particular subject is. But to suppose that any mistake made by the private linguist is going to be undetectable entails that he has absolutely no basis for any view about the frequency of his errors. And that in turn entails that he has no entitlement to regard any of his opinions as likely to be correct. So one who favours this preemptive way with the line of reasoning developed in the preceding section immediately pays a significant price: he surrenders not merely Cartesian authority but even the weaker authority which the fallibilist is likely to want to claim for his descriptions of those of his mental states which he conceives as private. Ironically enough, he thereby places himself in position to meet the demand which his strategy was designed to avoid: the demand that he give *operational* content to the (a) and (b) contrast. For he now has reason to say that states of information of type (iii) are available, the fact of his believing '*P*' to be true invariably providing absolutely no reason for supposing it to be so. Of course he is no closer than before to explaining how he could perfectly *rationally* enjoy such a state of information, since he has no evident defence against the thought that to allow himself to have any beliefs at all with the relevant sort of subject matter is a kind of passive irrationality. But, in any case, the availability of states of information of type (iii) is no longer to the dialectical purpose: the distinction demanded by Wittgenstein's argument has already been drawn if the private linguist can indeed attain so deeply realist a conception of the truth conditions of his private 'statements'. The question remains whether he can.

There are a number of reasons for doubting it, even if we forgo invocation of the general considerations about concept-acquisition and concept-display on which Dummett, for instance, builds a global anti-realist case. One important line of attack would pivot on whether it is permissible to think of meaning as possessing the strong objectivity which this defence of private language demands: the objectivity implicit in the idea that the meaning of a statement can be settled by a presumably finite set of behavioural and intellectual episodes in such a way as to determine truth value (with appropriate assistance from the world) quite independently of any actual or possible response from those whose understanding might naturally be held to constitute the meaning of the statement. An opposing conception would be that the responses of those who understand it stand to the meaning of a statement rather as someone's behaviour stands to his character: there is conceptual space for a failure of fit—acting out of character, misuse of the statement—but the relationship is somehow, at bottom, still a constitutive one. If anything like this latter conception is right, the meaning of the private linguist's statements could not possibly sustain the utterly fortuitous connections with his preferred uses of them which the realist defence of private language demands. A strong case can, I believe, be made for this conception without invoking anything which should be regarded as question-begging anti-realist presupposition.[21] But it would take us too far afield to review it here.

There are, however, two rather more specialised lines of thought. Both contend, in different ways, that the realist defence puts the ordinary idea of *intention* under intolerable strain. First, the realist owes an account of the precise mechanism which, quite independently—as we have seen—of the private linguist's beliefs, determines the truth values of his statements. What makes it the case that, say, 'A sensation of type S_2 is occurring' is true, when it is true, independently of the private linguist's view? The answer has to be: resemblance between the occurrent sensation and those of its predecessors whose association with the label 'S_2' established its meaning. But what determines what kind, or degree, of resemblance is *good enough*—

21. Cf. Wright (1986d) (this volume Essay 3).

what qualifies the sensation as a member of the relevant class? Pain, for example, can vary in duration, in intensity, and in a host of other qualitative ways. What is going to settle how far an S_2 sensation may vary, and in what parameters, before it is disqualified? The issue has to turn on the subject's intentions on the baptismal occasions: the resemblance is close enough when it is the kind of resemblance that the subject intended. But the concept of intention has a breadth far in excess of the concept of thought: I need not have explicitly entertained a detailed scenario comprising a specific course of action in specific background circumstances before it can be true to say of me that I intended that that course of action should take place in those circumstances. It is unclear how it would be possible for the concept of intention to have this breadth if we did not take a subject's actual responses as criterial for the character of his former intentions. Suppose now, however, that the private linguist has a sensation which—if you think you understand what it means to say so— is strictly qualitatively unlike any of the baptismal cases, but which he has no hesitation in describing as a further instance of S_2. The realist defence is committed, as we have seen, to the view that there can be no better reason for regarding this response as correct than as incorrect—committed, therefore, to surrender of the ordinary criterial connection just noted. So what is to be regarded as establishing the *content* of the intention which settles whether or not this particular response is correct?

It is very unclear that the materials are to hand for a satisfactory reply. Suppose the private linguist did not envisage this precise case (again, assume we know what it is to envisage a *precise* case). Then, when we are forced to regard the character of his present response as irrelevant, it is baffling what could give the intention the requisite determinacy, could make it true, or not, that the occurrent sensation should be described as an instance of S_2. Suppose instead, more conveniently, that the private linguist did envisage the precise case. Then the question is whether that can be true indefinitely often; whether, in other words, his intention could have had the *general* content necessary in order to establish a meaning, that is, a rule. Is it possible to envisage indefinitely many 'precise cases'? The requisite rule would have taken a form, I suppose, something like:

> Whenever a situation occurs exactly like this one, 'A sensation of type S_2 is occurring' is true.

But that is open to the simple-minded reproach that a situation 'exactly like this one' is never going to occur again: something is bound to be different. The rule needs some notion of *relevant* similarity. But now the class of 'relevantly similar' situations has got to be indefinitely various, since its members may vary indefinitely in the putatively irrelevant respects. So the question recurs: what can make it true that each of these was intended to count as a case of relevant similarity when all that is available to fix the content of the original intention is the explicit thoughts which the subject entertained at the time, and when only a proper subclass of these situations can have been so explicitly thought about?

The foregoing is, of course, strongly reminiscent of a central line of thought in Kripke's Sceptical Argument. But it would be wrong to conclude that it presents a real difficulty for the would-be private linguist only if Kripke's sceptic argues cogently. For there is a difference. Kripke's sceptic gulls his interlocutor into accepting that the content of his previous intentions has to be recoverable—if it is determinate at all—from his previous thoughts and behaviour. The possibility is thereby passed over that the subject be granted non-inferential recall of previous intentions, that it be analytic of the concept of intention that people are, by and large, authoritative about their own intentions past and present. The *special* problem to which the realist defence of private language is vulnerable is that, by transcendentalising the notion of mistake and hence that of the subject's reliability, it abrogates the right to call on this aspect of the concept of intention (and thereby—I suggest—leaves Kripke's sceptic with a clear run on goal).

The second way in which the realist defence places the concept of intention under strain is perhaps more immediate. Meaning, it is again platitudinous to say, is normative: it is because statements have meaning that there is such a thing as correct, or incorrect, use of them.

This is a platitude which the truth-conditional conception of meaning, like any other, must respect. The story will be, presumably, that the making of a statement is basically correct when its truth conditions are realised (though it may be criticisable on all sorts of other grounds); and is basically incorrect when its truth conditions are not realised (though it may then be excusable on all sorts of grounds). But this story respects the normativity of meaning only if the making of statements just when their truth conditions are realised constitutes a feasible policy. And it is important to realise that its feasibility is not guaranteed if one merely accepts—which of course an anti-realist would not in certain controversial cases—that there is such a thing as the truth conditions of the statement being realized or not. It is necessary, additionally, that there can be such a thing as *aiming* at making or assenting to a statement only when its truth conditions are realised. It is about this that there is a doubt in the present case.

The trouble, once again, flows from the consequence of the realist's defence that the private linguist's believing 'A sensation of type S_2 is occurring' is no longer even the weakest ground for supposing it true. The truth of an 'observation statement' in the private language has become utterly dissociated from any practical criterion. Can the private linguist still aim at making such statements only when they are true—is there any such thing as having that intention? The question, in effect, is whether there can be such a thing as aiming at a transcendent target such that there is no criterion for saying of any particular shot whether it hits, or is likely to hit, or not, and when hitting or missing can have no consequences for the course of your own or another's future experience.

To sample the flavour of the difficulty, try the following thought experiment. Suppose you are confronted with a pair of sealed boxes, one empty and the other containing an Egyptian scarab. The scarab will vaporise instantaneously and without trace if the seal on its box is disturbed. And there is no exterior sign—no difference in weight, rattle and so on—to betray which box is which.[22] Suppose finally that the

---

22. The empty box is lined with a quantity of the same volatile material sufficient to equalize the weights.

craftsman who originally made and sealed the boxes is dead and has left no record to help you, although it is quite certain that one and only one of the boxes does contain a scarab. And now suppose you are invited to pick the box containing the scarab by placing your finger on top of it. Can you so much as *try* to do so? What exactly will distinguish your performance from a response to the invitation to pick the empty box, or just to pick a box? Not, at any rate, the exact form taken by your behaviour; that will be consistent with its being a response to any one of the three invitations. Nor the fact that it is a response to one in particular of the invitations, since—if each of the three aims really is possible—it ought to be possible, out of contrariness, to aim, say, at the scarab when invited to pick the empty box. So the distinguishing feature or features have to be purely *interior*. What are they?

If the circumstances were different, the distinction could emerge in your response to the discovery that your chosen box did, or did not, contain the scarab—disappointment, self-satisfaction, relief, indifference and so on. So could it not, in the circumstances described, be true of you when you make your choice that if it *were* possible to uncover the scarab and if it *were* in your chosen box, then your response *would* be one of relief, for example? Perhaps. But making the sought-for difference reside in the truth or falsity of such counterfactual conditionals doesn't make it any clearer how it is supposed to be apparent *to you* which intention you have; the problem merely shifts to that of explaining how you can tell which among such counterfactuals are true of you. And there would, in any case, be a strong suspicion of circularity about an attempted counterfactual analysis of the relevant differences, since it would have to be stipulated that the counterfactual circumstances be ones in which your intentions had *remained the same*. But most serious of all: the obstacles for the detection of the beetle are at best causal; whereas the realist defence of private language makes it a *conceptual* truth that there is no detecting the truth value of the private linguist's 'observation statements'. Once that is recognised, it ought to seem quite unclear what is being said if it is claimed to be true of the private linguist for instance that if he *were* to get an independent check on the truth value of 'a sensation of type S_2 is occurring', he would be gratified, or whatever.

X. CONCLUSION

The net effect of the foregoing is to confront a proponent of the possibility of private language with a dilemma. One way or another he has to draw the 'seems right'/'is right' contrast. If he accepts the need to do so operationally, by reference to practical criteria, our finding was that he will be able to do so in a satisfactory way only in very special, at best unlikely circumstances; and that an element of contingency will thereby intrude into his central claim which is quite foreign to his original conviction. If, on the other hand, he claims the distinction need not be operational but may be drawn purely truth-conditionally, he commits himself to the unwelcome consequence that the private linguist can have no satisfactory basis for his belief in his general competence to practise the private language; and this, besides involving a substantial hostage to fortune in his commitment to a highly objective notion of meaning, generates special difficulties in explaining what constitutes the truth of a statement in the private language and what constitutes the private linguist's aiming at the truth. The answer which all this suggests to the title question is therefore: 'Probably'. The ball, anyway, is in the opposition's court.

✒

This material originated in one section of a paper on Kripke's interpretation presented to the seventh International Wittgenstein Symposium at Kirchberg-am-Wechsel, Austria, in 1982, and grew under the stimulus of seminars given in 1983–4 and 1984–5 at the Universities of Pennsylvania, Glasgow, Cambridge, Durham, Lampeter, Leeds, and Edinburgh; and at a Wittgenstein 'Workshop' held in Paris under the auspices of the Collège International de Philosophie. I am grateful to those who participated for many helpful comments and criticisms, especially R. Rockingham Gill, Hugh Mellor, James Ross, Flint Schier, Bob Sharpe, John Skorupski and Scott Weinstein. I should particularly like to thank Warren Goldfarb for his work, at my request, on the problems of the Appendix. The proof of claim (d) is due, in all essentials, to him. I also thank Simon Blackburn, Peter Carruthers, O. R. Jones and Leslie Stevenson for useful comments on an earlier draft.

APPENDIX   On the number of classical truth
            functions in n variables
            which are congenial to the
            Blackburn/Harrison purpose

(This is not an exclusive for formal logicians. I have tried to present the reasoning which follows in a way which should be intelligible to a *patient* and logical, rather than logically expert, reader with a memory of school arithmetic that can at least be jogged, and a rudimentary grasp of elementary logic and set theory.)

I

The assignment block (cf. p. 267) consists of 2^n distinct n-fold rows of Ts and Fs. Let us say that one such row is an m-transform of another just in case they differ in exactly m places, $1 \leq m \leq n$. A truth function, ϕ, in n variables may be identified with that subset of these rows for which it yields the value T. Call the members of such a subset, ϕ, the ϕ-selected rows. Our question is this:

> How many subsets are there, as a function of n, with the feature that for each variable there is *both* a ϕ-unselected row where that variable is assigned T, which has a ϕ-selected 1-transform involving change in just that assignment, and which has no other ϕ-selected 1-transform, *and* a ϕ-unselected row where that variable is assigned F, which likewise has a ϕ-selected 1-transform involving change in just that assignment, and which has no other ϕ-selected 1-transform?

I can at present provide no general answer to this question; nor even a proof that the ratio of the number of such *congenial* subsets over 2^{2^n}—the number of all possible classical truth functions (theories) in n variables—is strictly decreasing as n increases. But, where $\lambda(n)$ is the number of such congenial subsets, we can justify the following claims:

(a) for $n = 2$, $\lambda(n) = 0$;

$$\text{(b) for } n = 3, \ \frac{\lambda(n)}{2^{2^n}} = \frac{1}{64};$$

$$\text{(c) for } n = 4, \ \frac{\lambda(n)}{2^{2^n}} = \frac{1}{8,192};$$

$$\text{(d) for } n \text{ in general, } \lim_{n \to \infty} \frac{\lambda(n)}{2^{2^n}} = 0.$$

I conjecture that $\dfrac{\lambda(n)}{2^{2^n}}$ is strictly decreasing as n increases. And I suggest that the *philosophical* import of claim (d) is the same as that of the truth of this conjecture.

II.   CLAIMS (A), (B) AND (C)

It will be apparent that any congenial subset will contain more than one row, selected from opposite halves of the assignment block (given the usual conventions for listing the Ts and Fs). More generally, the selected rows must collectively involve assignments of both T and F to each of the n variables. Each selected row is associated with n 1-transforms. Let us say that an unselected row is *useful* with respect to a variable or the negation of a variable, just in case it is a 1-transform of a selected row in which that variable is assigned F/T and of no other selected row. So: we have to select rows in such a way as to generate at least $2n$ useful unselected rows, each useful in a different respect. (I shall say that a selected row gives a *decision* with respect to a variable or its negation just in case some unselected 1-transform of it is useful with respect to that variable or its negation.)

Case (a), $n = 2$:
ϕ must generate at least $2n$, = 4, useful unselected rows. But the assignment block contains only four rows. So there is no such ϕ; whence claim (a).

Case (b), $n = 3$:
ϕ must generate at least $2n$, = 6, useful unselected rows. The assignment block contains only eight rows. Hence ϕ must contain at least and

at most two rows, which—since they must together involve assignments of both T and F to each of the three variables—must be *complementary* (where rows a_i and a_j in the n-variable assignment block are complementary just in case they are n-transforms).

So

$$\frac{\lambda(3)}{2^{2^3}} = \frac{2^{3-1}}{2^{2^3}} = \frac{1}{64}.$$

Case (c), $n = 4$:
Note the following three points. First, each ϕ-selected row is potentially associated with four useful rows. This potential is frustrated, however, if ϕ contains rows which are 2-transforms of each other, for then some of their 1-transforms will coincide, so will not be useful. If, for example, ϕ contains [TFTT] and [TTFT], we lose the potentially useful rows [TFFT] and [TTTT] since they are each 1-transforms of both those rows. More generally, a pair of selected 2-transforms can be associated with only four, rather than eight, useful rows; and these four can be useful in only two respects—[FFTT] and [FTFT], for example, are both still useful when ϕ is as above; but they are useful in the *same* respect, namely, with respect to the negation of the first variable.

Second, there is no point in ϕ's containing rows which are 1-transforms of each other since the useful rows associated with them will be useful in the same three respects—determined by the assignments of Ts and Fs shared by the selected rows—and no useful rows will be associated with them with respect to the variable over whose assignment they differ, nor with respect to its negation. So: if ϕ is congenial and contains a pair of 1-transforms, there is a congenial ϕ which omits one member of the pair. *Lemma:* if there are no k-fold congenial sets not involving 1-transforms, there are no $k + 1$–fold congenial sets which do involve 1-transforms. So we can, for the moment, disregard the possibility of selecting 1-transforms.

Third, if ϕ contains (at least) three rows, no two of which are 1-transforms, then it must contain at least one pair of 2-transforms.[1]

---

1. *Proof.* Let α_i, α_j, α_k be three distinct rows no two of which are 1-transforms. Suppose, for reductio, that no two are 2-transforms either. So α_i is a 3- or 4-transform

Consequences:

(i) No *ϕ*, not involving 1-transforms, containing exactly *three* rows can be congenial. *Proof:* since at least two must be 2-transforms, their associated useful rows can be so only in the same two respects, as noted above. The third row can generate at most four more associated useful rows—so we finish with only, at most, six decisions out of the eight we need.

(ii) No *ϕ*, not involving 1-transforms, containing exactly *four* rows can be congenial. While a fully explicit proof would be a bit involved, the reason, basically, is that any such *ϕ* includes four three-fold subsets, each of which must contain at least one pair of 2-transforms. There are then two possibilities. *Either ϕ* includes two *disjoint* pairs of 2-transforms—in which case we get at most four decisions out of the eight we need. Or *ϕ* includes a *transitive triple* of 2-transforms—a_i a 2-transform of a_j; a_j a 2-transform of a_k; and a_i a 2-transform of a_k—which, as the reader may verify, can collectively contribute only a *single* decision so that, given that the fourth selection can contribute at most a further four, *ϕ* can yield at most five decisions out of the eight we need.

I leave it to the reader to verify that as *ϕ* increases to five, six, seven or eight rows, the proliferation of disjoint pairs, and/or of transitive triples, of 2-transforms invariably results in fewer than the requisite eight decisions. As with $n = 3$, the only congenial sets for $n = 4$ are pairs of complementary rows.

So

$$\frac{\lambda(4)}{2^{2^4}} = \frac{2^{4-1}}{2^{2^4}} = \frac{1}{2^{13}} = \frac{1}{8,192}.$$

---

of α_j and α_j is a 3- or 4-transform of α_k. If α_i is a 4-transform of α_j, then $\alpha_i = \alpha_k$, contrary to hypothesis, if α_k is a 4-transform of α_j; and α_i is a 1-transform of α_k, contrary to hypothesis, if α_k is a 3-transform of α_j. So α_i must be a 3-transform of α_j. Likewise α_j must be a 3-transform of α_k. But then, if $\alpha_i \neq \alpha_k$, they must be 2-transforms, since α_k must differ from α_j both in that assignment which α_j and α_i have in common and in two over which they differ.

It is not true, however, even for $n = 5$, that every congenial ϕ consists in a pair of complementary rows. For example, [TTFFT, FFFTT, FTTTF] is a congenial *three*fold ϕ and [TTTTT, TTFFF, FFFTT, FFTFF] a congenial *four*fold ϕ (each selected row being at least a 3-transform of all the others). So the natural conjecture, that

$$\frac{\lambda(n)}{2^{2^n}} = \frac{1}{2^{(2^n - n) + 1}}$$

is false.

III. CLAIM (D)

Strategy of proof:

First some further definitions. Let $\tau_i \alpha$ be the 1-transform of row α which differs from it in the ith place. (Let $\tau_0 \alpha = \alpha$.) Let an r-tuple $[\alpha_1, \ldots, \alpha_r]$ of rows from the assignment block be *F-good*, respectively *T-good*, iff the ith place of α_i is F, respectively T. Let such an r-tuple *fit* a particular subset (truth function) ϕ iff, for each α_i, $\tau_i \alpha_i \in \phi$ but neither α_i itself nor any other 1-transform of $\alpha_i \in \phi$.

Plainly, where n is the number of variables with which we are concerned, ϕ is congenial iff it is fitted both by a T-good n-tuple and by an F-good n-tuple. (For the constituents of the two n-tuples will thereby comprise $2n$ useful rows, each useful in a different respect.)

Let S be the set of all rows in the 2^n-fold assignment block. And let $Y(\alpha_1, \ldots, \alpha_r)$ be the set consisting of some $\alpha_1, \ldots, \alpha_r, \in S$, and all their 1-transforms. Let an r-tuple $[\alpha_1, \ldots, \alpha_r]$ be *independent* if $\alpha_1, \ldots, \alpha_r$ are all distinct and none is a 1- or 2-transform of any other. And let an $(r + 1)$-tuple $[\alpha_1, \ldots, \alpha_r, \alpha_{r+1}]$ be *barely dependent* if $[\alpha_1, \ldots, \alpha_t]$ is independent but α_{r+1} is a 1- or 2-transform of at least one of $\alpha_1, \ldots, \alpha_r$.

Finally let $m = n/2$ if n is even, $(n + 1)/2$ if n is odd. Let C be the set of subsets, ϕ, of S such that some independent F-good m-tuple fits ϕ. And, for each $r \geq 1, \leq m$, let D_r be the set of subsets, ϕ, of S such that some barely dependent F-good $(r + 1)$-tuple fits ϕ.

The proof of claim (d) hinges on the observation that if ϕ is congenial, then $\phi \in \{C \cup D_1 \cup D_2 \cup .. \cup D_{m-1}\}$.

Proof. If ϕ is congenial, it is fitted by an F-good n-tuple $[\alpha_1, \ldots, \alpha_n]$. Let $[\alpha_1, \ldots, \alpha_m]$ be the first m terms of $[\alpha_1, \ldots, \alpha_n]$. If $[\alpha_1, \ldots, \alpha_m]$ is independent, then $\phi \in C$. If $[\alpha_1, \ldots, \alpha_m]$ is not independent, let $[\alpha_1, \ldots, \alpha_i]$ be its longest independent initial segment (which might just be α_1). In that case $[\alpha_1, \ldots, \alpha_i, \alpha_{i+1}]$ is a barely dependent F-good $(i+1)$-tuple which fits ϕ; so $\phi \in D_i$.

Accordingly the number, $\lambda(n)$, of congenial such subsets, ϕ, is less than or equal to the cardinality of the union of $C, D_1, D_2, \ldots, D_{m-1}$; which is in turn less than or equal to the sum of the cardinalities of C, $D_1, D_2, \ldots, D_{m-1}$. The proof now proceeds by estimation of upper bounds on the cardinality of these sets. We establish

Lemma A: $\overline{\overline{C}} \leq 2^{2^n - n}$ for arbitrary n, and

Lemma B: $\overline{\overline{D_1}} + \overline{\overline{D_2}} + \cdots \overline{\overline{D_{m-1}}} \leq 2^{2^n - (n/2+1)}$ provided that $n \geq 32$.
It follows that, for $n \geq 32$,

$$\lambda(n) \leq 2^{2^n - n} + 2^{2^n - (n/2+1)}.$$

Since, for $n > 2$, $2^n - n < 2^n - (n/2 + 1)$, we may infer that

$$\lambda(n) < 2 \times 2^{2^n - (n/2+1)}, = 2^{2^n - n/2}, = 2^{2^n} \times 2^{-n/2}, = 2^{2^n} \times \frac{1}{2^{n/2}}, = \frac{2^{2^n}}{2^{n/2}}.$$

Hence, dividing each side by 2^{2^n}, we have

$$\frac{\lambda(n)}{2^{2^n}} < \frac{1}{2^{n/2}}, \text{ for } n \geq 32.$$

Whence, since

$$\lim_{n \to \infty} \frac{1}{2^{n/2}} = 0,$$

claim (d) follows.

Let us therefore establish the two lemmas.

Proof of Lemma A

We prove three sublemmas:

Lemma A1: if $\alpha_1, \ldots, \alpha_r$ are any rows in S, the number of subsets ϕ such that $[\alpha_1, \ldots, \alpha_r]$ fits ϕ is less than or equal to $2^{\overline{S-Y(\alpha_1, \cdots, \alpha_r)}}$, that is, 2 to the power of the number of rows in S which are distinct from $\alpha_1, \ldots, \alpha_r$ and are not 1-transforms of them; which is the number of sets of such rows.

Proof. If $[\alpha_1, \ldots, \alpha_r]$ fits ϕ, then the only members of $Y(\alpha_1, \ldots, \alpha_r)$ which are members of ϕ are each $\tau_i \alpha_i$, $1 \leq i \leq r$. Hence if $[\alpha_1, \ldots, \alpha_r]$ fits distinct ϕ and ϕ', then the membership of ϕ and ϕ' must be the same as far as $\alpha_1, \ldots, \alpha_r$ and their 1-transforms are concerned. Hence ϕ and ϕ' must differ by virtue of one, or both, containing k-transforms, $k \geq 2$, of some $\alpha_1, \ldots, \alpha_r$ which the other does not. So the number of distinct such sets cannot be greater than the number of sets of such k-transforms of $\alpha_1, \ldots, \alpha_r$, $= 2^{\overline{S-Y(\alpha_1, \cdots, \alpha_r)}}$.

Lemma A2: if $[\alpha_1, \ldots, \alpha_r]$ is independent, then

$$\overline{Y(\alpha_1, \cdots, \alpha_r)} = r \times (n + 1).$$

Proof. Clearly $\overline{Y(\alpha_p)} = n + 1$; that is the set consisting of α_p and all its 1-transforms is an $(n + 1)$-fold set. So it suffices to reflect that, since each element of $\alpha_1, \ldots, \alpha_r$ is at least a 3-transform of every other, they have no 1-transforms in common.

Lemma A3: for each r, there are at most $2^{r \times (n-1)}$ independent F-good r-tuples.

Proof. For each i, there are 2^{n-1} rows with F in the ith place. Hence there are $(2^{n-1} \times 2^{n-1} \times 2^{n-1} \times \ldots r$ times) ways of selecting an F-good r-tuple, so $2^{r \times (n-1)}$ F-good r-tuples altogether.

By Lemma A1, the number of subsets, ϕ, such that a particular (independent) $[\alpha_1, \ldots, \alpha_m]$ fits ϕ is less than or equal to

$$2^{2^n - \overline{Y(\alpha_1, \cdots, \alpha_m)}}$$

By Lemma A2, if $[\alpha_1, \ldots, \alpha_m]$ is independent, then

$$\overline{\overline{Y(\alpha_1, \cdots, \alpha_m)}} = m \times (n + 1)$$

So the number of subsets fitted by a particular independent $[\alpha_1, \ldots, \alpha_m]$ is less than or equal to

$$2^{2^n - (m \times (n+1))}$$

Since, by Lemma A3, there are at most $2^{m \times (n-1)}$ independent F-good m-tuples, the number of subsets fitted by some independent F-good m-tuple or other, $= \overline{\overline{C}}$, can be at most

$$2^{2^n - (m \times (n+1))} \times 2^{m \times (n-1)}, = 2^{2^n - mn - m + mn - m}, = 2^{2^n - 2m}.$$

Since $2m \geq n$,

$$\overline{\overline{C}} \leq 2^{2^n - n}, \text{ Q.E.D.}$$

Proof of Lemma B

We prove two further sublemmas:

Lemma B1: if $[\alpha_1, \ldots, \alpha_{r+1}]$ is barely dependent, then

$$\overline{\overline{Y(\alpha_1, \cdots, \alpha_{r+1})}} \geq (r \times (n + 1)) + (n + 1 - 2r).$$

    Proof. By Lemma A2, $\overline{\overline{Y(\alpha_1, \cdots, \alpha_r)}} = r \times (n + 1)$. And $\overline{\overline{Y(\alpha_{r+1})}}$, of course, is $n + 1$. So Lemma B1 holds provided $Y(\alpha_{r + 1})$ does not contain *more* than $2r$ members which are also members of $Y(\alpha_1, \ldots, \alpha_r)$. Suppose, for reductio, that there are more than $2r$ such. Then (*) there must be some α_p in $[\alpha_1, \ldots, \alpha_r]$ such that $Y(\alpha_p)$ and $Y(\alpha_{r + 1})$ have at least three members in common. Now α_p and $\alpha_{r + 1}$ cannot be k-transforms, for any $k \geq 3$, or $Y(\alpha_p) \cap Y(\alpha_{r + 1})$ would be empty. But they are distinct, by the definition of 'barely dependent'. Hence there are two cases:

Case (a): α_p and α_{r+1} are 1-transforms. Then $Y(\alpha_p) \cap Y(\alpha_{r+1}) = \{\alpha_p, \alpha_{r+1}\}$, contrary to (*).

Case (b): α_p and α_{r+1} are 2-transforms, differing in the ith and jth places. Then $Y(\alpha_p) \cap Y(\alpha_{r+1}) = \{\tau_i\alpha_p, \tau_j\alpha_p\}$, again contrary to (*).

Lemma B2: for each r there are at most

$$\frac{r \times n \times (n+1)}{2} \times 2^{r \times (n-1)}$$

barely dependent F-good $(r + 1)$-tuples.

Proof. Each such $(r + 1)$-tuple is constituted by an initial independent F-good r-tuple, plus a 1- or 2-transform of one of the first r elements. By Lemma A3, those first r elements may be chosen in at most $2^{r \times (n-1)}$ ways. Now, any a, ϵS, has n 1-transforms and $(n - 1 + n - 2 + \ldots + 1)$ 2-transforms; so

$$\frac{(n+1) \times n}{2}$$

1- and 2-transforms. Hence, given that the first r elements have been chosen, the $r + 1^{\text{st}}$ may be chosen in at most

$$\frac{r \times n \times (n+1)}{2}$$

ways. (Of course, some of these choices will not be consistent with F-goodness. But remember that we are estimating an *upper* bound.) Thus the total number of ways of choosing the first r, plus the $r + 1^{\text{st}}$ element, will not exceed

$$\frac{r \times n \times (n+1)}{2} \times 2^{r \times (n-1)}.$$

Now $\overline{\overline{D_r}}$, = the number of subsets, ϕ, of S which are fitted by some barely dependent F-good $(r + 1)$-tuple, will not exceed the product of the maximum number of subsets fitted by a particular $(r + 1)$-tuple and the maximum number of barely dependent F-good $(r + 1)$-tuples.

By Lemma $A1$ and $B1$, the first is less than or equal to $2^{2^n - ((r \times (n+1)) + (n + 1 - 2r))}$.

By Lemma B2, the second is

$$\frac{r \times n \times (n + 1)}{2} \times 2^{r \times (n-1)}.$$

So

$$\overline{\overline{D_r}} \leq \frac{r \times n \times (n + 1)}{2} \times 2^{r \times (n-1)} \times 2^{2^n - ((r \times (n+1)) + (n+1-2r))}$$

which is

$$\frac{r \times n \times (n + 1)}{2} \times 2^{rn-r+2^n - ((rn+r)+(n+1-2r))}$$

$$\text{i.e.} \quad '' \quad \times 2^{rn-r+2^n - rn - r - n - 1 + 2r},$$

$$\text{i.e.} \quad '' \quad \times 2^{2^n - (n+1)}.$$

Hence

$$\overline{\overline{D_1}} + \cdots + \overline{\overline{D_{m-1}}} \leq \frac{n \times (n + 1)}{2} \times 2^{2^n - (n+1)} \times \left[1 + 2 + \cdots + m - 1\right],$$

$$= \frac{n \times (n + 1)}{2} \times 2^{2^n - (n+1)} \times \frac{(m - 1) \times m}{2},$$

$$= \frac{n \times (n + 1) \times (m - 1) \times m}{4} \times 2^{2^n - (n+1)}.$$

Let

$$\alpha = \frac{n \times (n + 1) \times (m - 1) \times m}{4}$$

$$\text{and } \beta = 2^n - (n + 1),$$

$$\text{and } k = \overline{\overline{D_1}} + \cdots + \overline{\overline{D_{r-1}}}.$$

So we have shown that $k \leq \alpha \times 2^{\beta}$.

Now an interesting arithmetical fact: for values of $n \geq 32$, and only for such values,

$$\alpha \times \frac{1}{2^{n/2}} \leq 1.$$

So $\alpha \leq 2^{n/2}$.

So $k \leq 2^{n/2} \times 2^{\beta}, = 2^{2^n - (n+1) + n/2}$,

$$= 2^{2^n - (n/2+1)}, \text{ which is Lemma B.}$$

Q. E. D.

9

Wittgenstein's Later Philosophy of Mind: Sensation, Privacy and Intention

I want to point, very schematically, to a connection, well worth further study, between the kind of doubt about the possibility of private language which *Philosophical Investigations* §258 should be seen as suggesting and an idea about our knowledge of our own intentional states—beliefs, desires, intentions, etc.—for which I have also claimed a Wittgensteinian origin in recent papers.[1] But I shall try to presuppose no familiarity with those discussions.

The basic ideas in §258 are two: first, that the 'statements' in a private language of sensation would be contentful only if there were a substantial distinction between what it seemed right to the user of a private language—a *Linguist*—to say or think, and what really was right; and, second, that there can be no such distinction. The connection of this thought with the nature of knowledge of one's own intentions turns on two plausible provisos: that the meanings of a Linguist's private expressions—like those of any expressions—would

---

1. See Wright (1987a) (this volume Essay 5); Wright (1989c) (this volume Essay 7). The present essay complements and enlarges on section IX of Wright (1986a) (this volume Essay 8). See also Wright (1989a) (this volume Essay 6).

have to be the children of convention; and that a Linguist could have no recourse but, one way or another, to generate the conventions governing a private language out of his own intentions. Roughly: a correct private identification of a sensation would involve applying the identifying symbol to a sensation of the type which the Linguist *intended* that it should be associated with in doing whatever he did do to establish that symbol's meaning. The supporter of private language has an obligation, therefore, to ensure that there is a notion of intention robust enough to serve the generation of meanings, and hence truths, in the way which the Linguist needs; specifically, a notion of intention such that the formation of intentions, even in circumstances of privacy, can create facts about the proper description of sensations which await him in the future. That is an obligation which, on any view about knowledge of one's own intentional states along the broad lines I am later going to canvass, cannot be discharged.

I.   Wittgenstein and Cartesianism: A Brief Overview

Often in his later work Wittgenstein writes as though there were a clear—or clear enough—separation between our ordinary, as it were, first-order linguistic practices—which he believes stand in no need of justification and are not open to philosophical correction—and the kinds of thing (for instance, the sort of remark a mathematician might make about the objectivity and reality of mathematical facts) which we are inclined to say when we turn to philosophical reflection about those practices. This perspective will go against the grain for anyone who thinks that genuine conceptual tensions and confusions can be implicit in our ordinary thought. On the latter view, Wittgenstein's non-revisionary view of all but philosophical talk and thought—however they are to be demarcated from the rest—begs a substantial question. Rather, it will be a prime task of philosophy to check for genuine singularities in our ordinary thinking, usually presentable in the form of paradox; to formulate them in the sharpest possible form; and then to attempt to resolve them, either by showing that, on careful analysis, erroneous assumptions are involved—which is what we ordinarily think of a 'solution' to a philosophical problem as consisting in—or by devising and testing the consequences of revisions in the modes of thought which give rise to the difficulty.

Wittgenstein stands opposed to this sort of view. For him, it seems, there can be no genuine philosophical problems of the kind which it would be the task of philosophy, so conceived, to discover. There are merely knots of confusion into which we are prone to tangle ourselves when we incline to philosophical reflection—knots which can be untied only by assiduous attention to the details of the linguistic practices which motivate our reflections.

A challenge facing the interpreter of Wittgenstein's later writings is to reconcile this broad conception of the scope and limits of philosophical enquiry with the character of the philosophy of mind which emerges in the *Investigations* and later. For Wittgenstein's efforts are directed against a picture of the mind which is so intuitively natural and can seem to go so deep in our ordinary thinking that it seems quite perverse to regard it as *philosophical*. This picture does not feel like something we come to when we reflect, in perhaps misguided ways, on ordinary discourse concerning the mental. Rather, it seems to be imposed upon us, to be of the essence of the mind. If it is not appropriate, then we may well feel that we do not really understand some of the most salient features of our discourse concerning our own and others' mental states—that we do not really know what, in talking the way we do about the mental, we are about.

The picture in question constitutes what is often, though probably inaccurately, referred to as the *Cartesian* idea of the mind. According to it, each of us inhabits, in effect, two worlds. There is the ordinary material world existing in public space, to whose ingredient objects and states of affairs we all have access in principle. But each of us in addition has exclusive access to what is literally a world of our own—a world whose denizens constitute the truth-conferrers for ascriptions to us—made by others or ourselves—of sensations, moods, emotions and intentional states like belief, desire and intention itself. Our cognition of each world is mediated by distinctive respective sets of concepts. We sense the material world and, by organising our sensings under appropriate concepts, come to perceive it. We experience our sensations, for example, and, by organising these experiences under appropriate concepts, come to introspective awareness of our interior lives. The difference is only that the exclusivity of our access to our inner worlds means that it is, for each of us, a matter of conjecture whether anything of the taxonomy of our own interior states is replicated in others—whether the words which provide our common stock of descriptions of such states individuate, when used in one mouth, events, objects, processes and so on, of kinds similar, or quite different, to those which they specify when used by another. So human consciousness is apparently set in a predicament: the things which, minute by minute, are most intimately constitutive of us—our thoughts, feelings and emotions, and the 'contents' of our heads in general—are strictly our prisoners and are barred from another's (literal) sympathy.

Any nervousness which this conception may cause us is misplaced if Wittgenstein's view is correct that it is merely a product of misguided philosophical theorising. But what reason is there to see it as mere 'theory'—on what data is it based? And why, if it is, is it a bad theory?

The 'data' are linguistic, and familiar. Descriptions of one's own sensations, moods, emotions, beliefs and desires are characteristically (though not invariably) offered in the form of *avowals:* claims about one's own psychology which are standardly received as groundlessly authoritative. For others to have reason to believe that you are sincere in making such a claim is for them *eo ipso* to have reason to believe you. And when you make such a claim, you neither will be able, nor in general may be appropriately asked, to produce reasons for it. Of course, we say things like 'Well, it is my headache; I ought to know how bad it is'—but such remarks only serve, by emphasising the first-personal pedigree of a claim, precisely to excuse the absence of reasons. These features mark contrasts with our use of statements concerning the psychology of others. My evident sincerity in claiming that Jones is bored does not *eo ipso* give you any reason to believe me—you need in addition to have reason to think that I am in position to have formed a justified view; and justification here always depends upon the possession of reasons, grounded in the say-ings and doings of the subject, features of the context and back-ground knowledge.

These asymmetries in the 'grammar' of psychological discourse are apparently quite satisfyingly explained by Cartesianism. Imagine a walled garden which I and only I can physically observe—I have a uniquely suitable vantage point and no one else is in position to see in at all. And suppose that you know that this is the situation. Then you can be expected, barring doubts about my sincerity or competence in the language which I am using, to treat my assertions about the gar-den as authoritative, and as standing in no need of justification; it is justification enough that I am understood to be in sole position to see what is happening within the walls. For what is happening, by con-trast, you have only the evidence of what I say and do, and your general knowledge of gardens. You are thus restricted, broadly, to inference-based opinion about my garden. Thus, at first sight, the 'grammar' of psychological reports can seem closely to resemble that of observational privilege. That we benefit from a kind of observa-tional privilege in reporting our psychological states and goings-on is exactly the Cartesian thought.

There is, certainly, one important difference between the garden scenario and its Cartesian counterpart: genuine observation involves the exercise of *fallible* perceptual abilities—I may assert falsehoods from my vantage point not out of insincerity or incomprehension but because I misperceive. By contrast, the 'inner eye' is prone to no such frailty. However, rather than view that as an obstacle to the model, Cartesianism sees it as a distinctive feature of the epistemology of the inner realm that its ingredients are given to consciousness *immedi-ately,* so that no analogue of misperception can get a toehold.

The best—indeed, the only—way of showing that this is merely a picture, superintendent upon rather than immanent in anything which deserves to be regarded as 'our ordinary thought about the mental', is to disclose that it is not really in harmony with all aspects of our linguistic practice. As I read it, the *Investigations'* attempt to do this follows a two-pronged strategy. The first prong assembles argument in detail that particular psychological states are not items *for* consciousness in the way the Cartesian picture represents them. The Cartesian picture elevates (a certain conception of) sensation, and of the awareness of sensation, to the status of paradigms of the mental. The thrust of the first part of Wittgenstein's critique is that this quite misrepresents belief, desire, hope, fear, expectation, intention, meaning and understanding.

Part of the polemic here is provided by a repeated insistence that an honest introspective attempt to find the constituents of such states of mind within the occurrent phenomena of consciousness simply fails. There is nothing introspectible by which intending, understanding, believing, etc., even *seem* to be distinguished. But a more fundamental point is that the details of the phenomena of consciousness which may be associated with understanding, expecting, intending, hoping, etc., are neither in general called upon, nor able, to sustain the kinds of internal connection with aspects of a subject's (subsequent) doings and reactions which mental states of this kind essentially sustain. To take a very familiar instance: if coming to understand 'in a flash' the rule governing a decimal expansion were a matter *purely* of the occurrence of certain events in consciousness, then it would be a point of contingency that people who so come to understand something are able subsequently to deliver appropriate kinds of performance. But this is not a contingency; it is a conceptual requirement on the propriety of describing someone as having understood that they be able to perform properly. Ascribing understanding is ascribing (something very like) an ability.

Likewise, if expecting someone to tea were a matter purely of the occurrence of certain states and processes of consciousness, then it would be a contingency how it correlated with any subsequent goings-on which can be matters of public awareness. But such correlations are not invariably points of contingency: an expectation is constitutively identified by the distinction it effects between states of affairs which comply with it and those which do not; and we are quite at ease in drawing this distinction by reference to aspects of a subject's subsequent reactions—of anticipation, surprise and, of course, what she has to say—without any regard to the question whether the distinction thereby drawn was somehow prefigured in—could have been 'read off' from—her conscious phenomenology at the time the expectation was formed. If Jones's name is written in your diary and you react with no surprise when he appears on your doorstep, but welcome him in, the case for saying that you were expecting him—although defeasible by considerations of various kinds—does not have to answer to the events and processes within your consciousness in the earlier part of the day.

The general drift of the first prong of Wittgenstein's critique, then, is that although the Cartesian picture can seem well-motivated by certain elements in the 'grammar' of psychological ascriptions, it actually lacks the resources to give a satisfactory account of certain crucial aspects of our talk of intentional states—of states with a content which may be verified, acted upon, complied with, fulfilled, etc., by subsequent performances, states of affairs and events. We shall return to the point later. Clearly, however, by taking this line about intentional states, Wittgenstein reserves a need for a further, separate treatment of the kind of states of mind to which, putatively, the Cartesian mistakenly assimilates the intentional—the range of occurrent phenomena of consciousness which, in pursuing the first prong, Wittgenstein is content, at least *pro tempore*, to contrast with understanding, intending and their kin.

How is this range demarcated? Well, not sharply and there is no reason to expect otherwise. Wittgenstein adverts to a class of states which display the temporality of ordinary processes: states which, like a sensation or mood, ringing in the ears or a visual disturbance, typically have a determinately dated onset and departure, are interruptible by breaks in consciousness, may without incongruity be said to have been enjoyed (or suffered) continuously over a certain period, to have intensified in the last hour and so on. But our ordinary thinking makes another distinction which nets a large number of the same fish: very small children and animals, we suppose, have pains and tickles, can suffer tinnitus, can become anxious or elated—so these are states whose occurrence, at least in a central class of cases, makes no demands upon the conceptual resources of the subject.

Surely it cannot be an error to treat *these* as states of consciousness; if they are not states of consciousness, nothing is. So what is the Cartesian error here? That—even here, in the case of pure states of consciousness, where it might have seemed most harmlessly apt—the imagery of observer and observatum is misimported into the concept of introspection, whatever the etymology of the word might suggest. Even the purely phenomenological does not provide 'a world of one's own'. The authority which a first-personal ascription of a sensation, for instance, typically carries, is not to be explained by reference to the model of privileged observation of something within, excluded from others' scrutiny. A state there certainly is, of course, and it is harmless to describe it as 'inner' or 'interior', providing we merely advert thereby to such a familiar phenomenon as the possibility of concealing a pain. But such states are not objects for consciousness in any sense which would render it moot whether others could know their real character, or knowingly share the concepts under which the subject brings them in judgement. And that those things should be moot is the inevitable consequence of the Cartesian conception of the manner in which sensations, for example, are interior to their subject. Wittgenstein argues, by contrast, that the ability to make judgements about one's sensations—in particular, to classify them—can call only on concepts which are, at least potentially, public property and may justifiably be regarded as such. Since judgements concerning one's own sensations would not, on the Cartesian model, comply with such a constraint, it follows that the model is inadequate—a misunderstanding of the relation between a subject and his states of consciousness, founded upon a misreading of the grammar of avowals and phenomena like stoicism and pretence. All this is the gist of the second prong in the overall strategy—the extended examination of the idea of psychological privacy and, in particular, the 'private-language argument'.

In sum and reversing the order: the Cartesian philosophy of mind is guilty, in Wittgenstein's view, of misunderstanding the relation between a conscious subject and those of its states for which the bogus epistemology of inward observation is most attractive to us; and of compounding this misunderstanding by mis-assimilating great sweeps of the mental to such states of mind, so misconceived.

II. THE NEED FOR THE SEEMS RIGHT / IS RIGHT DISTINCTION

According to the broadly Cartesian conception of the mental which Wittgenstein is examining, the truth of any of a Linguist's judgements concerning his sensations will originate somewhat in the fashion of the truth of a contingent report of observation: it will be a matter of depiction of an appropriate—albeit interior—truth-conferring state of affairs, something manifest to consciousness but distinct from the judging, whose content is precisely that such a state of affairs obtains. The existence of a contrast between what seems right to the Linguist and what is right is simply a requirement of this comparison: something demanded if it is to be appropriate to think of matters in terms of a possible *fit*, or congruence, between the Linguist's judgements concerning his sensations and the character which those sensations actually have.

It is no cause for concern about the propriety of this demand that we are concerned with judgements about states which the Linguist is necessarily aware of. For—to stress a point made a moment ago—the Linguist's—and our ordinary—conception of sensations allows for their occurrence in subjects, like animals or very young children, who lack the conceptual wherewithal to judge and classify them. So the point stands: if judgements about sensation are to be viewed on the Cartesian observational model, we should conceive of their correctness, when they are correct, as rendered by something distinct from the judgement—the character of the brute sensation, the fact that it falls under the concept which it is thereby judged to fall under.

If a seems right/is right distinction is necessary, what would suffice to constitute a content for it? The implied answer of §258 is: some independent 'criterion' of correctness—some method whereby the Linguist could further appraise judgements which initially strike him as correct. But the privacy of the subject matter, and of the concepts under which the Linguist is putatively bringing it, necessarily pre-empt, Wittgenstein seems to suggest, the possibility of any such criterion. So, he ventures to conclude, no content can be established for the needed idea of congruence between the Linguist's successive convictions and the putative states of affairs they concern. And hence 'here we can't talk about "right"'.

There are two salient lines of defence open to the friend of privacy. One of them[2] contests whether the Linguist does irremediably lack all means for a principled appraisal of his own judgements. The suggestion is that by constructing sufficient of a system—a *theory*—around his judgements, the Linguist could establish conditions of acceptability which related not just to the judgements' initial appeal but to principled holistic constraints. And he could thereby have, in certain circumstances, compelling reason to overturn initially appealing judgements which he would otherwise have accepted. That would surely be to possess a 'criterion of correctness' in the sense material to §258.

This proposal is investigated in some detail in Essay 8. It's prospects turn out to be extremely unpromising. But our present business is to review an argument to the effect that the friend of privacy has no alternative to it.

The second response questions whether, in order for the Linguist to be entitled to the needed distinction between his judgements and the states of affairs to which they are supposed to correspond, a further *criterion* is necessary for their acceptability beyond their commanding his initial assent. On the contrary: difficulty in making out a contrast between what seems right to the Linguist and what is right is exactly to be expected if, as we naturally suppose, one's judgements about

2. See Harrison (1974), chaps. 3, 6; esp. p. 161; Blackburn (1984), concluding pages.

one's own sensations are *infallible*. In that case, so far from wanting a criterion for the correctness of his judgements, the Linguist has a decisive such criterion in the very phenomenon of judgement itself. No other criterion is necessary or, if it is intended that it should dominate and, on occasion, correct the Linguist's impressions, possible.

A seems right/is right distinction was demanded in order to vindicate the idea that the Linguist has a genuine class of recognitional judgements in play, answerable to a genuine range of situations of which it is possible—if only for the Linguist—to have a reasonably definite conception. The second response brings out that no fast-track demonstration that these ideas have no content can be based purely on the impossibility of *ascertainable* contrasts between what the Linguist is/was inclined to think and what is/was actually so. For *if* there can be such a thing as infallible judgement, of any subject matter, then there will be both a genuine distinction between the judging and the states of affairs judged and no possibility of that kind of ascertainable contrast. Our infallibility, no less than the contentlessness of the distinction, would explain our inability to tie it to operationally effective criteria of application. Pleading infallibility, as it were, does not, to stress, *establish* the needed distinction;[3] but the prima facie possibility of the plea seems to point up a lacuna in Wittgenstein's reasons for thinking that it cannot be established.

III. INFALLIBILITY

How, though, can judgement, even about so intimate a matter as one's own sensations, ever be infallible? It is true, of course, that there are many ways in which one *cannot*, apparently, go wrong in making such judgements. There is, for instance, no distinction between a

---

3. Rather, the propriety of regarding a class of judgements as genuinely infallible, as opposed to merely *incorrigible*, depends precisely on making out the distinction. The point is made in Wright (1980), pp. 356–7 (but note that 'incorrigible' is there, unhappily, used as I am now using 'infallible').

sensation's appearance, as it were, and its reality, so no ways in which appearances can deceive; there are no analogues, for sensation, of bad lighting, illusions of perspective and background noise. There is also no analogue of the distinction between how a perceived object seems to a particular subject and how it publicly seems; for the way a sensation feels to someone *is* the way it feels, *simpliciter*. But such considerations, though limiting the range of possible sources of error, do not establish infallibility. Classifying a sensation properly, as the Linguist conceives it, is a matter of responding with an appropriate concept to a token of a type of interior state of affairs which could have been instantiated in his consciousness even had he lacked the capacity to make judgements about it altogether. So it should still be viewed as a substantial cognitive accomplishment—a simple but genuine feat of phenomenological taxonomy. As such, it calls, one would imagine, for wheels to turn within one's cognitive apparatus—for presumably causally based classificatory mechanisms to fire. Why can't they misfire? Is it even intelligible that they might somehow be proof against misfire? Consider *Investigations* §271, where Wittgenstein has his interlocutor say:

> Imagine a person whose memory could not retain *what* the word 'pain' meant—so that he constantly called different things by that name—but nevertheless used the word in a way fitting in with the usual symptoms and presuppositions of pain.

Wittgenstein continues *in propria voce*

> —In short, he uses it as we all do. Here I should like to say: a wheel that can be turned though nothing else moves with it, is not part of the mechanism.

Here the 'idle wheel' is that putative ingredient in being competent in the ascription of pain to oneself and others which is supposed to involve the proper classification of interior objects, and hence to depend on success in remembering how such objects have to be if they are rightly to be classified as 'pain'. Wittgenstein's suggestion is that we ought to be doubtful whether any such interior classificatory ability is essentially involved in understanding 'pain' if somebody could lack it yet apparently function in all respects normally in his use of the word. Well, suppose we are unimpressed by that suggestion; does not the example at least force the Linguist to acknowledge one kind of fallibility? Clearly the sincere use of a private *language* cannot be infallible. For if the Linguist can establish private meanings, he can also lose track of them and use symbols in ways which diverge from the requirements of the meanings which he himself established.

The infallibilist will rejoin that no one, of course, intended to deny that merely *verbal* mistakes—slips of the tongue and so forth—are possible in the description of a subject matter about which we are infallible. There are questions here, however, about what we ought to include under the heading of 'verbal' slips. A springboard is provided by a remark at *Investigations* II, §xi, p. 272. Wittgenstein writes: 'Always get rid of the idea of the private object in this way: assume that it constantly changes, but that you do not notice the change because your memory constantly deceives you.' I shall not now consider how the fantasy of such a constant memory deception is supposed to undermine the 'private object'. Ask instead: what exact shape is the envisaged memory deception supposed to take? Consider this possible parallel: you watch a coloured light which varies between red, green and blue, and report its colour at specified intervals; you do so correctly, but at each stage you misremember both how the light was at the last stage and how you classified it, in such a way that it seems to you that there has been no variation in colour at all and that you have all along been describing the colours correctly.

In that way of taking the example there is no question about your continuing competence with colour concepts—for all your judgements are correct. Your failings belong entirely to your memory of facts. It is different in the following case. This time—when it comes, say, to reporting the light's colour for the second time—you *correctly* remember what judgement you previously made but misremember how the light then looked, taking it that there has been no change. Finding yourself now inclined to a different judgement, you may be inclined to disown the previous one; but equally, its precedent may stifle your inclination to what would in fact be the correct judgement about the present colour of the light. In this way, persistent failures of factual memory might destabilise your judgements of colour. Would these slips be 'merely verbal'?

Well, such a destabilisation need not merely involve your use of colour *vocabulary*. Someone learning a second language might occasionally muddle the names of colours, calling purple 'amarillo', for instance, or orange 'rojo'. However the *beliefs* about colours which, thus incompetently, the subject tried to express would be beliefs whose contents were determined by our ordinary concepts of colour. It is not merely an analogue of this kind of muddle to which the Linguist has to be liable in principle. Consider instead the case of a child learning to classify colours in English as his first language. Here it is not a matter of mapping a vocabulary onto an antecedently grasped set of concepts; rather, the boundaries of the concepts are set by the linguistic practice being acquired. And mastery of the vocabulary is not an all-or-nothing matter; various degrees of grasp are possible. There will be stages at which the child is acquainted with some but not all familiar colour terms; and, more significantly, there may be stages at which his grasp of the use of particular colour terms is partial. He may, for instance, reliably classify blue things as 'blue', and red things as 'red', but be inclined, until corrected, to classify most shades of purple as 'blue'and some—but not all—of the remainder as 'red'. Now normally, if we say that someone has made a verbal error, we credit him with the right beliefs about the facts—ergo the concepts necessary to grasp the contents of those beliefs. So it would be unhappy to say that the child's errors are merely verbal. If they were merely verbal, then he would be misusing the sentence, 'This is blue', to express the *right* beliefs, ergo beliefs which he has the conceptual resources to entertain, about the colours of purple things. But the right beliefs are precisely to the effect that the objects in question are *purple*. So to regard his errors as verbal would commit us to ascribing the concept of purple to him which, since grasping it involves mastery of the very linguistic boundaries to which he is insensitive, is exactly what he lacks.

In the example as described, it would be proper to credit the child with *some*—not yet the correct—concepts of red, blue and purple. There are degrees of grasp of colour concepts, and, correlatively, degrees of confusion. Normally people move through such intermediate degrees of grasp to attain a standard competence in colour judgement which stays with them for the rest of their lives. But the durability of the competence is a contingency, like the durability of the capacity to skate, or balance on a bicycle. A kind of *recidivism* is evidently possible, and might have been quite usual; human existence supplies many examples, after all, of gradual loss of capacities which, in the earlier part of our lives, we may have worked hard to acquire. Bizarre lapses of memory, as in the example above, might generate such recidivism.

What goes for the public classification of colours must go, on the Cartesian model, for the private classification of sensations. The Linguist, then, who would conceive of his ability to classify his sensations as an inward-looking recognitional skill, must recognise two potential kinds of error which the fallibility of his memory may engineer. First, he may suffer *linguistic amnesia*—forget which expressions respectively denote which kinds of sensations—although retaining a grasp of the various sensation *kinds* which, in the language as originally instituted, he had determined the use of the various classificatory terms to signal. Second he may suffer from a kind of *conceptual recidivism* parallel to that of someone who, having once mastered the system of colour concepts reflected in the standard vocabulary in English, slips back into, for example, classifying a large class of shades of purple with the blues. The Linguist may slip, that is to say, into classificatory practices which, judged in the light of his own previous practice, would reflect a merely partial grasp of the concepts which were constituted therein. And this may happen while his dominant intention is to conserve his original classificatory scheme.

Such recidivism is, evidently, merely one among a variety of possible forms of conceptual slippage: departures from the (putative) system of concepts enshrined in the Linguist's original practice may take all kinds of, perhaps unprecedented, directions. There is also the more drastic possibility of slippage to the point where no determinate concepts are being exercised at all: a subject's colour classifications, after a stroke or during the influence of a powerful drug, might come to be quite chaotic and irregular in circumstances which betray no abnormality in her vision of colour—she shows, for instance, no impairment in her capacity to discriminate among coloured objects, recognises the cat configured by a pattern of red dots among green dots and so on. Such a subject might naturally be decribed as having (temporarily) lost her colour concepts—even if, as it seemed to her, she was continuing to classify colours as she always had. A corresponding possibility must apply to the Linguist.

Do these reflections effect any progress against infallibilism? The point of the infallibilist's original protest, that he had not, of course, meant to exclude verbal error, was to emphasise that the claim of infallibility related to judgements about sensation, not their proper form of expression. Have we done anything to dislodge that claim? Only, it might seem, if linguistic amnesia with respect to colour adjectives, or recidivism with respect to colour concepts, or drastic slippage would involve false judgements of colour. But in none of these cases does that need to be so. The linguistic amnesiac forms a true belief which he forgets how to express. The recidivist's grasp is in doubt of the concepts which, in ascribing to him the false belief that a particular purple object is blue, we should apparently be crediting him with. On the other hand, there is no reason to suppose that he errs in the belief he forms using the degenerate colour concepts into which he has lapsed. Finally, the drastic slipper, so to say, makes no judgement of colour at all. So it seems that the infallibilist's stonewall response to the need for a seems right/is right distinction is so far quite undilapidated.

We might demur. Consider a recidivist who affirms of a purple patch the sentence, 'That is blue'. There is, as noted, no basis for ascribing to her the (false) belief that the patch is blue; and no basis for thinking that the belief which that sentence now expresses in her idiolect is false. Still, let her recidivism be unwitting and let her intention be to conform to the linguistic practice of her community. Then, although now lacking the concepts needed to grasp its content, she will nevertheless hold false beliefs *about* the belief actually expressed by her tokening of 'That is blue'—the belief that the demonstrated object is blue—viz. that she holds it, and that it is true. The same goes for the drastic slipper who continues—as it seems to him, smoothly and normally—to use his original colour vocabulary: he will repeatedly believe, falsely, that he holds the beliefs actually expressed by tokens of sentences containing that vocabulary, and, falsely, that those beliefs are true. And indeed, the point is good for the sort of linguistic amnesiac who, while retaining his grasp of the concept purple, forgets that it is expressed by 'purple' and essays to predicate it by uses of 'blue' instead.

Analogues of each case must hold for the Linguist too, so long as we suppose that he was originally successful in endowing the symbols of the private language with determinate content and that his dominant intention remains to use the language in conformity with that original endowment. The same sort of second-order error will have to be a possibility: instances where he falsely believes that he holds the belief expressed, courtesy of the original semantics, by a token of a particular private sentence, and falsely believes that the belief in question is true.

Does this puncture infallibilism? Well yes, if infallibility about a particular subject matter is held to demand not merely that a subject cannot form false beliefs about it but that there be no possibility of his being deluded into thinking that he holds, truly, a particular such belief when he does not hold it and it is false. But the issue begins to seem terminological. The important point is that the dialectical situation set up by the possibility of such second-order failings is just as it would be if we had demonstrated the possibility of first-order error. In either case, mistakes—perhaps ineradicable mistakes—must be possible about what constitutes correctly using a token sentence of the private language, by original standards of correctness which it remains the Linguist's dominant intention to preserve. The possibility of first-order error would merely open up additional ways in which such mistakes might occur. But the crux for the Cartesian is to attach sense to their occurrence in any way at all.

IV. PRIVACY AND INTENTION

We should make a distinction before we proceed. There is bigger and smaller game to go after here. One way of understanding the goal of a 'private-language argument' is exactly as the phrase suggests: an argument to the effect that a subject could not deliberately institute a *language,* a conventionally driven system of symbols for the annotation of recurrent features of a range of states and objects which were essentially private to him.[4] It would not follow immediately that there was no possibility of bringing such a subject matter under *private concepts*—that a subject could not make it the object of private thoughts. That is the bigger game. We can capture both if we have the lemma in place that there is nothing in which such thought could consist except the manipulation of a private language.

Now, this lemma can seem obviously wrong. If a private language exists by grace of conventional connections between its symbols and its subject matter, then must not that subject matter have been conceptualised in advance of the institution of the conventional connections? Surely, it is only when there is already a taxonomy of the subject matter in thought that one can determine to express it in particular conventional ways.

That seems right for the case of the deliberately instituted symbol. But when we think of the semantics of our ordinary public language as conventional, we do not, of course, imagine that it is in general the product of deliberate institution, against a background of concepts grasped independently. To think that is to embark on a high road to

---

4. Aspects of Wittgenstein's own presentation—that deliberate decisions are imagined to be taken by the Diarist, for instance—might seem to invite such a reading.

Platonic innatism. Wittgenstein's later philosophy presents, familiarly, a different perspective: one in which a child's learning of a first language is assimilated not to the mapping of symbols onto concepts—as if, as in the Augustinian picture at the start of the *Investigations*, there was no important difference between learning a first and a second language—but to *training*, in the same sense in which an animal is trained in certain routines. For this perspective, the formation of concepts is co-eval with the development of intentional linguistic activity. The having of a concept—at least in a very wide class of cases—is immanent in, rather than underlies, competent linguistic performance.

If the Linguist's private concepts would be constituted, if by anything, then by his very use of the private language, the bigger game can be captured with the smaller. Private concepts will require the conventional use of private symbols. And conceptual recidivism/drastic slippage will involve loss of grip on conventions governing the use of those symbols, unwitting failure to deploy them in a fashion conservative of those conventions, an overarching conservative intention notwithstanding. The challenge to explain how those possibilities might afflict the Linguist becomes the challenge to explain how he might lose track of the rules which, by his overarching intention, constitute proper practice of the private language.

How might such an explanation proceed? In terms of the second proviso I mentioned at the beginning, there is only one possible shape. The conventions of which the Linguist now has at best an imperfect grasp have to be thought of as constituted in his previous intentional linguistic activity. Inadvertent breaches of the conventions must involve not using the language in the way he previously intended to. To say that the Linguist has, for example, gone recidivist in his uses of S is to say that he is endorsing uses which he would not endorse were he to keep faith with intentions which previously informed his mature practice of the language, despite the overarching intention that his present practice be consonant with them—and this not because of any sort of misapprehension of 'the facts', for which the Cartesian epistemology of sensation provides no scope, but because of a loss of grip on the intentions themselves. Whence the connection of the private-language issue with our knowledge of our own intentions and of our intentional states in general.

An awareness of the philosophically perplexing character of this type of self-knowledge seems to have intensified recently. How, broadly, is it possible to have such knowledge? Two familiar paradigms are liable to blinker our response to the question: the paradigms of knowledge by inference and of knowledge by observation. But the idea that knowledge of one's own intentional states is anything but unusually arrived at inferentially misrepresents both their phenomenology and their 'grammar'. We do not in general have any account to offer of the grounds on which we take ourselves to have the beliefs, intentions, etc., which we do, and it is normally quite out of place to expect such an account. Intentional states are *avowable*: they are subject to groundless, authoritative self-ascription, and it belongs to their essence that they are so.[5]

The Cartesian conception of knowledge of one's own intentional states opts for the other, observational paradigm: the intentional state is, typically, simply an object for consciousness, and is directly recognised by the subject for what it is. This idea, as noted earlier, is a major target of Wittgenstein's destructive effort in the *Investigations*. A currently widely discussed sort of reason for discontent with it, emanating from the writings of Hilary Putnam, Tyler Burge and others,[6] would reflect that the content of intentional states in general is determined as a function of factors—for instance, aspects of the physical and/or social environment—which lie beyond the subject's consciousness; so the identity of an intentional state cannot in general be ascertained merely by scrutiny of elements which lie within con-

5. As noted by Paul Boghossian, it is in fact incoherent to suppose that all self-knowledge of intentional states could be inferential. See Boghossian (1989a).

6. The *locus classicus* is Hilary Putnam's (1975a) 'The Meaning of "Meaning"'. See also his 'Is Semantics Possible?', in Putnam (1975b), pp. 139–52. Tyler Burge's ideas concerning the contribution of social considerations are introduced in Burge (1979). See also Burge (1982a); Burge (1982b).

sciousness.[7] Wittgenstein's own objections to the observational model are somewhat different. In part they are once again phenomenological, though there is no space here to review any of the details. But perhaps the most arresting difficulty which his writings disclose has a similar structure to that deriving from the writings of Putnam and Burge. It issues from the requirement, imposed by the observational model, that intentional states can be fully determinate objects of inner contemplation before they issue in anything outward, before they are acted on—and hence that they can be fully identified without any consideration of events, reactions and performances lying in the future. For, on the contrary, the ascription of intentional states to a subject appears answerable to what he goes on to say and do in the broadly identificatory or constitutive fashion in which the ascription of dispositions and capacities is so answerable.

One of the most basic of the philosophical puzzles about intentional states is that they seem to straddle two conflicting paradigms: on the one hand, they are avowable, so to that extent conform to the paradigm of sensation and other 'observable' phenomena of consciousness; on the other, they answer constitutively to the ways in which the subject manifests them, and to that extent conform to the paradigm of psychological characteristics which, like irritability or modesty, are properly conceived as dispositional and—one would like

7. Two points about this train of thought. First, its thrust cannot be that second-order beliefs become additionally fallible on an externalist view of content; on the contrary, if the content of the belief that P is in part externally determined, so—and in exactly the same way—is that of the belief that I hold the belief that P. Externalism poses no *new* obstacle to the idea that *if* I believe that I believe that P, then I do believe that P. The question is, rather, how I am to tell introspectively what second-order belief I hold. Second, the train of thought is, of course, utterly unconvincing as formulated: it is rather as if someone were to argue that it was impossible to recognise a friend in the street since the identity of the approaching person would depend on considerations of history and origin which could not be salient to contemporary observation. There is much more to say. For disbelieving responses to the train of thought, see Davidson (1987) and Burge (1988). For defence of the train of thought as a weapon against the observational model, see Boghossian (1989a).

to say 'therefore'—give rise to no phenomenon of avowal but are identified inferentially, in ways which place the subject of the disposition at no special advantage. It appears that neither an epistemology of observation—of pure introspection—nor one of inference can be harmonised with all aspects of the intentional.

Perhaps the puzzle is somehow misconceived. But I want to gesture, in the briefest outline, to a way in which it might be resolved. When each of the horns of a dilemma seems unplayable, it is often good policy to look for a common assumption. And there is, of course, such an assumption here. It is the assumption that there must *be* a substantial epistemology of intentional states, a mode of cognitive *access* to those states which is distinctively available to their subject and which is somehow able to measure up to the epistemic security with which sincere avowals of intentional states are standardly credited. But then it seems that the only relevant possibilities—since one does not know a priori one's own beliefs, desires, etc.—are observation and inference, and neither seems to be at the service of a satisfying account. What if we reject the assumption, try to make sense of the idea that knowing one's own beliefs, desires and intentions is not really a matter of 'access to'—being in cognitive touch with—a state of affairs at all?

Can clear sense be made of this thought? I suspect that there is only one viable strategy for doing so. That is to recognise that the authority standardly granted to a subject's own beliefs, or expressed avowals, about his intentional states is a *constitutive principle:* something which is not a *consequence* of the nature of those states, and of an associated epistemologically privileged relation in which the subject stands to them, but enters primitively into the conditions of identification of what a subject believes, hopes and intends.

There are various more precise possible accounts and comparisons by means of which one might attempt to render this idea more concrete,[8] but I have no space to attempt to take the task on here, and we need, in any case, only a very general sketch for our present purpose.

8. See Wright (1989c) (this volume Essay 7); Wright (1998b).

The language-game of intentional states, so conceived, would function roughly like this. A subject's sincere dispositions of avowal concerning his intentional states—or, better, his beliefs concerning them so identified—would stand by default unless there was positive reason to reject them. Such reason might be provided by the inability of the intentional system so determined to rationalise his behaviour, together with the availability of an alternative story, generated by discarding the suspect ascriptions, which fared better. Or it might be that, while allowing his avowals to stand provided a rationalising system of sorts, certain constraints of harmony and intelligibility dictated a search for an improved account. Since the *telos,* in the most general terms, of the practice of ascribing intentional states to oneself and others is mutual understanding, the success of a language-game which worked this way would depend on certain deep contingencies. It would depend, for instance, on the contingency that taking the apparent self-conceptions of others seriously, in the sense involved in crediting their apparent beliefs about their intentional states, as expressed in their avowals, with authority, almost always tends to result in an overall picture of their psychology which is more illuminating—as it happens, *enormously* more illuminating—than anything which might be gleaned by respecting all the data *except* the subject's self-testimony. And that in turn rests on the contingency that we are, each of us, ceaselessly but—on the proposed conception—subcognitively moved to opinions concerning our own intentional states which will indeed give good service to others in their attempt to understand us. Thus: we do not *cognitively interact* with states of affairs which confer truth upon our opinions concerning our own intentional states; rather, we are, as it were, inundated, day by day, with opinions for which truth is the default position, so to say. They count as true provided that we hold them and that no good purpose is served, in another's quest to find us intelligible, by rejecting them.

To avoid misunderstanding, note that what is being highlighted is a (default) *sufficient* condition for a subject's being in a particular intentional state. There is no suggestion that the same condition is also necessary—so that to be in a particular intentional state is to believe that one is. Thus, to anticipate two readily foreseeable objections, nothing here need involve that there is always a regress of beliefs whenever anything is believed; or that un-self-conscious creatures, which lack the conceptual resources for second-order beliefs, are incapable of believing altogether.

Two crucial considerations are needed before we can bring these ideas directly to bear on the predicament of the Linguist. First, reflect that what we have done is, in effect, to identify the correctness conditions of ascriptions of intentional states with their interpretative utility, saving first-personal authority—the phenomenon of the avowability of such states—by assigning a certain pride of place, or 'default correctness', to the subject's self-conception in the construction of the interpretation. It follows that there is no place for the occurrence of *undetectable* errors within a subject's self-conception: no place for the idea that she may simply be mistaken in identifying her desires, intentions or hopes although neither she nor anyone else can get the weakest reason for saying so. Rather, her views are to be accounted correct unless a more satisfying rationalisation of (germane aspects) of her deportment can be constructed by discarding them. And if that is so—if a better account can be accomplished that way—then it can always in principle be recognised to be so by the very accomplishment, either by the subject or others, of such an account.

The second consideration is that the proposed, austere form of account ought, arguably, to be applied to knowledge not merely of current but also of *past* intentional states. It needs to be acknowledged, of course, that we speak, perfectly properly, of *remembering* what we intended. But it is unclear that in claiming such memories, we mean to claim any more than non-inferential knowledge of what we intended—(contrast the case where I *reason* that I must have had such-and-such an intention in view of my reaction when . . . , etc., etc.). And that we have such non-inferential knowledge is not in question; the issue is, precisely, its status.

Obviously, the proposed account *can* be extended to speak to this issue: our authority concerning our previous intentions or—what comes to the same thing, barring mistakes about other matters—the authority of our opinions concerning what would currently comply with them, may be viewed as likewise a matter of default correctness: our opinions stand unless the goal of making us intelligible licenses others to discount them or—as I expect the account should run—they clash with attested former opinions of ours concerning the same intentions which, apart from this very clash, there would be no reason to discount. (That is, roughly, attested former opinions concerning intentional states then current will, other things being equal, dominate present but conflicting opinions concerning those same states.)

What is questionable is whether it would be coherent *not* to extend the austere account in this way. The alternative would be a hybrid attempt to marry default correctness of opinions about current intentional states with the idea that non-inferential knowledge of past intentional states is a matter of full-blooded recollection, as it were—a matter of the operation of a faculty which tracks determinate antecedent states of affairs. And against this two thoughts seem compelling. First, this notion of 'full-blooded' recollection seems at home only as the retrospective counterpart of an epistemology of *observation;* full-blooded recollection ought to involve the representation of something which was a fully determinate object for consciousness at the time. But an observational epistemology of current intentional states was precisely one of the things the austere form of account was designed to avoid. Second, the hybrid view leaves us with no candidate conception of the state of affairs which is to be the object of the alleged full-blooded recall save those aspects of the subject's self-conception at the time which, it acknowledges, determine, other things being equal, what her intentions were. Yet it is a striking fact, beautifully illustrated in the discussion of the last sixty or so sections of part I of the *Investigations,* that the confident recollection of an intention—knowing, for instance what you were going to say before an interruption—need in no way depend on recollection of any *opinion* you held at the time. If evidence somehow comes to light that what you then believed about your intentions clashes with your current recollection, that will disconcert you; but your recollection does not depend on positive evidence that there is no such clash. Rather, we standardly move to non-inferential knowledge of our previous intentions with just the same effortless directness that characterises our knowledge of contemporary ones.

We are finally in position to address the target. Consider the background which we have worked through. Sensations and other occurrent phenomena of consciousness are conceived as private objects. The language of sensation, etc., is conceived in consequence as a vehicle for the operation of inward-looking classificatory competences, exercised over such objects. But genuine classifying must involve at least the kind of fallibility illustrated by recidivism and other forms of loss of conceptual grip. And that in turn demands the possibility of a split between the classification of an occurrent sensation which accords with those of the Linguist's erstwhile intentions which constitute the semantics for the language, and his actual classificatory response. The Linguist's semantically constitutive intentions have to be able to generate substantial correctness-conditions for uses of the language in response to sensations which have not yet occurred; and they have to be able to do this in ways which may clash with what, if any, uses he actually ventures when the sensations occur.

Well, the problem is obvious. Since the Linguist's overarching intentions are conservative, his actual uses will reflect his impressions about what constitutes compliance with the semantically constitutive intentions. So the sort of clash whose possibility is demanded involves mistaken such impressions. But the austere view allows room for the idea of such a mistake only when a better interpretation of the subject is purchased thereby. And in the context of a *private* language no interpretation can be better or worse. There is, simply, no possible interpretative project to undertake.

When one first reads Wittgenstein's discussion, it is natural to have some such thought as the following: that he is merely mysteriously refusing to acknowledge the possibility of forming certain determinate intentions about the use of a symbolism, which one then determinately either conforms to or breaks, whether one can recognise it or not. But that thought cannot be squared with the austere view.

Simply: there is nothing for an intention, conceived as determining subsequent conformity and non-conformity to it autonomously and independently of its author's judgements on the matter, to *be*. What would suit the Linguist's needs is a *Platonised* intention, an interior mental state sustaining response-independent relations of fit to prospective courses of action rather as a rule, Platonically conceived, determines its own proper applications indefinitely far down the tracks, as it were—leaving the human subject, in both cases, only with the task of following through a predeterminate commitment. That is mythology. And the austere view has no place for it.

There is only one possible recourse for the friend of privacy. That is to introduce into the scene a possible interpretative project. Only if the Linguist is in the business of *self-interpretation* can space be made, consistently with the austere view, for recidivism and other forms of lapse. Any residual hope for private language must depend upon the Linguist's turning explanatory theorist with respect to his own basic classificatory responses—seeking to devise criteria whereby they may be appraised, criteria whereby default-correctness might on occasion be overridden. As I have said, I do not believe that there is really any hope in that direction.[9] But the target here was to outline an argument that there is no hope in any other direction.

V.   Concluding Remarks

It is worth emphasising that the conclusion to which these thoughts point is a purely negative one: a certain model of the way the self-ascription of states of consciousness works—the model of the inward-looking observation statement—is shown to be untenable. Nothing positive is put in its place; nothing to replace the imagery of the walled garden. In particular, nothing follows about the assertoric status of avowals. Even for one who has sympathetically followed the dialectic thus far, the situation can seem intensely unsatisfying. The

---

9. For the reasons elaborated in Wright (1986a) (this volume Essay 8).

philosophical consciousness abhors a vacuum. If the model of the inward-looking observation statement fails, must there not be something better with which to replace it?

It is precisely with this (sort of) craving, I believe, that Wittgenstein's emphasis upon the error of seeking philosophical *explanations,* and the contrast with what he regards as the proper descriptive method, is meant to engage. Are we really clear what we are looking for when we seek a 'positive account' to explain the features of psychological language which Cartesianism tried to explain? Why should self-knowledge, and the language in which we express it, allow of illuminating comparison, if not with reports of observation, then with anything else? Yet the sort of account which can seem to be needed could only consist ultimately in such comparison. One of the hardest lessons which the pursuit of Wittgenstein's later thought may have to teach us is to know when philosophy can tell us nothing further.

Earlier versions of this essay were composed for the conference on Metaphysics and Epistemology held at the University of Queensland in May 1989, and read at the University of Wisconsin, Milwaukee, in September 1989, and at the Eastern Division meeting of the American Philosophical Association held at Atlanta in December 1989. I am grateful for helpful discussion to Andre Gallois, John Koethe, David Velleman and Joan Weiner; and to Bob Hale, Paul Boghossian, Stephen Yablo, Catherine Wright, Peter Carruthers and Gideon Rosen for comments on an earlier draft.

10

The Problem of Self-Knowledge (I)

It is only in fairly recent philosophy that psychological self-knowledge has come to be seen as problematical; once upon a time the hardest philosophical difficulties all seemed to attend our knowledge of others. But as philosophers have canvassed various models of the mental that would make knowledge of other minds less intractable, so it has become unobvious how to accommodate what once seemed evident and straightforward—the wide and seemingly immediate cognitive dominion of minds over themselves.

My programme in this and the next essay will involve characterising this dominion with some care. We need to have it as clear as possible why one form of traditional thinking on the matter has seemed so attractive—even unavoidable—and what a satisfactory account of the issues in this region must accomplish. I shall review various recent proposals. But my underlying and primary concern will be with the later Wittgenstein's contribution to the question. Ultimately I think we are provided with a most vivid illustration—and can perhaps gain an insight into the intended force—of something which I do not think has so far been very well understood: the *anti-explanatory* motif that runs through the pronouncements on philosophical method occurring in *Philosophical Investigations*.

I

People can be variously deluded about themselves, self-deceived about their motives, for instance, or deluded about their strengths of character and frailties. But it is nonetheless a truism that for the most part we know ourselves best—better than we know others and better than they know us.

In one kind of case, the explanation of this would seem straightforward. It is (merely) that our own presence is, for each of us, a constant factor in the kind of situation, usually but not always social, in which the evidence emerges which bears on various of our psychological characteristics. No one else is so constantly around us. So no one else observes as much of us or is as much observed by us. Selves have the best evidence about themselves.

Evidently, however, this form of explanation of the truth in the truism can run only in cases where one's own and another's knowledge of oneself must draw on the same kind of evidence. So it is restricted, it would seem, to broadly dispositional characteristics like honesty, patience, courage and conceit—cases where there is no essential self/other asymmetry in the means of knowledge. And this is not, of course, the most salient type of case, in which we not merely know ourselves best but also *differently* from the way in which we know others and they know us. The distinction is complicated, admittedly, by the fact that many apparently dispositional psychological characteristics are distinctively manifested not by raw behaviour, as it were, but by psychological performance in respects that may themselves exhibit self/other epistemological asymmetries. Conceit, for instance, will be, inter alia, a disposition to form certain kinds of belief. It remains that the type of case that sets our problem is that which gives rise to the phenomenon of *avowal*—the phenomenon of authoritative, non-inferential self-ascription. The basic philosophical problem of self-knowledge is to explain this phenomenon—to locate, characterise and account for the advantage which selves seemingly possess in the making of such claims about themselves.

The project will be conditioned by whatever more precise characterisation we offer of the target phenomenon. It seems safe to suppose that we must begin by distinguishing two broad classes of avowal. The first group—what I will call *phenomenal avowals*—comprise examples like 'I have a headache', 'My feet are sore', 'I'm tired', 'I feel elated', 'My vision is blurred', 'My ears are ringing', 'I feel sick' and so on. Such examples exhibit each of the following three marks.

First, they are *groundless*. The demand that somebody produces reasons or corroborating evidence for such a claim about themselves—'How can you tell?'—is always inappropriate. There is nothing they might reasonably be expected to be able to say. In that sense, there is nothing upon which such claims are based.

Second, they are *strongly authoritative*. If somebody understands such a claim, and is disposed to make it sincerely about themselves, that is a guarantee of the truth of what they say. A doubt about such a claim has to be a doubt about the sincerity or the understanding of its author. Since we standardly credit any interlocutor, absent evidence to the contrary, with sincerity and understanding, it follows that a subject's actually making such a claim about themselves is a criterion for the correctness of the corresponding third-personal claim made by someone else: my avowal that I'm in pain must be accepted by others, on pain of incompetence, as a ground for the belief that I am.

Finally, phenomenal avowals exhibit a kind of *transparency*. Where P is an avowal of the type concerned, there is typically something absurd about a profession of the form 'I don't know whether P'—don't know whether I have a headache, for instance, or whether my feet are sore. Not always: there are contexts in which I might be uncertain of a precondition—(for instance, whether I have feet.) But in the normal run of cases, the subject's ignorance of the truth or falsity of an avowal of this kind is not, it seems, an option.

None of the examples listed is an avowal of a *content-bearing* state. It is the hallmark of the second main group of avowals—what I shall call *attitudinal avowals*—that the psychological characteristics, processes and states which they concern are partially individuated by the propositional content, or intentional direction, which they contain—for instance, 'I believe that term ends on the 27th', 'I hope that noise stops soon', 'I think that professional philosophers are some of the most fortunate people on earth', 'I am frightened of that dog', 'I am thinking of my mother'. In order to see what is distinctive about an author's relation to avowals of this kind, we need first to take account of the fact that such claims can also be made as part of a process of *self-interpretation*—in the kind of context when we say that we have *learned* about our attitudes by finding that certain events cause us pleasure, for instance, or discomfort. Consider the following passage from Jane Austen's *Emma*:

> Emma's eyes were instantly withdrawn; and she sat silently meditating in a fixed attitude, for a few minutes. A few minutes were sufficient for making her acquainted with her own heart. A mind like hers, once opening to suspicion, made rapid progress. She touched—she admitted—she acknowledged the whole truth. Why was it so much the worse that Harriet should be in love with Mr. Knightley than with Mr. Churchill? Why was the evil so dreadfully increased by Harriet's having some hope of return? It darted through her, with the speed of an arrow, that Mr. Knightley must marry no-one but herself.[1]

Here Emma has just been told of the love of her protégé, Harriet, for her—Emma's—bachelor brother-in-law, a decade older than Emma, a frequent guest of her father's and hitherto a stable, somewhat avuncular part of the background to her life. She has entertained no thought of him as a possible husband. But now she realises that she strongly desires that he marry no one but her, and she arrives at this discovery by way of surprise at the strength and colour of her reaction to Harriet's declaration, and by way of a few minutes reflection on that reaction. She is, precisely, not moved to the realisation immediately; it

---

1. Austen (1987), p. 398. I was reminded of this apt example by Julia Tanney, who uses it in Tanney (1996).

dawns on her first as something she suspects and *then* recognises as true. It *explains* her reaction to Harriet.

In such self-interpretative cases, none of the three features we noted of phenomenal avowals are present. There is no groundlessness: the subject's view is one for which it *is* perfectly in order to request an account of the justifying grounds. There is no strong authority: mere sincerity and understanding will be no guarantee whatever of truth—it is for Jane Austen to stipulate, as it were, that Emma's self-discovery is the genuine article, but in any real context such a conclusion could be seriously mistaken. Finally there is no transparency: within a context of self-interpretation, it is in no way incongruous if the subject professes ignorance of particular aspects of her intentional psychology. However, what is vital to note for our present purpose is that such self-interpretative cases, although common, cannot be the *basic* case. For the body of data on which self-interpretation may draw is not restricted to recollected behaviour and items falling within the subject matter of phenomenal avowals. When Emma interprets her reaction to Harriet's declaration as evidence that she herself loves Knightley, there is an avowable ground—something like 'I am disconcerted by her love for that man and—more so—by the thought that it might be returned',—which is a *datum for,* rather than a product of, self-interpretation. That is to say, self-interpretation will typically draw on non-inferential knowledge of a basic range of attitudes and intentionally characterised responses. These will not be distinguished, I think, from non-basic, interpretative cases by any generic features of their content; rather they will reflect matters which, for the particular subject in the particular context, happen to require no interpretation to be known about— matters which are precisely *avowable*. It is these basic examples which comprise the attitudinal avowals.

Such avowals will have the same immediacy as phenomenal avowals and will exhibit both groundlessness and transparency—groundlessness rather trivially in so far as, any interpretational basis having been excluded, there will naturally be nothing a subject can say to justify such a self-ascription; transparency in the sense that, except where the matter is one of interpretation, we think a subject ought to know without further ado what she believes, or desires, etc., so that any profession of ignorance or uncertainty, unless coupled with a readiness to allow that the matter is not basic but calls for (self-) inter-pretation, will seem perplexing. However attitudinal avowals do not exhibit the strong authority of phenomenal avowals: to the extent that there is space for relevant forms of self-deception or confusion, sincerity-cum-understanding is no longer a guarantee of the truth of even basic self-ascriptions of intentional states. Any avowal may be discounted if accepting it would get in the way of making best sense of the subject's behaviour. But with attitudinal avowals it is admis-sible to look for other explanations of a subject's willingness to assert a bogus avowal than those provided by misunderstanding, insincerity or misinterpretation. This is the space occupied by the ordinary notion of self-deception; but the more general idea is just that we can be caused to hold mistaken higher-order beliefs in ways—wishful thinking, for instance—which do not go through misguided self-inter-pretative inference.

It is striking that attitudinal avowals would appear to exhibit a form of weak authority nevertheless: that is, they provide criterial—empirically assumptionless—justification for the corresponding third-personal claims. Since it cannot be attributed, as with phenomenal avowals, to the fact of sincerity-cum-understanding guaranteeing truth, what does this weak authority consist in? It might be suggested that it is nothing other than the presumptive acceptability of testimony generally. And certainly that proposal would be enough to set our problem: for the presumptive acceptability of *original* testimony—testimony for which the source is not itself testimony—extends no fur-ther than to subject matters which an informant is deemed competent to know about. So the question would recur: how is it possible for sub-jects to know about their intentional states in ways that involve no consideration of the evidence on which a third-party must rely?

Actually, however, I think the suggestion is wrong. What distin-guishes the presumptive acceptability of attitudinal avowals from anything characteristic of testimony generally is that the authority which attaches to them is, in a certain sense, *inalienable*. There is no such thing as showing oneself chronically unreliable in relation to the distinctive subject matter of attitudinal avowals. I may have such poor colour vision that you rightly come to distrust my testimony on matters of colour. I may, unwittingly, have a very bad memory and, learning of this, you may rightly come to a state of wholesale suspicion about my testimony on matters of personal recall. But no corresponding wholesale suspicion concerning my attitudinal avowals is possible. You may not suppose me sincere and comprehending and yet chronically unreliable about what I hope, believe, fear and intend. Wholesale suspicion about my attitudinal avowals—where it is not a doubt about sincerity or understanding—jars with conceiving of me as an intentional subject at all.

II

Both groups of avowals exhibit a further feature which it is worth attending to briefly. In a famous passage in the *Blue Book,* Wittgenstein writes:

> There are two different cases in the use of the word 'I' (or 'my') which I might call the 'use as object' and 'the use as subject'. Examples of the first kind of use are these: 'my arm is broken', 'I have grown six inches', 'I have a bump on my forehead', 'the wind blows my hair about'. Examples of the second kind are: 'I see so-and-so', 'I hear so-and-so', 'I try to lift my arm', 'I think it will rain', 'I have toothache'. One can point to the difference between these two categories by saying: the cases of the first category involve the recognition of a particular person, and there is in these cases the possibility of an error or as I should rather put it: the possibility of an error has been provided for . . . (but) it is as impossible that in making the statement 'I have toothache', I should have mistaken another person for myself, as it is to moan with pain by mistake, having mistaken someone else for me.[2]

2. *Blue Book,* pp. 66–7.

The characteristic to which Wittgenstein here calls attention is now standardly called *immunity to error through misidentification*.[3] In a large class of cases when someone makes a subject-predicate claim, they may mistake or misidentify the subject in a way for which, it appears, there is no provision in the case of an avowal. If I see someone running along the beach and, taking it to be my colleague NN, I say 'NN will catch up with us in a minute', I may be mistaken in ways which correspond either to the subject identified or to the predication I make: it may be that the character approaching is not NN at all, and it may be that he will turn away before he reaches us. But if I avow my indifference to a forthcoming ballot, for instance, then there is a provision for correction only for my predication—I can't be mistaken about whom I'm making that predication of.

Sydney Shoemaker writes that the absence of the possibility of misidentification "is one of the main sources of the mistaken opinion that one cannot be an object to oneself, which in turn is a source of the view that 'I' does not refer".[4] The line of thought he has in mind would run from the impossibility of *misidentifying* myself to the conclusion that, in reflection about myself, there is no identification of *any* object, that no object is attended to in such thought and that 'I' accordingly has no referential function.

Wittgenstein may, indeed, have been inclined to such an idea, for the passage from which I quoted continues:

> To say, 'I have pain' is no more a statement *about* a particular person than moaning is.[5]

But whether he was so inclined or not, it is simply a mistake to suppose that where there is no fallible identification, there is no reference either. It will be clear what's wrong with that idea once we have a bet-

---

3. The term is originally Sydney Shoemaker's, I believe. It is taken up in Evans (1982), see esp. chap. 7, section 2.

4. See Shoemaker (1968), pp. 568 ff.

5. *Blue Book*, p. 67.

ter characterisation of what immunity to error from misidentification (IEM) consists in. And we shall also thereby learn why, in the present context, the phenomenon need not be of primary concern.

The key point is that IEM is not a characteristic which a statement has simply by virtue of its subject matter. It depends upon the kind of ground which a speaker has for it. Specifically, the ground has to be such that in the event that the statement in question is somehow defeated, it cannot survive as a ground for the corresponding existential generalisation. Consider again the case of the chasing figure on the beach and suppose that, having asserted 'NN will catch up with us soon', I turn to see NN standing just a little in front of me. In that case, my original thought is defeated; but the basis for it survives as a ground for the claim, 'Someone will catch up with us soon'. Or suppose I catch sight of my reflection passing a shop window and I say to myself, 'My hair is blowing in the wind'. If it becomes apparent that the reflection I saw was not mine but someone else's, the basis for my claim will still remain as a ground for the existential generalisation, 'Someone's hair was blowing in the wind'. A claim, made on a certain kind of ground, involves IEM just when its defeat is *not* consistent with retention of grounds for existential generalisation in this kind of way.

Now, avowals do characteristically so behave. If an avowal of mine is somehow defeated, there is no question of my original entitlement surviving, without my gathering additional information, in such a way that I may justifiably claim that someone—though not me— exhibits the property which I avowed. However, two points are evident in the light of the characterisation just offered. First, the idea that Wittgenstein's 'as subject' uses of 'I' are somehow shown to be non-referential by their having IEM should have been strangled at birth by the reflection that a similar immunity is characteristic of many *demonstrative* claims—in whose case there is of course no question but that reference to an object is involved. If I see an object hurtling towards us and I say, 'That thing is approaching very fast', there is no way in which that claim can be defeated and yet my original grounds for it survive as grounds for the claim,

'Something is approaching very fast'. Second, it is clear that many *non-psychological* claims about the self can exhibit the same feature. Consider, for instance, my assertion 'My hair is blowing in the wind' when based not on the shop-window reflection but on certain characteristic feelings of the scalp and face and my auditory sensations. Or consider 'The bedclothes have fallen off my leg', uttered by an unwitting recent amputee. In neither case is there the possibility of a justified fall-back to an appropriate existential generalisation if the claim is defeated. Immunity to error through misidentification is not a distinctive characteristic of *psychological* self-ascriptions or, more specifically, of avowals.

When I said a moment ago that a better characterisation of IEM would teach us why this feature need not be of special concern to us in the present context, I was not merely anticipating this point. That the phenomenon extends to examples like those just given will seem to be quite consistent with its still betokening something essential about avowals once the plausible thought occurs that the *source* of IEM in non-psychological first-personal claims is always their being based on avowable psychological matters (for instance, my sensations of scalp and face and the rushing in my ears, or the amputee's sensations as of a draught around his foot.) The IEM of non-psychological self-ascriptions, when they have it, is presumably to be viewed as an inheritance from their basis in an underlying possible avowal. It is not the fact that IEM is not the exclusive property of psychological claims which entitles us to bracket the phenomenon in the present context but rather the reflection that avowals' exhibition of it is a *derived* feature, as it were—effectively, a consequence of respects in which we have already noted their distinction from third-personal psychological claims. Specifically it is a consequence of their being groundless while the corresponding third-personal claims demand evidential support. For if an avowal, 'I am φ', did not exhibit IEM, then its defeat would be consistent with the subject's retention of an entitlement to the corresponding existential generalisation—'Someone (else) is φ'— which could then be asserted *groundlessly*. But to suppose that such a claim could be both admissible and groundless would clash with the original asymmetry. Claims about the psychological states of others are acceptable only when grounded, one way or another; that goes both for particular such claims and for generalisations of them as well.

III

It is natural to wonder what if any independent, general characterisation may be possible of the psychological distinction marked by the contrast between phenomenal and attitudinal avowals, as outlined. Here I can only observe that neither of two initially suggestive proposals seems to be quite right. Familiarly, the *Investigations* repeatedly counsels against construing understanding, hoping, fearing, intending, etc., as mental *states* or *processes*. Wittgenstein's idea was not, of course, that there are no such things, strictly, as mental processes, or the states that would constitute their end-points, so to speak, but only that understanding, etc., will be misunderstood if assimilated to them. So the suggestion invites consideration that the distinction he is making, between mental events and processes strictly so termed—'turns' in consciousness, if you like—and other psychological states, corresponds nicely to that between phenomenal and attitudinal avowals: that phenomenal avowals register states or processes of mind which Wittgenstein was content to describe as such, whereas attitudinal avowals mark the cases where—he thought—danger lurks in that description.[6] The exegetical question is worth marking, but I shall not now pursue it.[7] Suffice it to say that some

---

6. See, e.g., *Philosophical Investigations* §§34, 146, 152, 154, 205, 303, 330–2, 427, 577, 673; also part II, §vi, p. 181; §xi, pp. 217–8. The distinction is prominent in the *Remarks on the Philosophy of Psychology* as well, where Wittgenstein uses the terminology of *dispositions* versus *states of consciousness;* see, e.g., Volume II, §§45, 48, 57, 178.

7. No speedy resolution is to be expected, for Wittgenstein was content to gesture at his distinction quite loosely—perhaps believing that it is vague, that the concept of a 'mental process' is a family resemblance concept, or whatever.

things which are surely 'turns in consciousness' in anyone's book—for instance, having a lover's face pass before your mind's eye, or having the thought occur to you that you should have called home twenty minutes ago, or being startled at an opponent's outburst at the umpire—such cases are, unlike any of our prototypes of the phenomenal-avowable, also *contentful;* moreover, the proper description of such an episode is, at least in some cases, something about which a subject might just conceivably be self-deceived.

Another mark of many phenomenal-avowable states—and certainly of each example I originally cited—is that, at least as we ordinarily suppose, creatures may be subject to them while *having no concept of them:* a dog can be tired, or afraid, or have an itch without having any concept of those states. But this distinction too seems not to coincide quite cleanly with that between the phenomenal- and the attitudinal-avowable. Some phenomenal-avowable conditions do appear to require the subject to have a concept of them. I doubt, for instance, that a dog can have *Auld Lang Syne* run through its head, although that is presumably a process amenable to strongly authoritative avowal by a suitably endowed subject—(though I suppose it depends what you regard as required by an understanding of "I am imagining a rendition of *Auld Lang Syne*"). Conversely, we tend quite freely to ascribe attitudinal states to (sufficiently intelligent, adaptable) creatures—primates and dogs, for instance—who presumably have no concept of such states.

In any case, we have sufficient focus for our central question. The cardinal problem of self-knowledge is that of explaining *why* avowals display the marks they do—what is it about their subject matter, and the subject's relationship to it, which explains and justifies our accrediting her sincere pronouncements about it with each of Groundlessness, Strong Authority and Transparency in the case of phenomenal avowals, and with Groundlessness, Weak Authority and Transparency in the case of attitudinal avowals? How is it possible for subjects to know these matters non-inferentially? How is it (often) impossible for them *not* to know such matters? And what is the source of the special authority carried by their verdicts?

IV

There is a line of response to these questions that comes so naturally as to seem almost irresistible—indeed, it may even seem to ordinary thought to amount merely to a characterisation of the essence of mind. According to it, the explanation of the special marks of avowals is that they are the product of the subject's exploitation of what is generally recognised to be a position of (something like) *observational privilege*. As an analogy, imagine somebody looking into a kaleidoscope and reporting on what he sees. No one else can look in, of course—at least while he is taking his turn. If we assume our Hero perceptually competent, and appropriately attentive, his claims about the patterns of shape and colour within will exhibit analogues of each of the marks of phenomenal avowals:

   (i)   The demand that he produces reasons or corroborating evidence for his claims will be misplaced—the most he will be able to say is that he is the only one in a position to see, and that is how things strike him;
   (ii) Granted his proper perceptual functioning, it will be sufficient for the truth of his claims that he understands them and is sincere in making them; so that for anyone who understands the situation, our Hero's merely making such a claim will constitute a sufficient, though defeasible reason for accepting its truth; and
   (iii) Where P is any claim about the patterns of shape and colour visible within, there will be no provision—bearing in mind Hero's assumed perceptual competence and attentiveness—for his intelligibly professing ignorance whether or not P.

The analogy isn't perfect by any means. In order to construct it, we have had to assume normal perceptual functioning and full attentiveness on the part of our observer. And no such assumption conditions our reception of others' avowals. But once into one's stride with this type of thinking, this difference will not seem bothersome. The idea will be that in the *inner* observational realm, in contrast to the outer, there is simply no room for analogues of misperception or of oversight or occlusion—for the objects and features there are necessarily salient to the observing subject. Or at least they are so in the case where they are objects and features recordable by phenomenal avowals. In the case of the subject matter of attitudinal avowals, by contrast, space for an analogue of misperception can and should be found—that will be what explains the failure of Strong Authority in those cases. In brief: this—Cartesian—response to the problem of avowals has it that the truth values of such utterances are non-inferentially known to the utterer via her immediate awareness of events and states in a special theatre, the theatre of her consciousness, of which others can have at best only indirect inferential knowledge. In the case of phenomenal avowals, this immediate awareness is, in addition, infallible and all seeing; in the case of basic attitudinal avowals, it is merely very, very reliable.

So presented, the Cartesian picture, of the transparency of one's own mind and, by inevitable contrast, the opacity of others', emerges as the product of a self-conscious attempt at philosophical explanation. That may seem congenial to John McDowell's claim that we "need to be seduced into philosophy before it can seem natural to suppose that another person's mind is hidden from us".[8] McDowell recoils against the idea that anything like the Cartesian picture might be part of ordinary unphilosophical thought. But I think he is quite wrong about this, the theoretical setting I have just given to the picture notwithstanding.[9] No doubt it is unclear what should count as a 'seduction into philosophy'. But if every manifestation of the Cartesian picture is to rate as the product of such a seduction, then the seductive reach of philosophy is flatteringly wide. I do not imagine, of course, that people typically self-consciously follow through the train of thought I outlined. But we ought not to balk at the notion that

8. McDowell (1991), p. 149.

9. You might as well say that we have to be seduced into philosophy before we can interest ourselves in time travel.

no intellectual routine characteristically pursued by those in its grip should capture exactly the best reconstruction of why an idea appeals. The privacy of the inner world is a recurrent idea in philosophically unprejudiced literature.[10] It is arguably a presupposition of the whole idea of the continuation of one's consciousness after death. The thought of the undetectable inverted colour spectrum is something which can engage quite young children without too much difficulty. And in each of these cases what comes naturally is essentially nothing other than the notion of a kind of privileged observation of one's own mind which (up to a point) works, in the ways we have reviewed, to explain the first/third-personal asymmetries in ordinary psychological discourse.

The privileged-observation explanation is unquestionably a natural one. What it *does* need philosophy to teach is its utter hopelessness. One very important realisation to that end is that nothing short of full-blown Cartesianism can explain the asymmetries in *anything like the same way*—there can be no scaled-down observational model of self-knowledge which preserves the advantages of the Cartesian account while avoiding its unaffordable costs. The problem is that the kind of authority I have over the avowable aspects of my mental life is not transferable to others: there is no contingency—anyway, none of which we have any remotely satisfactory concept[11]—whose suspension would put other ordinary people in position to avow away on my behalf, as it were. So the conception of avowals as reports of inner observation is saddled with the idea that the observations in question

10. A particularly striking example—also from a Victorian novelist—is provided by George Eliot's *The Lifted Veil*, whose hero—Latimer—is depicted as afflicted with what is portrayed as a kind of involuntary eavesdropping—a persistent and reluctant witnessing of others' mental states as if they were his own.

11. In particular, I do not think that we have any satisfactory concept of what it would be to be in touch with others' mental states *telepathically*. I do not mean, of course, to rule it out that someone might prove, by dint of *his own* occurrent suspicions and afflictions, to be a reliable guide to the states of mind of another. But that possibility falls conspicuously short of the idea that a subject might share direct witness of another's mental states.

are ones which *necessarily* only the subject can carry out. And once that conception is in place, others' means of access to the states of affairs which their subject (putatively) observes is bound to seem essentially second-rate by comparison and to be open to just the kinds of sceptical harassment which generate the traditional problem of other minds—the unaffordable cost referred to.

V

If this is right, then a deconstruction of the privileged-observation solution to the problem of self-knowledge is the indispensable prerequisite of an overall satisfactory philosophy of mind. It seems to me that it was Wittgenstein who first accomplished such a deconstruction, and in the remainder of this essay I shall try to defend a certain conception of the way that deconstruction goes. In essentials, what he does is to mount a two-pronged attack on the Cartesian picture, with the two prongs corresponding to the distinction between the two main kinds of avowals. It is the so-called private-language argument—the batch of considerations that surface in §§243 to the early 300s in the *Investigations*—which targets the idea of phenomenal avowals as inner observation reports, while the corresponding conception of attitudinal avowals is challenged by the various phenomenological and other considerations which Wittgenstein marshals in the, as we may call them, 'not a mental process' passages recurrent throughout the text.[12]

We need some preliminaries about *Investigations* §258—the famous passage in which Wittgenstein suggests that the 'private linguist' lacks the resources to draw a distinction which is essential if the 'reports' that he logs in his diary are to have a truth-evaluable content, the distinction, namely, between what seems right to him and what is really right. It seems clear that such a distinction is called for if these 'reports' are to have anything of the objectivity implicit in the very

12. See note 6.

idea of an observational report, the objectivity implicit in the idea of successful representation of some self-standing aspect of reality. But it is not just obvious that such a distinction is in good standing only if it can be drawn *operationally*—only if, that is, the diarist has the resources for making principled, presumably retrospective, judgements about occasions when he has been ignorant or mistaken. It ought to be enough if what constitutes the fact of the correctness of a report and what constitutes the diarist's impression of its correctness are not all the same thing so to speak, even if no one can ever be in the position of ascertaining the one without the other.

Some commentators have taken it that Wittgenstein has missed this: that his objection here is implicitly verificationist—implicitly demands *contrastive uses* for locutions corresponding to the two halves of the distinction, and thus in effect begs the question against the idea that a subject might be *infallibly* aware of aspects of her inner life which are nevertheless constitutively independent of that awareness in the manner the seems right/is right distinction, properly understood, demands. This accusation seems to me mistaken. Any idea that the private diarist's jottings might be subject to a non-operational but still valid seems right/ is right distinction comes into collision with an important aspect of Wittgenstein's discussion of the notion of intention. Broadly: the fact of an aspect of the diarist's inner world being as one of his reports states it to be demands—if it is to be constitutively independent of his impression of the fact—the existence of facts about what is required by the *semantics of the private language,* which are likewise constitutively independent of his impressions of facts about them. Since the semantics of the private language are to be constituted in certain original intentions of the diarist, the upshot is that a similar constitutive independence is required between facts concerning what really complies with the diarist's original semantic intentions and his own subsequent impression of those facts, even under best conditions—conditions of the utmost lucidity, perfect recall, etc. But that will be a sustainable demand only if the content of an intention is objectionably *Platonised,* in a fashion which, after Wittgenstein's discussions (especially in *Investigations* §600 onwards), we should know better than to do.

That, of course, is merely to sketch a line of interpretation which I have pursued before but have no time to elaborate here.[13] But the sketch should be enough to set the stage for three objections which John McDowell has lodged,[14] to which I now turn.

VI

The first objection is a perfectly natural one. Is there not a prior, rather obvious doubt about the whole idea that the semantics of a private language could be constituted in certain original intentions of its practitioner? We should ask, McDowell says,

> how an intention could be constitutive of a concept, as opposed to annexing an independently constituted concept to a word as what it is to express. The private linguist's semantical intention is supposed to be inwardly expressible by something like 'Let me call this kind of thing 'S' in future'. But for this story even to seem to make sense, the classificatory concepts supposedly expressed, with the help of an inward focusing of the attention, by 'this kind of thing' would need to be at the linguist's disposal already; it cannot be something he equips himself with by such a performance. If a new classificatory concept can be set up by focusing on an instance, that is only thanks to the prior availability of a concept that makes the right focus possible, in the presence of the instance, by fixing what kind of classification is in question.[15]

McDowell's suggestion is that my putative difficulty with the idea of a report's complying with the semantics of the private language is a distraction, that the place at which the real difficulty is to be found is in the idea that the diarist could intentionally constitute a semantics for his language in the first place. For how exactly is the private ostensive

13. See Wright (1991) (this volume Essay 9).
14. In McDowell (1991).
15. Ibid., pp. 164–5.

definition supposed to work? If focusing the attention has to be mediated by concepts—surely one of the prime intended morals of Wittgenstein's discussion of ostensive definition—then a private ostensive definition could take place only in a context akin to the Augustinian setting introduced right at the start of the *Investigations,* wherein the trainee is assumed already to be a *thinker*—already to be master of a range of concepts of which, as a result of ostensive training, he will for the first time acquire means of expression. That won't do.

There is no doubt about the Wittgensteinian resonances of this line of thought. But there is nothing in it to disturb the essentials of the Cartesian view. The reason is that the self-directive role which Wittgenstein gives to his diarist in §258 is actually quite inessential to the putative upshot—the operation of a private language. We are not, after all—or had better not be—tempted to say that a similar difficulty must afflict normal, public ostensive teaching. We don't think that a child must somehow already be equipped with concepts of colour if he is to benefit from a normal ostensive training in the use of colour words—that indeed is the point of the *Investigations'* contrast between ostensive definition proper and what Wittgenstein calls ostensive *teaching.*[16] But if that's right, there is in general no barrier to the idea that something conceptless—a colour-sensitive machine, say—might serve to do the teaching in place of a normally colour-concepted adult. Better, there ought to be no difficulty in the idea that a blind man, taking himself to have some form of prosthetic indication of variations in colour, might successfully introduce a normally sighted child to a range of colour concepts which he himself lacked. But *that's* essentially the model that Cartesianism, in so far as it figures in ordinary thought, offers of the teaching of sensation concepts. According to that model, I am screened from the inner goings-on when my child exhibits pain behaviour. But I take it that the behaviour gives me a kind of prosthesis—that it betokens inner phenomenal saliences which I can accordingly train him to vocalise, and thereby to conceptualise.

16. *Investigations* §6.

In short, the diarist/private linguist doesn't have to be an auto-didact. So no essential difficulty with the Cartesian conception of sensation language is disclosed by drawing out problems inherent in the idea of such auto-didacticism. At some point, the Cartesian should say, a subject's competence in the linguistic routines in which, both in the inner and outer cases, he is trained, will amount to the possession of concepts. And the identity of the concepts then possessed will supervene on the linguistic intentions of the subject: on the patterns of use which he will be willing to uphold. So there is no alternative but that a discussion of the idea of a subject's unwitting and undetectable departure from a prior intention must take centre stage if Wittgenstein's deconstruction is to succeed.

VII

McDowell's second objection is that the interpretation I offer winds up saddling Wittgenstein with the denial of platitudes. My claim was that we should elicit from Wittgenstein's discussion of intention and cognate concepts the moral that, as I put it in the discussion to which McDowell is responding, "there is nothing for an intention, conceived as a determining subsequent conformity and non-conformity to it autonomously and independently of its author's judgements on the matter, to *be*."[17] McDowell glosses this as

> [T]here is nothing but platonistic mythology in the idea that an intention determines what counts as conformity to it independently of its author's judgements.

He continues:

> So [Wright's] thesis is that what the private linguist needs in his semantical intentions is something that cannot be true of any intentions at all, on pain of platonism.

17. Wright (1991), p. 146 (this volume Essay 9).

But suppose I form the intention to type a period. If that's my intention, it is settled that only my typing a period will count as executing it. Of course I am capable of forming that intention only because I am party to the practices that are constitutive of the relevant concepts. But if that is indeed the intention which—thus empowered—I form, nothing more than the intention itself is needed to determine what counts as conformity to it. Certainly it needs no help from my subsequent judgements. (Suppose I forget what a period is.) So there is something for my intention to type a period, conceived as determining what counts as conformity to it autonomously and independently of my judgements on the matter, to be: namely, precisely, my intention to type a period. An intention to type a period is exactly something that must be conceived in that way. This is commonsense, not platonism. . . .[18]

This response is indeed commonsensical, but it completely misses the point. Yea verily, if I form the intention that P, what will comply with it is only and exactly the bringing it about that P; and it will typically be a matter independent of my subsequent judgements whether or not just that has indeed been effected. The role of subsequent judgement is indeed not to mediate somehow in the connection between the content of an intention and its execution—to be sure, that idea jars with the very idea of an intention's having a determinate content—but rather (of course) to enter into the determination of *what* the content of an anterior intention is to be understood as *having been*. If I form the intention to type a period, then sure, only typing a period will do. The anti-Platonist point is rather that there is nothing for my intention's having had *just that content* to consist in, if the fact has to be constitutively independent of anything which I may subsequently have to say about compliance or non-compliance with the intention, or about what its content was.

The Platonist mythology is a mythology of such constitutive independence. And it is exactly what the private linguist needs if the required seems right/is right distinction is to exist in the kind of way we are currently considering. Against this Platonism I want to set what I take to be an idea of Wittgensteinian authorship, although it is

18. McDowell (1991), pp. 163–4.

also familiar from the writings of Donald Davidson: that the content of a subject's intentional states is not something which may merely be *accessed,* as it were indirectly, by interpretative methods—rather as, on a Platonistic philosophy of mathematics, a good proof is merely a means of *access* to a mathematical truth—but is something which is intrinsically sensitive to the deliverances of best interpretative methodology. That is a methodology which in principle must include within its conspectus the whole sweep of a subject's sayings and doings, including future ones, without bound.

VIII

The foregoing concerns the first prong of Wittgenstein's deconstruction of the Cartesian view—the anti-private-language argument. The second prong, according to my reading, concerns certain special difficulties in the idea that attitudinal avowals describe introspectable mental occurrences. The suggestion of mine to which McDowell principally takes exception here is that one such special difficulty concerns the answerability of ascriptions of intentional states like expectation, hope and belief to aspects of a subject's outward performance that may simply *not be available* at the time of avowal. If an expectation, say, were a determinate, dated occurrence before the mind's eye, then in any particular case it would either have taken place or not, irrespective of how I subsequently went on to behave. So we ought to be guilty of a kind of conceptual solecism if we held claims about expectation to be answerable to subsequent sayings and doings in a fashion broadly akin to the way in which the ascription of dispositional states is so answerable. Yet that is exactly what we actually do.

The point was meant to be, then, that the conception of attitudinal avowals as reports of inner observation enforces a view of their subject matter which is at odds with another, fundamental feature of their grammar—their 'disposition-like theoreticity'.[19]

19. This idea is elaborated in Wright (1989c), pp. 237 ff (this volume Essay 7).

McDowell—this is his third objection—thinks this is wrong, both in substance and as a reading of Wittgenstein. There cannot, he contends, be a difficulty of this kind if there are examples of unquestioned phenomena of consciousness which nevertheless bear the same kind of internal connections to the outer. Yet there surely are. The coming of a picture before the mind is an episode in consciousness if anything is; yet the relation between the picture and the real scene it pictures, if there is one, is presumably comparable in relevant respects to that between an expectation and its fulfilment. So intentional states can certainly be mental occurrences—indeed, we noted this earlier. And equally, non-intentional occurrences—including the proto-example of pain itself—are in similar case: if a pain isn't an inner scenario, nothing is—yet the ascription of pain is, likewise, answerable in complex but constitutive ways to the subject's outward performance.

McDowell lodges this objection in the context of a reading which takes me to be attempting a rigorous and exhaustive division between strict phenomena of consciousness—Rylean 'twinges and stabs'—which, McDowell thinks I think, involve no intentionality and whose occurrence is independent of the conceptual resources of the subject, and intentional states and processes which are never, properly speaking, occurrent phenomena of consciousness. That's a misreading, and the second prong of Wittgenstein's attack does not require any such clean distinction. All that is required is that there be a difficulty along the indicated lines for at least one wide class of avowals. Still, the objection remains: isn't any such difficulty defused by the perfectly valid observation that items which certainly ought to be counted as mental *occurrences* do after all sustain internal relations to the outer?

I don't think so. For one thing, remember that the dialectical setting is one in which even the claim of twinges and stabs to count as pure occurrences before an inner eye is under question. As conceived by the Cartesian, a pain and the behaviour which expresses it are *quite distinct existences,* the one visible only to the subject, the other in public view. There *is* an incongruity, on that conception, in the conceptual linkage between the two which conditions ordinary psychological discourse. It is an instance of a more general incongruity which the sceptic quite rightly—when mentality is conceived as on the Cartesian view—finds in our empirically ungrounded reliance upon what is outer as a guide to subjects' mental lives.

The real counter to McDowell's objection, however, comes with a second consideration. When an image, or picture, comes before my mind, it presumably can't constitute a more explicit or substantial presence than the coming of a real physical picture before my physical eye. And when the latter happens, it is of course consistent with my being in full command of all manifest features of the object that I remain ignorant precisely of its intentionality—of what it is a picture of. I want to say that, analogously, in the sense in which an image or mental picture can come before the mind, its intentionality cannot. Wittgenstein himself is making this point when he asks 'What makes my image of him into an image of *him?*',[20] and his answer—having said that the same question applies to the expression, 'I see him now vividly before me' as to the image—is: 'Nothing in it or simultaneous with it'. But this aspect—the intentional content—of expectation, belief and their kin still falls firmly within the province of the non-inferential authority which we accord to attitudinal avowals. And it remains that the model of inner observation is bankrupt to explain the fact.

McDowell writes:

> Wright's reading actually puts it in doubt whether anything could be an occurrent phenomenon of consciousness. . . . The kinds of connection that raise the problem for intentional states are, as I said, connections involving the 'normative' notion of accord. But such connections are a species of a wider genus, that of internal relations. If Wright's a priori argument worked, it would have to be because nothing introspectable could sustain internal relations to anything outer.[21]

I have already said that I think there *is* a doubt whether things adequately conceived as occurrences in a Cartesian theatre of consciousness could sustain the kind of conceptual connections with outward performance which sensations, as we actually conceive of them, do

20. *Investigations* II, §iii.
21. McDowell (1991), p. 152.

---

sustain. But this ought to be consistent with the ordinary idea that a pain, say, is an item for introspection. It is a misunderstanding of the argument if it seems that, were it successful, nothing introspectable could sustain internal relations to anything outer. It all depends on the character and source of the internal relations in question. Both a sunburned arm and a triangle can be presented as ordinary objects of observation, and each sustains, *qua* presented under those particular respective concepts, certain internal relations: the sunburned arm to the causes of its being in that condition, and the triangle to, for instance, other particular triangles. And the point is simply that while the identification of the triangle as such can proceed in innocence of its internal relations of the latter kind—maybe the subject has no knowledge of the other triangles at all—recognition of the sunburned arm as just that cannot proceed in like innocence but demands knowledge that its actual causation is as is appropriate to that mode of presentation of it. The general form of the point that I take Wittgenstein to be making in the second prong of his attack is that the internal relations to the outer which are constituted in the intentionality of psychological items, of whatever sort, are all of the latter—sunburn-style—kind; and hence there is indeed a standing puzzle in the idea that an appropriate characterisation of them, incorporating such intentionality, is somehow vouchsafed to their subject by something akin to pure observation, a fortiori in the idea that it is the privileged character of this observation which underlies first-personal authority about such states. This thought, it seems to me, continues to be convincing.

IX

Interpreting Wittgenstein on these issues is a subtle and difficult matter, and not just because of the subtlety and difficulty of his thinking. McDowell's own positive reading[22] construes the target of the

22. Which needs in any case to be taken in the context of the more general ideas about the interface between thought and the external world since presented in his John Locke lectures, McDowell (1994).

private-language argument as a version of the Myth of the Given, transposed to the inner sphere; and he holds that the correct interpretation of the 'not a mental process' passages should still be consistent with the capacity of items such as meanings, intentions and their kin to 'come before the mind', as he likes to say.[23] I have not tried to respond to him here.[24] Rather I have been concerned to say at least a minimum to explain my continuing conviction that the reading of Wittgenstein I have defended should lead one to recognise deep incoherences in the Cartesian response to our problem—incoherences that are *prior to* its inordinate sceptical costs. And if what I said earlier is right—viz. that there is no alternative for one disposed to pursue the privileged observation route than to see the privilege as *necessarily* the exclusive property of the observing subject—then the incoherence of the Cartesian response is the incoherence of *any* broadly observational model of a subject's relation to their ordinary psychological states. That's the lesson I want to carry forward. It is a lesson which is broadly accepted by the philosophers—Tyler Burge, Donald Davidson and Christopher Peacocke—some of whose recent thoughts about this topic will occupy us in the next essay.

23. McDowell (1991), p. 158.
24. For some initial moves, see the second Postscript below.

11

The Problem of Self-Knowledge (II)

In Essay 10 I reviewed the basic linguistic data—the groundlessness, authority, and transparency of avowals—which combine to set the problem of self-knowledge. The most natural account of these features—it can seem, indeed, inevitable—involves resort to a picture in which each person's psychological states characteristically inhabit a kind of inner theatre to which they stand in a relation of uniquely privileged observation. This privilege, however, rapidly destabilises into unbreakable privacy, with the familiar epistemological costs of Cartesianism. And if one thought those costs, though steep, might still be affordable, *Philosophical Investigations,* I suggested, accomplishes a critique in depth of the Cartesian view after which we really have no alternative but to discard the inner observational model altogether.

I

So—what should we think instead? In this essay, I'll begin by reviewing responses to the problem of two of the most distinguished modern philosophers of mind. Both Donald Davidson and Tyler Burge have

345

taken the self/other asymmetries in knowledge of the psychological very seriously. Davidson begins a well-known recent discussion of the issues by writing:

> When a speaker avers that he has a belief, hope, desire or intention, there is a presumption that he is not mistaken, a presumption that does not attach to his ascriptions of similar mental states to others. Why should there be this asymmetry between attributions of attitudes to our present selves and attributions of the same attitudes to other selves. What accounts for the authority accorded first person present tense claims of this sort, and denied second or third person claims?[1]

And Burge writes:

> Descartes held that we know some of our propositional mental events in a direct, authoritative, and not merely empirical manner. I believe that this view is correct.[2]

Now, as is familiar, both Davidson and Burge accept forms of *semantic externalism:* the broad idea, originating in the writings of Putnam, that the semantic contribution of terms standing for natural kinds, in the first instance, as well as perhaps a variety of other kinds of expression, is determined by factors external to the minds of speakers—by relations in which they stand to objects and events in the real, material or social world—so that the contents of their thoughts must in principle be sensitive to certain kinds of variation in their material or social environment of which they may have no knowledge at all, let alone any form of special or privileged knowledge. The resulting tension has been much discussed. If I am unwittingly transported to Twin Earth long enough for the reference of my uses of the term 'water' to be to *twater,* then the content of those of my thoughts that I express using the term 'water' will change, although on the inside, as it were, everything will seem the same. So how can I be authoritative about

1. Davidson (1994), pp. 101–2.
2. Burge (1988), p. 649.

the content of my thoughts or, consequently, about the content of any of my attitudes? Davidson's and Burge's writings about self-knowledge are structured by this subplot: the special knowledge selves seemingly have about themselves has to be reconciled with semantic externalism. We should be mindful, however, that, fashionable though it may be, it is *only* a subplot. One might succeed in that project—succeed in showing that no special difficulty for first-personal authority, for instance, is posed by semantic externalism—without succeeding in saying anything very illuminating at all about the source and nature of the authority itself.

To a philosopher preoccupied with the subplot, it will seem substantial, maybe even decisive progress to notice that the kind of opacity—the 'behind one's back' component—introduced by semantic externalism can introduce no special risk of error about the content of occurrent thoughts. There can be no question, that is to say, of my thinking that I'm thinking that water is tasteless when I'm actually thinking that twater is tasteless, since the environmental contribution to the content of the thought that I express by the words 'Water is tasteless' will be the same for both the first and the second-order thought. You can't think second-order thoughts about water if you don't have a term for water; and the scenario in question is one in which, unbeknownst to you, you don't.

Davidson may have been the first to remark this. What the point shows is that if some element of opacity of content is indeed introduced by externalism, it will have to show in the possibility of a different kind of error—not a misfit between the contents of *contemporaneous* first- and second-order attitudes. And of course, once we drop the assumption that the attitudes in question are contemporaneous, it is clear exactly where the damage is done. What, for example, the externalist assumptions implicit in the water–twater example introduce is precisely the (bare) possibility of *cross-temporal* misidentification of thoughts which owes nothing to lapses of memory or confusion. The opacity introduced by externalism resides exactly in the fact that no matter how lucid I may be, nor how perfectly my memory functions, changing circumstances could in principle cause me unwittingly to misidentify thoughts I've had on other occasions. Maybe, though, that's a limitation which we ought just to take in stride; if more traditional intuitions about self-knowledge seem compromised at this point, perhaps that is just where they overstep the mark.

But what of the main plot? Davidson's well-known proposal[3] about attitudinal avowals takes off from an analogue of the last point—that there cannot be one kind of mismatch between contemporaneous first- and second-order thought—and from a point about disquotation. Any claim made about what a (putative) fellow English-speaker means by a particular sentence, even one that uses that very sentence to specify the content in question, is hostage to the evidence of interpretation. Aberrant use may defeat any opinion I hold, even disquotationally formulated ones, about others' meanings. By contrast, when I use a sentence to specify disquotationally what *I* mean by it, there is no such hostage. For whatever interpretation may teach *you* about the content I attach to the sentence in question will apply to both the mentioned and the used occurrences in my specification: whatever I mean by a sentence, S, I am guaranteed to be able to say with perfect accuracy what that sentence means merely by using it. Suppose, then, that I now assent to S. Both you and I can, so to speak, observe my assent. But I am proof against error about *what* I have assented to in a way that you are not. We are both in position to conclude that I believe something. But I am uniquely assured of no error in the specification of *what* I believe. Therein, suggests Davidson, lies the source of my special authority.

This is an ingenious suggestion. But it is likely to impress as ultimately quite unsatisfactory and it's worthwhile being clear why. It would not be fair to complain that it admits of no generalisation to avowals of non-content-bearing states. For one thing, Davidson explicitly sets those aside; and for another, it cannot in any case be ruled out that the best accounts of the authority respectively carried by phenomenal and attitudinal avowals may differ. It *would* be fair to

3. Davidson (1994).

complain that Davidson's account admits of no obvious generalisation to attitudes other than belief. The account cannot generalise because there is nothing which stands to hoping, desiring and fearing, for instance, as assent stands to believing. And there is, I suggest, a strong presumption that a correct account of the marks carried by attitudinal avowals should be uniform: it's not to be expected that the ground for my authority about my beliefs and the ground for my authority about my desires, say, should turn out to be quite different. But the real objection to Davidson's proposal is that it fails even for the case of belief. A simple dilemma arises over the interpretation of 'assent'. Davidson takes my assent to S to be available as a datum to both me and you. So 'assent' ought to mean: overt assenting behaviour (however that is characterised). But in that case we get no explanation for my authority on the matter of whether I *really do* believe that S. Overt behaviour as of assent is one thing; genuine belief another. True, I am proof against misidentification of the content of the belief, *if* I hold it. But part of the phenomenon to be explained is that I can know, effortlessly and non-inferentially, whether I hold it or not. When 'assent' is interpreted behaviourally, Davidson's reconstruction leaves me no better placed on that matter than you are. If, on the other hand, 'assent' is interpreted as behaviour expressive of a *genuine* belief, then there is an asymmetry in our knowledge of the supposed datum—my assent to S—about which his proposal says nothing, and which is effectively the very thing it was supposed to account for.[4]

Actually, it is clear, stepping back, that Davidson has simply missed the matter for explanation. What he offers is the correct observation that I cannot mis-specify the content of a belief of mine if I confine myself to disquotation within my idiolect. But the authority over my beliefs with which you will normally credit me pertains to what I say about them *after* you take it that you are interpreting those remarks correctly—when my distinctive advantage, construed as by Davidson,

---

4. There is also a doubt whether Davidson can in any case provide the right kind of account of what he *can* explain. His explanation has nothing particularly to do with psychology. It extends to "My thoughts about water are originally caused by water".

has already been neutralised, as it were. This authority cannot, accordingly, be grounded merely in an immunity to misinterpretation of myself that I enjoy but you do not. It kicks in after that asymmetry is allowed for. It shows in the way that, *after* you assume the correctness of your interpretation of my ungrounded, unsupported claims about my beliefs, you are required to treat them as a criterion of what my beliefs are.

II

Tyler Burge's discussions, like Davidson's, are in many respects preoccupied with the subplot of finding a reconciliation with externalism. But, as is well known, he has made a striking suggestion about our leading question as well. There is, he claims, an important category of self-knowledge which he terms *basic;* and the reason why self-ascriptions of states which are apt to compose the subject matter of basic self-knowledge are authoritative is because we are, with respect to this subject matter, *infallible*. As an example of a judgement which illustrates basic self-knowledge, Burge offers:

> I think (with this very thought) that writing requires concentration.

Such judgements—judgements of the form 'I think that P'—are paradigms of authoritative self-ascription. And about them, Burge writes as follows:

> When one knows that one is thinking that P, one is not taking one's thought (or thinking) that P merely is an object. One is thinking that P in the very event of thinking knowledgeably that one is thinking it. It is thought and thought about in the same mental act.[5]

In such cases, he claims,

5. Burge (1988), p. 654.

the object, or subject matter of one's thoughts is not contingently related to the thoughts one thinks about it. The thoughts are self-referential and self-verifying. An error based on a gap between one's thoughts and the subject matter is simply not possible in these cases.[6]

The idea is, I take it, that such second-order judgements—thoughts about what one is occurrently thinking—are constructed *upon* an appropriate first-order thought in such a way as to preclude any possibility of misfit: when I think such a second-order thought, there is no possibility of its untruth—because, say, I'm not thinking the relevant first-order thought, but some other, or no first-order thought at all—for the very having of the second-order thought involves rehearsing the very thought whose occurrence makes it true. In relevant respects, the situation is exactly comparable to that in which I say:

I am *saying* (with these very words) 'Writing requires concentration'.

There is no possibility of my falsely saying that sentence, for the very saying of it at all incorporates an occurrence—the utterance of the words 'Writing requires concentration'—which is sufficient for its truth.

The observation is well made. But its limitations are immediately apparent. For one thing, to explain *infallibility* is to explain too much, since in the cases that most interest us—par excellence, the self-ascription of attitudes like belief and desire—we are only *fallibly* authoritative; self-deception and other forms of confusion are not to be excluded. Moreover, Burge's account turns essentially on the *episodic* character of thinking (on one understanding of 'thinking'.) It is this which renders the relevant second-order judgements verifiable by an intellectual *performance*. But it is of course something of a peculiarity of thinking that is both episodic *and* content-bearing. Most of the attitudinal states which fall within the province of authoritative self-ascription are not episodic in the relevant kind of

6. Ibid., p. 658.

way. That's enough to show that there is no prospect of generalising Burge's observation.

Burge is under no illusion about these limitations. In another recent publication on the topic[7] he continues to place emphasis on such self-verifying ('*cogito*-like') judgements but presents in addition a quite different, potentially very important observation of much greater generality:

> To reason critically—to consider reasons bearing on the truth of some matter, to suspend belief or desire, to weigh values under a conception of the good—one must treat one's own commitments as matters to be considered and evaluated. Critical evaluation of one's own commitments is central to forming them and to rationally changing one's mind or standing fast.
>
> So critical reasoning requires thinking about one's thoughts. But it further requires that that thinking be normally knowledgeable. To appreciate one's reasons as reasons—to check, weigh, criticise, confirm one's reasons—one must know what one's reasons, thoughts and reasoning are. One need not always be knowledgeable, or even right. But being knowledgeable must be the normal situation. . . .[8]

The point, simply, is that in order to be a critical reasoner, in order to be capable of implementing changes in my attitudes under rational constraints, I have to be able not merely to subject *hypothetical* sets of attitudes to such constraints but to recognise the attitudes which I myself actually hold. That there should, at least potentially, be self-knowledge of any type of attitude whose assumption or persistence might be subject to rational criticism is the indispensable precondition of being a full-fledged, self-critical reasoner.

Burge develops this idea with subtlety and in detail, arguing in particular that the immediacy of the bearing which critical reasoning has on the tenability of attitudes being reviewed in any particular case cannot be saved if self-knowledge is thought of in terms of even the most vestigially perceptual model, whose key point would be merely

---

7. Burge (1996). This material was presented in his Whitehead Lectures in 1994.
8. Ibid., pp. 100–1.

that it is *causal* relations between our first- and second-order attitudes which make knowledge out of the latter. That contention merits a discussion which I cannot attempt here. But it remains that there seems to be an evident gap between what can be yielded by Burge's new consideration and the terms of our original problem. What is sure is that any episode of rational self-evaluation must proceed within a context of knowledgeable identification of the attitudes evaluated. But that, as far as it goes, is equally true of any episode of rational *other*-evaluation: I have to know what your attitudes are before I can form a view about whether they are as they rationally ought to be. No self/other asymmetry is entrained by this unquestionable component in Burge's discussion. Certainly, if my knowledge of your attitudes should be viewed as depending on causal connections they have with their manifestations, and on causal connections in turn between those manifestations and the opinions I form, then a self/other asymmetry *is* entrained if Burge is right, in addition, that the immediacy of self-directed critical reasoning precludes even the most vestigially perceptual model of self-knowledge. But the upshot would still be merely that critical self-directed reasoning demands a reasoner who knows herself *differently* to the way others know her. It would not follow that she knows herself *better*—that she has any kind of dominant (albeit defeasible) authority concerning her intentional states—nor that they will typically be transparent to her in a way they are not to others. But that is the asymmetry which we are challenged to explain

In general, it is one thing to point out a precondition for an ability with which ordinary thought does not hesitate to attribute to us; quite another to explain how that precondition is indeed generally satisfied, or what entitles us to suppose that it is.

III

The Cartesian conception of the origins of first-personal authority is *substantial* in a sense in which the proposals of Burge and Davidson are, by contrast, *deflationary*. According to the Cartesian conception, the distinctive features of avowals are to be attributed to the subject's occupation of a position of cognitive privilege with respect to their subject matter. Burge's and Davidson's instinct, by contrast, is to seek, in their different ways, an account of the authority of avowals which somehow makes something of the fact that one's beliefs about certain of one's first-order attitudes are not merely *about* those attitudes but embed them, or at least their contents, in some sort of constitutive way, a way preempting a misfit between them. It may be tempting to think that any approach must fall into one of these two broad camps: that a response to our leading question must either make out that subjects enjoy some special cognitive advantage in relation to their own phenomenal and attitudinal states or it must explain how harmony between one's first- and second-order attitudes is secured not by dint of any cognitive 'tracking' but by some kind of constitutive inter-dependence between them. In fact, though, neither of these broad rubrics happily covers the next two approaches we shall consider.

First to an interesting suggestion of Christopher Peacocke.[9] His concern in Peacocke (1992) was with the elaboration and defence of a framework which takes it that concepts are individuated by the statement, in a certain canonical form, of what it is for a subject to possess them, and which is driven by the hope that many questions of traditional and recent philosophical concern about particular concepts can be illuminated by the provision of such statements of possession conditions and the exploration of their consequences and inter-relations. Peacocke's target, in the parts of his book which will concern us, is the concept of *belief*. But it is to be expected that he would want to extend similar proposals to the other concepts of propositional attitude over which first-personal authority extends.

What would a correct statement of the possession conditions for the concept of belief look like? The part of Peacocke's formulation relevant to our present concerns runs as follows:

A relational concept R—[possessed by a particular thinker]—is the concept of belief only if

9. I refer to his discussion of belief in Peacocke (1992), chap. 6.

(F) the thinker finds the first-person content that he stands in R to P primitively compelling whenever he has the conscious belief that P, and he finds it compelling because he has that conscious belief; and. . . .[10]

That's the clause pertaining to possession of a concept of one's own beliefs. The account continues with a statement of a clause for the third-personal case—the condition for the possession of the concept of another's believing P—which need not concern us.[11] Recall that finding a judgement *primitively* compelling, in Peacocke's technical sense, involves finding it compelling on no inferential ground.[12]

Peacocke applies this formulation to the question of how a subject's second-order beliefs amount to knowledge. His discussion has some intricacy, but we can bracket it for our immediate purposes.[13]

---

10. Ibid., pp. 163–4.

11. The third-personal clause reads: "(T) In judging a thought of the third-person form *a*RP, the thinker thereby incurs a commitment to *a*'s being in a state that has the same content-dependent role in making *a* intelligible as the role of his own state of standing in R to P in making him intelligible, were he to be in that state."

12. There is more to the notion; but nothing that I'm going to say will depend on that extra.

13. The application goes via two principles. The first is that reference should always be assigned to a concept in such a way that any proposition embedding that concept is true in circumstances in which, according to the possession condition of the concept in question, that proposition is found primitively compelling (ibid., p. 157). That dictates that if a thinker has a concept R which obeys the proposed clause, its reference must be to a relation which obtains between the thinker and a given proposition P whenever that thinker consciously believes P—thereby ensuring, Peacocke obviously intends (it is another question whether he is right), that its reference must be to the relation of *belief*. The second is the "highly intuitive" principle that '[i]f your reasons for a belief ensure its truth and do so as a consequence of the nature of the concepts it contains, you are in the best possible epistemic position with respect to the content of the belief'(ibid., p. 158). Accordingly, someone who is moved to the judgement that they believe that P after the fashion schematised in Peacocke's clause is in the best possible epistemic position with respect to that judgement, and ought therefore—the idea is—to be deemed to *know* it. The upshot is thus to be that the possession condition for the concept of belief is such that it is constitutive of that concept that a subject who does possess it and who consciously has the belief that P, will *know* that they do.

For *knowledge* is not really the immediate point. The prior question is just to understand the strong standing presumption that an avowal of belief is true—it is a secondary question why, when it is, it should be held to be an expression of knowledge. Now, the bearing of Peacocke's proposal on this prior question is as follows. The first-personal clause of the possession condition tells us that it is part and parcel of your concept, R, being the concept of belief that you will find the judgement that you stand in R to P primitively compelling when you have the conscious belief that P. So, just by crediting you with the concept of belief, I credit you with the propensity to form true but non-inferential beliefs about your beliefs whenever the latter are conscious. Since *unconscious* beliefs of yours fall outside the sphere of what you can avow, it may seem that we have, if the possession condition is correct, exactly what is needed. Merely by taking you to be capable of second-order belief (and hence a possessor of the concept of belief), I am committed to accepting that your conscious beliefs will each be earmarked by an appropriate higher-order belief.

Is the possession condition correct? One possible concern about that turns on the status of the view which counsels that we should anticipate the disappearance of the concepts of ordinary intentional psychology from a mature behavioural science. I myself hold no brief for this eliminativist view. But I do not think that it is a trivial undertaking to show that it is incoherent. Suppose that it is *not* in fact incoherent, but that it *is* nevertheless false—in particular, that conscious beliefs, desires, intentions and so on do feature among the springs of human action. Then the eliminativist, like everyone else, and whether he likes it or not, *does* have certain conscious beliefs. But he also presumably has the concept of belief: he knows what kind of thing it is that he is claiming a mature behavioural science will eschew. So he is, it would seem, a standing counterexample to Peacocke's possession condition. For he will not, whenever he has the conscious belief that P, find the judgement 'I believe that P' primitively compelling. He will not find any such judgement compelling in any way, since he does not believe that he has any beliefs.

If that is not a serious objection, then I offer it for fun. A more immediate concern about Peacocke's formulation is whether sense can be made of the idea of a *conscious belief* that is not also the object of a second-order belief. (If not, then the account is not merely trivial but effects no connection between first- and second-order belief.) But I shall assume that can be satisfactorily addressed. The real short-coming in the proposed account is that the connection effected by the possession condition between a subject's first- and higher-order beliefs *goes in the wrong direction* to illuminate first-personal authority. The condition as formulated ensures that any possessor of the concept of belief who has conscious beliefs will believe that he has those beliefs in a compulsive but groundless fashion. That ensures something like *transparency*. But what we require in order to obtain, in Peacocke's kind of way, an account of the *authority* of attitudinal avowals is the reverse: an explanation of how—if Peacocke's general instinct is right—it flows from the very concept of belief that one who ground-lessly and compulsively endorses a self-ascription of belief should be presumed to be right. Peacocke's formulation has nothing to say about that. It is consistent with it that a subject could possess the con-cept of belief by dint of satisfying the two clauses he delineates (the second is no help with our concern here), and thereby be prone, in accordance with Peacocke's first clause, correctly to self-ascribe the conscious beliefs he actually has, while at the same time being prone to self-ascribe *no end* of beliefs and other intentional states which he *lacks*. The authority that we invest in others' attitudinal avowals ex-cludes that possibility. But Peacocke's account does not.[14]

Might the proposal be modified so as to cover the point? Well, not, so far as I can see, straightforwardly. In particular, it would not do to

14. It is arguable, indeed, that even attitudinal transparency is not adequately accommodated by Peacocke's proposal. For transparency involves not merely that one's conscious attitudes be reflected in one's second-order beliefs but that conscious attitudes are the *normal case*. The idea, as characterised early in Essay 10, is that a subject ought normally to know without further ado what she wants, believes or intends, etc.; Peacocke's possession condition has no bearing on that.

strengthen the first-personal clause to a biconditional. To propose that a possessor of the concept of belief must find the judgement that they believe P primitively compelling *when and only when* they have the conscious belief that P, (and to find it compelling because they have that conscious belief, etc.), would be to write it in that (non-inferential) self-deception, or related failings, about one's first-order beliefs are impossible. Doubtless there is a lot more to say, but I shall not now further speculate about what other repair might be proposed.

IV

It is time to review a quite different, rather more traditional, response to the problem. At *Investigations* §308 Wittgenstein writes:

> How does the philosophical problem about mental processes and states and about behaviourism arise?—The first step is the one that altogether escapes notice. We talk of processes and states and leave their nature undecided. Sometime perhaps we shall know more about them—we think. But that is just what commits us to a particular way of looking at the matter.

And a little earlier (§304) he urged that we need to

> make a radical break with the idea that language always functions in one way, always serves the same purpose: to convey thoughts—which may be about houses, pains, good and evil, or anything else you please.

These sections advance the diagnosis that our difficulties in this neighbourhood are generated by 'the grammar which tries to force itself on us here' (§304). They go, Wittgenstein suggests, with a conception of avowals as *reports* and the associated conception of a self-standing subject matter which they serve to report. We take it that there are mental states and processes going on anyway, as it were—the 'first step' that escapes notice—and that each person's avowals serve to report on such states and processes as pertain to her. The immediate effect is to set up a dilemma. How, in the most general terms, should we think of the states of affairs which confer truth on these 'reports'? There is the Cartesian—events-in-an-arena-accessible-only-to-the-subject—option; this does a reasonable job of explaining the distinctive marks of avowals, at least at a casual muster, but it relies on an 'analogy which . . . falls to pieces'(§308)—the analogy between avowals and observation reports made from a privileged position. But the only other option seems to be to 'go public': to opt for a view which identifies the truth-conferring states of affairs with items which are somehow wholly manifest and available to public view—an option which Wittgenstein expects, writing when he did, will naturally take a behaviourist shape so that now 'it looks as if we had denied mental processes'. Of course, a philosopher who takes this option—whether in behaviourist or other form—will want to resist the suggestion that she is *denying* anything, according to *her* recommended understanding of 'mental process', just as Berkeley resisted the suggestion that he was denying the existence of matter. But the manifest problem is to reconcile any such conception of the truth conditions of avowals with their distinctive marks: for as soon as you go public, it becomes obscure what advantage selves can enjoy over others.

This line of difficulty seems to point to an obvious conclusion. Conceiving of avowals as reports of states and processes which are going on anyway appears to enforce a disjunction: *either* accept the Cartesian view, which cannot accommodate ordinary knowledge of others, *or* accept some form of externalisation—perhaps behaviourist, more likely physicalist—which cannot sustain the special place of self-knowledge. So we should reject the parent assumption. And one tradition of commentary, encouraged especially by *Investigations* §244,[15] interprets Wittgenstein as doing this in a very radical way: as denying that avowals are so much as *assertions*—that they

---

15. But see also *Remarks on the Philosophy of Psychology* Volume I, §§450, 501, 593, 599, 832.

make statements, true or false—proposing to view them rather as *expressions* of the relevant aspects of the subject's psychology.[16]

'Expression'? To give expression to an aspect of one's mental life just means, presumably, to give it display, in the way in which wincing and a sharp intake of breath may display a stab of pain, or a smile may display that one is pleased, or a clenching of the teeth that one is angry. Propositional attitudes too can be open to natural expression of this kind: a prisoner's rattling the bars of his cell is a natural expression of a desire to get out. (It is not a way of acting *on* that desire, of course—it is not *rationalised* by it.)[17] Wittgenstein's famous suggestion in §244 is that we should see the avowal of pain as an acquired form of pain behaviour—something one learns to use to supplant or augment the natural expression of pain and which—the *expressivist* tradition of commentary suggests—is no more a *statement*—something with a truth-evaluable content—than are such natural forms of expression.

The immediate question is how well an expressivist treatment of avowals can handle their distinctive marks. And the answer appears to be: not badly at all. For instance, if the avowal, 'I am in pain', is not a statement, true or false, then naturally it is inappropriate to ask its author for grounds for it (Groundlessness) and naturally there is no question of her ignorance of its truth value (Transparency). And if, when uttered with proper comprehension, it is to be compared to an episode of pain behaviour, then only its being a piece of dissimulation—not sincere—can stand in the way of a conclusion that the subject really is in pain (Strong Authority). (And of course it will provide a criterion for the subject's being in pain in just the way that ordinary pain behaviour does.)

Nevertheless the expressivist proposal has come to be more or less universally viewed as a non-starter, for reasons preponderantly to do with the perceived impossibility of making coherent philosophy of language out of it. The claim that the avowal 'I am in pain', serves to

---

16. The sometime popularity of this interpretation is traceable to its being advanced by several of the first reviewers: P. F. Strawson (1954), for instance, in his critical study of *Philosophical Investigations;* and Norman Malcolm in Malcolm (1954).

17. Unless, of course, he believes the bars may come loose.

make no statement, true or false, has to be reconciled with a whole host of linguistic phenomena whose natural explanation would exploit the opposed idea that it is, just as it seems, the affirmation of a truth-evaluable content. Here are four of the snags:

(i) What has the expressivist proposal to say about transformations of tense—'I was in pain' and 'I will be in pain'? If either is a genuine assertion, doesn't there have to be such a thing as an author's making the *same* assertion at a time when doing so would demand its present-tense transform? If on the other hand they are regarded likewise merely as expressions, *what* do they serve to express? (Doesn't an act of expression have to take place at the same time as what it expresses?)

(ii) How is the proposal to construe a locution like 'He knows that I am in pain'? If there is a use of the words 'I am in pain' so embedded, which I can use to express the content of someone else's possible knowledge, why may I not *assert* that very same content by the use of the same words?

(iii) There are genuine—for instance, quantified—statements which stand in logical relations to 'I am in pain'. It entails, for instance, 'Someone is in pain'. How can a genuine statement be entailed by a mere expression?

(iv) 'I am in pain' embeds like any normal assertoric content in logical constructions such as negation and the conditional. 'It's not the case that I am in pain' and 'If I am in pain, I'd better take an aspirin' are syntactically perfectly acceptable constructions. But how can a mere expression, contrast; assertion, be *denied*? And doesn't the antecedent of a conditional have to be understood as the hypothesis that *something is the case*?

This kind of point—I shall dub the whole gamut 'the Geach point'[18]— has often been used as a counter to various forms of expressivism,

---

18. After P. T. Geach's (1965) emphasis of such difficulties for moral expressivism, Austin's performatory account of knowledge, etc.

notably in ethics, and much ingenuity has been expended (squandered?) by moral philosophers of expressivist inclination in the attempt to meet it. But in the present case I don't think it ought to have been influential at all. In the ethical case, the expressivist thesis is, crudely, that there are *no* real moral states of affairs; so the occurrence of what are apparently truth-evaluable contents couched in distinctively moral vocabulary has to be some kind of illusion. In that case the Geach point represents a very serious challenge, since it seems to show that everyday moral thought, in exploiting perfectly standard syntactic resources like those afforded by ordinary sentential logic, requires to the contrary that truth-evaluable moral contents exist. By contrast, it is no part of the present, allegedly Wittgensteinian expressivist proposal that there is no such thing as a statement of ordinary psychological fact. No one is questioning that '*He* is in pain' is an assertion. The expressivist thesis distinctively concerns *avowals*.

How does that difference help? Well, it is clear that we have to draw a distinction in any case between the question whether an indicative sentence is associated with a truth-evaluable content and the question whether its characteristic use is actually *assertoric*. For the two notions routinely come apart in the case of standard performatives like 'I promise to be on time', 'With this ring, I thee wed', 'I name this ship . . .' and so on. Each of these locutions embeds in all the ways the generalised Geach point focuses on; and none of them is standardly used, in the atomic case, as an assertion. We should conclude that what the Geach point signals is merely the presence of truth-evaluable content. It is powerless to determine that the standard use of a locution is to *assert* such a content. And now the expressivist thesis about avowals can be merely that the typical use of such sentences is as expressions rather than assertions. There need be no suggestion that one *cannot* make assertions about one's own psychology. But the suggestion—now initially rather exciting—will be that the appearance of the *epistemic* superiority of the self which avowals convey is an illusion created by attempting to find a home for features of such utterances which they carry *qua* expressions in the context of the mistaken assumption that they are ordinary assertions. When selves *do* make strict assertions about their own psychology, the story should continue, any epistemic advantages they enjoy are confined to those of superiority of evidence which I briefly noted at the beginning of Essay 10.

That, it seems to me, is, in outline, how the best expressivist proposal should go. Now, alas, to its real problems. Perhaps the most immediate awkwardness, if a general account of avowals is to be based upon the §244 idea, is that, even in the case of sensations, the range of cases where there are indeed *natural,* non-linguistic forms of expression—cases like pains, itches and tickles—is very restricted: contrast for instance the sensation of coolness in one foot, or the smell of vanilla. In the latter kind of case, the suggested model of the acquisition of competence in the avowal simply won't grip, and the theorist will have to try to live with the idea of a range of sensations whose *only* expression consists in their avowal. The same is evidently true in spades of psychological items other than sensations. This threatens a worrying dilution of the key notion of *expression.*

That's a worry that might, I suppose, be worked on. But the next one seems decisive. Suppose a highly trained secret agent under torture resolutely gives no ordinary behavioural sign of pain. However his torturers are men of discernment, with subtle instruments, who know full well of his agony nonetheless: they know the characteristic signs—patterns on the electro-encephalograph, raised heart rate, activation of reflexes in the eye, changes in surface skin chemistry, etc. If the suggestion really is to be that the superiority of the first-personal viewpoint is *wholly* an artefact of a grammatical misunderstanding—the misconstrual of expressions as assertions—then, any *knowledge,* strictly so conceived, which the victim has of his own pain has to originate in the same way as that of his tormentors. But by hypothesis he isn't expressing pain behaviourally. And the signs that leave them in no doubt are things which, in his agony, he may not be attending to, or which, like the print-out on the electro-encephalograph, he may not be able to see or interpret if he could see. So in such a case, when it comes down to knowledge, it looks as though the expressivist account must represent the victim as actually *at a disadvantage.* And that's evident nonsense.

In general, merely to conceive of avowals as expressive does not, when it goes in tandem with an acceptance of the reality of the states of affairs which they express, provide any way of deflecting the question: how, broadly speaking, should we conceive of the kind of state of affairs which is apt to confer truth on psychological ascriptions, and in what sort of epistemological relationship do their subjects themselves in general stand to such states of affairs? If this relationship is in any way more than evidentially privileged, we have our original problem back. If it isn't, we seem to get absurdities like that just illustrated.

A different way of seeing the unplayability of the expressivist position is to reflect that the content of an avowal is always available to figure just in a subject's thoughts, without public expression. You may sit reading and think to yourself 'My headache has gone' without giving any outward sign at all. And anyone versed in ordinary psychology will accept that *if* you have that thought, not by way of merely entertaining it but as something you endorse, then you will be right (Authority); that there is no way that your headache could have passed unless you are willing to endorse such a thought (Transparency); and that your willingness to endorse it will not be the product of inference or independently formulable grounds (Groundlessness). Thus analogues of each of the marks of avowals that pose our problem engage the corresponding unarticulated thoughts. It must follow that the correct explanation of the possession of them by avowals cannot have anything to do with illocutionary distinctions.

We should conclude that the expressivist proposal flies rather further than is usually thought. But it is a dead duck all the same.

V

We have now reviewed five very different approaches to our problem. Some contain points of local validity, but none appears to promise a generally satisfactory account. We seem no closer to understanding what we wish to understand. Why should this be so difficult? What direction can a fresh approach take?

And what, for that matter—if he has one—is Wittgenstein's *own* view? For sure, the textual evidence for attributing the expressivist view to him was always pretty exiguous. *Investigations* §244 in particular may be contrasted with much more cautionary and nuanced remarks elsewhere.[19] Such apparent equivocations, of course, are fuel for the common complaint that while Wittgenstein has suggestive criticisms to offer of certain tendencies in the philosophy of mind, he left any intended positive contribution shrouded in fog. What exactly—or even roughly—is Wittgenstein saying about avowals, if he is not proposing the expressivist view? How exactly does he propose we should liberate our thinking from Cartesian tendencies? What did he think we should put in their place?

I don't think it is all that difficult to glean what his positive recommendation is, at least in general outline. The difficulty is, rather, to find it intellectually sufficient. The first essential in interpreting him here is to give due prominence to the *Investigations*' explicit conception of the genesis of philosophical problems and of proper philosophical method. Wittgenstein wrote, recall, that

> we may not advance any kind of theory. There must not be anything hypothetical in our considerations. We must do away with all *explanation* and description alone must take its place. . . . [Philosophical problems] are solved, rather, by looking into the workings of our language, and that in such a way as to make us recognise those workings: *in despite of* the urge to misunderstand them. . . . Philosophy is a battle against the bewitchment of our intelligence by means of language.[20]

---

19. For instance *Investigations* II, §ix:

> [A] cry, which cannot be called a description, which is more primitive than any description, for all that serves as a description of the inner life.
>
> A cry is not a description. But there are transitions. And the words, 'I am afraid', may approximate more, or less, to being a cry. They may come quite close to this and also be *far* removed from it.

20. Ibid., §109

And, very famously:

> Our mistake is to look for an explanation while we ought to look at what happens as a 'proto-phenomenon'. That is, where we ought to have said: *this language game is played.*[21]

The bearing of these strategic remarks is immediate if we reflect that our whole problem is constituted by a demand for explanation. We are asking: what is the *explanation* of the characteristic marks of avowals? And we easily accept a refinement of the question along the lines: what is it about the subject matter of avowals, and about their authors' relation to it, which explains the possession by these utterances of their characteristic effortless, non-inferential, authority? Cartesianism takes the question head-on, giving the obvious, but impossible, answer. And the expressivist proposal, radical though it is in its questioning of the assumption that the authority of an avowal is the authority of a claim to truth, is not so radical as to raise a question about the validity of the *entire explanatory project.* But Wittgenstein, seemingly, means to do just that. Against the craving for explanation, he seemingly wants to set a conception of the 'autonomy of grammar'.[22] The features of avowals which set our problem—the features which seem to betray something remarkable about self-knowledge—do so only if we suppose that they are in some way *consequential* upon something deeper, for instance the nature of their subject matter and of their author's relationship to it. But what imposes that way of looking at the matter? Why shouldn't psychological discourse's exhibition of these features be regarded as primitively constitutive of its being *psychological,* so that the first/third-personal asymmetries that pose our question belong primitively to the 'grammar' of the language-game of ordinary psychology, in Wittgenstein's special sense—'grammar' which 'is not accountable to any reality' and whose rules 'cannot

21. Ibid., §654. It doesn't matter that this is said in the context of discussion of a different issue (recollection of the content of a prior intention.)
22. As Baker and Hacker style it.

be justified by showing that their application makes a representation agree with reality'?[23]

What did Wittgenstein suppose entitled him to this standpoint? In his later work, as everyone knows, he radically rethought his early conception of the relation between language and reality. It is to this readjustment, I suggest, that we must look if we are to understand the doctrine of the 'autonomy of grammar'. As I read the early 300s, the obstacle which Wittgenstein sees as lying in the way of our understanding 'mental processes and states' is not the assumption of truth-evaluability of avowals, as the expressivist interpretation has it, but rather a general picture of the working of *truth-evaluable* language. Wittgenstein means to reject a certain picture of what truth evaluability involves: the picture gestured at in §304, that our statements always serve 'the same purpose: to convey thoughts—which may be about houses, pains, good and evil, or anything else you please.' The picture involves thinking of assertions as expressing propositions which are laid over against reality in the manner of the *Tractatus,* so that there have to be self-standing states of affairs to correspond to avowals, when they are true, and it has therefore to be possible to raise general questions about the nature of these self-standing states of affairs and the nature of the subject's knowledge of them. And then, when we are mindful of the distinctive marks of avowals, it appears that the states, and the mode of knowledge, must be something rather out of the ordinary—the relevant states of affairs have to be conceived as somehow especially transparent to the subject, or, at the least, as working on her by some form of curiously reliable 'blind-sight'—(whose curious reliability, moreover, would have to be common knowledge if the authority credited to avowals is to be explained). Wittgenstein's diagnosis is that the 'philosophical problem about mental processes and states and about behaviourism' arises because we insist on intepreting the truth evaluability of avowals—the source of the linguistic features on which the Geach point fastens—as imposing a conception of their being true, when they are, in

23. *Philosophische Grammatik* X, §§133–134.

terms which have to raise these constitutive questions about nature and access. But these are the very questions—Wittgenstein is saying—which we must free ourselves of the temptation to raise; they are the questions which lead to the fast-track into the fly-bottle.

Of course, the conception of truth and truth-makers which, in Wittgenstein's diagnosis, is here at the root of our difficulty is the core of the outlook which Hilary Putnam has called 'metaphysical realism'. Perhaps the single most significant departure effected in Wittgenstein's later philosophy is his coming to believe that we have to stop thinking about the relationship between language and reality, and about the truth predicate, in that kind of way.

VI

Wittgenstein's stance deserves a much finer-grained depiction than I can attempt here—(not just because I lack the space.) If we abstract from the globally anti-explanatory background mantra, the cash value of the proposal, just for the issue of self-knowledge, involves a generalisation to all avowable subject matter, phenomenal and attitudinal, of a view which might be characterised like this:

> [T]he authority standardly granted to a subject's own beliefs, or expressed avowals, about his intentional states is a *constitutive principle*: something which is not a consequence of the nature of those states, and an associated epistemologically privileged relation in which the subject stands to them, but enters primitively into the conditions of identification of what a subject believes, hopes and intends.[24]

I'll call this general viewpoint the Default View. According to the Default View, it is just primitively constitutive of the acceptability of psychological claims that, save in cases whose justification would involve active self-interpretation, a subject's opinions about herself

24. Wright (1991), p. 142 (this volume Essay 9).

are default-authoritative and default-limitative: unless you can show how to make better sense of her by overriding or going beyond it, her active self-conception, as manifest in what she is willing to avow, must be deferred to. The truth conditions of psychological ascriptions are primitively conditioned by this constraint. In particular, it is simply basic to the competent ascription of the attitudes that, absent good reason to the contrary, one must accord correctness to what a subject is willing to avow; and limit one's ascriptions to her to those she is willing to avow.

It would be a great achievement of Wittgenstein's discussion if it made it possible to understand how the Default View need not be merely an unphilosophical turning of the back. But it is anything but clear, actually, how a repudiation of the metaphysical realist picture of truth could just by itself directly enjoin this conception. Moreover it is very difficult to rest easy with the general anti-explanatory mantra. For it is seemingly in tension with a diagnostic thought very important to Wittgenstein: that philosophical problems characteristically arise because we are encouraged by surface-grammatical analogies to form expectations about an area of discourse which are appropriate only for a particularly salient surface-grammatical analogue of it. That is *exactly* Wittgenstein's diagnosis in the present case: the target analogy is that between the use of avowals and ordinary reports of observation. So then that diagnosis itself requires that the explanatory questions which we are required *not* to press in the case of avowals are, by contrast, perfectly properly raised, and answerable, in the case of ordinary reports of observation. There cannot, accordingly, just be a blanket prohibition against explanatory questions of that kind. Put that simple thought alongside the plausible claim that there are perfectly legitimate modes of *conceptual* explanation—informal mathematics, in particular, is full of them—and it appears that it cannot in general be merely a confusion to seek to explain features of the practice of a discourse a priori by reference to our concepts of the kind of subject matter it has and of the epistemic capacities of speakers. Thus the insistence that these questions are misplaced in the target case of psychological self-ascriptions begins to seem merely dogmatic.

Is there any way this impression of dogmatism might be dispelled? In the analogy, used in Essay 10, of the kaleidoscope, our conception is that of a range of independent features and events—evolving patterns of shape and colour—to which the privileged observer is sensitive—responsive—by dint of his situation and his possession of certain germane cognitive capacities, notably vision. There is a story to be told about the kind of things on display and how things of that kind can elicit a response from someone with a suitable cognitive endowment. Now, one way to try to exculpate the Default View from the charge of dogmatism, it seems to me, is to seek a framework which places controls on the relevant idea of *responsiveness*.[25] One form of control might be elicited from pursuing recently much-discussed issues to do with judgement-dependence and the *Euthyphro contrast:* we may pursue the details of the relations, in different regions of thought, between best opinion and truth, attempting thereby to arrive at a conception of what it is for them to relate too closely, so to speak, for their congruence to count as a *success in tracking.* Another control might emerge from consideration of the question how wide the potential *explanatory range* has to be of a certain type of states of affairs if we are to think of our judgements about them as genuinely responsive to their subject matter at all (*width of cosmological role*). We can seek a framework of such controls and try to show that first-personal psychological discourse emerges on the wrong side of the tracks, so to speak, under the application of such controls. Then, if its apparent urgency does indeed derive from a tacit assumption of the *responsiveness* of selves to their own psychological states, the general explanatory question about self-knowledge, which official Wittgensteinian philosophical method would have us ignore, can emerge as something which we can understand *why* we ought not to ask.

By contrast, lacking such a framework, and the right kind of upshot within it concerning psychological discourse, it is hard to see how

25. This would be a programme of what John McDowell disparagingly calls 'constructive philosophy'.

the Default View can come to much more than a take-it-or-leave-it recommendation: a mere invitation to *choose* to treat as primitive something which we have run into trouble trying to explain, and to do so just on that account. Wittgenstein notoriously came to view philosophical problems as akin to a kind of self-inflicted intellectual *disease;* they would thus contrast starkly with *mathematical* problems as traditionally viewed (not by Wittgenstein, of course)—a kind of sublime, objective puzzle whose force can be felt by any rational intellect. If philosophical problems are justly deflated in Wittgenstein's way, then a kind of 'Here: think of matters this way, and you'll feel better' remedy might be the best we can do. But the prospect immensely disappoints. For most of us, after all, the attraction of philosophy is all about gaining understanding. Except in cases where one can *explain* a priori why the demand for understanding is inappropriate, it is apt to seem like a mere abrogation of philosophy to be told one mustn't make it at all.

VII

Our brief discussion has been, unsurprisingly, inconclusive, but let me try to pull things together a little. First, nothing we have reviewed impresses as a satisfactory explanation of the distinctive marks of avowals. We must not underestimate our colleagues' resourcefulness, of course, but the smart money will bet we are not going to get one. Second, we owe to Wittgenstein the insight that we are making an assumption in feeling this as a deficiency of understanding. The assumption is, roughly, that those distinctive marks must be *consequential*: that they must either derive from the nature of the subject matter—something which therefore drives our discourse about it into the relevant characteristic turns—or else they must derive from some unobvious feature of the semantics of first-personal psychological discourse (its being, for instance, expressive rather than assertoric.) So, according to the assumption, there must be an explanation which we have yet to assemble and get into focus. Third, there is a frontal collision between this way of thinking and the conception of the nature of legitimate philosophical enquiry seemingly quite explicit in Wittgenstein's later official methodological pronouncements. According to Wittgenstein, the limit of our philosophical ambition should be to recognise the assumptions we are making in falling into philosophical difficulty and to see our way clear to accepting, by whatever means, that nothing forces us to make them. It is, for Wittgenstein, with the very craving for legitimising explanations of features of our talk about mind, or rules, or mathematics that we are led into hopeless puzzles about the status—the epistemology and ontology—of those discourses. Philosophical treatment is wanted, not to solve these puzzles but to undermine them—to assuage the original craving that leads to the construction of the bogus models and interpretations by which we attempt to make sense of what we do, but which are the source of all our difficulties, and yet whose want is felt as a lack of understanding. The problem of self-knowledge is a signal example. It can have—I believe Wittgenstein's holds—*no solution* of the kind we seek; for that very conception of a solution implicitly presupposes that there must be a something-by-virtue-of-which the distinctive marks of avowals are sustained. But those marks are part of 'grammar' and grammar is not sustained by anything. We should just say 'this language game is played'.

The generalisation of this position—the execration of all philosophical explanation—seems to me vulnerable to a version of what one might call the 'paradox of postmodernism'. The paradox is that while, like all deflationists, Wittgenstein needs to impress one of the illegitimacy of more traditional aspirations, *argument* for that is hard to foresee if it is not of the very coin which he is declaring to be counterfeit. For what is needed here is precisely a *philosophical explanation*. Sure, what belongs to 'Grammar', in Wittgenstein's special sense of that term, requires no explanation. *Of course;* that's a matter of definition. But even a sympathetic reading of him will find a frustrating inattention to the question when something may legitimately be taken to be part of 'grammar'. It may be a crucial first step to recognise that the problem of self-knowledge is occasioned by an assumption of explicability—an assumption that may be discarded with a clear conscience if the special position of subjects in determining what is true of their psychology is indeed 'grammatical'. But, one wants to say, what shows that? Once one recognises the Default View as a possibility, the immediate instinct is to ask what might *justify* the idea that it is the whole truth? That is the instinct to attempt to understand when and why it is a good move to dismiss the attempt to understand. To succumb is to reenter the space of explanatory philosophy. To resist is to have no reason for the Default View.

To feel this dissatisfaction is not to have a reason to deny the insight that in a wide class of cases philosophical perplexity does indeed take the form of a casting about for what strike us as satisfying explanations of features of our language and of failing to find any that do not generate singularities, of one sort or another. (Just briefly to mention a second prominently Wittgensteinian example: how are we to make sense of the intelligibility of the distinction between whether a statement is really true and whether anybody ever takes it to be true unless the rule incorporated in its truth condition may be thought of as issuing its verdict autonomously and independently of any human judgement? So isn't the very idea of unratified truth an implicit commitment to 'rules-as-rails' Platonism?!) But to accept Wittgenstein's insight, that some of the hardest-seeming philosophical problems take this form, is not a commitment to an explanation-proscribing view of philosophy. Even if it is misguided to persist in assuming that there must be *something* satisfactorily to take up the explanatory slack left by the demise of Platonism, or Cartesianism, it may yet be possible to explain why such an assumption needn't be true in particular cases. It does not seem merely confused to seek, in particular, to characterise with some care the conception we have of the kinds of ways the marks of avowals might in principle be explained. It is even foreseeable that such a characterisation might lead to a clear-headed realisation that nothing could fulfil it. *That* would be the discovery that, in this area, 'gives philosophy peace'.[26]

26. *Investigations* §133.

PART FOUR

RULE-FOLLOWING
AND MATHEMATICS

These two essays centre on the bearing of Wittgenstein's ideas on issues in the philosophy of mathematics.

Essay 12 is my contribution to a symposium of the same title in which Paul Benacerraf and I participated at the Joint Session of the Mind Association and Aristotelian Society held at Leeds in 1985. In his paper, Benacerraf did a wonderful job of bringing out the likely confusions of those who argued that the Löwenheim-Skolem theorem, and its various extensions, show that we need a relativistic understanding of cardinality notions in set theory, and that no absolute uncountability exists. I found myself in complete agreement with his remarks on this, and the early part of the essay expands on this agreement. But I felt that three issues deserved a somewhat clearer separation than perhaps they received in Benacerraf's paper:

whether the Löwenheim-Skolem theorems cut the ground from under 'Cantor's paradise' by imposing a relativistic understanding of key set theoretic notions;

whether the thought that they do stands or falls with Hilary Putnam's generalised 'model theoretic argument' against metaphysical realism;[1] and

whether the Löwenheim-Skolem theorems present any other compelling line of difficulty for the classical interpretation of set theory.

Most of the paper is taken up with arguing, partly with the aid of material supplied by Benacerraf himself in others of his writings, that the answer to the third question is positive. The Löwenheim-Skolem theorem (in its transitive countable submodel version) would seem to show that nothing in an acceptance of the usual set-theoretic axioms, with the sole non-logical primitive, 'ϵ', interpreted as meaning set membership, involves commitment to the existence of uncountable sets. Accordingly, if there is such a commitment, it has to flow from some other aspect of the informal understanding of those axioms which the classical set theoretician believes she has. So the question arises what that aspect of the informal understanding is, and how it might be supposed to be acquired or properly explained. In fact it's clear that the vehicle of the commitment has to be the informal understanding of the intended range of the quantifiers. But in order to grasp that intended range, one must grasp the notion of an arbitrary subset of a countably infinite set—par excellence, the notion of an arbitrary infinite subset of the natural numbers. The concluding section of the essay proceeds to argue that the classical understanding of this notion rests on only the flimsiest analogy with the corresponding notion in the finite case—in particular that it severs the explanatory ties which ground the notion of set in the ideas of predication, and/or selection—and that the real philosophical import of the Löwenheim-Skolem is to highlight how stretched and thin the informal understanding of classical set-theoretic notions, in which Benacerraf reposed such confidence, really is.[2]

1. Putnam (1977).
2. Benacerraf has since responded: see Benacerraf (1998).

The explanation of the inclusion of this essay in the present volume, however, turns on a suggestion mooted in its section III. This concerns Putnam's attempt to generalise the Löwenheim-Skolem argument in order to show that metaphysical realism has no resources to account for determinate reference. The essence of his argument is the thought that, by the Löwenheim-Skolem theorem, any total empirical theory will (provided it is formulated in a first-order language) allow of no end of alternative truth-preserving interpretations. How is the realist to make a case that one of these in particular is *the* interpretation—that it captures the real semantic relations between our language and the (metaphysically separated) world? The problem, as presented by Putnam, is that anything the realist says to try to nail down the intended interpretation of the theory will itself be open to alternative interpretations (so long as it is expressed in first-order terms) and so it seems that determinacy of meaning and reference simply cannot be secured.

There are, familiarly, all kinds of questions and possible misgivings about this argument.[3] But I was concerned with the central assumption—which, indeed, it shares with Quine's famous arguments for the indeterminacy of translation and with the routine pursued by Kripke's sceptic—that meaning is no more determinate than *interpretation* is, and hence that to show that, consistently with its truth, a theory allows of a variety of incompatible interpretations—or more generally, that consistently with its practice, a discourse allows of a variety of incompatible interpretations—is to show that it involves no determinate content. It is often supposed—explicitly so by Quine and Putnam—that to resist this idea must involve a retreat to psychologism: to the 'Myth of the Museum' (Quine), or the fiction of a mysterious metaphysical 'glue' (Putnam) connecting our words and thoughts with their true objects. But the psychologistic move is to *retain* the

---

3. Most especially: even if it works, what gives it its selective bearing against metaphysical realism—why is it not just one more meaning-sceptical paradox? For discussion of this and other issues, see Hale and Wright (1997).

idea that the determinacy of meaning consists in the determinacy of interpretation, and then to suppose that what determines correct interpretation is internal and transcends use. The contrast is therefore stark with the response which Wittgenstein himself makes to his own 'regress of interpretations' paradox at *Philosophical Investigations* §§198–201:

> What this shows is that there is a way of grasping a rule which is *not* an *interpretation,* but which is exhibited in what we call 'obeying the rule' and 'going against it' in actual cases.

If following a rule in general and understanding an expression in particular, is not a matter of interpretation, then determinacy in the rule one is following—in what one means—need not require determinacy of interpretation. Thus Wittgenstein draws a conclusion in §201 which, could we properly understand and sustain it, would quite cut the ground from under that genre of meaning-sceptical argument which regards multiple interpretability as a ground for semantic indeterminacy and which has overshadowed so much late-twentieth-century analytical philosophy.

Essay 13 reverts to Wittgenstein's own philosophy of mathematics. It was written for presentation in the Royal Institute of Philosophy's public lecture series for Wittgenstein's centenary, and I was concerned to try to make as accessible as possible something of the general character of Wittgenstein's concerns in the *Remarks on the Foundations of Mathematics.* The essay outlines an intuitive Platonism about pure mathematics, applied to the case of arithmetic, and illustrates Wittgenstein's opposition to it. It then moves to its central contention that, whether taken as interpreted by Kripke or merely as having some yet-to-be-specified bearing on questions to do with mathematical objectivity, the rule-following considerations may do a great deal to explain Wittgenstein's antipathy to a Platonist conception of the *subject matter* of mathematics, but they do little, unsupplemented, to explain his distinctive views about *proof.* The core of those views would seem to be the contention that the acceptance of a proof *as* a proof is always the acceptance of an internal relation, and that the ratification of an internal relation is never a purely *cognitive* response. The essay pursues one strategy, suggested by various of Wittgenstein's examples, of how this claim might be argued, and closes in doubt about the sufficiency of that argument.

12

Skolem and the Sceptic

I

Like Paul Benacerraf, I have found it difficult to see how a cogent version of the argument for 'set-theoretic relativity' might seem to run. But it is worth separating what I think are two quite different lines of thought.

Moral relativism, for instance, is (or could be) the view that there are no absolute moral standards, and (hence?) that moral judgements take on a content which is conditioned, in part, by the local moral standards of the culture(s) to which their makers belong. Someone who took this view might hold, for example, that there is no genuine conflict between enlightened English-speaking opinion on capital punishment and the views of Islamic fundamentalists, since there is sufficient cultural diversity between the respective sources of these judgements to ensure that the moral concepts involved are not the same. Deeply confused as this thinking may be, it at least serves to remind us that relativism is a classic form of escape from *contradiction:* the relativist postulates an ambiguity—a hidden parameter—in order to avoid a collision.

The first line of thought belongs in this sort of relativistic tradition. The Löwenheim-Skolem theorem (LST) *about,* say, Zermelo-Fraenkel set theory (ZF) is presented as contradicting Cantor's theorem *in* ZF. Cantor's theorem entails that the power set of the integers cannot be put into 1–1 correspondence with the integers; whereas LST entails— at this point we begin to struggle—that ZF deals in at most countably many objects, and hence that the power set of the integers, as an object dealt with in the theory, is itself at most countably infinite. As Benacerraf says, this is, so far, a tissue of confusion. Bluntly: LST entails neither that ZF deals only in a countable infinity of objects nor that it deals only in objects which are at most countably infinite. It says that ZF, if it has a model at all, has a countable model. There is not even the appearance of a contradiction. All we have—or so the Cantorian is so far at liberty to contend—is a proof that ZF, if consistent, has non-standard models.

In order to get a line worth considering we must, I think, go for something like the more sophisticated reconstruction of the argument which Benacerraf builds on the transitive countable submodel version of LST (= SMT). The intended interpretation for ZF involves, I take it, a transitive model: that is, every member of every set which the intended interpretation would include in the subject matter of set theory is likewise part of that subject matter. According to SMT, then, if ZF can sustain its intended interpretation at all, it may be interpreted in a countable subdomain of the sets involved in the intended interpretation, in such a way that 'ϵ' continues to mean set membership and every set in the domain of the new interpretation is itself at most countably infinite.

Even now it is apt to seem pretty unclear how exactly there is supposed to be an appearance of contradiction. The thought, presumably, will be something like the following. Consider the Power Set Axiom:

$$(\forall x)(\exists u)(\forall t)[t \in u \leftrightarrow (\forall y)(y \in t \rightarrow y \in x)]$$

And let x be Z_0, the set of positive integers. (It could be, in fact, any denumerably infinite set which features both in the domain of the intended interpretation and in that of the countable submodel—there has, presumably, to be some such set.) Let D be the domain of the intended interpretation, and D′ that of the submodel. Since—the argument is supposing—Z_0 is an element both of D and D′, and since the Power Set Axiom holds *under its intended interpretation* with respect both to D and D′— (for, remember, 'ϵ' is not reinterpreted in the submodel and is the sole non-logical constant in the Power Set Axiom)—the power set of Z_0, $\wp Z_0$—the u whose existence the Power Set Axiom stipulates—must be an element both of D and D′. And now we do appear to have shown contradictory results about it. Cantor's theorem, proved within ZF, entails that there is no 1–1 correspondence between Z_0 and $\wp Z_0$; but if $\wp Z_0$ is an element of a transitive, countable submodel of the ZF axioms, it must itself be countable—that is, there must indeed be such a 1-1 correspondence.

One response would be to regard the situation as demonstrating that ZF, and indeed any set theory adequate for the demonstration of Cantor's theorem, is, if not actually inconsistent, at least *unsound:* a misdescription of what is really true of sets. The relativist response, in contrast, would be to introduce an ambiguity, so that the two results are not really in conflict. Cantor's theorem, proved within the system, should—the relativist would contend—be seen as a result about the mapping-defining power of the system: no 1-1 correspondence between Z_0 and $\wp Z_0$ can be defined *within* the system. And this claim is quite consistent with the reflection that such a 1-1 correspondence can be defined *outside* the system, using methods, presumably, for whose formalisation ZF is inadequate.

Well, that this could not be a satisfactory response is evident, it seems to me, from the mundane reflection that it is so far utterly unclear why the purported Z_0: $\wp Z_0$ mapping, mysteriously unformalizable in ZF set theory, is not confounded by Cantor's reasoning when presented *informally.* For Cantor's reasoning *seems* entirely general: it invites us, presented with any purported 1-1 correspondence, R, between the integers and their subsets, to form a set of exactly those which are not members of their correlates under R. Intuitively, there *ought* to be such a set in the case when the relation in question is the one which establishes—allegedly—the extra-systematic countability of $\wp Z_0$; and, on pain of contradiction, this set cannot itself be correlated with an integer under R. So something is wrong here; if the relativist argument were correct up to the point where there is an apparent contradiction and a relativistic response might seem to be called for, that response could not possibly be intuitively adequate.

Benacerraf seems to me to bring out perfectly what has gone wrong. The trouble is in the supposition that if Z_0 is an element both of D and D′, then the fact that the Power Set Axiom holds for both domains, without reinterpretation of its sole non-logical constant, is a guarantee that $\wp Z_0$ is an element of both domains as well. This is simply incorrect. What the Power Set Axiom guarantees is that each domain will contain, for Z_0, a set u which contains every t in that domain which satisfies the condition on the right-hand side of the biconditional vis à vis Z_0. But whether these should intuitively be regarded as *the same* set depends, of course, on the respective ranges of t in the two domains. If those ranges are not the same, it cannot be assumed that the '$\wp Z_0$' which is an element of D′ is indeed the true $\wp Z_0$, the full-blown power set of the integers. And without that assumption, the transitive countability of D′ is in no sort of tension with the uncountability of $\wp Z_0$. So we simply do not get to the point when we appear to confront contradictory claims about one and the same object—the point where relativisation of the content of those claims might seem to be an appropriate strategy for dissolving the problem. We don't get to that point because the supposition is so far totally unjustified that it is one and the same object with which the claims are concerned.

This seems to me a decisive and helpful point, and I think that Benacerraf's conclusion—in effect that there simply is no coherent relativistic argument of the classic sort to be gleaned from SMT (or LST)—is justified. However, I think the situation with the second train of thought is different.

II

Here is a passage from a justly influential article:

> [N]umbers are not objects at all, because in giving the properties . . . of numbers you merely characterise an *abstract structure*—and the dis-

tinction lies in the fact that the 'elements' of the structure have no properties other than those relating them to other 'elements' of the same structure. . . .

. . . That a system of objects exhibits the structure of the integers implies that the elements of that system have some properties not dependent on structure. It must be possible to individuate those objects independently of the role they play in that structure. But this is precisely what cannot be done with the numbers. To *be* the number 3 is no more and no less than to be preceded by 2, 1, and possibly 0, and to be followed by 4, 5, and so forth. And to *be* the number 4 is no more and no less than to be preceded by 3, 2, 1, and possibly 0, and to be followed by. . . .

. . . *Any* object *can play the role of* 3; that is, any object can be the third element in some progression. What is peculiar to 3 is that it defines that role—not by being a paradigm of any object which plays it, but by representing the relation that any third member of a progression bears to the rest of the progression.

Arithmetic is therefore the science that elaborates the abstract structure that all progressions have in common in virtue of being progressions. It is not a science concerned with particular objects—the numbers. The search for which independently identifiable particular objects the numbers really are (sets? Julius Caesars?) is a misguided one.[1]

The argument which precedes these conclusions is well known. Suppose that someone has received satisfactory definitions of '1' (or '0'), 'number', 'successor', '+', and 'x' on the basis of which the laws of arithmetic can be derived. Let him also have confronted, if you like, an explicit statement of Peano's axioms. Suppose further that he has been given a full explanation of the 'extramathematical' uses of numbers[2]—principally, counting—and has thereby been introduced to the concepts of cardinality and of cardinal number. Then it is possible to claim that, *conceptually* at least, the subject's arithmetical education is complete: he may be ignorant of all sorts of aspects of advanced (and less advanced) number theory, but his deficiencies, if any, are not

1. Benacerraf (1965). The quotation is taken from the reprint in Benacerraf and Putnam (1983), p. 291.
2. Cf. ibid., p. 277.

in his *understanding*—at least not if he has followed his training properly. Yet the striking fact is—the argument runs—that someone who in this way perfectly understands the concept of (*finite* cardinal) number has no basis for (non-arbitrary) identification of the numbers with any objects given in some other way. Benacerraf makes the point vivid by comparing two hypothetical logicist-educated children, each of whom takes zero to be Λ but one of whom identifies successor (following Zermelo) with the unit set operation while the other (following Von Neumann–Berneys–Gödel) identifies the successor of a number with the set consisting of that number and all its elements. Each of the set-theoretic frameworks is perfectly adequate for the explanation of the arithmetical primitives, and the derivation of the Peano axioms, and supplies the background against which the application of arithmetic can be satisfactorily explained. Yet a dispute between the two children as to the *true* identity of the numbers is intractable.

The moral drawn is that the concept of number has no content sufficing to resolve such disputes, has indeed no content sufficing genuinely to individuate the numbers at all. When the explanations, formal and informal, are in, a good deal will have been said to characterise the *structure* which the numbers collectively exemplify, and which, in Benacerraf's view, is the real object of pure number-theoretic investigation; but nothing will have been said to enable a subject to know which, if any, sets the numbers are—or which, if any, objects of any sort they are. If the numbers *really were* objects of some kind, however, surely someone who perfectly understood the concept of number should be able, at least in principle, to identify them. Since we do not have the slightest idea how such an identification might be defended, we ought to contrapose. Whence Benacerraf's anti-Platonist conclusion.

I have elsewhere[3] tried to give reason for thinking that the force of this argument is qualified both by certain internal weaknesses—the concept of finite cardinal number is determinate in ways the argument

3. Wright (1983), esp. §xv, pp. 117–29.

overlooks—and by the company it keeps—for instance Frege's 'permutation' argument and the various Quinean arguments for inscrutability of reference. But what is the point of reminding you of the argument here? Simply that it may be contended to furnish somewhat strange company for the direction Benacerraf would have us take in response to his Skolemite Sceptic. He writes:

> The meaning of 'ε' and the range of the quantifiers must constrain the class of permissible interpretations if the formalized version is to retain the connection with intuitive mathematics with which set theory began—if it is to be a formalization *of set theory*.[4]

And later:

> The reason we don't have a Skolem paradox, and the reason set-theoretic notions *aren't* relative in Skolem's sense, is that there is no reason to treat set theory model-theoretically—which is *not* to say that there is no reason to study its model theory. What a set-theoretical statement *says* can simply not be identified with what is invariant under all classical models of the theory (i.e. models that allow 'ε' to take on whatever binary relation will satisfy the axioms). . . . Axiomatized set theory took its roots in informal mathematics and in order to retain its sense through axiomatization and formalization it must retain these points of contact.
>
> After all, Zermelo . . . chose *these* particular axioms because they give us *these* theorems, which have an independent intuitive meaning of their own. Why turn our backs on this ancestry and pretend that the sole determinant of meaning of the axioms is their first order structure?[5]

In common with many, I imagine, I find the general train of thought here attractive; at least, if there is a coherent line of resistance to 'Skolemism' in general, it must surely involve taking issue with the assumption that the meaning of a sentence, or class of sentences, can

---

4. Benacerraf (1985), p. 106.
5. Ibid., pp. 108–9.

aspire to no greater determinacy than is somehow reflected in the common ground between its, or their, defensible (by some criterion or other) interpretations. But I am not clear why, on the *specific* issue concerning uncountability, the Skolemite—Benacerraf's Sceptic—needs to take this line on determinacy of sense. His argument is better put, it seems to me, in a form which, superficially at least, closely resembles Benacerraf's own argument against arithmetical Platonism. Let somebody have as rich an informal set-theoretic education as you like— which, however, is to stop short of a demonstration of Cantor's theorem, or any comparable result, since these findings are, after all, supposed to be available by way of *discovery* to someone who has mastered the intuitive concept of set. And let him recognise the axioms of ZF as a correct formal digest of his informal notion. Then SMT entails that a commitment to these axioms, plus possession of the intended grasp of 'ϵ'—the sole non-logical primitive—need involve no commitment to the uncountable; someone who rejects it need not say or do anything at variance with acceptance of all the standard set-theoretic axioms interpreted *as* set-theoretic axioms. In other words, just as—according to Benacerraf's argument—a full and complete explanation of arithmetical concepts is neutral with respect to the identification of the integers with any particular objects, so— the Sceptic will urge—a full and complete explanation of the concept of set is neutral with respect to the existence of uncountable sets. But if there really were uncountable sets, their existence woul surely have to flow from the concept of set, as intuitively satisfactorily explained.

Here, as it seems to me, there is no assumption that the content of the ZF axioms cannot exceed what is invariant under all their classical models. It is granted that they are to have their 'intended interpretation': 'ϵ' is to mean set-membership. Even so, and conceived as encoding the intuitive concept of set, they fail to entail the existence of uncountable sets. So how can it be *true* that there are such sets?

Benacerraf's reply is that the ZF axioms are indeed faithful to the relevant informal notions only if, in addition to ensuring that 'ϵ' means set-membership, we interpret them so as to observe the constraint that 'the universal quantifier has to mean *all* or at least *all sets*.[6] It follows, of course, that if the concept of set does determine a background against which Cantor's theorem, under its intended interpretation, is sound, there is *more* to the concept of set that can be explained by communication of the intended sense of 'ε' and the stipulation that the ZF axioms are to hold. And the residue is contained, presumably, in the *informal* explanations to which, Benacerraf reminds us, Zermelo intended his formalisation to answer. At least, this must be so if the 'intuitive concept of set' is capable of being explained at all. Yet it is notable that Benacerraf nowhere ventures to supply the missing informal explanation—the story which will pack enough into the extension of 'all sets' to yield Cantor's theorem, under its intended interpretation, as a highly non-trivial corollary.

The dialectical position then—according to this second Sceptical line of thought—is not that we have been given what is, by ordinary criteria, a perfectly satisfactory explanation of the intuitive concept of set—but an explanation whose very expression some uncooperative individual now persists in 'Skolemising'. Rather, it is unclear whether the 'intended interpretation' has been satisfactorily explained, formally or informally, at all. At any rate, if the 'intuitive conception of set' *is* satisfactorily explained by informal characterisation of the meaning of 'ε' and stipulation of the ZF axioms, then the Cantorian—Benacerraf?—owes an explanation, I believe, of why the Sceptic about uncountability does not have an argument strategically identical to that which Benacerraf brought against arithmetical Platonism. And if, on the other hand, such is not a satisfactory explanation of the intuitive concept, and more, in particular, needs to be packed into the interpretation of the quantifiers, then an appropriate informal explanation is owing of the residue. (I shall return to this.)

A successful Skolem-Sceptical argument has somehow to provide a bridge from the non-categoricity of the ZF axioms to the realisation that all is not well with the classical concept of set in general or indenumerability in particular. Benacerraf represents the Sceptic as seeking to effect the bridge via some such assumption as that 'the *only*

---

6. Ibid., p. 103.

mathematical concepts we have are those that are embodied by all models of our mathematical theories under first-order formalisation'[7] and hence that the content of the ZF axioms cannot have a greater determinacy than that reflected by whatever properties are invariant through all those axioms' models. He complains, rightly as it seems to me, that such a contention not merely seems quite arbitrary but has in addition a self-defeating character: the very formulation of the contention requires recourse to certain concepts—'model', 'first–order theory', etc.—which it must take to have *intuitive content*. The last thing which the Sceptic intends, presumably, by such a contention is something dilute enough to be shared by all admissible interpretations of it! If the Sceptic is happy to rely on specific intuitive concepts in the formulation of his claim, why does he refuse his Cantorian opponent the same right?

This is surely a fair point *ad Scepticum*. But, whatever Skolem or any other actual relativist may have said, the second line of thought I have described would not attempt to give the bridge this shape. The non-categoricity of the ZF axioms must concern anyone who, while granting Benacerraf that there is a genuinely intuitive, informal concept of set to be had, inclines to view the standard axiomatisation as something akin to an *explication* in Carnap's sense. The essence of explication, of course, is that the *explicans* preserves everything essential to the *explicandum;* unlike strict analysis, or definition, however, it is permissible that elements of determinacy, or precision, be introduced. At any rate, a good explication cannot be *weaker* than the intuitive concept it supplants, cannot be neutral on points on which the latter is committed. Accordingly if the ZF axioms, with '∈' interpreted as set membership, did constitute a satisfactory *explication* of the extension of the intuitive concept of set, the fact that they do not, so interpreted, entail the existence of uncountable sets would force the conclusion that there is no such entailment from the intuitive concept of set either. So I do not think it is enough for Benacerraf to urge, on behalf of the Cantorian, that we recognise that set theory is

7. Ibid., p. 109.

answerable to intuitive concepts. So much *is* recognised by one who looks to the ZF axioms for an explication, and the difficulty still arises. The Cantorian claim has to be something stronger: that the intended range of the quantifiers in the ZF axioms is precisely *not* susceptible to explication by axiomatic stipulation at all. It is not so much a matter of paying due heed to the informal roots of the discipline as recognising, in the Cantorian view, that no satisfactory formal explication of the concept of set can be given, even when we hold fixed the interpretation of the only set-theoretic primitive—'390'— which need feature in such an explication. It does not seem to me that only a theoretical position which drew on the assumption which Benacerraf complains about could inspire misgivings about this.

III

One reason why it can be hard to hear the modest criticisms which, in my view, SMT can properly encourage is because of the clamour raised by the much less modest generalisation of 'Skolemism' developed by writers such as Hilary Putnam. The last third of a century has, indeed, been a bad time for the notion of determinacy of meaning in general. W. V. Quine, Putnam, and Saul Kripke (on behalf of Wittgenstein) have all developed arguments which, notwithstanding important differences, would each, if sustained, have the effect that the traditional notion of meaning simply could not survive. Quine, Kripke's Wittgenstein, and Putnam all seem to believe that we can, and should, pay this price: whether by a more resolute adherence to the models of explanation displayed in theoretical physics, or by the adoption of some form of 'Sceptical Solution', or by a shift to a more constructivistic conception of meaning, intellectual life can flourish without the traditional notion of meaning. Like many, I am sceptical whether this is so. To mention but one cause of anxiety: the notion of meaning connects, in platitudinous ways, with that of truth—whether a particular utterance expresses a truth is a function of what, in context, it succeeds in saying, which is in turn a function of the meaning of the type-utterance of which it is an instance. If we really decided that there is no such thing as determinate meaning, *what* would be the determinants of the truth of an utterance? Nothing is more likely to make us sympathise with the kind of response which Benacerraf wants to make to 'Skolemism' about the classical notion of set than the belief that the argument involved is simply a restricted precursor of the heavyweight meaning-sceptical arguments which have commanded so much recent philosophical attention. We are not, most of us, in the market for purchase of the conclusion of these arguments; they can at best have a status of paradoxes, rather than findings, even if there is no general agreement about how to disinfect them. So, for as long as it seems that Skolemistic doubts about the determinacy of the classical concept of set can be sustained only if we are prepared to admit their wholesale generalisation, we are likely to want to sympathise with Benacerraf's point of view: Cantorianism may carry its own intellectual discomforts, but it's a good deal more comfortable than what appears to be the alternative.

It seems to me that the dichotomy should be false. I have great sympathy for Benacerraf's 'direction' as a response to *generalised* Skolemism, and I shall try in a moment to indicate why. But this sympathy is quite consistent with the sort of doubt about the good standing of the classical concept of set which, I believe, SMT may contribute towards motivating.

I have no space here to attempt to review the detail of Quine's, Kripke's, and Putnam's arguments. But someone who is familiar with them will recognise, I think, that they involve a common assumption. The assumption is a version of the later Wittgenstein's idea that meaning cannot transcend use. One of Quine's claims is exactly that whatever the extent of her data about our use of an expression, a radical interpreter would still be confronted with indefinitely many mutually incompatible hypotheses about the meaning of that expression each of which would serve adequately to rationalise the data. Kripke's sceptic persuades her victim to accept that his previous use of an expression cannot rationally constrain its interpretation to within uniqueness, and hence that the fact—assuming, at this stage of his dialectic, that there is such a fact—in which the determinacy of what he meant by the expression consists must be sought elsewhere. And—if I may repeat the quotation cited by Benacerraf—Putnam writes:

> If we are told, 'axiomatic set theory does not capture the intuitive notion of a set', then it is natural to think that *something else*—our 'understanding'—does capture it. But what can our 'understanding' come to, at least for a naturalistically minded philosopher, which is more than *the way we use our language?* And the Skolem argument can be extended, as we have just seen, to show that the *total use of the language* (operational plus theoretical constraints) does not 'fix' a unique 'intended interpretation' any more than axiomatic set theory by itself does.[8]

The dilemma is this. If we hold that meaning cannot transcend use, we seem to be committed to the contention that there cannot be more, or more specificity, to the meaning of an expression than would be apparent to someone who engaged in purely rational reflection upon a sufficient sample, or an otherwise adequate characterisation, of its use. The various sceptical arguments then all take the form of contending—with a good degree of plausibility, which is what gives them their interest—that no amount of data about the use of an expression, and no (axiomatic) characterisation of its use, can rationally constrain its interpretation to within uniqueness. But if we lurch to the opposite wing and allow that meaning can somehow transcend use, the price we pay for securing determinacy of meaning that way is to be beggared for a satisfactory epistemology of understanding (= knowledge of meaning). Meaning, it seems, will have to be the object of some sort of direct intellection, since inaccessible to mere rationalisation of perceived use. So, if the sceptical arguments are sound, the choice would appear to be between dropping the idea that there is such a thing as determinate meaning or retaining it at the cost of an

8. Ibid., quoting Putnam (1977), p. 424.

awkward silence when charged to explain how meanings can be public, how they can be known, and so on.[9] In these circumstances, since the response of allowing meaning to transcend use seems so utterly futile, one feels there *has* to be something amiss with the sceptical arguments. But what?

Consider Benacerraf's response to Putnam's generalisation of Skolemism:

> Even if we agree with Putnam that the determinants of mathematical meaning must lie somewhere in our *use* of mathematical language, why think use to be captured (or capturable) by axioms . . .? Or that the proper way to treat the *explanation* is to de-interpret it and add it to our axioms to form a new first order theory of the world, an extension of our old theory, itself de-interpreted and a candidate for Skolemisation? [Putnam's] view *builds in* the systematic undercutting of any ground there could be for explaining not only *what* we mean, but *what it is to mean anything at all.* That is the effect of adding the explanation to the theory and ignoring the meaning of the terms in the extended theory in order to treat it model-theoretically.[10]

Now, Wittgenstein wrote, in response to the sceptical paradox which Kripke interprets, that the solution consists in seeing that 'there is a way of grasping a rule which is *not* an *interpretation*' (*Philosophical Investigations* §201). What Benacerraf is urging, comparably, is that there is a way of receiving an explanation which is not an *interpretation*. So if someone, for example, lays down the ZF axioms and then adds some informal remarks by way of explanation of the intended concept of set, these remarks, Benacerraf is urging, can have a determinacy of content, and so an explanatory force, which far exceeds the constraints which they impose on any model of their first-order union with the original axioms.

---

9. I have not been able to understand how Putnam's espousal of verificationism ('internalism') gets to grips with the dilemma.
10. Benacerraf (1985), p. 111.

But *what* is the way of receiving an explanation which is not an interpretation? Has not Benacerraf in effect simply begged the question against the sceptic, assuming that there is such a thing as determinacy of meaning when the least the sceptical arguments teach us is that the right to suppose so is bought only at extortionate epistemological cost? I do not think so, since I believe we can glimpse the possibility of an alternative to the Platonism which, pending disclosure of some internal flaw in the sceptical arguments, was all that seemed available as an alternative to the sceptical conclusion. Wittgenstein is very inexplicit about his 'way of grasping a rule which is not an interpretation' but he does at least say that it is something 'which is exhibited in what we call "obeying the rule" and "going against it" in actual cases' (ibid.) What we need to win through to, I suggest, is a perspective from which we may both repudiate any suggestion of the Platonic transcendence of meaning over use *and* recognise that meaning cannot be determined to within uniqueness if the sole determinants are rational interpretative methodology and an as-large-as-you-like pool of data about use. Wittgenstein wanted to suggest that the missing parameter, the source of determinacy, is human nature. Coming to understand an expression is not and cannot be a matter of arriving at a uniquely rational solution to the problem of interpreting witnessed use of it—a 'best explanation' of the data. Still less is it a matter of getting into some form of direct intellectual contact with a Platonic concept, or whatever. Rather, it is a matter of acquiring the capacity to participate in a practice, or set of practices, in which the use of that expression is a component. And the ability to acquire this capacity is something with which we are endowed not just by our rational faculties but to which elements in our sub-rational natures also contribute: certain natural propensities we have to uphold particular patterns of judgement and response. Crudely, then, what makes it possible to derive something more specific from an explanation than whatever is invariant through the totality of 'models' of the 'theory' containing that explanation is that one's response to the explanation will be conditioned by other factors than the attempt rationally to interpret that 'theory'.

These remarks, indeed, also constitute 'merely a direction'. But it is a hopeful direction: it holds out the promise of an explanation of how, without Platonising meaning, we can uphold the right to maintain that some particular interpretation—of set theory or of anything you like—is what is intended, and what is communally understood to be intended, without suffering the probably hopeless commitment to defending the claim that *only* that interpretation can rationalise our use of the relevant concepts.[11]

IV

To come back to earth, however—if to resume consideration of the uncountable can be to do that—let me conclude by trying to explain why I still think that the classical concept of set, which concept requires the existence of uncountable sets, is indeed something to stumble over. The Cantorian may, of course, disclaim the need for explanation altogether, though if he does he can scarcely hope for much respect for his views. What we have seen is that if the intuitive concept of set is indeed satisfactorily explicable—and how else could it be communicable?—the explanation has to be, at least in large part, informal; and it will not suffice informally to explain the set–membership relation and then to stipulate, for example, that the ZF axioms are a correct digest of the principles of set existence. If the Cantorian wishes it to follow from his explanation that there are

11. There is, admittedly, little cause to be sanguine that a development of this response could be effective against the strong form of Quinean indeterminacy: the version which holds that there are, *ab initio* as it were, rival interpretations which will each serve to explain any amount of a subject's lingusitic behaviour (rather than the weaker claim that for any amount of data about linguistic behaviour, there are rival interpretations, etc.). Wittgenstein's idea is addressed to the question how the patterns of linguistic practice constitutive of a particular concept can be apparent in a finite sample. But if the strong claim is right, shared patterns of linguistic practice cannot justifiably be taken to constitute shared concepts. The crucial question, of course, is whether Quine succeeds in presenting cogent reason for this claim.

all the sets which, intuitively, he believes that there are, he has to do something more. But what?

He has to say something which entails that there are uncountably many sets. And that is not the same as stipulating an axiomatic framework in which Cantor's theorem may be proved, since the difficulty is exactly that if his preferred set theory can take its intended interpretation at all, it can take a *set-theoretic* interpretation under which Cantor's theorem cannot be interpreted as a result about uncountability. So how does the Cantorian get across to a trainee that interpretation (of the range of the individual variables of the theory) which will enforce conceiving of Cantor's theorem as a cardinality result? Now, the reason why it can seem as if there is no very great difficulty here is the point noted earlier, that Cantor's theorem, and indeed his Diagonal Argument, are apt to impress us as having unrestricted applicability as examples of *informal* mathematics. That is why the original relativistic position on the uncountability of, for example, the reals seems so unconvincing: the extra-systematic enumerability of the 'reals' in a countable model for ZF ought, intuitively, to be disruptible by diagonalisation—there ought to be something with, intuitively, perfect credentials to be a real number which is nevertheless not, on pain of contradiction, in the range of the enumerating function. Is it not this that makes us feel entitled to regard any countable set model for the ZF axioms as an *unintended* model, something that only imperfectly embodies our intuitive set-theoretic concepts? For the fact is that there is an informal set-theoretic result which we can achieve— the beautifully simple result which Cantor taught us—which we can prove *about* this model, which is not to be identified with the corresponding result *within* the system when the latter is interpreted in terms of this model, and which *shows* that the model does not include everything which the *intended* interpretation of the system embraces.

These remarks are intended to be diagnostic. I am suggesting that Cantor's reasoning—it doesn't matter at present whether we concentrate on the power set theorem or the Diagonal Argument—plays a role in the *formation* of our conception of what the intended interpretation of set theory is. Its role is less to articulate a surprising consequence of concepts fixed in some other way than to lead the determination of an inchoate concept of set in a particular direction. At any rate, we have absolutely no right to the idea that a countable set model of the ZF axioms has to be 'non-standard', a misrepresentation of our intuitive intentions, *unless* we buy Cantor's reasoning as a piece of informal mathematics, something that defeats *any* candidate for a 1–1 correlation of the integers and reals, however characterised in whatever sort of system.

The question, accordingly, is whether Cantor's reasoning is cogent as (contributing to) an *introduction* to the intended conception of the range of the individual variables in set theory; whether it does indeed lead us to a concept of set of which no countable model can be an adequate realisation. Well, the answer, I believe, for reasons which you can probably all too easily anticipate, is that it does not. Let us informally rehearse the Diagonal Argument that the reals are uncountable. We know that the rationals are countable, and that the union of any pair of countable disjoint sets is itself countable. So the reals are uncountable if and only if the irrationals are. Each irrational can be represented as an infinite non-recurring decimal; to suppose that they are countable is therefore to suppose that there is some array

a.	a1	a2	a3	a4	a5	. . . . .
b.	b1	b2	b3	b4	b5	. . . . .
c.	c1	c2	c3	c4	c5	. . . . .
d.	d1	d2	d3	d4	d5	. . . . .
e.	e1	e2	e3	e4	e5	. . . . .

. . . .

(where each letter to the left of the decimal point represents some numeral, while those to the right represent any of 0–9) in which every non-recurring decimal occurs somewhere. But then, Cantor observes, it is easy to see that no such array can be complete; we have only to reflect that there is a decimal which differs at the ith place from each ith decimal in the array. However, in order to imbue Cantor's observation with its intended significance, we need to make a substantial assumption. Suppose we restricted our attention to *effectively computable* infinite decimals—those whose every ith place can (at least in principle) be calculated; and suppose we stipulated, in addition, that the whole array must itself be effective, which is to say that for each i, it should be effectively determinable what the ith decimal in the array should be. Under these restrictions, the Diagonal Argument takes on a wholly constructive character; we can now effectively compute a decimal which, on pain of contradiction, is no member of the array. But just for that reason, we no longer have a result about uncountability. At least, we have no such result if we suppose that Church's Thesis holds. For in that case all the decimals in the array, and each successive diagonal decimal which we care to define, will correspond to recursively enumerable sequences of numerals. And we know independently that the totality of recursive functions is only countably infinite, since they are all definable in a finitely based vocabulary. Under these restrictions, then, Cantor's argument takes on a quite different significance: rather than showing something about uncountability, it shows that there is no recursive enumeration of all recursively enumerable infinite decimals. (The reader will easily see how similar considerations may be applied to the informal proof of the power set theorem.)

What goes for real numbers goes for subsets of natural numbers, since every infinite decimal has a unique binary equivalent, and an infinite binary expansion may be regarded as determining a unique subset of natural numbers in accordance with the principle that the ith natural number will be a member of the subset in question just in case the ith element in the binary expansion is 1. So, under the restrictions, the result is, again, that there is no effective/recursive enumeration of all effectively/recursively enumerable subsets of natural numbers. And, again, we know that the finite and recursively enumerable infinite subsets of natural numbers form a countable set. So the moral is simple: before the Diagonal Argument, or the informal proof of the power set theorem, can lead us to a conception of the intended range of the individual variables in set theory which will allow us to regard any countable set model as a non-standard truncation, we need to waive the restrictions. And in order to understand the waiver, we need to grasp the notion of a *non- effectively enumerable denumerably infinite subset* of natural numbers.[12]

This is what, if he is in the business of giving explanations, the Cantorian needs to explain. Now there are, I suppose, two routes into the informal notion of a subset of a given set. One is formally reflected in the *Aussonderungsaxiom*: a subset of a given set is determined by any bona fide *property*. The other route proceeds via the notion of a *selection*: a subset of a given set corresponds to every way, rule-governed or arbitrary, of selecting some of its members. Neither of these routes, it seems to me, holds out any very plausible promise of meeting the Cantorian's needs. Certainly, whichever he chooses, there are extremely awkward challenges to face. For instance, it is evident that the requisite properties cannot all be identified with the content of a possible predication (open sentence) in something we could recognise as a single language. Intuitively, there are indeed non- effectively enumerable infinite subsets of natural numbers which can be characterised in a finite and perfectly definite way; an example would be the set of Gödel-numbers of non-theorems of first-order logic. But the Cantorian cannot give us the slightest reason to think that *everything* which he wishes to regard as a subset of natural numbers would allow of an intelligible, finite characterisation in this manner. Let him be granted that such a characterisation need not be constructive, that is, that there need be no effective way of determining whether a particular natural number qualifies for membership. Still, a property is something which it should be possible to *claim* to be exemplified by a particular object, even if the claim cannot be

---

12. We could hardly attain the conception of a non- effectively enumerable denumerably infinite array of infinite decimals without grasping this notion first.

assessed. If the Cantorian believes that a notion of a subset (of natural numbers) can be gleaned by this route which is sufficiently fertile for his purposes, he commits himself to the belief—if he respects the connection between *property* and *possible predication*—that there are *uncountably many finitely expressible properties* This is an enormously problematic idea. Naturally, no single language—at least no finitely based language—can be adequate to express them all. Since any intelligible language is, presumably, finitely based, and hence can express at most countably many distinct properties, the Cantorian who takes this line is committed to a potentially uncountable infinity of languages no two of which are completely inter-translatable. Perhaps there is no contradiction in such a conception but it is, at best, a highly unfortunate consequence of something which was supposed to be an intuitive explanation. And it is, besides, a very nice question—where inter-translatability is missing—what would make a pair of the relevant properties, each expressed in one of these languages in a manner not translatable into the other, *distinct.* (It would of course be circular in the present context to attribute their distinction to that of the subsets which they respectively define.) If, on the other hand, the Cantorian severs the connection between *property* and *possible predication* he is open to the charge that he is obscurantising the notion of a property and thus can use it to explain nothing.

Matters are no better if we focus instead on the notion of a selection. The selections in question—if they are to generate enough subsets for the Cantorian's purposes—have to be thought of as uninformed by any sort of recursive procedure. But they also have to be thought of as *complete,* since it is only when infinitely many selections have actually been made—in a non-recursive way—that we actually have a non- recursively enumerable infinite subset of natural numbers. So long as only finitely many selections have been made, the constitution of the subset so far determined will be consistent with supposing it to be recursively enumerable. So in order to arrive at the intended notion of subset, we have to understand what it would be *actually to complete* an infinite but arbitrary selection from the set of natural numbers. Of course some philosophers, notably Russell, have found no difficulty in crediting us with such a conception. But I do not think that anyone who follows up the literature on 'Supertasks' is likely to feel at ease with the idea. Someone who is inclined to think there is no problem should ask himself what it would be like to have reason to think that he had, magically as it were, acquired the capacity to complete such a selection. Benacerraf himself writes:

> [T]here is probably no set of conditions that we can (nontrivially) state . . . whose satisfaction would lead us to conclude that a supertask had been performed . . . no circumstance that we could imagine and describe in which we would be justified in saying that an infinite sequence of tasks had been completed . . . there is nothing we can describe that it would be reasonable to call a completed infinite sequence of tasks.[13]

Can we claim to understand what a certain capacity would be if we do not know what it would be like to have exercised it? And what can the idea of an arbitrary actually infinite selection come to if we do *not* know what the capacity to perform one would be?

I am, of course, aware that what counts as adequate clarity in an explanation is, inevitably, to some extent a subjective business. What I claim is that the analogies which underpin the *further development* of the notion of subset—for that is what it is—with which the Cantorian wishes to work are very, very stretched. If someone is pleased to think that they are nevertheless good enough, I have no decisive counter-argument. But I hope to have reminded you that there are certain not very heavily theoretical—'anti-realist' or whatever—reasons for dissatisfaction with 'the intuitive concept of set', and 'the intended interpretation' of classical set theory. And, more importantly, to have made it plausible that we need not, in sympathising with these reasons, be receiving the thin end of a meaning-sceptical wedge.

---

13. Benacerraf (1962). The quotation is taken from the reprint in Salmon (1970), pp. 125–6.

13 Wittgenstein on Mathematical Proof

Close to one-half of Wittgenstein's writings after 1929 concerned mathematics, and the roots of his discussions, which contain a bewildering variety of underdeveloped and sometimes apparently conflicting suggestions, go deep to some of the most basic and difficult ideas in his later philosophy. My aims in what follows are forced to be modest. I shall sketch an intuitively attractive way of thinking about mathematics and illustrate Wittgenstein's opposition to it. I shall explain why, contrary to what is often supposed, that opposition cannot be fully satisfactorily explained by tracing it back to the discussions of following a rule in *Philosophical Investigations* and *Remarks on the Foundations of Mathematics*. Finally, I shall try to indicate very briefly something of the real motivation for Wittgenstein's more strikingly deflationary claims about mathematical proof, and canvass a reason why it may not in the end be possible to uphold those claims.

I

Euclid is credited with the first proof that, among the series of positive whole numbers, the occurrence of prime numbers is endless. His reasoning, as you doubtless recall, was based on what is often called the Fundamental Theorem of arithmetic—the lemma that every number has a unique prime factorisation: that is, can be represented as the product of a multiplication sum in which only prime numbers occur as factors. (Thus 28 is $7 \times 2 \times 2$; 273 is $3 \times 7 \times 13$; and so on.) The proof then proceeds by reductio ad absurdum. Suppose there were a last prime—call it N. And consider the corresponding N!+1—the number we get by cumulatively multiplying N by each of its predecessors in turn and adding 1 to the total. If N is the greatest prime, as we have assumed, then this number is not prime but composite. Hence, by the Fundamental Theorem, it is the product of a unique set of prime factors. But what are they? They cannot comprise any number *smaller than or equal to* N, for, given the way that N!+1 is constructed, none of those numbers divides into it without a remainder—they all leave remainder 1. So the prime factors of N!+1 must be *greater* than N—but then that contradicts our hypothesis, that N is the greatest prime, which is therefore refuted. If there were a greatest prime, then, by the Fundamental Theorem of arithmetic, there would have to be prime numbers greater than it; so there is no greatest prime number—the primes run on without end.

It is natural and attractive to view this pleasantly accessible and economical reasoning as constituting a *discovery*. The basic concepts of number theory—the branch of pure mathematics that deals with zero and the positive whole numbers that succeed it—are very straightforward: they include the concept of zero itself, the idea of one number succeeding another, the idea of an endless array of such numbers getting larger and larger ad infinitum, and elementary operations upon them such as addition, multiplication, exponentiation and so on. In terms of this basic and easily intelligible set of notions, all the concepts and operations of pure number theory can be defined and all the problems which exercise the interest of the number theoretician can be formulated. And because of the simplicity of the basic concepts, and the straightforward character of many of the consequential definitions, some of these problems are extremely easy to understand.

The alleged 'last theorem' of Fermat—now finally proved—that the equation $x^n + y^n = z^n$ has no solution among the natural numbers for values of n greater than or equal to 3, and Goldbach's Conjecture, still unresolved, that every even number is the sum of two primes, are two such easily grasped examples.[1]

Confronted with such examples, our inclination is to think that they raise interesting questions which must have answers, but answers which we may not at present know. It would be quite possible, before I knew anything of Euclid's proof, to wonder about Goldbach's Conjecture and then realise that, if true, it would require the infinity of the primes, and to proceed to wonder about that. Euclid's proof would then naturally present itself as a discovery that at least one necessary condition for the truth of the Goldbach Conjecture was met. And it would remain to wonder whether a similar but, no doubt, more complex feat of human ingenuity will some day disclose that the Conjecture itself is indeed true, or whether, rather, far out into the series of natural numbers, occurs an even number which is the sum of no two of its prime predecessors.

A striking aspect of this intuitively natural way of thinking is the separation it effects between the concepts of truth and proof in mathematics. We wonder whether the Goldbach Conjecture will ever be proved or refuted. But the statement of the conjecture is so easily grasped, and its meaning so apparently sharp, that we are not at all inclined to doubt that it must be, determinately, either true or false. For the series of natural numbers itself, we conceive, is a perfectly definite structure, in which the even numbers are a sharply defined subseries. And of each particular even number it is, surely, a definite question with a definite and (in principle) ascertainable answer, whether it is the sum of two primes or not. And now, how can the question whether *all* items of a certain kind have a certain characteristic fail to have a determinate answer—even if perhaps we cannot know what the answer is—if the items in question are a sharply

1. For n = 2, of course, it has been familiar since the Greeks that there are 'Pythagorean' solutions—for instance, 3, 4 and 5; 5, 12 and 13; and so on.

defined class and the characteristic in question is something which *each* of them determinately either possesses or not?

We are thus instinctively drawn, at least in the case of number theory, to mathematical realism. According to mathematical realism, the number theoretician is a kind of *explorer*. His project arises because, whereas the natural numbers are infinite, the capacities and opportunities possessed by the human mind are finite. Perhaps a deity could somehow mechanically check each even number and determine whether it was the sum of two primes or not—and then remember whether, in the course of this infinite labour, any counter-examples to the Goldbach Conjecture had turned up. But *we* can do no such thing. For us, the only way of determining the truth or falsity of such a statement is, as it were, indirectly, by cunning. So proof comes to be seen as merely a kind of cognitive auxiliary for cheating infinity, a method of investigation which we are forced to use because, in dealing with infinite totalities, our human finiteness leaves us with no other recourse.

To conceive of the truth of number-theoretic statements in this way invites, of course, the question: what, when such a statement is true, *makes* it true? And it is no answer to say: the way things are with the natural numbers. What the questioner is requesting is advice about how, in general terms, the states of affairs which—perhaps quite independently of any possibility of human knowledge—confer truth on number-theoretic statements, should be conceived as constituted. A very ancient answer is that the world contains numbers and other kinds of mathematical objects much as it contains mountains and seas; that there is an abstract substance to the world as much as a physical one. Such a view is, remarkably, still a topic of ongoing professional debate.[2] But the view of most contemporary philosophers of mathematics would be that it is no more than a metaphor for the kind of objectivity which, driven by the sort of intuitive realist thinking

---

2. Kurt Gödel (1947) is widely regarded as having endorsed the ancient answer. Penelope Maddy (1980) was also a long-time champion of it.

which I briefly sketched, we would like pure mathematics to have. What, I suspect, with our realist hats on, we really think about the constitutive question is something more anthropocentric. Kronecker said, famously, that whereas all the rest of pure mathematics was the work of man, the natural numbers were created by God. But no realist need think anything of that sort. It is enough if we are capable of creating, in thought, a sufficiently definite concept of the series of natural numbers to give substance to questions about its characteristics which we may not know how to answer. And is that so puzzling an idea? The rules of Noughts and Crosses, for instance, are perfectly definite, yet it is not totally trivial to show that the second player can always force a draw; and it is possible to understand the rules perfectly yet be unaware of the point. Is it not, nevertheless, a perfectly objective feature of the game which, when it finally dawns on one as a child, it is proper to think of oneself as *finding out?* And is not Noughts and Crosses a human invention for all that? As the small child with Noughts and Crosses, so the adult mathematician with number theory; the difference is only that there is, in the case of Noughts and Crosses, no analogue of the infinity of the number series to set up the possibility that truth and verifiability, even verifiability 'in principle', might come apart.

We now have on display almost all the ingredients in our intuitive thinking about pure mathematics against which Wittgenstein's later philosophy reacts. The conception of mathematics as a kind of investigative science; the notion that it explores a special domain of states of affairs, which are constituted by acts of human concept formation yet somehow acquire the autonomy to outstrip what is transparent, or even in principle accessible, to the human subject; the view of proof as an exploratory tool, albeit a kind of cognitive prosthetic on which we are forced to rely because of finitude—each of these ideas is roundly criticized throughout Wittgenstein's later writings on mathematics. It remains only to include our sense of a proof as somehow excluding all rational options but assent to its status as proof—what Wittgenstein famously characterized as the 'hardness' of the logical 'must'—and the associated idea, which even Descartes' scepticism did not prompt him seriously to call into question, that proof in mathematics is a source of an especially sure and certain genre of knowledge—add these and we have both a thumbnail sketch of the lay philosophy of pure mathematics which we find most attractive and an inventory of the principal confusions to which Wittgenstein regarded our thought about these matters as prone.

For Wittgenstein, pure mathematics is not a project of exploration and discovery; mathematical proof is not an instrument whereby we find out things; conceptual structures cannot have the kind of autonomy to allow their characteristics to outstrip what can be ratified by human thought; there is no external compulsion upon us when we ratify proofs—we are driven, but not by cognition of an external, normative constraint; and insofar as there is a special sureness about at least some mathematical propositions, it does not amount to a superlative genre of knowledge—such propositions do not enjoy a *cognitive* certainty at all.

Here are some passages illustrative of each of these deflationary lines of thought. On mathematics as an investigative science in which we explore the characteristics of our own conceptual constructions and rules, Wittgenstein writes:

> What, then—does [mathematics] just twist and turn about within these rules?—It forms ever new rules: is always building new roads for traffic; by extending the network of the old ones.
>
> But then doesn't it need a sanction for this? Can it extend the network *arbitrarily?* Well, I could say: a mathematician is always inventing new forms of description. Some, stimulated by practical needs, others from aesthetic needs,—and yet others in a variety of ways. And here imagine a landscape gardener designing paths for the layout of a garden; it may well be that he draws them on a drawing board merely as ornamental strips without the slightest thought of someone sometime walking on them.
>
> The mathematician is an inventor, not a discoverer.[3]

3. *Remarks on the Foundations of Mathematics* I, 166–67.

He speaks with suspicion of the idea of

> [a]rithmetic as the natural history [mineralogy] of numbers. But *who* talks like this about it? Our whole thinking is penetrated with this idea.[4]

And in the discussion of Cantor's Diagonal Argument he remarks:

> 'Fractions cannot be arranged in an order of magnitude'.—First and foremost, this sounds extremely interesting and remarkable.
>
> It sounds interesting in a quite different way from, say, a proposition of the differential calculus. The difference, I think, resides in the fact that *such* a proposition is easily associated with an application to physics, whereas *this* proposition belongs simply and solely to mathematics, seems to concern as it were the natural history of mathematical objects themselves.
>
> One would like to say of it e.g.: it introduces us to the mysteries of the mathematical world. *This* is the aspect against which I want to give a warning.
>
> When it looks as if . . . , we should look out.[5]

Against the conception of proof as an instrument of conceptual discovery, Wittgenstein urges a quite different picture:

> I am trying to say something like this: even if the mathematical proposition seems to point to a reality outside itself, still it only expresses acceptance of a new measure (of reality). . . . We have won through to a piece of knowledge in the proof? And the final proposition expresses this knowledge? And is this knowledge now independent of the proof (is the navel string cut)?—well, the proposition is now used by itself and without having the proof attached to it.
>
> Why should I not say: in the proof I have won through to a *decision?* . . .
>
> The proposition proved by means of the proof serves as a rule. . . .[6]

4. *RFM*, IV, 11.
5. Ibid., II, 40–1.
6. Ibid., III, 27.

I go through the proof and say: 'yes, this is how it *has* to be; I must fix the use of my language in *this* way'.

I want to say that the *must* corresponds to a track which I lay down in language.

When I said that a proof introduces a new concept, I meant something like: the proof puts a new paradigm among the paradigms of the language . . . the proof changes the grammar of our language, changes our concepts. It makes new connections, and it creates the concept of those connections. (It does not establish that they are there; they do not exist until it makes them.)[7]

Proofs do not *draw to our attention* to what must be the case, nor is it right to think of them as commanding our assent:

What is the transition that I make from 'it will be like this' to 'it *must* be like this'? I form a different concept. One involving something that was not there before. When I say: 'if these derivations are the same, then it *must* be that . . .', I am making something into a criterion of identity. So I am recasting my concept of identity. . . .

Can I say: "A proof induces us to make a certain decision, namely that of accepting a particular concept formation"?

Do not look on a proof as a procedure which *compels* you, but as one which *guides* you.—And what it guides is your *conception* of a (particular) situation.[8]

What is unshakably certain about what is proved?

To accept a proposition as unshakably certain—I want to say—means to use it as a grammatical rule: this removes uncertainty from it.[9]

And again, on mathematical (logical) compulsion:

We say: 'If you really follow the rule in multiplying, you *must* all get the same results'. Now if this is only the somewhat hysterical way of putting things that you get in university talk, it need not interest us overmuch.

7. *RFM*, III, 30, 31.
8. Ibid., IV, 29, 30.
9. Ibid., III, 39.

It is however the expression of an attitude towards the technique of calculation, which comes out everywhere in our life. The emphasis of the *must* corresponds only to the inexorableness of this attitude both to the technique of calculating and to a host of related techniques.

The mathematical Must is only another expression of the fact that mathematics forms concepts.[10]

Finally, on a mathematical problem structurally similar to that posed by the Goldbach Conjecture—namely, the question whether seven consecutive '7's occur in the decimal expansion of π—Wittgenstein writes:

> The question—I want to say—changes its status when it becomes decidable. For a connection is then made which formerly *was not there*. . . .
>
> However queer it sounds, the further expansion of an irrational number is a further expansion of mathematics. . . .
>
> I want to say: it looks as though the ground for the decision were already there; and it has yet to be invented.[11]

It does indeed look as though the 'ground for the decision were already there'. How could it not be? For is not the decimal expansion of π determined by rule at every step? So how can there be any indeterminacy, before we get any mathematical result on the matter, about what is the correct answer to the question? Either, we want to say, seven consecutive '7's do occur—and necessarily so, since their occurrence, where they occur, is built into the identity of π—or, again necessarily, they do not. The question could be indeterminate—'the ground for the decision' not yet exist—only if there were some indeterminacy in the proper expansion of π. But there is, surely, none. Yet Wittgenstein challenges these intuitive and seemingly unassailable thoughts head-on:

> Might I not say: if you do a multiplication, in any case you do not find the mathematical fact, but you do find the mathematical proposition? For what you *find* is the non-mathematical fact, and in this way the

10. Ibid., VII, 67.
11. Ibid., V, 9.

mathematical proposition. . . . A mathematical proposition is the determination of a concept, following upon a discovery. . . .

The concept is altered so that this *had* to be the result. I find, not the result, but that I reach it. And it is not this route's beginning here and ending here that is an empirical fact, but my having gone this road, or some road to this end.

But might it not be said that the *rules* lead this way, even if no one went it? For that is what one would like to say—and here we see the mathematical machine which, driven by the rules themselves, obeys only mathematical laws and not physical ones.

I want to say: the working of the mathematical machine is only the *picture* of the working of a machine. The rule does not do work, for whatever happens according to the rule is an interpretation of the rule.[12]

What moves Wittgenstein to these implausible-seeming and unattractive views?

II

More than two decades ago, in a systematic study of Wittgenstein's later philosophy of mathematics,[13] I was, I think, the first to offer and develop in print the suggestion that the critical examination of the concept of following a rule, pursued both in the *Remarks on the Foundation of Mathematics* and the *Investigations,* is central to the interpretation not just of Wittgenstein's later thought about mathematics but of his later philosophy as a whole. This perspective seems to have been an idea whose time had come. Subsequently Saul Kripke published his highly influential *Wittgenstein on Rules and Private Language* [14] outlining a vivid 'Sceptical Paradox' which it presents as the heart of Wittgenstein's thought about rule-following, and whose

12. *RFM*, IV, 47, 48.
13. Wright (1980).
14. Kripke (1982).

resolution purportedly generates the argument against private language. Kripke's book concentrates almost exclusively on the Sceptical Paradox and the accommodation with it—the Sceptical Solution—which, in Kripke's view, underlies Wittgenstein's ideas about privacy and the self-ascription of sensation and other psychological states. But he anticipates a perfectly direct application of his interpretation of the ideas about rules to the philosophy of mathematics,[15] and doesn't hesitate to suggest that both the philosophy of mind of the *Investigations* and the philosophy of logic and mathematics expounded in *RFM* should be seen as driven by them.[16]

This is a natural thought which it is worth filling out briefly. Kripke's Wittgenstein holds, crudely, that there are no facts of the matter about what an expression means, how it is generally understood, what accords or fails to accord with a particular rule, what behaviour constitutes implementation of a particular intention, and so on. This is the Sceptical Paradox. We habitually talk as if there were normative realities, constituted by the contents of our sentences, rules, thoughts, intentions, and so on, but the truth is that there are none such. The whole conception of facts to do with meaning and its cognates is mythology.

This wild and absurd-seeming thesis is backed by an arresting argument. In the first instance, Kripke's Wittgenstein constructs a debate about a token claim concerning any past meaning of mine—say,

15. Ibid., pp. 3–5.
16. For the record let me say that Kripke's ideas about these issues and mine seem to have developed in complete isolation from each other. Kripke's interpretation originated, as he recounts, in graduate seminars given in Princeton as early as the spring of 1965 and was subsequently developed through a series of conferences and colloquia from 1976 onwards. I first proposed such an interpretation of aspects of Wittgenstein's later thought on mathematics in my Cambridge Ph.D. thesis ('Two-valuedness, Meaning and Intuitionism', 1968); and the material that constitutes the first six chapters of Wright (1980) was first written up for graduate seminars given in All Souls College in the summer of 1974. Kripke and I were, indeed, colleagues for several months at All Souls in the academic year 1977–8, when he held a Visiting Fellowship there. But we never discussed the interpretation of Wittgenstein.

the claim that by '+' I formerly meant addition. I am to defend the claim and the sceptic is to contest it. You might think that even if I were to lose the debate, no conclusions about the *reality* of meanings, rules, etc., would be in prospect—the only conclusion licensed would be that the *epistemology* of claims about meaning was no more straightforward than, under sceptical pressure, the epistemology of *the past* or *the material world* has turned out to be. But that would be wrong. Traditional forms of scepticism make much issue of what are taken to be intrinsic cognitive predicaments of ours—it is contended that we are, necessarily, screened from direct knowledge of others' mental states, the past and the characteristics of matter, and are therefore restricted to problematical inferences from behaviour, the present and our own experience. By contrast, the debate with Kripke's Wittgenstein's sceptic proceeds under conditions of *cognitive idealisation:* in my attempt to justify my claim that by '+' I formerly meant addition, I am presumed to have perfect recall of all aspects of my former behaviour and mental life. And the governing strategic thought is precisely that, *were* there a fact about what I formerly meant by '+', it would have somehow to be constituted in aspects of my former behaviour and mental life; and should therefore, under the idealisation, be salient to me. Accordingly, if I still lose the debate with the sceptic, even so idealised, it follows that there can indeed be no such fact. This conclusion is then easily developed to generate, successively, that there are no facts about what I presently mean, no facts about what anyone else presently means, nor, therefore, any fact about what any expression means nor, correlatively, about what uses comply with such facts.

Such, in briefest outline, is the overriding strategy of the argument for the Sceptical Paradox. And now it might seem quite straightforward how these ideas, if sustained, would dislodge the realist conception of pure mathematics and support the opposed Wittgensteinian ideas which we rehearsed. The basic conclusion is that there are, necessarily, no facts about meaning. It follows that there can be no such thing as a reflective exploration within the domain of meanings, no such thing as creating a concept and then, by analysis and proof, verifying characteristics of it which, unwittingly, we have put into our creation. There simply is no coherent conception to be had, if the Sceptical Paradox is accepted, of the subject matter to which such an investigation would be responsive. So pure mathematical proofs cannot be instruments of discovery concerning such a subject matter—there are no such discoveries to be made. A fortiori, they cannot be a source of a special, *cognitively earned* certainty; and any sense of constraint, or compulsion, which they inspire in us cannot properly be conceived as a by-product of recognition of our obligations, so to speak, to conceptual structures which we ourselves have erected.

On further reflection, however, the ability of the meaning-scepticism, developed by Kripke's Wittgenstein, to motivate the philosophy of mathematics propounded by the actual Wittgenstein comes to seem less clear. Wittgenstein, as the passages quoted above illustrate, did not merely repudiate the intuitive realist conception of mathematical proof and objectivity; he proposed, in addition, a suggestive alternative conception—the conception of the mathematician as the developer of 'new measures' of reality, the architect of 'new roads for traffic', new tracks for the use of language to follow. The proper exegesis of this positive direction in his thought would be a matter of detail which I cannot undertake here. But this much seems to be clear: the general drift of the proposal has to be *conservative* of our intuitive understanding of rules and rule-governed practices. If the pure mathematician is to be seen, broadly, not as the explorer of a special domain but the inventor of new forms of description, new rules linking together concepts which we are already accustomed to apply outside pure mathematics, then there has to be such a thing as *changing and extending* the way a discourse is properly practised. And that is a notion of which we can make sense only under the aegis of the distinction between practices which conform with the rules as they were before and practices which reflect a modification in those rules generated by some pure mathematical development. Unless, then, there is such a thing as practice which is in line with a rule, contrasting with practice which is not, there is simply no chance of a competitive construal of Wittgenstein's positive proposals. But that distinction, it would seem, is precisely what is subverted if what is driving the negative proposals is the meaning-scepticism propounded by Kripke's Wittgenstein.

Someone familiar with Kripke's text may want to protest that this is to ignore the role of the so-called Sceptical Solution, which attempts an accommodation with the Sceptical Paradox. A proponent of the Sceptical Solution grants that there are indeed no substantial facts about meaning, understanding or any of the other cognate notions; but disputes that the propriety of ordinary discourse in which such notions are implicated has to be a casualty of that concession. The casualty is rather a certain conception of the kind of content which such discourse has—the conception, precisely, that it is a *kind* of content which may be explicated in terms of the idea of correspondence to fact. The role of a statement like

The rules of addition dictate that 29 + 13 is 42

is not to report a state of affairs but, for instance, to express a condition compliance with which we treat as a criterion for competence in adding.[17] According to the Sceptical Solution, then, our right to continue with our ordinary talk of rules, and of what complies with them and breaches them, is not jeopardised by the Sceptical Paradox. What we lose is only a certain philosophical picture of what, when we engage in such discourse, underwrites the distinction between correct and incorrect assertions within it.

But it is doubtful whether this helps. Let us describe as *content-committed* all discourse which, in one way or another, deals with meaning or any of its cognate notions—in general, all discourse which falls within the scope of the Sceptical Solution if the Sceptical Paradox is accepted; and as *robustly truth-conditional* all putatively factual discourse whose status as such can survive the Paradox. It is a matter of

17. It might be said, similarly, by an opponent of moral realism that the role of the sentence 'Lying is wrong' is not to describe a moral fact, but to express a condition compliance with which is a necessary condition for avoiding moral disapprobation.

controversy whether a proponent of the Sceptical Solution can provide in plausible detail the sort of semantic proposals for content-committed discourse which he owes. One, as it seems to me, very impressive reason for doubting so is that the scope of content-committed discourse threatens, given three natural assumptions, to become universal.

The first assumption is the platitude that the truth value of a statement, as used on a particular occasion, is a function of its content, so used, and the then obtaining state of the world in relevant respects. The second is that it is an a priori truth, for anyone who understands English, that the result of substituting any truth-apt sentence in English for 'P' in the following schema will generate a truth:

'P' is true if and only if P.

The third is that no a priori true biconditional can have as its constituents a fact-stating sentence—one about whose content a robust, truth-conditional conception is appropriate—and a sentence which is not apt for truth and falsity at all, since it is not in the business of depiction of states of affairs but has a quite different role.

With these premises in place, we may reason as follows. Since, by the first, platitudinous assumption, truth value on an occasion is always a function, in part, of content, and since—by the Sceptical Paradox—what it is correct to think about the content of a sentence, as used on a particular occasion, is not a substantial question, it follows that the truth value of the sentence, as used on that occasion, is not a substantial question either. So no matter *what* English sentence we substitute for 'P', '"P" is true' is never a robustly truth-conditional claim. And since, by our second assumption, it is a priori co-acceptable with the claim that P, it follows—by the third assumption—that the claim that P is not robustly truth-conditional either. So nothing is robustly truth-conditional.[18]

This reasoning may, perhaps, be resisted. Paul Boghossian (1989c) independently develops a somewhat different argument to similar

18. Cf. Wright (1984), p. 769 (this volume, Essay 4).

effect. Reacting to this argument, Simon Blackburn believes himself to find in it a confusion between use and mention; that is, he believes it illicitly jumps a gap between establishing a result, in point of robust truth-conditionality, about the *metalinguistic* assertion that 'P' is true, and justifying a conclusion in that respect about the object-language assertion that P.[19]

Which, precisely, of the two assumptions—the second and third—which just now enabled us to argue for the validity of that transition would Blackburn want to deny? That is a matter of speculation. But prescinding from the detail of that argument, and of Boghossian's, it is hard to see in general terms how the result about the metalinguistic assertion could fail to be transferable. How could the claim that P escape the fate of its metalinguistic counterpart if the latter's fate is sealed merely by the involvement of content? Language is not a mere clothing for thought. We have no wordless contact with the thought that P: if we are to assess it, it has to be given to us *linguistically*. And our assessment will then be a function of the content which we find in its linguistic mode of presentation and of what we take to be the state of the world in relevant respects. Knowing what claim a particular use of a sentence makes is not and could not be a matter of pairing the sentence with an item that was somehow identified non-linguistically. If your and my sole language is English, then, in order to assess my claim that the cat is on the mat, it will be no less necessary for you to form a judgement about the content of 'The cat is on the mat' than if I had said that 'The cat is on the mat' is true. We have no grip on the question of the truth status of a claim that does not make it into the question whether a tokening of a sentence is true.[20]

If all claims are content-committed—depend, in this way, upon facts about meaning—then a proponent of the Sceptical Solution faces the daunting task of providing not merely a reconstructive, non-robustly truth-conditional semantics for all our declarative discourse, but also of explaining—when there are, perforce, no examples now to

19. Blackburn (1990).
20. For further discussion, see Wright (1992), chap. 6.

draw upon—what exactly it is that is being repudiated: what exactly robust truth-conditionality should be supposed to come to. And there is in addition a specific concern about how the *cogency* of the argument to the Sceptical Paradox can survive a non-truth-conditional reconstruction of its premises, lemmas, and conclusion. These issues are all very discussable. But at present there seems every reason to question whether Kripke's Wittgenstein has the materials for a coherent philosophy of language.

That the package of Sceptical Paradox and Sceptical Solution is (if it is) unstable provides, of course, no conclusive reason for refusing to ascribe it to Wittgenstein or for denying that it could have provided a key motive for his distinctive ideas about mathematics. But prudence, and the urge to learn, would dictate that we look for something better. What, if not that there are no substantial facts about the content of rules and about what complies with or breaches them, should the principal conclusion of Wittgenstein's discussion be taken to be? And is there any prospect of a spin-off which, as Kripke anticipated, makes a case for each of the key features of Wittgenstein's philosophy of mathematics?

Since, for reasons that may already be apparent, the answer to the second question must, I believe, be negative, there is no point in getting embroiled—on this occasion—in the first. But I cannot forbear to say a little. Wittgenstein's general point, as I read him, is that coming to understand a particular rule, and acquiring thereby the ability to follow it in new cases, is not a matter of learning to keep track of something whose direction is dictated, somehow or other, independently of the judgements on the matter of anyone who might be regarded as competent. Wittgenstein's discussion of rule-following is directed against the mythological sublimation of rules and content, crystallised in traditional Platonism, which allows the course assumed by the proper application of a rule—for instance, the identity of the series generated by an arithmetical function—to be thought of as generated purely by the rule itself, and of our judgements, when we competently follow it, as responses to states of affairs which are constituted quite independently. Such a picture seems to provide simultaneously both a certain cognitive dignity for our rule-governed practices and an explanation of *why* we are able, by and large, to agree about what constitutes proper performance within them. It is rather as if we all had hold of the same railings. But for Wittgenstein, on the contrary, the conception of the content of a rule, thus sublimated, is unintelligible, and the kind of epistemology of rule-following for which it calls—the account demanded of how we are able to recognise the requirements of rules when they are so conceived—impossible. In consequence, no real explanation is provided of our ability to concur in our use of language and in other rule-governed practices. And it is, indeed, a philosophical error to think that such an explanation is needed. No ulterior cognitive accomplishment underwrites our disposition, on receipt of similar explanations, to proceed to follow rules in similar ways.[21]

A host of questions arise, of course. The position outlined can maintain its distinction from that of Kripke's Wittgenstein, for instance, only if there can be an *unsublimated* conception of the content of rules, which nevertheless conserves our right to think of the requirements of rules as somehow substantial, and questions about whether a particular move is in or out of line as factual. Moreover, it is all very well to say that we should not think of the requirements of a rule on a particular occasion as constituted, as it were Platonically, in all independence of our judgements, but must there not also be some positive story: some account of the precise form of the dependence which we are being urged to recognise? Wittgenstein, it seems, thought not. And if so, then that view too requires explanation.

Whatever the correct upshot of engaging these various questions would be, it is hard not to feel that Wittgenstein is in range, in his discussions of rule-following, of a most profound insight, even if philosophers have yet to clinch it definitively. And I think it is right that the general direction of his remarks, as just briefly characterised and without further analysis, does suffice to explain *some* aspects of his philosophy of mathematics. If our ongoing judgements are some-

21. For further discussion of these ideas, and of the perplexities they generate, see Wright (1989a) (this volume Essay 6); Wright (1989c) (this volume Essay 7).

how primitively involved in determining the content of the rules that compose the decimal expansion of π, would that not suffice to explain remarks like that quoted earlier:

> However queer it sounds, the further expansion of an irrational number is a further expansion of mathematics. . . .
>
> I want to say: it looks as though the ground for a decision were already there, and it has yet to be invented.[22]

It is *we* who compose the decimal expansion of π by the judgements concerning its expansion which, step by step, we find ultimately cogent; for in making these judgements we do not align ourselves with requirements that are somehow constituted independently of us, but apply concepts primitively, in the sense that the conformity of such applications to some externally constituted standard makes no sense.

The truth is that the ideas on rules can motivate much of what Wittgenstein says about Platonism in the philosophy of mathematics, and about mathematical objectivity and logical compulsion—and, in general, can explain his opposition to ideas about mathematics that overlook what we might call the 'anthropological contribution'. What they cannot explain are his distinctive remarks about proof and the status, in point of certainty, of the conclusions of proof. And we have, in effect, already glimpsed the reason for saying so, in the train of thought, levelled against the Sceptical Solution, that led to the conclusion that all discourse is 'content-committed'.

That train of thought was that, since the recognition of meaning is an inextricable ingredient in the appraisal of any statement whatever, any general thesis about the epistemology and objectivity of meaning will be liable to widen into a thesis about the epistemology and objectivity of discourse in general. If, as in Kripke's discussion, the thesis is taken to be that discourse concerning such matters is devoid of genuinely factual content, then, as noted, we get the dubiously coherent conclusion that that is the situation of all declarative discourse. If on the other hand the claim is the, in intention at least, more modest one

---

22. *RFM* V, 9, quoted above.

which we are now entertaining—not that meanings, rules, etc., have no reality but that the truth about them and their requirements is somehow constitutionally responsive to our ongoing judgements and reactions—then the conclusion will be that truth in general is constitutionally responsive in the same way. The argument appealed to the platitude that the truth value of a sentence, as uttered on a particular occasion, will be a function of its content and the state of the world in relevant respects. If its content, when so used—or, what comes to the same thing, the condition on how the state of the world in relevant respects has to be in order for the sentence to express a truth—is, so to speak, unmade in advance of appropriate, primitive judgements from us, then so is the truth value of the utterance of the sentence in question. And now it seems that, in whatever sense the ideas about rule following afford the consequence that the further expansion of π is a mathematical novelty, *all* discoveries, in whatever area of inquiry, are likewise novelties. We cannot keep our thumbs off the scales anywhere.

But it is unmistakable that Wittgenstein intended a *distinctive* thesis about proof. His claim was not that, in some hopelessly sublimated sense of 'discovery', exploded by the rule-following considerations, proofs are not instruments of discovery; it was that, even when the notion of discovery is viewed aright, and many ordinary things *do* stand as discoveries, mathematical proofs do not. If the foregoing thoughts are right, then the ideas about rules, whatever the best development of their general direction and detail, cannot substantiate this claim. So we should think again.[23]

III

How should the claim that something is, or is not, a technique of discovery be appraised? Well, whatever constitutes the *discovery* that a proposition is true had better be a process, or sequence of events, which leaves someone who fully understands that proposition with

23. This point was perhaps the most important factor determining the overall direction of my argument in Wright (1980).

no justifiable option but to assent to it. But of course one may always justifiably refuse assent to the conclusion of a proof in mathematics if one may justifiably refuse assent to the claim that what is presented is indeed a proof.[24] It follows that proofs are properly regarded as instruments whereby we discover mathematical facts only if there is in general no justifiable way whereby the status of a proof may be disputed—at least a wide class of proofs must be such that one who fully understands the concepts involved and works through all the steps has no justifiable option but to assent to the claim that what is presented is indeed a proof.

If this is right, then an effective way of attacking the mathematical realist conception of proof is to argue that a proper understanding of each of the notions in play in a proof and a full empirical awareness of its detail never completely constrain our assent; that the status of something as a proof is left underdetermined by its strictly cognitive aspects. When we ratify a proof, we go beyond anything that is required of us purely by acknowledgement of features of the presented construction.

This is, as we have noted, consonant with the general direction of Wittgenstein's remarks. Proofs do indeed do less than compel our assent:

> Do not look at the proof as a procedure that *compels* you, but as one that *guides* you.[25]

But what does Wittgenstein say to make it clear that this is a practical option? What would it be to *refuse* the 'guidance' offered by a particular (putative) proof? The whole point about good proofs is that they strike us as *cogent*. And Wittgenstein himself stresses that it is of the essence of proof that it produce complete conviction:

> A proof shows what OUGHT to come out.—And since every reproduction of the proof must demonstrate the same thing, while on the one

24. Provided, of course, that no other proof of the same conclusion is known to one.
25. *RFM* IV, 30.

---

hand it must reproduce the result automatically, on the other hand it must also reproduce the *compulsion* to get it.[26]

How can these remarks be made to cohere? How can it be of the essence of proof that it produce complete conviction and, at the same time, of the nature of proof that it merely guides towards the conception of things embodied in its conclusion?

Take a simple example: suppose I calculate that $26 \times 23 = 598$. The calculation constitutes a proof only so long as it secures my conviction that no other outcome than 598 is possible if I correctly multiply 26 by 23. For if I have any doubt about that, I will not consider that I have a proof. Yet—according to Wittgenstein—I am simultaneously supposed to be able to see the proof as providing guidance, rather than compulsion, as representing itself merely, as it were, as an advocate of the complex set of convictions involved in accepting its conclusion—the conviction, for instance, that if 598 two-inch square tiles do not suffice to cover a rectangular surface, which I have measured as 46 inches by 52, then I must have mismeasured. So I am simultaneously *both* to see no alternative to accepting the proof which the calculation accomplishes, and the ways of looking at things dictated by its conclusion—otherwise I will not be persuaded that I have a proof at all—*and*, following Wittgenstein's advice, to view the proof not as *teaching* that its conclusion is correct, but merely as guiding me towards a decision, as it were, to count it so. How is this schizophrenic feat to be carried off?

The tension is resolved when we take the remarks about compulsion to pertain to the *phenomenology* of proof, and the talk of guidance to relate to its *cognitive status*. Consider an analogy. No one but a theoretically prejudiced philosopher would think that the sense of humour is, literally, a cognitive sense—something which enables us to detect real comic values, out there in the world. Finding a situation funny involves, no doubt, cognition of many features of it; but the comic response itself is contributed by the affective, rather than cognitive, side of our nature. Nevertheless, we should not count as finding

26. *RFM*, III, 55.

a situation funny if our reaction to it were somehow a matter of choice. It is of the essence of comic responses that they seem to the responder to be elicited from without—you can simulate finding something funny, but you cannot bring it about by will that you do.

So also, in Wittgenstein's view, with the intellectual response—the conviction—generated by a proof. If a calculation is to impress us as proving its result, it has to convince us that no other outcome is possible if the sequence of operations which it contains are performed correctly. But it is one thing to say that we register that conviction in judging something to be a proof; another to say that the conviction is a purely cognitive accomplishment.

The question remains: given that the phenomenology of proof is essentially compulsive, wherein consists the cognitive freedom which Wittgenstein apparently thinks we nevertheless possess? To get a sense of the kind of thought which leads him here, we need to look at his repeated discussions of the relations between proof, especially calculation, and experiment.[27]

Typical proofs, and all calculations, involve a *process:* we start at a particular point, run through a series of prescribed operations—correctly, to the best of our ability—and get a certain result. So too with, say, a laboratory experiment: we set up an apparatus in a certain initial state, carry out certain operations upon it, and a certain result ensues. And both a proof, and an experiment which, when repeated, consistently gives the same result, may prompt our assent to a conditional statement along the following lines:

If, starting on such-and-such a basis, such-and-such procedures are properly carried out, then such-and-such results.[28]

---

27. A selection of relevant passages from *RFM* includes I, 36–57, 75–103, 156–64 and Appendix II; III, 55, 65–76; IV, 46–53; VI, 1–10, 15–16, 36; VII, 6, 17–18, 25–6. Cora Diamond's (1976) edition of the 1939 *Lectures on the Foundations of Mathematics* touches on the issues in lectures iii (pp. 36–9), vii (pp. 71 and following), x and xi passim, and xiii (pp. 128–30).

28. What I have elsewhere called the *corresponding descriptive conditional.* See Wright (1980), p. 452; cf. Wright (1986b), pp. 203–4; Wright (1989b), pp. 231–2.

This statement need not, in the case of proofs in general, be that which we regard the proof as primarily proving (though it always is precisely that in the case of a calculation). But one thing is clear. Our willingness to acknowledge a proof as a proof—what marks it off for us from an experiment—depends upon our willingness to accept that this conditional statement holds of *necessity:* our willingness to accept that there is, in the case of the process in question, an *internal* connection between basis, steps and outcome.[29]

You can begin to get a sense of Wittgenstein's concern if, bearing in mind the very analogy between proof and an experiment, you now ask: what is it about a calculation, say—about the routine of carefully running through a calculation—which puts us in position to make a *necessitated* assertion? What do we recognise about the calculation that justifies the claim that the particular result *must* result from that particular process on that particular starting point? Why is our entitlement not exhausted by the claim, merely, that this is what resulted when, so far as we can tell, the calculation was done correctly—and probably always will result when we are so convinced?

The point to be explained is not that we are supremely certain of the truth of the corresponding conditional in the case of a calculation and merely, say, highly confident in the case of an experiment. I may well be more confident about the repeatability of an experiment than about the conclusion of a complex calculation, but still prepared to assert both the relevant conditionals. The crux is rather that, in the case of a calculation, we make a claim of a quite different kind. The 'must' is an expression, not of certainty, but of the conviction that the conditional, if true, is sustained by factors quite other than those which sustain its experimental counterpart. Yet the confirmatory processes seem similar: in each case we have, surely, only ordinary empirical grounds for identifying the starting point and conclusion, and only ordinary empirical certainty that appropriate controls have been properly applied on the intervening steps.

29. This is what Wittgenstein means when he says—*RFM* IV, 41—that *causality* plays no part in a proof.

This is the problem that runs through much of Wittgenstein's discussion. A common thought, which will see no problem here, will want to credit us with a special intuitive faculty—a necessity-detector, as it were—which is summoned into action in 'reading' a proof. At the purely empirical level there is, it will be granted, no material difference between a proof and an experiment. And that just shows that, in order to detect the difference—to distinguish processes in which basis, steps and outcome are all internally related from processes in which they are not—more than merely empirical faculties are demanded.

But this response is at once obscure and ad hoc. And now we may feel the attraction of a simple opposing strategy of response: make out that the contrast between the two kinds of process, so far from needing explanation in terms of special cognitive faculties, is not properly speaking a *cognitive* contrast at all. Consider a favourite example of Wittgenstein's: a rule of conversion between units of measurement in distinct systems—say, 'One inch equals 2.54 centimetres'. If we were at a point in history when there had been no interaction between users of the Imperial and Metric systems respectively, we would have to set about appraising that statement empirically: measuring objects using instruments calibrated in each unit, and determining statistically the limit of the ratios in which the results stood. Yet the proposition, if true, is surely *no contingency*—it expresses an internal relation between the concepts of correctly measuring in centimetres and correctly measuring in inches. So a similar problem arises: how could we possibly verify an internal relation obtained by (broadly) statistical empirical methods?

The answer is that we do not. Rather, we *already* have the idea that there must be an internal relation in the offing, and what we identify empirically is the *best candidate* for what the internal relation is. And so too, in Wittgenstein's view, with a calculation: the calculation excites no special intuitive faculty—rather we are already 'in the market' for an internal relation between basis, process and outcome, and doing the calculation, perhaps with repeated checks, makes an ordinary empirical case for what the internal relation in question is.

The crucial issue accordingly becomes: what puts us 'in the market'? Do we recognise, by dint of which cognitive faculties we cannot say, that the rules of multiplication *can* only ever generate one result when correctly applied to a particular set of factors? Or is it rather that here 'correctness' precludes variation in the outcome as a matter of (something akin to) *convention?*

The contrast, thus expressed, is crudely drawn. But many commentators have found in Wittgenstein a view of the second broad sort— albeit one in which the notion of convention is softened by considerations concerning our natures and unreflective practices. We do not, as it were, explicitly lay it down that the rules of multiplication do not count as correctly applied in cases where variation in output is unaccompanied by variation in imput. It is merely that

> [*w*]*e do not accept* e.g. a multiplication's not yielding the same result every time.[30]

Our *practice* is not to tolerate such variation. And whereas, for the cognitivist, this practice is backed by a *perception*—an insight into what the rules of multiplication make possible—for Wittgenstein it may be accepted simply as primitive and groundless:

> This is use and custom among us, or a fact of our natural history.[31]

What are the options if our inclination is to try to underwrite the 'must' which we incorporate into the conclusion of a calculation, with a substantial epistemology? Only the two canvassed, it might seem: *either* the details of a specific calculation somehow excite an 'intuitional' recognition that what results must result, *or* there is only an empirical routine, but a routine which is informed by the general a priori insight that proper implementation of these rules cannot gener-

---

30. *RFM*, IV, 52.
31. Ibid., I, 63.

ate variable outcome. But either line precariously offers hostages for redemption by the theory of knowledge.

Wittgenstein's alternative, in contrast, promises what may seem the clear advantage of handling the mathematical 'must' within an empiricist epistemology. In Wittgenstein's view, the internal relations which articulate the inter-connections within a proof are acknowledged by way of institution or custom, following on empirical findings. And this background of unreflective custom is not something in which our participation is imposed by purely cognitive considerations. So a faultless understanding of each of the notions in play in a proof and a full empirical awareness of its detail do underdetermine assent to it; one needs, in addition, to be party to the relevant practices. And if that is right, then—by the criterion I offered at the start of this section—proofs are not instruments of discovery.

IV

It remains to record the advertised cause for dissatisfaction. This is that the two alternatives we canvassed for the cognitivist—construction-triggered intuitions, or background a priori insights—do not exhaust the field. The reason is that the simplest ingredient steps in a calculation, or in formal proofs in general, are typically certified by operations which are primitively given as *functions:* operations which are *identified,* in part, by the characteristic that only variation in input can generate variation in output.[32] Wittgenstein's view has it that a culture might deploy the same arithmetical concepts as we do, but without the institutional setting that leads us to dignify the products of calculation as necessary. That requires that there be fully adequate modes of explanation of arithmetical operations that are, so to speak,

32. I am here by-passing complications to do with rules of inference, like vel-introduction, which permit more than one conclusion from given premises. For further discussion, see Wright (1989b), pp. 234–5.

neutral on the question whether their output may vary for fixed imput. And that is most implausible. There is no hiatus between an understanding of arithmetical addition, for instance, and the knowledge that it is a function. Rather, it has to be an explicit part of any adequate explanation of the concept of addition that no pair of numbers has more than one sum. Not to know that is not to know what adding is. There is no stripped-down concept which is somehow neutral on the matter.

The crucial Wittgensteinian claim is that participation in the 'institutional setting' is no part of the conditions for understanding arithmetical operations. If that is wrong, then someone who fully understands those operations and properly assesses the empirical features of a correct calculation will have no rational option but to assent to its finding. And that will restore a scaled-down cognitivism, independent of intuitions and a priori insights: recognising the 'must' that underlies a calculation will simply be a matter of applying concepts as one was taught them to an empirically given construction. These matters need much fuller discussion, beyond the scope of this essay. But perhaps the preceding will convey at least something of the geography of the issues raised by Wittgenstein's mature thought about mathematical proof.[33]

33. For a somewhat fuller account, see ibid., section IV.

POSTSCRIPTS

Study Note on Wittgenstein on the Nature of Philosophy and Its Proper Method

No leading philosopher has been more self-conscious about the nature of philosophy, and philosophical method, than Wittgenstein.[1] This self-consciousness is a product of his conviction that the subject has been, for the most part, practised very badly, that what passes for 'philosophical' thought is very often nonsensical and that philosophy's problems tend to be philosophers' fault.

I

A more traditional conception sees philosophy as the "Queen of the Sciences": a region of enquiry in which, as in physics or mathematics, we aim to discover *truths*. But the truths at which philosophy aims are of an especially profound kind: *philosophy goes after the real essence of things*—the nature of truth, what moral goodness consists in, the nature of time, and so on—even, traditionally, the nature and existence of God.

---

1. The key passages in *Philosophical Investigations* include §§89–90, 109–33, 192–6, 216, 251–5, 309, 464, 593, 599.

The idea that pure thought could be a self-sufficient tool of enquiry in this kind of way originated before the development of modern empirical science, and doubtless initially drew strength from the failure to distinguish between the empirical and the a priori. But even after that distinction is made, philosophy has clung on to the idea that there is a special province of especially profound truths—the province of Metaphysics—whose secrets are accessible to the traditional methods of analysis, reflection and inference.

Going along with this way of thinking is a certain conception of the *objectivity of philosophical problems*. Philosophers tend to think of themselves not as creating philosophical problems—in the sense in which a troublemaker creates problems—but rather as their *discoverers*. The problems are thought of as objectively there, available to be appreciated by anyone of sufficient sophistication and reflective capacity. In this respect, they are thought of as analogous to mathematical problems (as *they* are usually thought of). Arithmetical concepts, for instance, are available in principle to any rational thinker, to whom it will then be open to wonder about the number and distribution of the primes, about how many perfect numbers there are, about the truth of what we call Goldbach's Conjecture (that every even number is the sum of two primes), etc. In the same way, according to the traditional conception, there are, for any sufficiently conceptually endowed, reflective thinker, objective problems about the possibility of knowledge of a material world, or of other minds, the nature of causation, the relationship between thought and language, and so on.

It belongs with this general conception that philosophical discovery is potentially *legitimately revisionary* of ordinary ways of thinking and of ordinary practice. If we misconceive the nature of time, for instance, it cannot be ruled out that the misconception may have seeped into quite specialised forms of scientific and mathematical thought; so changes may be enjoined in those disciplines when the misconception is put right. If we are ignorant about the real nature of knowledge, it may be that when we know better, we will recognise that much of our customary application of the notion is misguided—

for instance, that we ought not to see empirical science as, even in the best case, producing genuine knowledge.

On the traditional conception of philosophy, then, surprising—disconcerting or exciting—discoveries are on the cards. True, it is hard to think of many such discoveries that philosophers have actually made—they tend to be much better at confounding the argumentative constructs of their colleagues than at construction that actually works. But this lack of progress is not usually seen as a challenge to the picture of philosophy which I am outlining. You might think it would have to bring into question either the adequacy of philosophy's methods to its target subject matter—the availability of that subject matter to reason and analysis—or even the very existence of the subject matter: the ontology of deep conceptual truths which are supposed to be philosophy's proper concern. But philosophers are good at thinking up excuses for their lack of progress consistent with the traditional picture: P. F. Strawson, for instance, has—plausibly enough—claimed that philosophy's slow progress is largely owing to the fact that successive generations of philosophers cannot *inherit from their predecessors* in the way that is possible in science or mathematics, since each generation has to interpret and understand the problems and issues for itself—like adolescents, each generation of philosophers has to make its own mistakes if it is to understand why they are mistakes, and this puts limits on the extent to which their wisdom, when they get it, can surpass that of earlier thinkers.

II

Wittgenstein's conception of philosophy and philosophical method, as it emerges in *Philosophical Investigations,* is strikingly antithetical to all this. Set against the idea that philosophy is to penetrate to the (hidden) essences of certain difficult concepts—time, freedom, meaning, causation, truth, goodness, and so on—we find instead the notion that there are no hidden essences: that when a concept covers a seemingly diverse range of cases, that may just be the whole fact of the matter—there need be no underlying principle of unification. (This of course is the purpose of the notion of family resemblances.)

> [The traditional questions] see in the essence, not something that already lies open to view and that becomes surveyable by a rearrangement, but something that lies *beneath* the surface. Something that lies within, which we see when we look *into* a thing, and which an analysis digs out.
>
> 'The essence is hidden from us': this is the form our problem now assumes. We ask: '*What is* language?', '*What is* a proposition?' And the answer to these questions is to be given once and for all; and independently of any future experience. (§92)

For Wittgenstein, the analytical pursuit of hidden essences is an illusion. Everything we need to know is already on the surface. What the philosopher has to do is not penetrate behind the use of language, but to arrange the manifest facts of its use in the right kind of way, for it is thereby that our perplexities will be resolved.

> Philosophy simply puts everything before us, and neither explains nor deduces anything.—Since everything lies open to view there is nothing to explain. For what is hidden, for example, is of no interest to us. (§126)

> [W]e may not advance any kind of theory. There must not be anything hypothetical in our considerations. We must do away with all *explanation,* and description alone must take its place. And this description gets its light, that is to say its purpose, from the philosophical problems. These are, of course, not empirical problems; they are solved, rather, by looking into the workings of our language, and that in such a way as to make us recognise those workings: *in despite of* an urge to misunderstand them. The problems are solved, not by giving new information, but by arranging what we have always known. Philosophy is a battle against the bewitchment of our intelligence by means of language. (§109)

Notice the conception of a philosophical problem which emerges here. Gone is the traditional idea of the objective conceptual difficulty, appreciable in principle by any rational thinker. It is replaced with the notion, to the contrary, that philosophical problems are *muddles:* confusions into which we fall, seduced by superficial aspects of our language, and a natural propensity to misconstrue the way it works.

> The results of philosophy are the uncovering of one or another piece of plain nonsense and of bumps that the understanding has got by running its head up against the limits of language. These bumps make us see the value of the discovery. (§119)
>
> A philosophical problem has the form 'I don't know my way about'. (§123)

The task of the philosopher, then, is not to uncover conceptual truths (and hence conceptual mistakes) but rather to defuse the temptation to certain sorts of muddle:

> What we 'are tempted to say' in such a case is, of course, not philosophy; but it is its raw material. Thus, for example, what a mathematician is inclined to say about the objectivity and reality of mathematical facts, is not a philosophy of mathematics, but something for philosophical *treatment.*
>
> 255. The philosopher's treatment of a question is like the treatment of an illness. (§§254–5)

And of course, famously,

> What is your aim in philosophy?—to show the fly the way out of the fly bottle. (§309)

Somewhere it shouldn't have fetched up in the first place!

Given this conception of the nature of philosophical problems, and of the way in which they are to be resolved, the idea that philosophy might somehow sustain or undermine claims which are in some way foundational for our linguistic practice in a given area, and so prove potentially revisionary of it, is of course quite preempted. You get into philosophical trouble by failing to understand the way a particular language game works. Unpicking the knots of confusion, then, cannot possibly issue in a ground for criticism of that language game—

> Philosophy may in no way interfere with the actual use of language; it can in the end only describe it. For it cannot give it any foundation either. It leaves everything as it is. It also leaves mathematics as it is, and no mathematical discovery can advance it. A 'leading problem of mathematical logic' is for us a problem of mathematics like any other. (§124)

So: a quite new conception of philosophy—of its agenda and of its proper methods—is being proposed. The business of philosophy is not the pursuit of—a special rarefied kind of—truth, but the dissolution of confusion. Philosophical problems are not standing intellectual difficulties, but the effects of language's 'bewitching our intelligence'. They are to be resolved not by penetrating to conceptual essences, but by a descriptive examination of the surface: reflection on the way language actually functions. And philosophy will give us no theories or explanations—on the contrary, the inclination to theorise, and especially to generalise, across diverse but superficially similar language games and forms of expressions is a prime source of philosophical confusion.

III

So much for Wittgenstein's 'official' conception of what he is about. But it can seem difficult to relate these meta-philosophical pronouncements to the actual course of events in the *Investigations*. Which exactly are the problems there treated for which the diagnosis is that they arise because we are misled by superficial similarities between different areas of discourse? To what extent can we see Wittgenstein's discussions as assembling reminders of things we know already (§109) and thereby correcting our misunderstandings of certain forms of expression?

I think it's fair to say that a *real* integration of Wittgenstein's official conception of philosophy with his own practice is something which has so far eluded even the best commentary. But we are at least in position to identify two quite striking instances, each a fundamental problem, where Wittgenstein's procedures may be made out to accord pretty well with his official conception of the way philosophical problems arise and how they may be treated.

(i) Rule-Following and the "Predetermination" of Applications in Advance

(A) Recall §§188 ff of the *Investigations*. Wittgenstein writes:

> 188. Here I should first of all like to say: your idea was that that act of meaning the order had in its own way already traversed all those steps: that when you meant it your mind as it were flew ahead and took all those steps before you physically arrived at this or that one.
>
> Thus you were inclined to use such expressions as: 'The steps are *really* already taken, even before I take them in writing or orally or in thought'. And it seems as if they were in some *unique* way predetermined, anticipated—as only the act of meaning can anticipate reality.

This passage is concerned with the idea that it can be perfectly proper to say that one meant a pupil, for example, to continue a series in a particular way at a particular stage even in circumstances when one gave no explicit thought to that particular stage. So I can perfectly properly say, for example, "Look: I meant you to continue, '1002, 1004, . . . etc.' even in a case where no thought was given to the continuation after 1000. What §188 does is to portray *an interpretation*—a particular way of taking—the propriety of such a remark. So the thought is: we are prone to misunderstand claims like 'I meant you to do so and so' as reporting a queer process of mind which somehow had the power, without involving anything which amounted to an explicit contemplation of the case, to determine what would and wouldn't do at every *n*th place. And, as Wittgenstein argues, we are bereft of any conception of what a state of mind could be which would do that, and when we look within, we find nothing remotely resembling such a thing. In short: we are inclined to misunderstand the avowal 'I meant you to do so and so at the *n*th stage' as a report of our anterior state of mind which mysteriously anticipated the *n*th case. But that's not what the avowal does.

Now recall what happens next:

> 'But *are* the steps then *not* determined by the algebraic formula?'—the question contains a mistake. (§189)

What mistake? As remarked, we are inclined to misunderstand 'I meant you to do so and so at the nth place' or 'This formula determines the correct continuation of the series at every stage'. But the misunderstanding comes so naturally that we are inclined to react to criticism of it as though it invited *denial* of locutions of the kind in question—as though an intention left what should count as implementing it *open*, or as though a formula like $x_n = (x_{n-1})^2$ did *not* determine the *n*th element of the series. The 'mistake', then, is to think that in discarding the misinterpretation, we have to discard the locution. The locution is in good standing:

> We use the expression: 'The steps are determined by the formula . . .'. *How* is it used?

What Wittgenstein is now going to do is to draw our attention to what the use of such a claim actually accomplishes—given that what it does *not* accomplish is to mark the fact that the formula in question expresses a Platonic rule-as-rail. And §189 proceeds to explain two harmless, legitimate uses which such locutions do indeed have:

It may be used to call attention to the uniformity of response which training in arithmetic is intended to and does secure—to such facts as that people will respond alike to the order 'add three,' or all work out the same value for y given a value for x and the formula $y = x^2$. The implied contrast is then with the behaviour of people who are bewildered by such orders, or that of people whose responses are positive but various. Alternatively:

We may be effecting a distinction among formulae, contrasting their different kinds of use. For example, '$y = x^2 + 1$' determines the value of y as a *function* of x; whereas '$y < x^2 + y$', or '$y = x^2 + z$' does not. Dropping the idea of the 'rule-as-rail' doesn't mean abandoning the distinction between these two kinds of formula, abandoning the notion of an arithmetical *function*. (Though it does of course mean that we can't explicate that notion in Platonistic terms.)

(B) Another example in the area of rule-following (not explicitly treated by Wittgenstein) is provided by the fact that, in very many areas, ordinary thought makes space for a contrast between what a majority or even a whole community may think and what it may really be correct to think.

Here comes the misunderstanding. 'Correct to think'—that must mean, surely: what the rules governing the use of various relevant expressions require of us, modulo relevant aspects of the world. But now, if that can be independent of our actual considered judgement, how can we think of the rules other than as determining verdicts in isolation from us and hence as, in effect, the hyper-objective kind of rule-as-rail that Wittgenstein's discussion targets?

That picture, however, is *not* imposed upon us by the mere legitimacy of locutions like 'The currently accepted hypothesis is that P, but we could all be wrong". Rather invoking the rule-as-rail is an *explanation*—an interpretation—of what such a locution is expressing, and a bad one at that, because of its attendant hopeless philosophical difficulties. The therapy is to review the circumstances in which we do have practical use for a contrast between what whole communities, or bodies of experts, may think and what is really the case. When we review the circumstances in which such locutions have their home, we shall see that they are grounded in the defeasibility of ordinary standards of evidence, for example, and in the consequent improvability of any particular point of view, and that an objectionable Platonism simply doesn't have to be in the picture. ('Objectivity of judgement' and 'objectivity of meaning').[2]

(ii) First-Personal Psychological Ascriptions

An equally important example, however, has to be that of avowals. In various of the essays in this volume, we have noted features that first-personal ascriptions of sensation, for example, distinctively carry: their non-inferential character, their strong authority, the incongruity of their embedding within expressions of doubt. Those are 'grammatical' facts. And they sustain a superficial analogy, as we saw, with ordinary observational reports made under optimal conditions. So ordinary thought, always prone to generalise, tries to see them as just that—and is rapidly embroiled in all the difficulties of the Cartesian philosophy of mind. The Wittgensteinian solution is to realise that the Cartesian picture attempts a lay-philosophical *explanation* of something which needs no explanation—aspects of the 'grammar' of avowals: the rules of the ordinary psychological language game.

IV

We are perhaps in a position, finally, to shed some light on an outstanding puzzle for the interpreter of the *Investigations:* the extent to which, his self-imposed 'grammar-descriptive' brief notwithstanding, Wittgenstein indulges in *criticism* of various notions—par excellence, the Cartesian conception of the meaning of ascriptions of mental states. The solution is simply that there is no real tension: philosophical puzzles arise, according to Wittgenstein, from bad pictures, misinterpretations, generated by the desire to find explanations for features

2. Cf. Essay 3.

which belong to the 'grammar' of our language, and to let the—already misguided—search for these explanations be constrained by craving for generalisation. The *products* of these misguided tendencies are, of course, open to analytical criticism. And they need to be criticised if we are to see them for what they are. The role of 'description' is rather in letting us see what really belongs to our linguistic practices and what to our interpretation of them. With that distinction in relatively sharp relief, it will be possible to understand how our troublesome interpretations flourish by ignoring differences, and also to canvass other pictures—by way of therapeutic counterweight—to allow us to free our thinking from the habits of those interpretations. (It is presumably as such 'counterweights'—rather than as alternative theoretical proposals of the very kind he warns against—that we are meant to take Wittgenstein's suggestions, for instance, that avowals are a form of *expression,* and his analogy between mathematical statements and commands.)

On *Mind and World*

This note is a reaction to John McDowell's reply to my contribution to a *Philosophy and Phenomenological Research* book symposium on his *Mind and World*.[1] Responses to responses risk diminishing returns. But there is more to say and, since McDowell believes he has Wittgenstein for an ally in some of his more distinctive claims, much of it is directly relevant to the concerns of the present volume. I will offer a few orientational remarks but will otherwise presuppose the reader's acquaintance with *Mind and World* and with the contents of the book symposium.

To recap a little: the problem McDowell is urging on us—and I do not deny that it is a good one—is how best to conceive of experience if it is to exert a *rational* influence on basic empirical beliefs. The poles of McDowell's 'oscillation' both think of experience in the same

---

1. *Philosophy and Phenomenological Research* 58 (1998), p. 2. My contribution (which is essentially an excerpt from Wright (1996)) is at pp. 395–402. McDowell's Reply to his Commentators—Brandom, Collins, Peacocke, Rorty and myself—is at pp. 403–31, with the discussion of my contribution at pp. 425–31. All page references are to his Reply unless otherwise stated.

way, as 'occurrences in consciousness that are independent of conceptual capacities' (p. 425)—a kind of brute impingement on awareness. One—Coherentism—accordingly concedes that experience is indeed not a rational influence (justifier) but is merely a *causal* source of beliefs, whose justification, properly so regarded, is then confined to their relations to other beliefs. The other—the 'Myth of the Given'—tries to maintain that experience, even conceived as a brute impact, can somehow justify basic empirical beliefs. But that, supposedly, is hopeless. So the see-saw is powered by two incompatible thoughts about experience conceived as brute: it had better be a justifier—but that's a Myth—so it cannot justify, and the best we can do is Coherentism—but that's radically unsatisfactory—so it had better be a justifier—but that's a Myth—. . . . etc.

Obviously it is crucial to McDowell's purpose that we cannot comfortably live with either station. I think the respective cases for thinking so developed in *Mind and World* remain incomplete (in the case of Coherentism) and unconvincing (in the case of the Myth). The principal weakness in the latter, to which I shall return, drives from McDowell's failure to characterise the targeted error sufficiently sharply. Notice again, that he does not dismiss the idea that something *is* 'given' in experience: he believes in a *conceptual* given—what he regards as mythical is, rather, the notion of relations which are both justificatory *and* merely causal. He doesn't argue for this incompatibility but just asserts it, and I do not know how he would rebut an awkward customer who just counter-asserted that 'occurrences in consciousness that are independent of conceptual capacities' can justify. But I believe we could agree with McDowell about that—and grant him that Coherentism is radically unsatisfactory—yet still be unpersuaded that his refashioning of experience is called for, with the key issue turning on the interpretation of the dangerously imprecise 'independent' in 'independent of conceptual capacities'. The weakness in the rebuttal of Coherentism, by contrast, remains its dependence on a thesis about the necessary conditions for empirical content—or 'objective purport' (p. 405)—which, correct or not, he leaves inchoate.

I shall confine my observations to three headings: McDowell's' reaction to my comments on his treatment of Coherentism; his attempt to enlist Wittgenstein's support in defence of his conception of experience; and his reactions to two suggestions I made about ways we might 'dismount the see-saw' without conceptualising experience.

COHERENTISM AND CONTENT

McDowell embraces not just essentially conceptualised experience but a view of the world as conceptual too: a world of *facts*—of conceptually structured states of affairs. It seemed to me useful, in trying to understand this, to consider a kind of half-way house position: an Extended Coherentism which allowed experience to carry conceptual content (without worrying too much about how it gets it) and regarded justification as a matter of coherence over a larger domain including both beliefs and experiences, but viewed experience itself as standing in merely causal relations to the world. The point of considering this position was to focus on the question of what McDowell's most fundamental dissatisfaction with Coherentism is. If it were the consideration which impels one side of the see-saw—the uncomfortable thought that Coherentism denies experience any properly justificatory role—then this adjustment would successfully still the movement without any need for the additional 're-enchantment' of the world involved in thinking of it as a totality of facts. So it seemed reasonable to conclude that the real dissatisfaction lay elsewhere: precisely in the point about which McDowell finds me 'gratifyingly clear', that there is an issue about how Coherentism, even of this extended variety, could make a place for anything amounting to genuine empirical content. It would follow, if that is a good concern, that it is a precondition of the objective purport of the beliefs based upon it that experience stands not (merely) in causal relationships to the world but sustains *internal* relations to it, which would accordingly demand the conceptually structured nature of the latter. In brief: the 're-enchantment' of the world would emerge as a precondition of the objective purport of the beliefs which experience is apt to justify.

Given that it led me to 'gratifying clarity' about a central point, it is odd that McDowell dismisses this train of thought as "a very uncooperative attempt at spelling out my drift" (p. 426). He complains that he wanted experience to be conceived as 'sensory consciousness of objective reality' from the start and that his thought never moved through a half-way house with experience *first* conceived as carrying conceptual content, and *then* construed as direct receptivity. But these complaints reveal a misunderstanding. I did not intend to ascribe to McDowell an 'interim conclusion'. My point was *meant* to be co-operative—but it was not to speculate about McDowell's actual ratiocinative sequence, still less to try to *spell out* the 'crucial transcendental thought' about the problem Coherentism is supposed to have with objective purport. Rather it was to eliminate a compromise position which might seem, to a Coherentist, to be responsive to the need to have experience as a justifier, and to bring out that, and why, McDowell had better have a further concern about Coherentism which would not be met by this compromise. That further concern is, again, the 'crucial transcendental thought': that, as I should express it, merely causal—hence external—relations to a subject matter cannot sustain beliefs'—or experiences'—being *about* that subject matter. But my attempt was not to spell this out—that is, not to make a case for its cogency (which I do not know how to do)—but to show how McDowell's position demands it, both to stop Extended Coherentism from stilling the oscillation and to enforce the first stage of 're-enchantment'.

McDowell continues to misread me when he writes that 'Wright charges the interim conclusion . . . with [an] oversimplification: it says nothing about theoretical beliefs' (p. 427). The charge is not of oversimplification but, again, of omission and it bears not on any 'interim conclusion' but on McDowell's master thought about the failings of Coherentism, that it cannot accommodate the 'objective purport' of basic empirical beliefs. Theoretical beliefs, for present purposes, are precisely those which do not concern aspects of reality which are open to direct awareness. One version of the master thought about basic empirical beliefs would be this: that in order for such a belief to be just that—to have a content concerning some aspect of objective empirical reality—it has to be possible for the facts in virtue of which it is true, or false, to exert a rational control over its acceptance. That seems to be McDowell's (nowhere elaborated) idea. Suppose it is right. Clearly *that* constraint cannot be met by any theoretical beliefs. A weaker version of the master thought would make it a necessary condition of a belief's having objective empirical purport that experience, conceived as direct awareness of states of affairs, exerts, perhaps indirectly, a rational constraint on it. And theoretical beliefs can meet *this* constraint, it would seem, since what controls their acceptability is how well they are able to participate (coherently!) in a system in which basic empirical beliefs also participate. But the question arises: what bestows the content on such beliefs in virtue of which they do or do not so participate? The stronger master thought addresses that question for basic empirical beliefs. But it would be merely dogmatic (or ostrich-like) to assert without further ado that their satisfaction of the weaker constraint is enough to do the job for theoretical beliefs. After all, that need demand no more than a network of *formal* liaisons with basic empirical beliefs.

In brief: McDowell wants to say that Coherentism has gone past a legitimate concern about empirical content. I want to say that, in so far as I have a sense of what this concern may be, McDowell's own response would seem to leave it unaddressed for empirical beliefs about non-observable subject matters. He responds that 'All I need is a version of the picture Sellars gives in §VIII of "Empiricism and the Philosophy of Mind"'. But Wilfrid Sellars in that section of his famous paper is concerned with repudiation of the *other* Myth of the Given—the 'Myth of the Synthetic Statement', if I may so put it.[2] McDowell presumably thinks that to see that and why there are no pure synthetic statements is to see how satisfaction of something like

2. Cf. Wright (1998a), p. 396, n. 3.

the constraint embodied in the weaker of the two master thoughts allows 'objective purport' to suffuse across the totality of our empirical beliefs. To appropriate his riposte to another of his commentators (p. 408), that seems like magic to me.

But I confess to shadow-boxing, absent any clear statement of what exactly the 'transcendental discomfort' about Coherentism and empirical content comes to, and a clear case that it is a discomfort that deserves to be felt. That omission remains *my* principal discomfort with McDowell's treatment of Coherentism. McDowell himself seems not to feel any deficiency here; but then Donald Davidson and his followers seem not to feel McDowell's 'transcendental discomfort' with their management of the notion of empirical thought.

ANIMALS, INFANTS AND WITTGENSTEIN

To conceptualise experience is to regard any episode of experience as involving *having it seem to one that P*. Someone might observe[3] that in an hallucination, or dream, one can also have it seem to one that P and hence that to describe experience in the same way invites an idea which McDowell precisely rejects: the conception of genuine sense experience and, for example, dreaming as sharing a common phenomenological factor, a type of event or state essentially ingredient in both. But that is presumably a cancellable implication. One can insist that there are variety of ways in which it can seem to one that P which have no factor in common in the sense McDowell is concerned to deny: that they are not, in particular, to be conceived as events of the same type differing only in their causes but rather, despite their subjective similarities, as occurrences of essentially differing ontological structure. To have it seem to one that P in the course of genuine sense experience is to stand in a relation of direct awareness to items in the objective world; to have it seem to one that P in the course of a dream, or hallucination, is quite otherwise. Sure, one can *mistake* one state

---

3. As William Wringe did to me, in discussion.

for the other; so there is undeniably a subjective similarity captured by the shared description 'having it seem to one that P'. But that no more enforces the idea that the items in question have a type of ingredient in common (besides, possibly, their content) than a parallel conclusion is enforced by the mistakability (in suitable circumstances) of a mirror image for the object from which it originates.

So, at least, is how I understand McDowell's view. In my contribution to the symposium I charged that such a conception of experience is radically unintuitive, since it must restrict the capacity for experience—both of the outer and of an 'inner' world—to conceptually endowed subjects. Only a thinker capable of grasping the thought that P can have it seem to them that P. McDowell tries to make out that this is a bearable consequence. He writes:

> Wright depicts the conception of experience I recommend as something everyone has reason to resist, because of its implications about non-possessors of conceptual capacities. He formulates an implication of my conception like this: 'It cannot be within a creature's consciousness in all respects as if it were experiencing pain—save that it lacks the concept pain.' And he says 'This does great violence'. But violence to what? A creature can be *feeling pain* though it lacks the concept of pain. (p. 429)

But this attempt at a distinction—in effect, between two ways of suffering: *feeling* pain and *experiencing* it—should seem merely sophistical, provided that we follow McDowell's own advice and keep a firm grip on the thought that, in the co-operation between 'receptivity' and 'spontaneity' the former 'does not make an even notionally separable contribution'.[4] That stops us thinking—and is precisely intended so to do—of something which a conceptless creature merely feels—its pain—as *of a kind with* something which goes on within our awareness when we experience pain in McDowell's fuller sense of 'experience'—for that would be a notionally separated contribution by

4. McDowell (1994), p. 9.

'receptivity' if anything was. So McDowell ought to regard the surface grammar of 'feeling pain' and 'experiencing pain' as misleading in its implication of a common component. Contrary to the impression suggested by the common occurrence of 'pain', the two conditions literally *have nothing in common*. An animal in pain does not stand in one kind of relation to (an instance of) a certain type of state to which a human in pain stands in another—a different modality of awareness, as it were. To think that way is exactly to make the prohibited notional separation.

What goes missing on this line is any role for empathy or projection in the range of broadly evaluative responses—sympathy, outrage, sadistic satisfaction, delight, etc.—which we have towards the suffering or pleasures of the conceptless. Events and states whose occurrence makes no conceptual demands on their 'owner' cannot be understood on the model of events and states which essentially draw upon a conceptual repertoire, events and states which essentially go with *thought*. So it seems that such responses become groundless, or even unintelligible: where do we look for a satisfactory conception of what is bad about the suffering of an animal or infant *per se* if its state cannot be conceived by analogy with the awful thing that we sometimes *experience*, and if what is awful about the latter depends essentially on its being experienced *as* awful? McDowell confidently reaffirms that no damage of this kind is done by his view. But I cannot see that he says anything to substantiate that claim.

Part of his misplaced confidence would seem to derive from the belief that the opposed conception is committed to something Wittgenstein exposed as hopeless: sensations as private. McDowell agrees that it is true

if you like (the wording is not mine), that, according to me, for such a [conceptless] creature to feel pain cannot be for things to be a certain way within its consciousness—the way they are within our consciousness when we feel pain. This does violence to an inclination to suppose that that is what feeling pain, as such, is. But that is not, as Wright suggests, a bit of philosophically uncontaminated common sense. On the contrary, the idea that for a creature to feel pain is for some state of affairs to obtain within its consciousness, from which it may or may not go on to an actualisation of a conceptual capacity, is just the supposed conception of the private object, which is conclusively exposed as hopeless by Wittgenstein. . . . [I]t is simply a way of taking Wittgenstein's point to say that the idea of states of affairs within consciousness is applicable only where we are already thinking in terms of actualisations of conceptual capacities. This leaves the fact that non-possessors of conceptual capacities can feel pain completely unthreatened. (ibid.)

McDowell's idea would seem to amount to this: that a conception of sensation as something which essentially draws on conceptual capacities represents the only escape from the dilemma between a Cartesian dualism of private objects and outward appearances on the one hand and, on the other, some form of reductive behaviourism. This is too large an issue to hope to explore adequately within a short compass, but I think neither that those three proposals exhaust the options nor that Wittgenstein's discussion either tends or was intended to establish that they do. Philosophising about sensation simply misses the intended subject matter if it leaves no place for those features of the concept from which the dualistic impulse springs—features which ground a perfectly *innocent* conception of privacy. Here are some examples:

it is often, just in the ordinary run of things, very difficult, even impossible to know what others are feeling;

a subject can in principle be as good as you like at concealing her sensations;

it is the merest platitude that my pains do not hurt anyone else, whereas my hand is a potential object of experience for anyone;

any of us, not just animals and infants, may on occasion be unable adequately to express our feelings; and may quite properly and intelligibly report that we cannot say how we feel;

sometimes it is necessary to experience a sensation for yourself if you are to know what it is like;

it is reasonable to suppose but not absolutely certain that a baby's finger, trapped in a door, feels much the way yours would; and that a biting horse-fly on a cow's skin feels much the way it would on yours.

The ways of thinking illustrated by these remarks are constitutive of our ordinary notion of sensation precisely in the sense that a range of putative states of a subject for which they were inappropriate would just on that account be disqualified as *sensations*. To be sure, they allow of—can seduce us into acquiescing in—a folk-explanation, or perhaps better, a *model* which does indeed view sensations, and feelings generally, as objects or states of affairs whose nature is Cartesian: a model which represents sensations as events within an inner arena to which, necessarily, only a single subject can bear witness. On that model, only the subject can know what her own sensations are like, with the consequence that there can be in the end no reason to suppose that any two subjects share the conceptual repertoires under which they respectively taxonomise their inner lives.

Whatever might be his view of the others, McDowell would seem to suppose that the sixth remark above not merely permits the Cartesian model but *demands* it—that to think of an animal's feelings in certain circumstances and those of an articulate human in similar circumstances as being of the same general kind cannot but be interpreted as a commitment to Cartesian privacy. But the sixth remark, as it seems to me, belongs with the others as, indeed, a 'piece of philosophically uncontaminated common sense'. What is under attack in the famous sections of *Philosophical Investigations* is not the conception of sensations as private—in effect, the conception of sensations as *sensations*—which is innocently at work in those various commonplace ways of talking, but the philosophical model of privacy to which we succumb when we accede to the Cartesian picture. It is on the implications of that model for the idea that we have genuine concepts under which we acknowledge and report our sensations that Wittgenstein's attack focuses: in brief, if it is successful, the result is that there is nothing for competence in such a concept to consist if the subject matter it may purportedly be used to characterise exists in Cartesian privacy. So the *model*—not the ways of talking to which it is applied—is undercut. The upshot of the attack, if it is sustained, is not that it is simply wrong to think of sensations as private but that the Cartesian model of privacy—the inner theatre of observation from which all but a single witness are excluded—merely induces misunderstanding of the kinds of ways of talking, illustrated above, which variously express their privacy. Sensations are indeed private, if to say so is merely to advert to the kinds of ways of talking about them illustrated; but they are not private in any sense which would require that it becomes a mere metaphysical hypothesis whether we respectively bring them under a common conceptual vocabulary.[5]

---

5. 'So in *what* sense are they private, then?' The question may seem almost irresistible. But it asks, in effect, for a better model: *another* way of underwriting the habits of thought and talk illustrated above. Let me remind you of Wittgenstein's response. This is from Philosophical *Investigations* §109:

> We must do away with all *explanation*, and description alone must take its place. And this description gets its light, that's to say its purpose, from the philosophical problems. These are, of course, not empirical problems; they are solved, rather, by looking into the workings of our language, and that in such a way as to make us recognise those workings: *in despite of* an urge to misunderstand them. . . . [p]hilosophy is a battle against the bewitchment of our intelligence by means of language.

Recall also *Investigations* §§654–5:

> Our mistake is to look for an explanation where we ought to look at what happens as a 'proto-phenomenon'. That is, where we ought to have said: *this language game is played.*
>
> The question is not one of explaining a language game by means of our experiences, but of noting a language game.

That we should settle for this kind of deflationary position seems to me to be one of the hardest things to accept in Wittgenstein's later philosophy. But that it should be accepted is, it seems unmistakable, his view. The Cartesian conception of privacy is exactly something to which we succumb when we misunderstand the workings of our language, and specifically the kinds of locution illustrated by the six examples. And his recommended moral is, not that we abandon any of those ways of talking, but that we resist the temptation of trying to *underwrite* them, that is, to construct a general

On this reading of Wittgenstein, McDowell's idea of inner experience as conceptual is exactly *not* 'a way of taking Wittgenstein's point'; for it is wholly anti-Wittgensteinian in spirit to see the effect of his work on this issue as being to correct ordinary linguistic practice, as reflected for example in the sixth remark, rather than to adjust a philosophical misunderstanding of that practice. It seems to me that it is simply no implication of that adjustment that conceptless creatures are barred from experiencing any of the sensations which we are accustomed to ascribe to other adult humans and ourselves. When we ascribe pain to an animal, we mean to ascribe to it a state which, *qua* pain, we think we fully understand and to whose assimilation to what we ourselves can experience there is no conceptual barrier. On McDowell's reading, taking Wittgenstein's thought on board would involve that this way of thinking is forfeit: that our mutual intelligibility can be safeguarded at the cost only of deep disanalogy between our inner lives and those—if it still makes any sense to think of them as having inner lives—of the conceptually inarticulate. That conclusion seems to me to be neither desirable nor required—either as a reading of Wittgenstein or as a self-standing proposal about what it takes to escape Cartesianism.

DISMOUNTING THE SEE-SAW (I)

If the foregoing is persuasive, then we now face a bind: how *are* basic empirical beliefs to be conceived as justified if not by intra-systematic relations of coherence—supposing the correctness of McDowell's 'crucial transcendental thought'—nor by experience conceived as a brute impingement on consciousness, nor by experience conceived as by McDowell? In Wright (1998a) I suggested two possibilities.

---

picture of the nature of their subject matter and our relations to it which would explain why it is alright to talk in such ways.

I have explored this general idea further in Wright (1998b) and in Essay 11 and the first Postscript in this volume.

One—I'll call it the fourth possibility—turns on discarding what I called the *quasi-inferential* conception of how non-inferentially justified beliefs are justified. The quasi-inferential conception (i) calls for something content-bearing to do the justifying (for example, having it seem to one *that P*) and (ii) requires the content of the justifier to stand in certain kinds of relation to that of the justified (in the best case: identity.) On this type of view, non-inferential justification is just like inferential except that it is not other *beliefs* that serve in, so to speak, the premise position, but the non-doxastic content-carrying *input* of certain presumed cognitive faculties—perception, on McDowell's view, but a similar story could be extended to memory, logical intuition and perhaps our faculty for self-knowledge.

I suggested that McDowell's thinking about his problem was controlled by this quasi-inferential conception, and that it is not mandatory. For a view is at least structurally possible which dispenses with the content-specific justifiers which, in their different ways, both a strictly inferentialist Coherentism and the quasi-inferential conception of McDowell believe in. On McDowell's view, justification for those basic empirical beliefs to which one moves directly, without any element of inference, is provided by the relation between their content and that of the experiences which move one to them. For Coherentism, their justification is a matter of the relations between their content and that of the beliefs already participant in one's presumed coherent system of belief. But for the view now canvassed—the fourth possibility— what justifies a belief to which one is just directly moved is one's concurrent entitlement to the presupposition that it is the product of the operation of some appropriate and effectively functioning cognitive faculty. This type of justification is content non-specific in the sense that the specific content of the targeted belief plays no role in determining that it is justified (save perhaps in the very general way that only a belief with a certain *type* of content could sensibly be deemed to be the product of a germane type of cognitive faculty.)

McDowell rejects the claim that his thinking is 'controlled' by the quasi-inferential conception (p. 430)—but it manifestly is. Look at what he actually says by way of riposte:

Unsurprisingly, I do not think this diagnosis fits. . . . If it were not for distortions inflicted on our thinking by philosophy, I think it would be obvious that the idea of observational judgement, in particular, involves 'a specific, content-sensitive justifier'—namely, the fact observed. The point of the idea of experience is that it is in experience that facts themselves come to be among the justifiers available to subjects; that does not represent experience as a quasi-inferential intermediary between facts and judgements, as in Wright's two-step reading of my thought. It strikes me as obvious enough that observational judgements have specific content-sensitive justifiers—apart, as I say, from philosophically generated distortions—for the thought to stand on its own feet. It does not need to be defended as a conclusion from something more general, such as a quasi-inferential conception of justification.

Part of this protest is spurred by the misreading I mentioned earlier: McDowell's reception of my play with Extended Coherentism as an attempt to depict the movement of his own thought. This seems to have encouraged him to equate a quasi-inferential conception of the justificatory role of experience with the idea that experience serves as an 'intermediary', in a fashion inconsistent with his direct realism. But the quasi-inferential conception is simply the general idea that, in order for any belief to be justified, something must justify it which stands in an internal relation to its specific content. This idea is quasi-inferential precisely because it inherits from inferential justification its insistence on the kind of relation between justifier and justified which obtains when the justifiers are a set of antecedent beliefs whose content precisely sustains an inference to that of the belief to be justified. And this conception is unmistakably in control of McDowell's thinking about the issue: when he talks of *facts* as doing the justifying for empirical beliefs, he precisely invokes what are, in his view, a range of justifiers which owe their justificatory relations to being individuated by their content—the fact *that P*—and to the content of the beliefs they purportedly justify. This is exactly an instance of the kind of thinking which, according to the fourth possibility, is not compulsory.

It is worth pursuing McDowell's riposte a little. We sometimes speak of proofs as justifying mathematical beliefs, but of course this is inept unless elliptical: nobody is justified in a mathematical belief by a proof of which he is *unaware,* even if it exists. Speaking of 'the fact observed' as a justifier is inept in the same way, since if facts really could carry the weight of the first term of the justification relation, there would be no need to experience them in order to be justified in one's empirical beliefs. McDowell should therefore stick to saying that it is indeed *experience* which justifies, with reminders when necessary that experience is being conceived as direct awareness of external fact. But now it is worth asking *how* exactly experience, so conceived, is supposed to *justify:* why should a having-it-seem-to-one-that-P which is as a matter of fact an 'episode of openness to the layout of reality' be taken to warrant the belief that P? The answer, even for one who conceives of such seemings as, in the best case, instances of 'openness to the layout of reality', must be that one is normally entitled to take them as precisely that. (For if one was for some reason agnostic about their status—if, say, one somehow had good reason to suppose (falsely) that now and for the next few hours it would be a strong possibility (as likely as not) that one would be suffering very extensive hallucinations while actually lying in a hospital bed—then one's (as a matter of fact) continuing direct experience of reality would lose its justificatory force.) Even McDowellian experience, then, is not an *unconditional* justifier: a suitably conducive background of collateral general belief is required in any case, however experience is conceived. There is therefore a question why/whether McDowell's account differs in any important respect from the fourth possibility, at least so far as its potential to save the justificatory character of experience is concerned.

The fourth possibility, outlined no further, says nothing about the nature of experience. It could be augmented by a view of experience as the carrier of conceptual content, or non-conceptual content, or no content at all—a 'brute impingement' on awareness. It doesn't matter what experience is: on this view, it can justify the beliefs it (causally) encourages if (but only if) placed in the correct collateral doxastic setting—one which, one way or another, entitles a thinker to take the content of the beliefs to which her experience inclines her as a likely reflection of the nature of the world. Whether or not content, of whatever sort, is assigned to experience as well is—once it is recognised that a conducive collateral doxastic setting is required in any case—a question with no bearing on its capacity to justify.

At this point, of course, it should begin to seem that the 'fourth possibility' is actually a bit of an impostor: we are presented not so much with an alternative idea about the justification of basic empirical beliefs, contrasting both with McDowell's and with those in play in the two "see-saw" positions, as with a more developed, counter-attacking version of Coherentism which, rather than conceding that experience is not a justifier at all, argues that, precisely because justification is always holistic, any *conscious phenomenon whatever* can be a justifier and need stand in no internal relation to the content of what is justified. Here again, then, is where it would be important for McDowell to be able to make good the claim, essential to his rejection of the Myth of the Given, that it is a kind of solecism to think of experience conceived as non-conceptual as capable of justifying anything. The Coherentist counter-attack, again, consists in the thought that even if McDowellised, experience won't justify in the wrong doxastic setting; and if the doxastic setting is right, letting experience carry conceptual content in common with a candidate empirical belief adds nothing to its justificatory power. The template in any case is that justification accrues by virtue of (one's being aware of) something's happening which one is entitled to take as an indicator of the truth of the candidate belief, and it is all the same whether that something is a McDowellian experience that P or, say, a loud noise. The 'fourth possibility', then, pursued a little, merely takes us back into and extends McDowell's debate with Coherentism. And as before, his master card will have to be the 'crucial transcendental thought' that conceptual experience, conceived as direct awareness of a conceptually structured reality, cannot be dispensed with in any account which can save the possibility of objective empirical purport. It is that issue, and not the question which drives the see-saw—the question of making out how experience can play a role in the rationalisation of belief—which turns out to be fundamental.

Dismounting the See-Saw (II)

I return, finally, to what I find most unconvincing about McDowell's main argument in the first part of *Mind and World*. Suppose that he is right that experience can only justify if conceived as carrying conceptual content. And grant the point that so conceiving of experience gains no advantage over Coherentism unless it is also thought of as directly responsive to the world: that is, as not just caused by it but *disclosing* it. These two points call, as we have noted, for a Tractarian ontology: the world of our experience must be a totality of *things that are the case,* facts that P. McDowell spends some time repudiating the idea that this metaphysics is idealist in any pejorative sense. But it would be just that if we supposed that facts—like experience, on McDowell's view—owe their being to *actual* conceptual activity: that any particular fact would not so much as exist unless actually conceived by some thinker. If the position is not to be idealist, then facts, as self-standing states of affairs, have to be mere conceiv*ables*. They are individuated by conceptual content, but do not depend for their existence on anyone's actually thinking—or even being capable of thinking—their content.

It seems to me just obvious to ask now: why cannot this conception of a fact, which McDowell enthusiastically embraces and to which he is anyway committed, be applied to episodes of brute awareness? Why should not a subject's sensory awareness of certain items in his environment—his experience of the cat sitting on the mat, say—be conceived as just such a (relational) fact: a fact consisting in his standing in a certain mental relation to a chunk of material reality? It would only be in bringing concepts to bear on this relational fact that it would be registered as an experience that P, and hence become able to contribute towards justifying the belief that P. But it could obtain unconceptualised in just the same way as the fact that P itself. So on this view, there is simply no good need so to refashion the concept of experience that it is barred to animals and infants.

When McDowell argues that, if we are to dismount the see-saw, we must cease to think of experience as consisting in 'occurrences in consciousness that are independent of conceptual capacities', he would appear to conflate a weaker and a stronger version of the claim. The strong version is just what he goes on to recommend: experience is an activity of conceptually endowed subjects that draws on their actual conceptual capacities. The weaker claim is: the justificatory *potential* of experience depends on its being, as it were, *readable;* it does not actually have to be read, however, in order to exist (any more than a newspaper). So the question is: even granting, against the more developed Coherentism latterly outlined, that experience has to be conceptual if it is to justify, why do we need more than the weaker claim in order to dismount the see-saw? To be sure, if we had *already* discarded the very idea of brute experience, there would only be the stronger option. But McDowell's reason for discarding it was precisely to safeguard the justificatory potential of experience. And to have justificatory potential, merely, it is enough for experience to be a relational fact, available for but not owing its existence to the operation of concepts.

McDowell responds (pp. 430–1):

> I am baffled by Wright's second suggested line of resistance. I cannot see the 'absolute parallel' he claims, between the idea of a fact as a thinkable that does not depend on anyone's thinking it, on the one hand, and, on the other, the idea of an occurrence in consciousness that is not an actualisation of conceptual powers but nevertheless such as to 'sustain' or 'command'

—my words in Wright (1996)—

> a particular conceptual articulation. If an item ontologically independent of anyone's thinking it is in view as a *thinkable,* there can be no problem about the idea that someone *might* think it. But there is a problem about 'sustaining' or 'commanding' conceptual articulations, the supposedly parallel optional extras in Wright's alleged counterpart. Can Wright separate the language of 'sustaining' and 'commanding' from the idea that one rather than another conceptual articulation is correct in the light of the supposed occurrence in consciousness? If not,

then the proposal is simply, and obviously, a version of the Myth of the Given. . . .

I am quite content not to 'separate the language of "sustaining" and "commanding" from the idea that one rather than another conceptual articulation is correct in the light of the supposed occurrence in consciousness'. McDowell's idea was that in experience, I bring a fact to conceptual awareness: it appears to me that P. So the fact that P 'sustains' and 'commands' that particular conceptual articulation—that's just a fancy way of saying that I recognise it for what it is. And, someone running the line that so baffles McDowell will say, my awareness of that fact is, in just the same way, recognised for what it is by the conceptual articulation: *it appears to me* that P.

McDowell charges that this is just the Myth of the Given all over again. But either it isn't or else it really isn't clear what the supposed Myth is, and what, according to *Mind and World,* is wrong with it. What McDowell officially *said* was mythical was: the notion that justification can accrue to a belief from something which merely causes it and stands in no conceptual (internal) relationship to it. But the weaker claim does not controvert that; it allows that an experience is justificatory only as and when actually conceptualised—'read', which is to say: recognised for what it is—questioning only whether this justificatory potential has to be actualised—via an actual 'reading'—in order for experience to exist at all.

Of course, the conception now in play of experience as material for recognition is just scheme/content dualism of the kind which Davidson famously rejects. McDowell too, for his rather different reasons, sets himself the task of 'overcoming' that dualism. But, the intentions of its author notwithstanding, the question which *Mind and World* leaves open is: why should we want to overcome it? Not, anyway, in order to explain how experience can justify. I need hardly add that the overcoming of dualisms is a good thing only when the duality is bogus; otherwise, it is just the missing of distinctions.

REFERENCES AND
ADDITIONAL READINGS

CREDITS

INDEX

References and
Additional Readings

d'Agostino, F. 1986. *Chomsky's System of Ideas*. Oxford: The Clarendon Press.

Austen, J. 1987. *Emma*. London: Penguin Books.

Ayer, A. J. 1954. "Can there be a Private Language?", *Proceedings of the Aristotelian Society* Suppl. vol. 28, pp. 63–76.

Baker, G. and P. Hacker. 1976. "Critical Notice of Wittgenstein's *Philosophical Grammar*", *Mind* 85, pp. 269–94.

—— 1983a. *Wittgenstein: Meaning and Understanding. Essays on the Philosophical Investigations* vol. 1. Oxford: Blackwell.

—— 1983b. *An Analytical Commentary on Wittgenstein's Philosophical Investigations*. Oxford: Blackwell.

—— 1984a. *Language, Sense and Nonsense*. Oxford: Blackwell.

—— 1984b. "On Misunderstanding Wittgenstein", *Synthese* 58, pp. 407–50.

—— 1984c. *Scepticism, Rules and Language*. Oxford: Blackwell.

Benacerraf, P. 1962. "Tasks, Super-Tasks and the Modern Eleatics", *Journal of Philosophy* 59, pp. 765–84, *reprinted in* Salmon (1970).

—— 1965. "What Numbers Could Not Be", *Philosophical Review* 74, pp. 47–73.

—— 1985. "Skolem and the Skeptic", *Proceedings of the Aristotelian Society* Suppl. vol. 59, pp. 85–115.

———— 1998. "What Mathematical Truth Could Not Be—I", *in* M. Schirn, ed., *The Philosophy of Mathematics Today.* Oxford: The Clarendon Press, pp. 33–75.

Benacerraf, P., and Putnam, H., eds. 1983. *Philosophy of Mathematics: Selected Readings.* Cambridge: Cambridge University Press.

Blackburn, S. 1969. "Goodman's Paradox", *in* Rescher (1969), pp. 28–43.

———— 1984. "The Individual Strikes Back", *Synthese* 58, pp. 281–301.

———— 1990. "Wittgenstein's Irrealism", *Proceedings of the International Wittgenstein Symposium* 14, pp. 13–26.

Boghossian, P. 1989a. "Content and Self-knowledge", *Philosophical Topics* 17, pp. 5–26.

———— 1989b. Review of Colin McGinn's *Wittgenstein on Meaning*, *Philosophical Review* 98, pp. 83–92.

———— 1989c. "The Rule-Following Considerations", *Mind* 93, pp. 507–49.

Brandom, R. 1994. *Making It Explicit*, chap. 1. Cambridge: Harvard University Press.

Budd, M. 1984. "Wittgenstein on Meaning, Interpretation and Rules", *Synthese* 58, pp. 303–23.

Burge, T. 1979. "Individualism and the Mental", *Midwest Studies in Philosophy* 4, pp. 73–122.

———— 1982a. "Other bodies", *in* Woodfield (1982).

———— 1982b. "Two Thought Experiments Reviewed", *Notre Dame Journal of Formal Logic* 23, pp. 284–94.

———— 1988. "Individualism and Self-knowledge", *Journal of Philosophy* 85, pp. 649–63.

———— 1996. "Our Entitlement to Self-Knowledge", *Proceedings of the Aristotelian Society* 96, pp. 91–116.

Butterfield, J., ed. 1986. *Language, Mind and Logic.* Cambridge: Cambridge University Press.

Byrne, A. 1998. "Interpretivism", *European Review of Philosophy* 3, pp. 199–223.

Byrne, D. 2000. "The Components of Linguistic Understanding", D.Phil. diss., Oxford University.

Carruthers, P. 1984. "Baker and Hacker's Wittgenstein", *Synthese* 58, pp. 451–79.

———— 1985. "Ruling out Realism", *Philosophia* 15, pp. 61–78.

Chomsky, N. 1959. "A Review of B. F. Skinner's *Verbal Behavior*", *Language* 35, pp. 26–58.

—— 1964. *Current Issues in Linguistics*. The Hague: Mouton.

—— 1966. *Cartesian Linguistics*. New York: Harper & Row.

—— 1967. "Recent Contributions to the Theory of Innate Ideas", *Synthese* 17, pp. 2–11.

—— 1986. *Knowledge of Language*. New York: Praeger.

—— 1987. "Replies to Alexander George and Michael Brody", *Mind and Language* 2, pp. 178–97.

Craig, E. 1986. "Privacy and Rule Following", *in* Butterfield (1986), pp. 169–87.

Davidson, D. 1973. "In Defense of Convention 'T'", *in* LeBlanc (1973), pp. 76–87.

—— 1987. "Knowing One's Own Mind", *Proceedings and Addresses of the American Philosophical Association* 60, pp. 441–58.

—— 1994. "First-Person Authority", *Dialectica* 48, pp. 101–12.

Diamond, C., ed. 1976. Wittgenstein's 1939 *Lectures on the Foundations of Mathematics*. Brighton: Harvester.

Dummett, M. 1973. *Frege: Philosophy of Language*. London: Duckworth.

—— 1975. "What Is a Theory of Meaning?", *in* Guttenplan (1975).

—— 1976. "What Is a Theory of Meaning? (II)", *in* Evans and McDowell (1976), pp. 67–137.

—— 1994. "Wittgenstein on Necessity: Some Reflections", *in* Peter Clark and Bob Hale, eds., *Reading Putnam* (Cambridge, Mass. and Oxford: Blackwell).

Edwards, J. 1992. "Best Opinion and Intentional States", *Philosophical Quarterly* 42, pp. 21–33.

—— 1998. "Response-Dependence, Kripke and Minimal Truth", *European Review of Philosophy* 3, pp. 149–74.

Eliot, G. 1985. *The Lifted Veil*. Harmondsworth: Penguin Books.

Evans, G. 1981. "Semantic Theory and Tacit Knowledge", *in* Leich and Holtzman (1981), pp. 118–37.

—— 1982. *The Varieties of Reference*. Oxford: The Clarendon Press.

Evans, G., and J. McDowell, eds. 1976. *Truth and Meaning: Essays in Semantics*. Oxford: Oxford University Press.

Forbes, G. 1984. "Skepticism and Semantic Knowledge", *Proceedings of the Aristotelian Society* 84, pp. 221–37.

Foster, J. 1976. "Meaning and Truth-Theory", *in* Evans and McDowell (1976), pp. 1–32.

Geach, P. T. 1965. "Assertion", *Philosophical Review* 74, pp. 449–65.

George, A. 1987. "Review of *Knowledge of Language*", *Mind and Language* 2, pp. 155–64.

George, A., ed. 1989. *Reflections of Chomsky*. Oxford: Blackwell.

Gödel, K. 1947. "What Is Cantor's Continuum Problem?", *American Mathematical Monthly* 54, pp. 515–25; *reprinted in* Benacerraf and Putnam (1983), pp. 470–85.

Goldfarb, W. 1985. "Kripke on Wittgenstein and Rules", *Journal of Philosophy* 82, pp. 471–88.

Goodman, N. 1954. *Fact, Fiction and Forecast*. London: Athlone.

Guttenplan, S., ed. 1975. *Mind and Language*. Oxford: Oxford University Press.

Hacker, P. 1972. *Insight and Illusion*. Oxford: The Clarendon Press.

Haldane, J., and C. Wright, eds. 1993. *Reality: Representation and Projection*. Oxford: The Clarendon Press.

Hale, R. V. 1989. "Necessity, Caution and Scepticism", *Proceedings of the Aristotelian Society* Suppl. vol. 63, pp. 175–202.

———— 1997. "Rule-Following, Objectivity and Meaning", *in* R. Hale and C. Wright, eds., *A Companion to the Philosophy of Language* (Oxford: Blackwell), pp. 369–96.

Hale, R. V., and C Wright. 1997. "Putnam's Model-Theoretic Argument against Metaphysical Realism", *in* R. V. Hale and C. Wright, eds., *A Companion to the Philosophy of Language* (Oxford: Blackwell), pp. 427–57.

Hamilton, A. 1987. "The Self and Self-Consciousness". Ph.D. diss., University of St. Andrews.

Harrison, R. 1974. *On What There Must Be*. Oxford: The Clarendon Press.

Heal, J. 1989. *Fact and Meaning*. Oxford: Blackwell.

Holton, R. 1993. "Intention Detecting", *Philosophical Quarterly* 43, pp. 298–318.

Holtzman, S., and C. Leich, eds. 1981. *Wittgenstein: To Follow a Rule*. London: Routledge & Kegan Paul.

Hume, D. 1975 (1748). *Enquiries Concerning Human Understanding and Concerning the Perfection of Morals*. Oxford: The Clarendon Press.

Kripke, S. 1982. *Wittgenstein on Rules and Private Language*. Oxford: Blackwell.

LeBlanc, H., ed. 1973. *Truth, Syntax and Modality*. Amsterdam: North-Holland.

McDowell, J. 1976. "Truth Conditions, Bivalence and Verificationism", *in* Evans and McDowell (1976).

———— 1981. "Non-Cognitivism and Rule-Following", *in* Leich and Holtzman (1981), pp. 141–62.

———— 1984. "Wittgenstein on Following a Rule", *Synthese* 58, pp. 325–63.

———— 1991. "Intentionality and Interiority in Wittgenstein", *in* Puhl (1991), pp. 148–69.

———— 1992. "Meaning and Intentionality in Wittgenstein's Later Philosophy", *Midwest Studies in Philosophy* 17, pp. 40–52.

———— 1994. *Mind and World*. Cambridge, Mass.: Harvard University Press.

———— 1998. "Response to Crispin Wright", *in* C. Wright, B. Smith and C. Macdonald, eds., *Knowing Our Own Minds* (Oxford: The Clarendon Press), pp. 47–62.

McGinn, C. 1984. *Wittgenstein on Meaning*. Oxford: Blackwell.

Mackie, J. 1976. *Problems from Locke*. Oxford: The Clarendon Press.

Maddy, P. 1980. "Perception and Mathematical Intuition", *Philosophical Review* 89, pp. 163–96.

Malcolm, N. 1954. "Wittgenstein's *Philosophical Investigations*", *Philosophical Review* 63, pp. 530–59.

———— 1986. *Nothing Is Hidden*. Oxford: Blackwell.

Miller, A. 1989. "An Objection to Wright's Treatment of Intention", *Analysis* 49, pp. 169–73.

———— 1998. "Rule-Following, Response-Dependence and McDowell's Debate with Anti-realism", *European Review of Philosophy* 3, pp. 175–97.

Miller, A., with J. Divers. 1994. "Best Opinion, Intention-Detecting and Analytic Functionalism", *Philosophical Quarterly* 44, 239–45.

Peacocke, C. 1981. "Rule-Following: The Nature of Wittgenstein's Arguments", *in* Holtzman and C. Leich (1981).

———— 1983. *Sense and Content,* Oxford: Oxford University Press.

———— 1992. *Study of Concepts*. Cambridge, Mass.: MIT Press.

———— 2000. *Being Known*. Oxford: The Clarendon Press.

Pettit, P., and J. McDowell, eds. 1986. *Subject, Thought and Context*. Oxford: Oxford University Press.

Puhl, K., ed. 1991. *Meaning Scepticism*. Berlin: de Gruyter.

Putnam, H. 1970. "Is Semantics Possible", in Putnam (1975b), Essay 8, pp. 139–53.

———— 1975a. "The Meaning of 'Meaning'", *in* Putnam (1975b), Essay 12, pp. 215–72.

———— 1975b. *Mind, Language and Reality: Philosophical Papers 2*. Cambridge: Cambridge University Press.

——— 1977. "Models and Reality", Presidential Address to the Association of Symbolic Logic, December 1977, *reprinted in* Benacerraf and Putnam (1983), pp. 421–44.

Rescher, N. 1969. *Studies in the Philosophy of Science, American Philosophical Quarterly Monographs* 3. Oxford: Blackwell.

Rhees, R. 1954. "Can there be a Private Language?", *Proceedings of the Aristotelian Society* Suppl. vol. 28, pp. 77–94.

Salmon, W. C., ed. 1970. *Zeno's Paradoxes.* Indianapolis: Bobbs-Merrill.

Shoemaker, S. 1968. "Self-Reference and Self-Awareness", *Journal of Philosophy* 65, pp. 555–78.

Stevenson, L. 1982. *The Metaphysics of Experience.* Oxford: The Clarendon Press.

Strawson, P. F. 1954. Critical Study of the *Philosophical Investigations, Mind* 63, pp. 70–99.

Sullivan, P. 1994. "Problems for a Construction of Meaning and Intention", *Mind* 103, pp. 147–68.

Tanney, J. 1996. "A Constructivist Picture of Self-Knowledge", *Philosophy* 71, pp. 405–22.

Travis, C., ed. 1986. *Meaning and Interpretation.* Oxford: Blackwell.

Thornton, T. 1997. "Intention, Rule-following and the Strategic Role of Wright's Order of Determination Test", *Philosophical Investigations* 20, pp. 136–47.

Walker, R. 1978. *Kant.* London: Routledge.

Wittgenstein, L. 1961 (1922). *Tractatus Logico Philosophicus.* Translated by D. Pears and B. F. McGuinness. London: Routledge.

——— 1953. *Philosophical Investigations.* Edited by G. E. M. Anscombe and R. Rhees. Translated by G. E. M Anscombe. Oxford: Blackwell.

——— 1956. *Remarks on the Foundations of Mathematics.* Edited by G. H. von Wright, R. Rhees and G. E. M. Anscombe. Translated by G. E. M Anscombe. Oxford: Blackwell.

——— 1958. *The Blue and Brown Books.* Oxford: Blackwell.

——— 1967. *Zettel.* Edited by G. E. M. Anscombe and G. H. von Wright. Translated by G. E. M. Anscombe. Oxford: Blackwell.

——— 1974. *Philosophical Grammar.* Edited by R. Rhees. Translated by A. Kenny. Oxford: Blackwell.

——— 1980. *Remarks on the Philosophy of Psychology.* Edited by G. E. M. Anscombe and G. H. von Wright. Translated by G. E. M. Anscombe. Oxford: Blackwell.

Woodfield, A., ed. 1982. *Thought and Object*. Oxford: Oxford University Press.

Wright, C. 1980. *Wittgenstein on the Foundations of Mathematics*. London: Duckworth.

——— 1981. "Rule Following, Objectivity and the Theory of Meaning", *in* Leich and Holtzman (1981), pp. 99–106 (this volume Essay 2).

——— 1982. "Strict Finitism", *Synthese* 51, pp. 203–82.

——— 1983. *Frege's Conception of Numbers as Objects*. Aberdeen: Aberdeen University Press.

——— 1984. "Kripke's Account of the Argument against Private Language", *Journal of Philosophy* 81, pp. 759–78 (this volume Essay 4).

——— 1985. "Skolem and the Skeptic", *Proceedings of the Aristotelian Society* Suppl. vol. 59, pp. 117–37 (this volume Essay 12).

——— 1986a. "Does *Philosophical Investigations* §§258–60 Suggest a Cogent Argument against Private Language", *in* Pettit and McDowell (1986), pp. 209–66 (this volume Essay 8).

——— 1986b. "Inventing Logical Necessity", *in* Butterfield (1986), pp. 187–211.

——— 1986c. *Realism, Meaning and Truth*. Oxford: Blackwell.

——— 1986d. "Rule-Following, Meaning and Constructivism" *in* Travis (1986), pp. 271–97 (this volume Essay 3).

——— 1987a. "On Making up One's Mind: Wittgenstein on Intention", *Logic, Philosophy of Science and Epistemology: Proceedings of the International Wittgenstein Symposium* XI, pp. 391–404 (this volume Essay 5).

——— 1987b. "Realism, Anti-Realism, Irrealism, Quasi-Realism", *Midwest Studies in Philosophy* 12 (Minneapolis: University of Minnesota Press), pp. 29–47.

——— 1988. "Moral values, Projection and Secondary Qualities", *Proceedings of the Aristotelian Society* Suppl. vol. 62, pp. 1–26.

——— 1989a. Critical Study of Colin McGinn's *Wittgenstein on Meaning, Mind* 98, pp. 289–305 (this volume Essay 6).

——— 1989b. "Necessity, Caution and Scepticism", *Proceedings of the Aristotelian Society* Suppl. vol. 63, pp. 203–39.

——— 1989c. "Wittgenstein's Rule-Following Considerations and the Central Project of Theoretical Linguistics", *in* George (1989), pp. 233–64 (this volume Essay 7).

——— 1991. "Wittgenstein's Later Philosophy of Mind: Sensation, Privacy and Intention", *in* Puhl (1991), pp. 126–47 (this volume Essay 9).

———— 1992. *Truth and Objectivity.* Cambridge, Mass.: Harvard University Press.

———— 1993. "Realism: The Contemporary Debate—Whither Now?", *in* Haldane and Wright (1993), pp. 63–84.

———— 1996. "Human Nature?", critical study of John McDowell, *Mind and World, European Journal of Philsophy* 4, pp. 235–54.

———— 1998a. "McDowell's Oscillation", *Philosophy and Phenomenological Research* 58, pp. 395–402.

———— 1998b. "Self-Knowledge: The Wittgensteinian Legacy", *in* C. Wright, B. Smith and C. Macdonald, eds., *Knowing Our Own Minds* (Oxford: The Clarendon Press).

Zalabardo, J. 2000. "Realism Detranscendentalized", *European Journal of Philosophy* 8, pp. 63–88.

CREDITS

Essay 1, "Following a Rule", was first published as chap. 2 of *Wittgenstein on the Foundations of Mathematics* (Duckworth/Harvard, London and Cambridge, Mass.) 1980.

Essay 2, "Rule-Following, Objectivity and the Theory of Meaning", was first published in S. Holtzman and C. Leich, eds., *Wittgenstein: To Follow a Rule* (Routledge) 1981. It is reprinted by permission of Routledge and Kegan Paul plc.

Essay 3, "Rule-Following, Meaning and Constructivism", was first published in *Meaning and Interpretation,* ed. C. Travis (Blackwell) 1986. It is reprinted by permission of Basil Blackwell Ltd.

Essay 4, "Kripke's Account of the Argument against Private Language", was first published in the *Journal of Philosophy* 71, 12 (1984), pp. 759–778. It is reprinted by permission of the editors.

Essay 5, "On Making Up One's Mind: Wittgenstein on Intention", was first published in *Logic, Philosophy of Science and Epistemology,* the *Proceedings of the XIth International Wittgenstein Symposium,* ed. P. Weingartner and Gerhard Schurz (Vienna: Holder—Pickler-Tempsky) 1987. It is reprinted by permission of the publishers.

Essay 6, excerpts from a critical study of Colin McGinn's *Wittgenstein on Meaning,* was first published in *Mind* 98 (1989). It is reprinted by permission of Oxford University Press.

Essay 7, "Wittgenstein's Rule-Following Considerations and the Central Project of Theoretical Linguistics", was first published in *Reflections on Chomsky,* ed. Alexander George (Blackwell) 1989. It is reprinted by permission of Basil Blackwell Ltd.

Essay 8, "Does *Philosophical Investigations* §§258–60 Suggest a Cogent Argument against Private Language?", was first published in *Subject, Thought and Context,* ed. P. Pettit and J. McDowell (Oxford) 1986. It is reprinted by permission of Oxford University Press.

Essay 9, "Wittgenstein's Later Philosophy of Mind: Sensation, Privacy and Intention", was first published in *Meaning Scepticism,* ed. Klaus Puhl (de Gruyter) 1991. It is reprinted by permission of Walter de Gruyter and Co. An earlier (abbreviated) version first appeared in the *Journal of Philosophy* 86 (1989).

Essays 10 and 11, "The Problem of Self-Knowledge (I)" and "The Problem of Self-Knowledge (II)", were given as the Whitehead Lectures at Harvard in spring 1996. They are previously unpublished.

Essay 12, "Skolem and the Sceptic", was first published in *Proceedings of the Aristotelian Society,* supplementary volume 59 (1985). It is reprinted by permission of the officers of the Aristotelian Society.

Essay 13, "Wittgenstein on Mathematical Proof", was first published in *Wittgenstein Centenary Essays,* ed. A Phillips Griffiths, Royal Institute of Philosophy Supplement 28 (Cambridge University Press) 1991. It is reprinted by permission of Cambridge University Press.

"Study Note on Wittgenstein on the Nature of Philosophy" is previously unpublished.

"On *Mind and World*" was first published as a Postscript to the reprinting of my "Human Nature?" (Critical Study of John McDowell's *Mind and World* in the *European Journal of Philosophy* 4, pp. 235–54), in Nicholas Smith, ed., *Reading McDowell: On Mind and World* (Routledge) forthcoming. It is reprinted by permission of Routledge and Kegan Paul plc.

INDEX

Index